Parents
MAGAZINE

It Worked for Me!

Parents

MAGAZINE

It Worked for Me!

From thumb sucking to
schoolyard fights, parents reveal
their secrets to solving the
everyday problems
of raising kids

Edited by ANNE PLESHETTE MURPHY

Foreword by SALLY LEE,
Editor in Chief, Parents **magazine**

ST. MARTIN'S PRESS
NEW YORK

Library of Congress Cataloging-in-Publication Data

Parents magazine's it worked for me! : from thumb sucking to schoolyard fights, parents reveal their secrets to solving the everyday problems of raising kids / edited by Ann Pleshette Murphy.

p. cm.

ly published: Emmaus, Pa. : Rodale Press, c1997.

Includes index.

ISBN 1-58238-015-5 (alk. paper)

d rearing.   2. Infants.   3. Parenting.   I. Parents (New York, N.Y. : 1993)

HQ769.P275   1997b   97-13572

649'.1—dc21   CIP

First published in the United States by Rodale Press, Inc.

First St. Martin's Press Edition: August 1999

10   9   8   7   6   5   4   3   2   1

To Rob and Gracie; and to Dorothy Lee and Josephine Niosi, who are never short of good advice
—*Sally Lee*

To Beth, Chris, Essie, Fin, Janet, Lauren, Molly, Ruth and Sonia. moms whose friendship, great advice and example make being a mom even more fun
—*Marge Kennedy (also known as Caitlin's mom)*

For Steven, Maddie and Nick
—*Ann Pleshette Murphy*

For the children in my life: Amanda, Kristi and Chelsi Kosarin, and Justin and Alexander Morelli
—*Linda Kosarin*

Contents

CHAPTER ONE

Baby's First Year - 1

CHAPTER TWO

Let's Eat! - 39

CHAPTER THREE

Bathtime and Grooming - 71

CHAPTER FOUR

Bedtime from A to Zzz - 96

CHAPTER FIVE

Potty Time - 113

CHAPTER SIX

Health and Safety - 132

CHAPTER SEVEN

Child Care Solutions - 184

CHAPTER EIGHT

Positive Discipline - 208

CHAPTER NINE

Family Relationships - 237

CHAPTER TEN

Your Child's Emotional Life - 267

CHAPTER ELEVEN

School Days: A Primer - 289

CHAPTER TWELVE

The Working Life - 317

CHAPTER THIRTEEN

Household Hints - 343

CHAPTER FOURTEEN

Fun and Games - 372

CHAPTER FIFTEEN

On the Road - 404

CHAPTER SIXTEEN

Time for You - 424

F O R E W O R D

Not long ago, I got a call from a *Parents* magazine reader desperate for advice. Her twenty-month-old son wouldn't stay in his new big-boy bed and was up half the night, begging to come sleep with her and shrieking until she gave in. To make matters worse (for both of them), she was already getting up two or three times each night to nurse his new baby brother. Frustrated and exhausted, this mom needed support and a quick-fix strategy.

I shared some of the expert advice we'd run in the magazine: Give the jealous big brother some extra "baby" time during the day, vary his bed-time routine at night, and tough out some sleepless nights by firmly, and quietly, returning him to his own bed over and over again until he gets the message that 2:00 A.M. is not cuddle time. She listened to every word, asking an occasional question about the whens and hows. Then I told her about the one special trick a friend had shared with me, and the entire conversation opened up. Suddenly, we were no longer speaking editor to reader but mother to mother, friend to friend.

"Try putting your son's mattress next to your bed," I suggested. "Every night tuck him in bed, but over the course of the next two weeks slowly move the mattress out of your room and into his. He'll get used to sleeping in his big-boy bed, but the transition won't be quite so rough on him."

For a magazine editor, there is nothing more satisfying than knowing you've reached your readers with information they need—information that makes their lives easier, better, happier. For more than seventy years, *Parents* has led the way in helping new moms and dads make a smooth, successful transition to parenthood with expert advice on everything from diapering to discipline. But many of the pros our readers turn to every month are other parents. Under various titles over the years, our popular column "It worked for me!" has dispensed tried-and-true solutions from the most knowledgeable sources: our readers.

Who else but another parent would have this handy tip for toilet-teaching: "Line your child's potty with disposable coffee filters. It makes cleanup quick and easy." Or this solution for getting kids to take their medicine: "If you have a child's tea set, throw an impromptu tea party. Mix the medicine with white grape juice and pour it into the tiny cups. Once you make a game of it, they'll drink it right up."

That kind of kitchen-table wisdom, which mothers share daily with friends and neighbors over coffee, at the playground, or on the checkout line, is more valuable than any textbook tip, because it comes from real-life experience and because it makes parents feel supported and connected in a job that can sometimes be overwhelming and isolating: raising young children. In today's world, where face-to-face connections are harder to make and keep, this book brings that coffee klatch right into your home.

There's nothing like the wisdom, warmth and humor of another parent's words to help put your own parenting questions in perspective, to ease your doubts and remind you that there are as many ways to solve a problem as there are people in this world—and to remind you that the more we share with one another, the more we grow as parents together.

—*Sally Lee, Editor in Chief*

CHAPTER ONE

Baby's First Year

Y*ou've got a new life to nurture, one that's unique in all the* world. As you look down into the bassinet, you feel overwhelmed by love—and perhaps by a little panic, too. You realize that nothing has quite prepared you for this moment. As hard as it might be to imagine, you will adjust to your newfound status as a parent. A few things will come naturally—but not as many as you may want. You'll learn a few tricks by trial and error. You'll pick up others from friends and family who have walked this path before. You'll even invent a few clever baby-raising tricks of your own. And pretty soon, you'll be the one that new parents will turn to for advice. For now, enjoy the surprises as they unfold. There's no need to hurry this first year. Instead, savor it.

Welcome Home!

While the idea of parenthood occupied your thoughts for nearly a year, the reality of family life really takes hold when you bring your newborn home. It's a wonderful and thrilling feeling to be on familiar ground, perhaps with friends and relatives gathered around, as you introduce your son or daughter to the world. The moment can also be trying. Who gets to hold her? Are the camera lights too bright? What does that funny face he's making mean? Is all the excitement too much for your baby—or for you? These parents have been there, and their suggestions can work for you.

Schedule visits

I was afraid that everyone would show up at our doorstep the minute we brought Jonathan home and I really wanted to have time to spend alone with my family for the first couple of days. My husband called everyone and arranged specific times for each family member or friend to drop by—*after* the third day. Everyone understood and by the time they came, I was ready for them.

Lisbeth Smythe, Chappaqua, New York

Enjoy the intrusion

Just about everyone on our close-knit block knew how difficult a time I'd had getting pregnant and were as thrilled as we were when Joshua was born. When we drove down the street coming home from the hospital, every mailbox had blue ribbons and balloons tied to it and our lawn was decorated with a giant It's a boy! poster. One neighbor caught the ride and our reaction to the sign on video, which helps us to remember how lucky we are to have Josh and such great neighbors. My advice to anyone who's lucky enough to have people who care about you and your baby is to be open to everyone's good wishes. There's no such thing as an intrusion when people really want to help you celebrate.

Linda and Donald Frank, Tucson, Arizona

Record the big moment

When we brought Cecelia home from the hospital, I walked her from room to room, showing her her new home. My husband took pictures of her first time in each place. We put all the pictures together in a Welcome Home album that Cecelia, now three, loves looking at.

Celia Sanchez, Highland, Michigan

Hire help

My daughter was born three weeks early and the house was not at all ready for her arrival. I was panicking about bringing her home when I didn't even have her crib set up. So I did something I never dreamed I'd do: I hired a cleaning service to come in and scrub the place from top to bottom. I also asked them to set up the baby's furniture, which they did. That was the best $100 I ever spent.

Emily Cranston, Arlington, Virginia

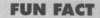

FUN FACT

More babies are born in September than in any other month. The fewest births occur in January.

Understand relatives' excitement

I had big plans for bringing my son, Demitri, home from the hospital. I was going to have a wonderful intimate time with my husband and baby with absolutely no interruptions. We planned to turn off the phone, draw the shades and just be together. Well, that was my fantasy. When we arrived at our door, we found two carloads of relatives waiting to greet us. At first I was heartbroken and felt really invaded. But I bit my tongue and now I'm glad I did. Yes, it was a bit overwhelming to have 10 guests in the house when I was so tired and didn't want the company. But before I let it get me down, I realized how lucky Demitri was to have so many people who care about him. I gave everyone a chance to hold him (even though they thought I was crazy to make them wear surgical masks and wash their hands first). After a few hours, they all went home and I got to have the quiet I wanted.

Theresa Popodopolus, Astoria, New York

Be prepared

If I had the coming-home event to do over again, I'd make absolutely sure that I had everything I needed—diapers, film, camera batteries, tiny-size stretchies, cotton swabs—before I got home. During the first day, my husband had to make at least 10 trips to the store as we kept finding that we needed things we didn't have.

Marge Lansky, Huntington, New York

Count on mom

I had a hard time explaining to my husband that I really wanted my mother here when we got home. He wanted us to be

PARENTS' BOOKSHELF

Great First-Year Advice

A trip to the bookstore or library will reveal many useful books on raising your child during his or her first year. These are a few of the most helpful.

Parents Book for Your Baby's First Year, by Maja Bernath (Ballantine Press)

Touchpoints, by T. Berry Brazelton, M.D. (Addison-Wesley)

What to Expect the First Year, by Arlene Eisenberg, Heidi E. Murkoff and Sandee E. Hathaway, B.S.N. (Workman Publishing)

Mothering the New Mother, by Sally Placksin (New Market Press)

Dr. Spock's Baby and Child Care, by Benjamin Spock, M.D. (Pocket Books)

alone for a few hours first. So I called my mother-in-law and asked her if *her* mother had been there when she'd brought my husband home from the hospital 32 years ago. "Of course, she was!" my mother-in-law answered. My husband laughed and said, "Well, if my grandmother was there, I suppose my son's grandma should be there, too."

Anna Lapinsky, Boston

Plan a celebration

I'm the youngest of three kids and my older brother and sister each had two children before my son was born. My husband's family, too, had grandchildren, so

PARENTS' CHECKLIST

What You Really Need for Your Baby's Nursery

Here's a list of basic items for a new baby. It's not meant to cover everything your baby will need, but you'll be off to a good start with this assortment.

Clothing

- 8 to 10 undershirts
- 3 "onesies"—snap-crotch T-shirts or bodysuits
- 4 to 6 sleeping gowns or kimonos
- 2 or 3 blanket sleepers (for winters in cool climates)
- 4 to 6 stretchies or coveralls with feet
- 1 or 2 sunhats or cooler-weather hats (depending on season)
- 1 or 2 sweaters (more for winter)
- 1 pram suit or bunting with attached mitts (for winter weather)
- 3 pairs socks or booties
- 3 washable bibs
- 1 special dress-up outfit
- 3 or 4 waterproof pants, diaper covers or diaper wraps (if you're planning to use cloth diapers)

Linens

- 2 waterproof mattress pads for crib
- 2 quilted mattress pads for crib
- 4 to 6 receiving blankets (depending on the season)
- 3 or 4 terry bath towels with hoods

- 4 dozen cloth diapers (1 for burping, 3 for diapering)
- 3 or 4 fitted sheets for crib, cradle, bassinet and/or carriage
- 2 washable crib or bassinet blankets or comforters (avoid long fringes and loose threads)

Toiletries

- Baby soap
- Baby shampoo
- Baby lotion and baby oil
- Diaper wipes
- Diaper-rash ointment
- Sterile cotton balls or swabs
- Blunt nail scissors or clippers and file
- Baby comb and brush
- Petroleum jelly

Furniture and features

- Crib

It's important to use a crib made after 1974 that meets the Consumer Product Safety Commission's standards. To be sure that your baby's crib meets current standards, inspect it carefully to see that

---

that by the time my baby came home, nobody in our extended families got too excited about a new baby. All of our siblings were too busy with their toddlers and preschoolers to be able to celebrate when

our turn at parenthood arrived. We decided that instead of letting ourselves feel bad about the lack of attention that we'd organize a big family party for when Liam was two weeks old. We invited the whole

the slats are spaced no more than 2⅜ inches apart and are in good repair; any corner posts are no higher than 1/16 inch; there are no cutouts in the footboard or headboard that would permit head entrapment; the mattress fits snugly with a space of less than two fingers' width between the mattress and crib sides; the mattress support is securely attached to the footboard and headboard and the sides are securely held in a raised position by latches that cannot be released by your baby; all screws and bolts are present and tight and the finish or paint is nontoxic.

•Changing table

Be sure it has easily accessible drawers and shelves, plus safety straps to prevent your baby from rolling off. It should also be stable, to prevent tipping.

•Comfortable rocking chair
•Hamper
•Diaper pail (for cloth or disposable diapers)
•Storage units

Choose pieces that allow for various uses now and in the future such as wheeled stacking bins, baskets or plastic crates for diapering supplies at first and toys later. Other good storage choices: bookcases with adjustable shelves for folded clothing, books and soft toys now, games and schoolbooks later; peg racks or hooks mounted on the walls; wheel-mounted under-the-bed storage containers; an artist's trolley with shelves.

•Nursery monitor (optional)
•Safety accessories

Electrical outlet covers; nonskid pads for underneath throw rugs; cord wraps to wind accessible electrical wiring and pull cords for window blinds or shades; window locks and window guards; smoke detector—with working batteries; locks on cabinets with cleaning supplies; lock on toilet; stair gates; bumpers around sharp edges.

•Mobile and/or artwork (for over baby's crib)

Newborns are drawn to black-and-white visuals. Infants over the age of three months will also like primary colors. Be sure to remove the mobile once your child is able to pull him or herself up—at about five months—-to prevent entanglement.

family and we even hired a clown to entertain the other kids. Because we knew that everyone, including us, was on a tight budget, I asked each person to bring a hand-me-down for our new baby and a dish of food to share. Everyone came and Liam, my husband and I got our moment in the spotlight—and a wardrobe that will last a year or so.

Ailis O'Connor, Albany, New York

Premature Infants

Almost all parents marvel at the smallness of their infants. Parents of babies measured in grams instead of ounces know that a baby's size does not correlate to their love or hopes for him. Nor does a baby's prematurity obscure her personality. One dad, who's son was born weighing less than three pounds and with health problems, says, "Even though I could hold him in one hand, I could tell that he had a feistiness, a tremendous spirit." And he adds of his now six-year-old, "By the time he left the hospital at two months, his sense of humor was already apparent." These parents offer advice and wisdom gained from their own experiences.

Get early intervention

If your child is born prematurely, enroll him in an Early Intervention Program (EIP) as soon as possible. They're free, state-sponsored programs designed to give at-risk infants, toddlers and preschoolers the extra boost they may need to catch up developmentally. My son, now two, has met regularly at home with physical and occupational therapists since he was seven months old, and a speech therapist since he was 20 months old. He's still behind cognitively and physically, but as long as there's progress, his doctors are pleased. Some premature babies catch up to their peers by the time they are two years of age; however, all preemies are different and some may take until they are three or four or even older. Call your local department of health or education for more information about how to sign your child up for an EIP.

Karyn K. Miller, Neptune City, New Jersey

Secure Social Security benefits

Apply for preemie perks immediately through your Social Security office. If your baby weighs less than two pounds, ten ounces at birth, you may be eligible for at least $400 a month starting the day that you apply. Call with an intent to file an application and set up an appointment. (SSI is not retroactive to the baby's birth, only to the day that intent to file was established.) And don't worry if you don't have a Social Security number yet for

PARENTS' RESOURCE

More for Preemies

- **Pediatric specialists:** For referrals to preemie specialists in your area, send a business-size SASE to the American Academy of Pediatrics, Pediatrician Referral Service, P.O. Box 927, Elk Grove Village, IL 60009-0927.
- **Clothing:** For the littlest children, call The Preemie Store . . . and More!/TLC Clothing (800-O-SO-TINY or 714-434-3740), which offers preemie clothing and accessories.
- **Information and support:** Parent Care (9041 Colgate Street, Indianapolis, IN 46268-1210, 317-872-9913) is a national clearinghouse of information on premature babies. Write or call for referrals to local support groups.

your child, because it can be taken care of on the day of your appointment. As the mother of preemie triplets, I know how valuable these benefits are.

Etti Siegel, Kew Gardens, New York

Focus on home care

Check whether your insurance company will cover home nursing care for your preemie. This was a lifesaver for my family, because it allowed me to continue my job—and without it we would have lost our health insurance coverage.

Joanna Lucas, R.N., Madison, Wisconsin

Find a specialist

Find a caring pediatrician who specializes in preemie care. My son's doctor took time to explain—in terms that I could understand—the lifesaving equipment and medications that my baby was on. Knowing that I could call her at any time, or just bring my son in to be weighed and measured, gave me peace of mind. Sometimes she even opened the office early so that my son wouldn't be exposed to other children's illnesses. She also helped me select other specialists, such as a cardiologist and a nutritionist. I realize that there's no perfect doctor, but if you're not satisfied, find another one.

Holly Froning, Rockton, Illinois

Apply for a parking permit

Apply for a temporary handicap sticker from the Department of Motor Vehicles while your baby is still on medical equipment. It will make your life much easier going to and from doctor's appointments.

Susan Rodbell, Bethesda, Maryland

Learn procedures

My husband and I were taught how to use a heel stick so that we didn't have to bring our triplets, four monitors and oxygen tank to the hospital every three weeks for a blood check. Instead, my husband just dropped off the blood samples at the lab.

Judy Stelmack, Wayne, New Jersey

Hang in there

I was scared to bring my premature twins home. I cringed at the thought of using CPR, but I knew it was the most vital skill I could learn. I didn't think that I could ever administer oxygen, but I did.

ASK THE EXPERTS

How Can I Ensure That My Pet Will Behave around My New Baby?

Veterinarians are all too familiar with the syndrome. Before couples have children, pets get all the attention. But when an infant arrives, Fido finds himself in the doghouse. Vets say that these tips will help ease the transition for their furry firstborns.

- If your pet has *not* shown aggression toward children in the past, ask a friend with a baby to visit so your pet can see and smell their child. Becoming familiar with any baby will ease the shock somewhat. If your pet has been aggressive toward children, talk to your veterinarian, an animal trainer or animal-behavior specialist before bringing your pet into contact with your child to learn what must be done before the baby arrives. Any animal that shows hostile feelings to a child must be kept away from children. If your pet growls, hisses, bares its teeth or if its hair stands on end when it is around a child, you may have to consider finding it a new home.

- Before your new baby comes home, bring an undershirt that he wore in the hospital for your pet to sniff. Also let it investigate the baby's room both prior to and after the baby's arrival, while the baby is not there.

- When you first bring your infant home, greet the dog or cat for 5 to 10 minutes while your spouse or someone else tends to the baby. After your pet has gotten over its excitement at seeing you, make formal introductions to the newest family member.

- Include your pet in family activities as much as possible, particularly those that the pet is used to partaking in, such as lazing on the sofa with you while you read or watch TV. Try to spend 10 to 15 minutes a day exclusively with your pet so that it doesn't feel neglected.

- When your pet behaves well in the baby's presence, offer praise.

- Never leave your pet alone with the baby, even if you're sure that the pet wouldn't harm your infant. Pets can be curious, and a cat or dog that cuddles up to a newborn can smother or otherwise harm the baby.

- If your pet begins to have urinary accidents, have a urine sample tested to rule out cystitis, diabetes and kidney disease, all of which can be treated with medication and dietary changes. If tests reveal that your pet is healthy, consult your veterinarian or an animal behavior specialist for behavior-modification training to help the pet adjust to the new arrival.

The thought of the apnea monitor going off kept my husband and me awake on countless nights, but eventually it gave us peace of mind. On some days I wanted to give up and scream, but I did what I had to do. Hang in there—things will get easier.

Cindy Cummins, Lawrenceville, Illinois

Have faith

Preemies do thrive! My daughter had heart surgery 36 hours after her birth, and was on an apnea monitor, oxygen and endless medications when she came home. Worst of all, the doctors gave her a poor prognosis. I'm proud to report that our preemie will soon be 11 years old. The only way you'd be able to tell that she was a preemie is by her chest-tube and heart-surgery scars. Otherwise, she's healthy, she excels in school and she's the tallest child in her class.

Sue Zandbergen, Caledonia, Michigan

Be prepared

Before any emergency, inform your local ambulance company that you have a premature infant and give them a map highlighting the most direct route to your house. Keep an updated record of your baby's medicines with you at all times. I also posted a large calendar on my refrigerator so that both my husband and I could track the dosages and the times we gave our son his medications. It was a good way to help us check on each other, especially when we were both feeling exhausted.

Karen S. Whitney, Collegeville, Pennsylvania

Alter clothing

I purchased a lot of onesie outfits that snap down the front so that I didn't have to cut holes in my son's T-shirts to attach the wires.

Lisa Prashach, Pearl River, New York

Give yourself time off

Take breaks; otherwise you'll burn out, as I did. My parents, sister-in-law, two nieces and baby-sitter took training in CPR and learned about the apnea monitor so that I could get out of the house sometimes. Now I exercise at the local YMCA, go for walks, read or just soak in a hot bath. Do whatever helps you unwind.

Lori Swanson, Marinette, Wisconsin

Hook up by phone

My lifesaver was a telephone support network of preemie parents. It was run by the newborn intensive-care unit in the hospital where my daughter stayed for seven months. I called my phone buddies anytime I felt lonely, frustrated, depressed or just excited that my child had accomplished something new. It's vital to connect with people who can truly understand what you're going through. Remember: Although it may feel like it at times, you are not alone!

Teresa M. Kwasnik, Winfield, Illinois

Join a support group

I felt cheated out of a full-term pregnancy. I was sad that I gave birth to an unhealthy baby and worried that he would develop at a slower rate. But once I resolved these issues with the help of a support group, I could rejoice in each of my son's milestones. The first time he rolled over or walked wasn't on schedule, but nevertheless, it was his first and it was exciting.

Georgeanne Roberts, Fort Worth, Texas

Is a Doula Right for You?

If your best friend, mother or mother-in-law isn't available or doesn't have the right personality for the job, you can still get help by hiring a doula. *Doula* is a Greek word for a woman whose job is to attend to the new mother.

Doulas take care of a mother's physical and emotional needs during the postpartum period. They know about breastfeeding, baby care and the mother's postpartum body. A doula will also take care of the baby or siblings or do chores like cooking, cleaning and laundry. Rates for doula services vary around the country, averaging $11 to $15 per hour.

To find a doula, look under Maternity Care Services or Postpartum Services in the Yellow Pages or check the advertising section of your local parents newspaper. To receive a list of doulas in your area, write to the National Association of Postpartum Care Services, P.O. Box 102, Edmonds, WA 98020, or call 800-45-DOULA.

Adjust your expectations

Have realistic expectations about your baby's cognitive and physical development. Think in terms of his adjusted age—that's his due date, not his birth date—if you compare his progress with milestone charts. Keep in mind, however, that these charts are only guidelines; not even all full-term babies accomplish each task on time.

Bridgette Nevola, Neshanic, New Jersey

Enjoy accomplishments

Ignore all the people who say, "He's so small." In time you'll be very surprised at what your child can accomplish. Although it may be hard to believe now, many of the painful memories will be just that—memories.

Karen Valk, Kingsport, Tennessee

Take lots of pictures

Don't forget to take lots of pictures of your premature child. You'll be amazed to

see how much the baby has changed. I took monthly pictures of my twin daughters with their stuffed animals, and it was encouraging to see how much they'd grown. Preemies are a bit more fussy than full-term infants—their tolerance level is not as high. I found that my preemies were soothed by the time they spent in their battery-operated swings.

Cassie Demerath, Appleton, Wisconsin

Mothering the New Mom

Rightly so, a new baby in the family brings out everyone's desire to coo, smile and make the little one smile back. Every new mother wishes that someone would take a moment or two to envelop her in that warm embrace of care. These moms tell about some of the best things their friends and families did for them in those early weeks of motherhood and the things they did for themselves, too.

This may be the page you want to leave open on the coffee table. After all, it never hurts to drop hints about what you'd like. Or better yet, tell those who love you what you need and want right now. They really do want to help, but may not know what to do.

Rely on friends

I felt so scared when I brought my baby home. Even though my husband was with me I knew the two of us were no match for the responsibility. I couldn't believe it when we got home and I found a dozen notes, arranged in a heart, on our front door. Each note was from a friend who promised a particular service. From a mother of four I got a promise to answer 100 questions about new babies. From my next-door neighbor, the note said, "Good for seven casseroles." Another friend's note said, "Good for one hour per day of time to yourself while I watch the baby." Each and every one was for something that I really needed and appreciated.

Moira Delaney, Yarmouth, Maine

Count on teen helpers

My teenage sisters got to our house before we did and had the nursery all ready for their new niece, Kate. They'd even put all the presents we received in the drawers. They also had a nice meal ready for us and a bath drawn for me. It was wonderful.

Kathleen Blaise, Indianapolis

Don't hesitate to ask

I'm a single mother and when I brought my daughter home I was both terrified and excited. I knew that I needed friends and family to help out, and I wasn't afraid to ask people to pick whole days to be with us for those first few weeks. Different people, including my sisters and brothers and friends and co-workers, each took a time slot. I'm sure that we would never have survived without their help. I think it's important to recognize that new motherhood is exhausting and that you can't do it all by yourself.

Heather Alexander, Address withheld

Take care of yourself

I arranged for a doula—a woman specially trained to take care of me—to meet us on the second day home from the hospital. She did things like massage my feet, make me tea, talk to me about everything on my mind and generally make me feel well-cared-for. Giving birth was harder than I thought it would be and being treated like I'd just joined a very exclusive club after the birth was fabulous. I hired Maryanne, the doula, for four hours a day for 10 days. I'd do it again, and I've recommended this service to every pregnant woman I know.

Sandy Carrithers, Poughkeepsie, New York

Great Gifts for New Moms

- A basket of body-care products, such as bath salts and lotions
- A gift certificate for a massage, facial, manicure/pedicure or other feel-good treat
- A new nightgown and a pretty robe
- Soothing music tapes or CDs
- Rocking-chair cushions for comfortably holding baby during feedings
- A basket or tin of delectable foods
- Time—in the form of offers to babysit, to go on errands or whatever the new mom requests

Enjoy some luxury

I loved getting all those cute little clothes for my daughter, Amy, but I think the favorite gift I received when she was a newborn was a basketful of things to make my life easier—bath salts, special teas, even new sexy underwear. My daughter is two now, and she's outgrown everything we received for her. But I still have my basket and the undies!

Caroline Cheo, Shaker Heights, Illinois

Hire a sitter

During my maternity leave, I arranged for a sitter to come in for one or two hours a day to give me a rest. Sometimes I just slept. Sometimes I took a long bath. A few times I met friends for lunch. My baby was fine without me and I was always refreshed when I came back to her.

Isabel Bailey, Oshkosh, Wisconsin

Share the care

It was really important to me that my husband be a hands-on dad. In theory that's what we both wanted. I was so sur-prised to find out, though, that I was afraid to let him take charge of our daughter, afraid he didn't do things right. I had to make a real effort to let him do all the normal things that parents do, like diapering and soothing her when she cried, even if he did them differently than I would have. By not interfering, I was able to rest, go out and take care of myself. Our daughter is now six and my husband knows as much as I do about raising her. My advice for new moms is to assume that dads can handle baby care. And by sharing the child care you'll have a lot more energy and time to take care of yourself, too.

Darlee Mavins, St. Catherine, Quebec

Eat well

Here's the perfect gift idea for a new mother: Decorate and fill a basket with decaffeinated teas and coffees, jellies, cereals, bagels, homemade breads and fruits. It's a welcome gift for new moms who need to eat healthful foods but are often too busy to cook.

Beth Wagner, Saylorsburg, Pennsylvania

Survival Guide for New Moms
10 Ideas to Make You Feel Good Now

1. Take a shower every morning.
2. Take a walk.
3. Sleep when the baby sleeps.
4. Get a sitter once in a while.
5. Accept help.
6. Find the right doctor, for both you and your baby.
7. Beg, borrow or buy good baby equipment, items that will mean more convenience for you and comfort for your baby.
8. Socialize.
9. Give yourself some credit. You deserve applause for all you do.
10. Indulge those loving feelings and cuddle your baby whenever you can.

Meet other moms

If you want mothering after you become a mother, seek out other moms. I was so lost in those first weeks that I thought I'd die. Thank goodness spring came and I walked to a local playground and found a dozen other women in the same boat. I've become good friends with a few of them. I recommend to every new mother that she find other moms in her neighborhood to spend time with. Just talking to someone else who's in the same position will do wonders for you.

Jessica Diaz, Center Moriches, New York

Learn to catnap

Not getting enough sleep is the hardest thing for new moms. After two weeks of sleepwalking because my baby never slept when I did, I learned to sleep when he did. Every time he took a nap, so did I. Changing your sleep schedule doesn't take as much getting used to as you might think. And it's a lot easier than learning to live on no sleep at all.

Maria Buxton, Akron, Ohio

Just for Dad

When everyone's attention is riveted on your child and your wife, you may understandably feel a bit left out. It's not at all unusual for new dads to want—and need— some of that special attention for themselves. These dads found ways to enjoy their new roles.

Realize you're not alone

At first I was surprised by how jealous I felt that I couldn't breastfeed my son. I was also too embarrassed to say that this was bothering me. Fortunately, when Connor was about 10 days old, another couple with a new baby visited us and the husband said, "I get to do everything but breastfeed." I was surprised to find another father who felt the same way. Somehow just knowing that I wasn't the only dad on the planet with this feeling made it go away. And now that Connor is seven months old and is drinking from a bottle, I do get to share in feeding him.

William Stacey, Address withheld

Get into the act

My wife and I have four children, ranging in age from eight months to 12 years. A lot has changed in that time. With my firstborn, I was like a visiting dad. I held her and took her for walks but didn't do much of the day-to-day stuff. Now, with the baby, I'm able to change a diaper while I'm finding a missing sneaker for the four-year-old. My advice to new dads is to get into the dad act right away. Don't wait until your wife is ready to scream at you for help before you do what needs to be done. The secret is realizing that when you're home, you're just as responsible for the kids as your wife.

David Fichlin, Pontiac, Michigan

Find your own style

I think it's important to be the kind of dad you want to be, not just the kind of dad that women's magazines write about. Maybe you'll never get the hang of diapering and burping or take paternity leave, but that doesn't mean that you can't be a really good father. There's a lot to be said for working hard and bringing home a paycheck, too. What's important is that you spend as much time as you can with your kids and that you talk to them a lot

and listen a lot. I'm close to my kids in a different way than my wife is and that's okay with both of us.

Mike Ross, Orlando, Florida

Get help

Becoming a father made me really think for the first time in my life about what kind of person I was and what I wanted to be. At the same time, I also found it very scary to feel so responsible, not just to the baby but to my wife. I became worried about money, the condition of the house and the safety of the neighborhood. At 27, I felt like I had to fix the whole world. For the first time in my life, I saw a therapist to talk about all the things that worried me. It really helped. It also helped to talk to my wife about my feelings and to find out that she had some of the same worries.

Glen Cunningham, Address withheld

Talk

When my son was a few weeks old, I planned a surprise weekend away for my wife and me, but when the time came to leave our son with my mother, Karen wouldn't go because she didn't want to leave Mikel. I had been looking forward to having a fun time, away from child care. I was pretty upset. That night, we sat down together and each wrote up a "Here's What I Need" list. (That was Karen's idea.) I wrote down that I needed time alone with her and a few other things. She wrote down that she couldn't handle surprises right at that moment. We found that we both wanted a nice dinner out. So that's what we did, the next night. Since then, we've made a point of telling each other

Great Gifts for New Dads

- Alarm clock (for 3:00 A.M. feedings)
- Bathrobe or pajamas
- Slippers (for nighttime walks with baby)
- Film, tape and batteries (for the camera and camcorder)
- Picture frame (for dad's desk or workshop)
- Stroller handle extenders (to make pushing the carriage easier for taller men)
- Baby-care book of his own
- Journal
- Baby backpack
- Diaper bag designed just for dads
- Gift certificate to a nice restaurant and a promise of an evening's babysitting so that he and his wife can have a night out

what we need instead of trying to guess. When Mikel was eight months old, we finally did get away for the weekend.

Sam Wasserstein, Oakland, California

Get in the picture

I spent the first few weeks taking about a hundred pictures of my wife and new son. It wasn't until after the pictures were developed that we realized that I wasn't in any of them. My advice for all new fathers is to pass the camera around and make sure that you have some of your own memories recorded for all time.

Anthony D'Angelo, Bayside, New York

Be helpful

Sometimes I felt left out when my wife was breastfeeding. But the surest cure for my blues was realizing how I could help her. I handed her the baby so that she wouldn't have to get out of bed. I propped pillows under her arms so that she'd be comfortable (breastfeeding can strain the back and neck). I made sure she had cold water next to her at all times (breastfeeding moms are thirsty). Finally, I'd snuggle up next to my wife and watch her breastfeed our son. This was my greatest joy and helped me feel connected.

Gabriel Lauro, Des Moines, Iowa

Mom's Self-Image

Advertisers would have you believe that new mothers are all models of serenity and composure. Shown with sleepy babies nestled to their breasts, they may not look an awful lot like the mom looking back at you in the mirror. Just remember that those models have had plenty of sleep and haven't been thrown up on lately. Becoming a mom changed you in a number of ways—psychologically as well as physically. Over the next few months, you will regain much of your former equilibrium as your mind and body adjust. Just as important, you'll move forward, discovering new things about yourself, fine-tuning both your self-image and the image you project to others.

Think pretty thoughts

I like to think of my body as a beautiful instrument that created and nourished my children. If I have to pay the price by being overweight for a while, it's worth it.

Sarah Cheslock, Hilliard, Ohio

Exercise and eat right

Drinking water and walking were key to getting me back into my pre-pregnancy jeans. I walked everywhere I could, I drank 10 or more glasses of water a day and I was careful to snack mainly on fruits and vegetables.

Dana Cohen, Ocean Park, British Columbia

Go for a new look

After my baby was born I changed my hairstyle and colored my hair. The immediate results made me feel like new.

Lea Caldwell, Elizabeth City, North Carolina

Shower early

The hardest but most rewarding thing I did for myself every day when my son was a newborn was to shower before my husband left for work and to dress in clean, comfortable, fashionable clothes. Looking good made me feel good.

Annette Coster-Blythe, Antioch, Michigan

Take it slow

I gained 70 pounds when I was pregnant with my twins. A month after they were born, I was still 22 pounds over my ideal weight. I knew I couldn't really diet because I was nursing. I asked my doctor about ways to lose weight and she said, "It took nine months to gain all that weight, so don't try to lose it all in one or two months." That was great advice. I decided to take it easy on myself about losing the weight immediately and to walk a lot, pushing the boys in their carriage, instead of cutting down on food. After nine months, I was back to my original size. Not paying too much attention to my weight really helped.

Lisa Morganstein, Bristol, Connecticut

Maintain your pleasures

Don't give up your real pleasures, whatever they are. I have to read my paper every morning and have a cup of coffee

Dressing Tips That Slim

V necks draw the eye downward to give the look of a longer neck and torso.

Dark colors seem to subtract inches. Try neutrals, such as navy or terra cotta.

Small prints create eye-catching interest without looking too loud.

Shoulder pads work waist-slimming magic.

Long necklaces work better than short, wide ones.

Tummy-trimming lingerie helps firm and flatten bulges.

without any interruptions. A friend of mine has to run at least a mile a day. Another friend loves to take long drives into the country. Whatever it is you love to do, keep doing it. Then you'll know that you're still you.

Peggy Kerrigan, Mt. Kisco, New York

Ask for compliments

Remind your husband at least once a day that you need to be told you're beautiful. In return, tell him that he's handsome, too.

Phyllis Carr, Des Moines, Iowa

Get new clothes

I bought new clothes after I gave birth and before I lost 25 pounds. It was too depressing to wear my maternity garb.

Teresa Nicklas, St. Mary's, Pennsylvania

Show off your baby

Though I was tired and not looking my best after Katelyn's birth, I made a point of dressing her up beautifully every day and taking her for a walk around the neighborhood. Having every one who saw us stop and comment on how beautiful she looked made me feel great.

Sally Houston, Chicago

Postpartum Blues

For some new moms, the time following your baby's birth can seem like a roller-coaster ride through a tornado. It seems like just hanging on is all you can do. Feeling blue after giving birth is a common phenomenon; roughly half of all new moms experience some form of post-birth baby blues. For most, the blues pass within a few days or weeks as your hormone levels return to normal. But for about 1 in 10 moms, it persists. These moms have been there and perhaps can help you through this difficult time.

Get support

I couldn't explain my weepiness after my son was born. I had every reason to be happy but I was miserable and ashamed to admit I was so sad. My husband was so worried that he called my doctor, who referred me to a psychiatrist. Taking antidepressants and joining a support group made all the difference. Now I'm able to enjoy my child and my life. If anyone can't face the days and weeks of dragging around, I say get professional help and get it right away.

Mimi Zigler, New York City

Take a break

I think my depression was exacerbated by suddenly being cooped up in the house with a newborn, seven days a week, during the winter. To help me, my husband and I designated Sunday as my day. While I sleep, my husband gets up with the baby and feeds her. Then he cooks me breakfast. Later I take a walk or a hike, get a massage, visit friends or see a movie. And I don't give in to the temptation to call home. I've learned to trust that my husband and baby will be fine without me for a few hours.

Sally Grenier, Niwot, Colorado

See a professional

My advice to any mother who's feeling depressed after giving birth is to get help

Help for Postpartum Pains

- **Engorged breasts:** Regardless of whether you breastfeed, your breasts can become engorged between 24 and 72 hours after birth. The hard, swollen and painful feeling won't last long, but in the meantime you can relieve the discomfort by wearing a supportive bra and applying hot or cold compresses to your breasts—whichever offers you the most relief. Hot showers work for some women. If you're nursing, try frequent, unlimited feedings.
- **Episiotomy pains:** Try a sitz bath or, even better, try standing in the shower with your back to the shower head and letting warm water flow over the incision for 15 minutes. When sitting, use a dough-nut pillow. If you're still in pain after the third day, your incision is extremely red or has a black or dusky appearance, see your doctor to check for infection.
- **Hemorrhoids:** Try an over-the-counter medication as well as a sitz bath. For many women, letting warm water from a squeeze bottle flow over the area after toileting also offers relief.
- **Afterpains:** These are severe contractions that occur during the first week postpartum, most often during nursing. Afterpains will diminish in duration and severity as the week progresses. You may want to ask your doctor to prescribe pain medication.

fast. If you tell your husband how you feel and he doesn't take it seriously enough, tell your doctor. If the doctor says something like "lots of women feel this way," demand a referral to a mental-health professional. The point is that your feelings are real and are potentially dangerous. I almost harmed my baby because I was so depressed. Four years later, I still shudder to think about it. If it hadn't been for a friend literally dragging me to a shrink, I might not now be having such a wonderful time with my little boy.

Andrea Melendez, Address withheld

Find the right medication

I had an anti-medication upbringing. Even taking an aspirin was frowned upon. But once my doctor and therapist convinced me that postpartum depression was not something I could control, I felt relieved. After taking medication for only a few months and going for several psychotherapy sessions, I began feeling better. My relationship with my husband has improved. I'm more relaxed and less critical. Overall, I feel like myself once again. And if that means being on medication for a while, I can accept that now.

Cathy Heppell, Los Angeles

Join a support group

Until I joined Depression After Delivery (DAD), a support group for mothers experiencing postpartum depression, I didn't know what was wrong with me or where to turn. I felt lost and confused and, most worrisome, felt no love for my child for the first three months after his birth. I'm now an active member of DAD and even counsel other mothers with postpartum depression.

Debbie Cassidy, Round Brook, New Jersey

Involve your husband

By going to counseling with me, my husband realized how much I missed my old life before the baby. I missed working, socializing, spending time alone and, most of all, spending time with him.

Somehow hearing me talk about my problems in front of a professional helped him understand the depth of my depression in a way that he hadn't before. Since then, our relationship has improved dramatically.

Maria Smith, Tulsa, Oklahoma

Admit your feelings

Through therapy I was able to learn that I wasn't a terrible mother because I had wished on occasion that I didn't have to be responsible for my two children all the time. My therapist also helped me realize that being a good mother is a hard job and that I should be proud, not embarrassed, about admitting that I needed help.

Lisa Argule, Hopewell Junction, New York

PARENTS' RESOURCE

Help for Moms with Postpartum Depression

There's no need to face your depression alone. The following can help.

Support groups

Depression After Delivery: Call 800-944-4773 or 215-295-3994, or write to DAD, P.O. Box 1282, Morrisville, PA 19067.

Postpartum Support International: Call 805-967-7636.

The American Psychological Association: Call 202-336-5700.

Postpartum Adjustment Support Services—Canada: Fax 905-844-5973, or write to PASS-CAN, P.O. Box 7282, Station Main, Oakville, Ontario L6J 6L6 Canada.

Books

The New Mother Syndrome—Coping with Postpartum Stress and Depression, by Carol Dix (Pocket Books)

Postpartum Survival Guide, by Anne Dunnewold, Ph.D., and Diane Sanford, Ph.D. (New Harbinger Books)

Talk to others

Once I started to open up and tell people what I was going through, an amazing number of women admitted that they, too, experienced postpartum depression. Knowing I wasn't alone helped me tremendously.

Laura Daminano, Antioch, Tennessee

Educate yourself

I learned the steps to wellness in my postpartum-distress group: education, sleep, good nutrition, exercise, time to yourself, time with your spouse, asking for and accepting help, referrals to postpartum specialists and, if necessary, medication and even hospitalization. I also learned that the worst things are denial and ignorance.

Susan Shields, Santa Barbara, California

Newborn Basics: Belly Buttons and Burping

Few first-time moms have ever seen a belly-button stump before, let alone actually cleaned one. And even though most have known that a baby's head needs gentle handling, not all are confident in handling their own baby's head gently enough. Hear how these moms handled their worries.

Use hospital services

I stayed at the hospital for only one day after my son was born. Even though all I wanted to do was sleep, I asked a nurse to spend some time with me reviewing all the basics. She showed me and my hus- band how to hold Jonathan, how to burp him and what to expect when his umbilical-cord stump fell off. I actually took notes. I felt much more confident because of her little lessons.

Myra Anna Tibett, Santa Monica, California

Check with professionals

When my son was just three days old, I called his doctor and asked if I could bring him in just so that I would be sure that I was doing things right. The office made a same-day appointment and assured me that everything I was doing was okay. I needed that confidence-builder.

Julia Johnston-Murphy, Grand Rapids, Michigan

Learn from experience

When I was diapering my newborn, I saw that the umbilical-cord stump was about to come off and I really panicked. I called a mother who lived in our apartment building whom I barely knew and screamed into the phone, "Her belly button's falling off and I don't know what to do!" She came over right away, with her two kids in tow. She showed me how to wipe the area clean gently and to put a tiny bandage over the small sore on my daughter's tummy. I recommend that all new moms have someone close by to call who can help if you're too scared yourself. I also found that by watching her carefully instead of letting my fear completely overtake me, I felt a little sense of competence returning.

Joleen Traiber, Fort Lee, New Jersey

Learn with your spouse

My husband is a real rough-and-tumble kind of guy and I was terrified that he'd play roughly with our infant daughter. I mentioned this to my doctor and asked him to go over baby care with us together at the hospital. I asked that he'd state specifically that a baby needs very gentle handling. The doctor gave us his talk and my husband took it all very seriously. Now he's even more concerned about accidentally jostling Caroline's head than I am. I feel much better that Jack, my husband, and I both take special care of our infant.

Rachel Haberstein, Brookline, Massachusetts

Relax

Over and over again, while my baby was a newborn, I kept reminding myself that babies have been surviving new moms for thousands of years. Because I'd read a lot, I knew much of what was ahead and wasn't too surprised when her bowel movements were green and when her belly-button stump became loose. I just kept saying, "This is normal; you'll get through it." We did.

Lenore Nunuez, Charlotte, North Carolina

Diapering

From the newborn days through the toddler years, you can expect to change about four to eight diapers a day—roughly 4,000 times in your child's young life. If the image seems bleak, don't despair. Diapering time can be playtime, talk time and teaching time all rolled into one. These moms offer some great tips to make the most of this routine.

Keep wipes moist

To keep baby wipes moist, store baby-wipe containers upside down every now and then. This way they all remain moist and the wipes that are on the bottom don't get overly soggy.

Anna Karski, Houston

Warm the wipes

The feel of cold wipes during diaper changes can be a chilling experience for babies. I keep my baby warm by storing the wipes next to the heat vent to assure her a cozy diaper change.

Susan Kade, Spokane, Washington

Give choices

My son used to put up a terrible fuss when I changed his diaper, until I gave him some control over the situation. When I allow him to choose where he wants me to change him—on his changing table or the floor, for example—he's easy to handle. He focuses on the power I've given him rather than on whether he wants to be changed or not.

Yvonne Wollenberg, Teaneck, New Jersey

Try the floor . . .

Because my son is such a squirmer while I'm diapering him, I switched from doing it on the changing table to the floor. It's much easier and I don't have to worry about him falling off.

Caryn Saunders, Albuquerque, New Mexico

. . . or the crib

I purchased an extra changing mat to keep in my son's room so that I can change his diaper safely without a fuss or a mess while he's in his crib. It comes in handy when my baby is in an especially wiggly mood and I don't want to put him on his changing table.

Lauren Goodall, San Diego

Rx for Diaper Rash

No matter how hard you try to keep your baby dry, diaper rash—reddish bumps or pink, scaly patches—can occur. Fortunately, it usually isn't painful and is easily treated. Try these ideas for preventing and treating the condition.

- Cleanse the affected area with water and moistened cotton balls or toilet tissue and pat or let air dry thoroughly before rediapering until the rash heals, usually in about one to two days. Avoid using scented wipes, which may further irritate your baby's skin.
- When a rash makes it painful for your baby's bottom to be wiped, try this: Fill a spray bottle with half a tablespoon of baking soda dissolved in 16 ounces of water. Vigorously spray your child's bottom with the solution to remove stool and urine and then gently wipe away any remaining soilage.
- Apply a thin coating of ointment containing zinc oxide or petroleum jelly at each diaper change.
- Let your baby go diaper-free for about 30 minutes several times a day.

Air helps heal the rash. *Caution: Never use a blow-dryer on your baby's skin; even a cool setting can burn your baby.*
- Change your baby as soon as he wets.
- Consult your baby's doctor if the rash does not heal within two days, if your child is in pain or if she has a fever.
- Always wash your own hands before and after changing a diaper and be sure that others who are caring for your baby do the same. If soap and water aren't handy, cleanse hands with an antiseptic baby wipe.
- Put your baby's diaper on as loosely as possible, rather than snug at the waist and, before putting the diaper on, snip some of the elastic from the bands around the leg openings to allow air to circulate around baby's bottom.

Get a puppet to help

To keep my baby from wriggling when I'm changing his diaper, I slip a funny puppet on my hand. My son is so busy watching the puppet help me that he stops squirming long enough for me to change him.

Sara McAllister, Seymour, Indiana

Keep an extra mat handy

I keep an extra changing mat in my living room so that I can easily change my son's diaper without having to run upstairs to his changing table. I also keep an extra mat in his carriage for quick outdoor changes.

Linda Lindner, Charlotte, North Carolina

Take cover

As the new mother of a son, I didn't know about getting sprayed when I changed him. Another mother taught me this trick: As soon as you remove the wet diaper, cover his penis with a clean diaper to catch any new urine stream. This gives you the few seconds you need to position the new diaper under him.

Adrienne Nichols, Arlington, Virginia

Play music

I turn on a soothing radio station whenever it's time to change my daughter. She lies back and looks for where the sound is coming from. The music seems to relax her while I change her.

Margo Mitchell, Address withheld

Hang a mobile

When I removed the mobile over my daughter's crib because she was getting strong enough to pull herself up to it, I rehung it over her changing table. Since she's never there alone, it's safe and it also does wonders for keeping her happy while I change her.

Nanette Gross, Farmingdale, New York

Teething Time

Cutting a first tooth is a momentous occasion, easily earning a place in your baby's record book. Typically, the first tooth comes in at around 7 months, though it's not uncommon for babies to get their first teeth anywhere between 3 and 12 months of age. When a baby's teeth come in, of course, says nothing about the rest of his development. As one mom of a child born with two teeth jokingly lamented, "I doubt they give scholarships for teething prodigies." No matter when your baby's baby teeth erupt, these teething tips should help ease the discomfort.

Freeze a washcloth . . .

A small, frozen washcloth rolled up is an ideal teether to relieve pain. The coolness relieves the baby's pain, and you always have washcloths on hand.

Marjorie Salzberg, Westchester, New York

. . . or a spoon

A silver spoon cooled in the freezer works well. Silver retains coolness for quite a while, and a spoon isn't a choking hazard for the baby. Don't, however, leave your baby alone with the spoon pacifier because your baby might hurt himself with it.

Linda Sprayreagan, Address withheld

Make an ice pack

Try a clean sock filled with ice chips and tied in a knot at the end. It's a simple but very effective way to provide comfort for a baby.

Elizabeth Crow, New York City

Ask your pharmacist

The pharmacist at our local drugstore recommended an over-the-counter ointment that really helped my son, James, during teething time. Even more than most doctors, I've found, pharmacists know what products parents buy again and again, and that's the best recommendation you can get.

Barbara Santucci, Address withheld

Stock up on teethers

Commercially made teethers, the kind with gel inside that you put in the freezer, are great. The trick is to have enough of them and to keep them handy. I pack a few in a wide-mouth Thermos for trips away from home. That way I always have one ready when Hannah needs one.

Debra Cole, Hartford, Connecticut

PARENTS' ALERT

Safe Teething Tactics

Here are some ways to make teething easier and safer for baby.

- Although chewing relieves teething pain, never give an infant hard or frozen foods to chew on. Small pieces can break off and pose a choking hazard. Instead, try a fluid-filled rubber teething ring chilled in your refrigerator or simply massage your baby's gums with your finger.
- Never tie a teether to a long string, which could wrap around your baby's neck.
- Don't apply brandy or other alcohol to your baby's gums. Even a small amount of alcohol can be toxic to an infant.
- Never use aspirin paste or other aspirin products to alleviate teething pain. Aspirin can be lethal for babies.

Colic and Crying

The crying jags that overcome some infants are probably harder on parents than they are on babies. Babies generally cry for a particular reason. Finding that reason and responding to it in ways that help alleviate an infant's discomfort are among the biggest challenges parents of newborns face. Crying is your baby's only means of letting you know that he or she needs you now. It's also important to realize that as infants grow, their crying spells grow considerably shorter. Colic usually ends by four months. Here are some thoughts on getting through these trying periods together.

Try the "colic carry"

While holding your baby, position her so that her stomach rests on your forearm. Her head should be turned to one side and supported with the palm of your hand. For some babies, this position relieves gas.

Jeanne Mitchell, Fairhaven, Massachusetts

Use your dryer

Run the clothes dryer and strap your child in his infant or car seat on top of it. The rhythmic motion and sound may help. Caution: Never take your hands off the seat, not even for a second.

Seferina Vega, Redwood City, California

Set a mellow mood

During my son's crying jags, I dimmed the lights, spoke softly and shut off the TV. This seemed to calm him down more often than not.

Jan Stearns, Waterville Valley, New Hampshire

Hold the baby close

I carried my daughter in a special sling designed for babies while I did the housework or grocery shopping or went for a walk. Within a short time, her fussy periods were over.

Molly L. Stone, Greenville, Texas

Change formulas

I changed my baby's formula to a hypoallergenic one that was made for babies who can't digest protein and his crying diminished considerably. Ask your doctor about this.

Rhonda Brooks, Livonia, Michigan

Check your diet

If you're breastfeeding, check your own diet. Something either bad-tasting or gas-producing was being passed along to my baby via my milk. When I cut out broccoli, cabbage, caffeine, onions and garlic, my son was fine.

Karyn Kreher, Clarence Center, New York

Rev up the blow-dryer

While holding and rocking my daughter in one hand, I held the dryer in the other (aiming the air stream away from the baby) because the motor's hum

PARENTS' RESOURCE

Baby Massage

To learn more about baby massage, contact the International Association of Infant Massage at 800-248-5432.

calmed her. Eventually, I made a tape recording of it as if it were a lullaby.

Josee Sauve, Cornwall, Ontario

Clean the floors

The vacuum cleaner saved me. My daughter would sometimes cry for six to eight hours nonstop. Then one day, when I was cleaning, I discovered her calmed response to the sound of the vacuum. From then on, I would turn it on just to soothe her cries.

Kim Lessnau, Allen Park, Michigan

Try static

Static on the radio was one remedy that worked wonders for my son. "White-noise" machines can be purchased from catalogs such as Hammacher Schlemmer (800-543-3366) and The Sharper Image (800-344-4444).

Laura Grodzicki, Waterford, Michigan

Give a massage

Babies love massages. I massaged my daughter's stomach with baby oil when she was fussy. Using gentle pressure, I ran my hands along the center of her stomach from just under the rib cage down to the pelvic area, from top to bottom only.

Bernadette E. Faris, Louisville

Get into the swing

Our little guy was mesmerized by the motion of his baby swing. When putting him in the swing didn't work, my husband gently bounced him on his knee in front of a mirror and chanted in a monotone. Sometimes I just held my son tight and walked around the house while humming motor noises.

Mary Ann Sieber, Cumberland, Maryland

Try car sounds

There is a device that replicates the noise and motion of a car doing 50 miles per hour and can be attached to the crib. SleepTight can be ordered by calling 800-NO-COLIC. We used it, and even though it was expensive ($79.95), we felt it was worth it.

Margaret Conte, Milford, Connecticut

Let water run

The sound of running water is soothing. So every night I put my son in his swing beside the bathroom door and took a bath. With the drain open, I kept the water running. The bath calmed my nerves and the running water calmed the baby.

Beverly Granger, Findlay, Ohio

Warm baby's feet

I put thick socks on my baby's feet when he began to cry. The warmth seemed to lull him to sleep.

Lisa Chipkin, Rego Park, New York

Try bicycling exercises

I placed a warm, wet washcloth on my son's tummy and gently exercised his legs in a bicycle-pedaling motion to help him expel gas.

Andria Kiel, North Plainfield, New Jersey

Warm baby's sleeping place

Warm your baby's sleeping area with a hot-water bottle before she typically starts to cry. Then put her down to rest. She may find the warmth relieving. Remember to check the area with your hand first to make sure it's not too warm.

Melissa Edmonds, Taylorsville, Kentucky

Head for the kitchen

Turn on just the stove light and fan and rock your child. My baby loved the glow of the light and the hum of the fan.

Katie Tibbits, Ballston Lake, New York

Hit the road

A car ride often works miracles. Many a night my husband could be found driving our daughter around the neighborhood trying to relax her.

Kim Kotlow, Franklin Park, Illinois

Go outside

Strap your baby in a front carrier and take a walk around the block. Fresh air can work wonders for both you and your baby. If you have a fussy baby, see if you can get someone to give you a break—even if it's just for 10 or 15 minutes on occasion. You need time alone to collect your thoughts and regain your strength before the next bout of crying begins.

Lisa Holden, Tecumseh, Michigan

ASK THE EXPERTS

How Will I Know If My Baby Has Colic?

Before assuming that your crying baby has colic, check with your pediatrician to rule out other conditions that may be causing your child's discomfort. And before assuming that you and your baby must simply endure the condition until he naturally outgrows it, take note. New approaches show that colic can be cured.

According to pediatrician Bruce Taubman, M.D., author of *Why Is My Baby Crying?* and clinical associate professor of pediatrics at the University of Pennsylvania, the key to reducing crying is learning to recognize and respond to your baby's cues. He suggests that parents keep a three-day diary, recording each incident of prolonged crying, to identify the incidents that trigger the tears. All babies, he points out, cry to express one of five basic needs: hunger, fatigue, the need for sucking, wanting to be held or the need for stimulation. Colicky babies—temperamentally more intense—simply turn up the volume in expressing these needs. Dr. Taubman suggests that by fine-tuning their responses to their baby's crying, parents can greatly reduce the intensity. He suggests the following adjustments in your response.

Fatigue: If your baby cries most prior to naps and bedtime, the crying may signal fatigue. Put the baby into his crib a few minutes prior to his regular sleeptimes rather than holding and rocking him off to sleep, which may be stimulating him into his fretful state. You'll know that this is the right move if, after allowing him a few unattended minutes, his cries diminish and he falls asleep. If the crying persists, he isn't sleepy.

Hunger: If your baby is crying even though you've just fed him or he isn't scheduled for feeding for a few hours, feed him anyway. If his crying stops, then you know his cries signaled hunger. Begin feeding him on demand rather than trying to follow any set schedule. If you're breastfeeding and your milk production doesn't keep up with his hunger, try offering a bottle of breast milk or formula after nursing.

The need to suck: Babies need to suck, independent of their need to eat. Sucking is comforting and calming. Offer a breast or pacifier to see if this need triggered his crying.

The need to be held: Babies need to be held, some more frequently than others. Don't worry that holding your infant too often will spoil him. If your baby only stops crying when you walk with him, however, the intent of his crying is not a need to be held, so try other calm-down methods.

The need for stimulation: Some babies cry out of boredom, especially if they're put down to sleep when they're not tired. Make sure your baby has some interesting things to observe—especially parents and siblings in action. Place him in an infant seat or swing where he can observe the action.

Swaddle

Even if it's warm outside, swaddle your baby in a receiving blanket. The snug feeling may make a crying infant feel so secure that he or she will stop crying.

Diana Kittredge, Fort Pierce, Florida

Be patient

I fought the colic demon with my daughter until she was four months old. My advice to other parents is "Hang in there." I also found that if I burped her more often than usual that this would reduce the amount of air she swallowed and would relieve gas.

Delores M. Middleton, Fort Riley, Kansas

Go fishing

Putting a fish tank in our son's room really helped relieve his colicky crying. The sound of the motor in the filter seemed to do the trick.

Erin Johnson, Stanford, California

Handling Everyday Routines

Simple things like taking a shower, getting dressed or talking on the phone are not quite so simple when a baby is demanding your attention. Though you now understand why nature endowed women with hips shaped to hold kids, you may wonder why mothers were not given four hands and, perhaps, an extra head, too. These moms figured out ways to meet the challenge.

For Shower Dilemma, the Answer's Transparent

When I was a new mother, I was afraid to leave my newborn alone while I took a

What about Pacifiers?

Pacifiers do not cause any harm to a baby's mouth and can provide much needed comfort. Here's what to keep in mind.

- Buy a pacifier with sturdy one-piece construction.
- Make sure it has a shield with ventilation holes.
- Look for pacifiers with an orthodontic shape.
- Never tie a pacifier around a child's neck, it presents a risk of strangulation. Opt instead for a commercially made clip-on holder that features a short ribbon.
- Never use homemade or makeshift pacifiers.
- Don't purchase pacifiers that contain imbedded squeakers or rattles.

shower, so I bought a transparent shower curtain. Now I put my daughter in her infant seat on the bathroom floor when I am showering. She watches me and listens to me sing while I keep an eye on her.

Melissa Hill, Tarpon Springs, Florida

Use baby slings

Whoever invented the baby sling deserves a medal. They're not just for taking trips outdoors, but are also perfect for holding your baby while you do things like write letters, pay the bills and do the dishes. Holding your baby close while leaving your hands free is a blessing.

Ellie Angelos, Nutley, New Jersey

Shop by mail

I was amazed at how many free or low-cost services are available that I'd never used before but need now. Since Caitlyn was born, I now order stamps by mail, have the groceries and newspaper delivered and the dry cleaning picked up and returned. I also found someone who'll cut my hair in my home, saving me a trip to the stylist.

Michelle Margolis, Tenafly, New Jersey

Get a portable telephone

Every new mother needs a portable telephone. I carry mine in my pocket around the house so I never have to interrupt what I'm doing to answer it.

Arabel Danson, Maui, Hawaii

Organize your errands

Make lists of things you need to do before taking your child for a walk. That ensures that you won't get home and find that you still need something. It also is nice to have a real agenda so that your walks feel more energizing and purposeful.

Linda Santucci, Brooklyn, New York

Keep watch

I put a ticking clock next to the infant monitor in my baby's room. Hearing the ticking through the intercom tells me the monitor is working and also lets me know when I am out of range.

Sandy Smith, Washington, D.C.

Entertain baby

To keep my one-year-old son, Jonathan, amused while I put on my makeup in the morning, I bought a two-sided mirror—one side for him and one side for me. From his infant seat he loves to look at himself, and his reflection keeps him occupied for the few minutes I need to put on my makeup.

Carrie Montoya, Park City, Utah

Set a schedule

I think it's important to help children, starting when they're a few months old, adjust to your schedule instead of trying to do everything around their schedule. I have three children and it would be im-

Getting Your Baby's Social Security Card

All children ages one and over must have their own Social Security number in order to be listed as dependents on their parents' tax returns. The card is free; to obtain one, call 800-772-1213 and request that Form #SS-5 be mailed to you. Then bring the completed form, your child's original birth certificate (with raised seal, not a copy) and your own identification to your local Social Security Administration office. Your child's card will be mailed to you within ten days. Ignore direct-mail solicitations from firms that offer to handle the paperwork for a fee. Although their mailings may look official, these firms are not affiliated with the government and there's no reason to pay for a service that is free.

possible for me to do everything when they want it. We'd have to have dinner at 3:00 p.m., at 6:00 and again at 8:00. My advice is to help the baby follow the same clock as you do, except that they need to be in bed earlier.

Dawna Suki, New York City

Keeping Your Baby Healthy

Nothing matters more than your baby's health. While you can't shield your baby from every germ, these moms have found ways to reduce their children's exposure to many common bugs and to work with their children's health care team.

Find a good doctor

Find a good team of doctors with a helpful office staff. I did and it makes a big difference. They never seem to tire of my telephone calls beginning with "I've got a little question for you . . ." If my questions can't be answered over the phone, they always squeeze my child in for an appointment.

Heidi Page, Petersborough, Ontario

Get fresh air

Being cooped up all day—even for a baby—can make you sick. Unless the weather is truly horrible, I take my twin sons out for a morning and an afternoon walk. Many of my friends are always keeping their children indoors at the slightest sign of illness or if the weather isn't perfect and their children have far many more colds than mine do.

Teresa Moran, Little Rock, Arkansas

PEDIATRICKS

- **To soothe a runny nose:** Put a bit of petroleum jelly, which can prevent chapping, on her tissues before wiping her nose.
- **To help the medicine go down:** If your infant spits up most of his liquid medicine or daily vitamins, try changing the way you give her the dosage. Instead of cradling your baby forward, as you would for bottle feeding, gently lean his head backward. Insert the dropper into your baby's mouth so that it is pressed against his cheek and tilted toward the back of his throat. Squeeze out the contents. He should swallow the entire dose quickly.
- **To prevent bedtime choking:** To make sure that your baby hasn't squirreled away food or a foreign object that she could choke on while sleeping, check her mouth before putting her to bed. Wash your hands and then gently sweep your finger along the inside of her cheeks and around her teeth and gums. Also, keep her sleeping area free of toys, pillows and other objects.

Avoid sneezers

Before I visit friends and relatives, I ask them if anyone is sick. I also ask that people not come over to my house if they know they aren't feeling well. Some are offended by my rules, but they make me feel better.

Tracey Grubb, Amelia, Ohio

Wash hands

Dress your baby properly and wash her hands and toys regularly with antibacterial soap. This may prevent common illnesses from recurring too often.

Christina Hoppy, Berwick, Pennsylvania

Avoid crowds

My son's pediatrician recommended that we spend a lot of time going out but also said that indoor crowds at malls and stores should be avoided since germs get trapped inside. One person's sneeze can infect a lot of other people in a closed space.

Lilleth Cowper, Lexington, Kentucky

Tracking Your Baby's First Year

"I never before had to put film on my list of budget items," laughs a mother of four-month-old twins, who admits to spending about $40 a month on film and processing. Many parents experience an overwhelming urge to snap pictures of just about everything their infants do. Others develop their talents as writers, recording all milestones in their journals. These parents share their ways of celebrating this remarkable year.

Keep a journal

Before the birth of my four-year-old daughter, I was given several baby showers by my family and friends. I purchased

PARENTS' ALERT

What You Should Know about SIDS

Each year more than 6,000 babies in the United States die of sudden infant death syndrome (SIDS). To reduce the number of babies who fall victim to SIDS, the U.S. Public Health Service and the American Academy of Pediatrics (AAP) are urging that healthy babies—even those who can turn over on their own—be put to sleep on their backs or sides. Many parents place their baby face down, believing that if an infant is laid on his back he may choke if he spits up. But research links the prone position to SIDS, the leading cause of death during the first year of life. (Researchers suspect that infants who sleep face down may breathe their own expired air and suffocate, particularly if they are placed on a soft surface.) "Keep your baby's crib free of soft pillows, comforters, sheepskins and other soft objects that can trap gas," advises John Kattwinkel, M.D., chairman of the AAP task force on SIDS. "Ideally, your baby should sleep on a standard infant mattress covered by a sheet." For the free brochure "Reducing the Risk of Sudden Infant Death Syndrome: What You Can Do" and a crib sticker that reminds caretakers of the proper sleep position, call 800-505-CRIB.

When to Call the Doctor during Your Baby's First Year

If you have *any* questions or concerns about your baby's health, call his or her health care provider. This guide can help you spot those symptoms that require medical attention.

Newborns to six weeks

Temperature: Any fever in a newborn infant is cause for a physician's attention.

Vomiting: Spitting up after eating is normal for many babies. Excessive vomiting, especially in the absence of eating, should be brought to your doctor's attention.

Yellowing of skin or eyes: If your baby was released from the hospital less than 36 hours after birth, be aware of any yellowing of the whites of his or her eyes or a yellowing of the skin. This is a sign of jaundice and needs to be treated.

Bring to your doctor's attention immediately.

Irregular breathing rate: Any breathing difficulty—faster or slower than normal, raspy, or labored—needs medical intervention.

Low appetite: Inability to eat or low appetite should be brought to a physician's attention.

Reduced urine output: Lack of urination or low output is a sign of dehydration, and a physician should be consulted.

Diarrhea: Loose, watery stools may lead to dehydration and should be

---

a pretty blank book as a keepsake, and I asked each guest to complete the following sentence: "The most important gift you can give a child is..." I treasure my book, and I find the wise words of the people I love inspiring.

Madeline Conover, Rochester, Michigan

Grow an afghan

When my 14-year-old grandson, Ted, was born, I knitted him an afghan using the basic granny stitch. Every few months,

as he grew taller, I added rows using a different-colored yarn each time. My daughter loves this keepsake.

C. M. Wegner, Minneapolis

Save the news

When my first daughter was born, I lived overseas because my husband was in the military. To keep connected to friends and family who lived in the United Sates, I wrote and asked each one to save the front page from their daily hometown newspa-

brought to a physician's attention.

Bulging or sunken fontanel: Any bulging or sunken appearance of the fontanel (the soft spot on baby's head) needs medical attention.

Six weeks to 12 months

Temperature: A temperature over 101°F should be brought to a doctor's attention immediately. Do not administer fever-reducing medication without a physician's instruction.

Vomiting: Excessive vomiting, especially in the absence of eating, should be brought to a doctor's attention.

Changes in bowel movements and/ or urination: Loose, watery stools can lead to dehydration; dry diapers may indicate dehydration. Bring it to the attention of a physician.

Changes in behavior: If your child is lethargic, excessively irritable, unusually drowsy, inconsolable and crying in a high-pitched, intense manner, has a greatly reduced appetite or is unresponsive, call his or her physician. A child's tugging on his or her ears may indicate that he or she has an ear infection.

Changes in appearance: If skin tone is pale or bluish, if there's an unexplained rash, if eyes are glassy, sunken or vacant looking, if there are any unusual nasal or other discharges, if lymph glands in neck appear swollen or if your baby just doesn't look right, call the doctor.

per that was published on my daughter's birthday. I had fun reading what was going on in America, and I kept each clipping in a special scrapbook as a memento.

Doreen E. Conner, Crownsville, Maryland

Stay organized

About the only thing I would do differently in terms of recording my son's first year is put pictures in albums as the photos were developed. When Bradley was about 11 months old, I was faced with an overwhelming pile of hundreds of photos

that needed to be organized by date and then put away. It was a lot of work. Since then, I have kept the photo albums up-to-date.

Monica Clark, Mayfield, Pennsylvania

Write a letter

On my daughter's first birthday, I wrote her a letter to tell her about this wonderful year that had just passed. I plan to write a letter on every birthday and give them all to her when *her* first child is born.

Marilyn Wells, Secaucus, New Jersey

ASK THE EXPERTS

What Are the First-Year Vaccines?

Vaccine	Birth	2 months	4 months	6 months	12 months
Hepatitis B	HB-1	HB-2		HB-3	
Diphtheria-tetanus-pertussis		DTP	DTP	DTP	DTP
Hemophilus influenza type B		Hib	Hib	Hib	Hib
Oral polio		OPV	OPV	OPV	
Measles-mumps-rubella					MMR
Varicella (chicken pox)					VVV

The vaccine name pinpoints the age at which the vaccine is recommended; the shaded bar represents the period during which it can be given. Notes on specific vaccines:

HB: At least 1 month should elapse between the first and second doses; the third can be given up until 18 months.

DTP: The fourth DTP can be given up until 18 months; starting at 15 months the DTaP (an acellular version of the DTP) can be given instead.

Hib: Depending on the Hib vaccine given at 2 and 4 months, children may not need a dose at 6 months; the next dose can be given up to 15 months.

OPV: The third OPV dose can be given up until 18 months.

MMR: Can be given up until 15 months.

VVV: The varicella vaccine is given between 12 and 18 months of age. Consult your doctor.

Children who do not have health insurance or are enrolled in Medicaid are eligible for free vaccinations through the federally funded, state-operated Vaccines for Children program: Call 800-232-2522 for your state's toll-free number.

Mark the calendar

Before my first son was born, I was looking forward to keeping a daily journal about his development. But I soon learned that there is no extra time with a new baby. Instead, I jotted down notes about the day's events on a calendar: "Today was quiet; Dad and Mom took you for a walk." "You sat up today!" "You love Winnie-the-Pooh!" These notes still trigger delightful memories.

Beth Zahn, Kenosha, Wisconsin

Record baby's growth

When my daughter was born, she received an oversize teddy bear, which my wife named Rosie in honor of the friend who'd given it to her. Every month during her first year, I took a picture of Beth lying next to or sitting next to Rosie. By the time of Beth's first birthday, she and Rosie were the same size.

Eric Neubal, Brooklyn, New York

Create a collage

It was impossible for me to individually frame all the great photos of my son's first year. Putting them in albums didn't allow me to display them. So my husband bought a huge plastic frame that we've used to create a collage of our favorite photos. It hangs in the kitchen for everyone to see.

Molly Parsons, New York City

Baby Play

To you, tossing a sock in the air and crawling to retrieve it might seem a bit boring. To your baby, it's a game of never-ending excitement. Will I catch it? Will it go farther this time? Where is it now? For small children, all things are play: eating, rolling over, getting a bath. Each activity offers a multitude of opportunities to learn and to interact with you and the world. Here are some great ideas for playful times.

Be there

Your three-month-old's most interesting toy is you! Laugh, talk, play with her hands and feet and tickle her gently. Babies also love looking in mirrors.

Ellen Perrich, British Columbia

Exercise together

I love to exercise with my two-month-old son. I place him on his back in front of me as I do push-ups. Every time I come down close, I kiss him. He giggles and squeals, anticipating my next kiss.

Colleen Corrigan, Quebec

PARENTS' BOOKSHELF

Great Books for Babies

Picture Books

Three Little Chicks, by Nicola Smee (Scholastic)

Baby Animals, by Gyo Fujikawa (Grosset & Dunlop)

Cyndy Szekeres' Counting Book 1 to 10 (Golden)

Garden Animals, by Sara Lynn (Macmillan)

"A" You're Adorable, illustrated by Martha Alexander (Candlewick Press)

Doggies, by Sandra Boynton (Simon & Schuster)

26 Letters and 99 Cents, by Tana Hoban (Greenwillow)

Pat the Bunny, by Dorothy Kunhardt

Storybooks

Are You My Mother? by P. D. Eastman (Random House)

The Little Engine That Could, by Watty Piper (Grosset & Dunlop)

Where's Spot? by Eric Hill (Putnam)

A Super Chubby Mother Goose Rhymes (Simon & Schuster)

Goodnight, Moon, by Margaret Wise Brown (HarperCollins)

Great Baby Games

Here are two games to play with your baby throughout the first year. Your baby's response to each one will change from month to month as he acquires more skills and experiences.

Spoon Flip

In this game, your baby learns that he can move one object with the help of another. To play, you'll need a toy block, a tablespoon and a lightweight object that fits into the bowl of the spoon (but not small enough to be a choking hazard), such as a plastic egg. Use the spoon as a seesaw with the toy block as its support. Put the plastic egg in the bowl of the spoon to weigh down the seesaw on that side. Then press down on the handle of the spoon so that the egg flips. At 6 to 7 months, your baby will watch you, but is not likely to imitate your action; by 7 to 9 months your baby will try to do the spoon flip himself and by 9 to 12 months, if you replace the plastic egg with another object—or use something instead of the spoon as a seesaw—your baby will recognize the game despite the differences and will pound on the seesaw so that the object flips.

Hide-and-Seek

This game teaches your baby that an object exists even when she cannot see it. You'll need a small toy and a cloth napkin. Place the toy in front of your baby and let her look at it for awhile, then cover it with the napkin. At 6 to 7 months, your baby will act as if the toy had never been there. (At this stage, it's out of sight, out of mind.) At 7 to 8 months, your baby will pick up the napkin to uncover the toy. At 8 to 9 months, try covering the toy, then distracting your baby for a while. When she sees the napkin, she will look for the toy underneath it, evidence that her ability to remember has increased. At 9 to 12 months, roll the toy under the couch. Your baby will go to the couch and look for the toy.

Try floor play

If you have an extra mattress at home, put a colorful sheet and soft toys on it, and keep it on the floor in your child's room. I find that it's an ideal spot for my daughter to play and roll around. Often she'll even lie down on her own to take a nap. It's also comfortable for breastfeeding my daughter in the middle of the night.

Sherri Altman, Okinawa, Japan

Read to baby

My daughter is certainly too young to read, but will sit still for 10 minutes or

PARENTS' ALERT
Safe Play

- Remove all playthings strung across a crib or playpen once a child reaches five months of age and has learned to push himself up. The U.S. Consumer Product Safety Commission also cautions against allowing toys to dangle into the crib; wall decorations with ribbons or streamers attached to them are also safety hazards if they are hung near a crib.
- *Never* shake a baby; even playful tossing and jostling may cause serious head and neck injuries that could result in blindness, brain damage or even death.

more while I read a book to her. Already she's let me know that she loves books because she takes a book out of the book basket I keep in the living room and crawls over to bring one to me.

Barbara Morganstein, Bethesda, Maryland

First-Year Money Savers

The best things in life may be free, but cribs and diapers and all the rest of your baby's needed gear usually require some cold cash or, as these parents found, a bit of creativity.

Use diaper liners

Instead of using a new diaper for each and every change, I purchased reusable diaper liners that work just fine for wetness. Now, instead of using six or eight disposable diapers a day, I use three or four.

Mary Ann Oliver, Edgewater, New Jersey

Buy used baby furniture

If you know anyone who has a baby about a year or more older than yours, ask if you can buy or borrow the baby things that they're saving for their next child or that are just taking up room. They'd probably be thrilled to have the garage emptied of used playpens and high chairs and the dressers emptied of outgrown clothing. Shortly before my son was born, I met a neighbor who had a four-year-old. She mentioned that she was saving for a trip to Disney World for him and that maybe she'd sell his baby furniture and some odds and ends to speed up the savings. I offered to buy all of the outgrown things myself. We agreed on $200, which we both considered a great deal.

Amelia Lord-Mazzola,
Hastings-on-Hudson, New York

Shop at rummage sales

Check out rummage sales—especially at nursery school fund-raisers. Babies' clothing that's hardly been worn sells for very little. I bought a large shopping bag full of goodies right before my daughter was born for less than $20.

Myra Hendricks, New York City

Make drawer liners from wrapping paper

Instead of throwing away the wrapping paper that was leftover after my wife's shower, we saved it and used it to line our baby's dresser drawers.

Bill Duarte, Atlanta

Buy store brands

Even though disposable diapers and diaper wipes are expensive, I can't live without them. But if I buy the store brand I save big. They are sold under the names of drugstore, supermarket or toy-store chains—and are about 40 percent less expensive than the brand-name products. Today's generic brands are often high quality: They don't leak any more than brand-name diapers do.

Kari Ming, Houston

Sign on for free samples

I asked my pediatrician for the addresses of drug companies that often supply free samples of over-the-counter medicines. I got on a few mailing lists and now receive coupons for many useful products.

Libby Smith, Fort Lauderdale, Florida

Ask for larger sizes

If anyone's offering to buy clothing gifts for your baby, ask them to buy larger than newborn sizes. During his first year, my son received dozens of 3- to 9-month size outfits but not much in larger sizes. By the time he was 6 months old, he was wearing a 12-month size. It was a shame that so many of the cute smaller outfits went unworn, while we had to go out and buy larger clothes.

Betsey McGuire, Redwood City, California

Avoid the stores

Every time I went out, I saw something adorable for my baby daughter. I spent a fortune on little outfits she really didn't need. To cut down on my spending, I had to avoid the stores—and opening catalogs—for a while.

Anna Carr, Green Bay, Wisconsin

CHAPTER TWO

Let's Eat!

Feeding provides your child more than physical nourishment. During your baby's first few months, it offers both of you a chance to snuggle up close, to learn more about each other and to practice reading each other's signals. (Fortunately, babies arrive fully prepared to let you know when they're hungry.) Reading other mealtime signals, however, takes a bit more practice to master. Is she breastfeeding enough? Is he ready for weaning? When should I begin to offer solid foods?

As your baby moves on to a more varied menu, feeding time evolves into a different kind of social experiment as your toddler learns the delightful texture of green peas squished between fingers or your preschooler insists that sandwiches cut into triangles really do taste better than squares.

Finding the right answers to feeding questions is more like attending a buffet than sitting down to a fixed menu. Substitutions are allowed! You can sample one method of enlisting your child's cooperation at mealtime to see if it works for you, or you can move on to something else. As your baby grows, his needs and tastes will change. You'll change, too, growing more confident, less worried, more attuned to your child's needs and more adept at meeting those needs. In time, you'll find that mealtime can be satisfying emotionally as well as physically.

Breastfeeding Success

Breastfeeding provides benefits to your baby and to you. Studies show that breast milk contains substances that boost your child's immunity and even raise his or her intelligence. Since breast milk lacks vitamin D, your physician may advise that you give your baby supplements. Breastfeeding offers you some protection against breast disease and weight control. It can also be one of the most intimate and satisfying experiences you'll ever know. But it's not always easy. Most moms need practical support and an extra dose of care for themselves to learn to breastfeed successfully.

Hang in there

I was totally unprepared for—and totally committed to—the idea of nursing my daughter. When an infection (in me) followed her C-section birth, even the nurses at the hospital told me to give up my plan to breastfeed. But I decided to

pump milk for the three days that I was sick. Meanwhile, she drank from a bottle. I called a lactation specialist and asked her to show me what I was supposed to do. Christina, my baby, was already used to the bottle, but after a few frustrating tries, we managed to work it out. I recommend that anyone who wants to nurse not give up on the idea too soon.

Kathy LaFont, Indianapolis

Working moms can nurse

I knew (or thought I knew) that I'd have to give up breastfeeding when I went back to work when my baby was three months old. At first that seemed okay, but since nursing was so pleasant, convenient and economical, I really wanted to keep it up. Pumping my breasts at work, however, was totally out of the question. So two weeks before I was due back at work, I cut

Nursing Help Hotline

For breastfeeding advice, call the La Leche League at 800-LA-LECHE or check your phone book for a local office. A representative can give you advice and support over the phone and, if you wish, put you in touch with a nearby lactation specialist who can visit and help you learn how to nurse, how to care for your breasts during nursing and answer any questions you have. Consultants are on hand Monday through Friday, from 8:00 A.M. to 5:00 P.M. CST.

Nutrition for Both of You

Breastfeeding moms need at least 1,800 calories a day, including 60 grams of fat, to ensure an adequate supply of milk. Discuss taking vitamin supplements with your physician. You need to be extremely careful of self-prescribing vitamins since mega-doses of some vitamins can be harmful to a baby. Limit alcohol consumption and don't smoke. And be sure to drink 8 to 10 eight-ounce glasses of water each day.

To get all the protein, vitamins and minerals you need, a nursing mother's daily diet should include the following:

- Milk—1 to 1½ quarts
- Fruits and vegetables—6 or more servings (2 should contain vitamin C and at least 1 dark green, leafy vegetable for vitamin A)
- Cereals, breads and pastas—3 or more servings
- Meat, poultry, fish and eggs—1 or 2 four- to six-ounce portions

down on nursing, doing it at night, before 8:00 A.M. and again after 6:00 P.M. I gave her bottles at the other times. Both my body and my baby got used to this schedule, and I was able to keep nursing her on this schedule for more than two years.

Marge O'Mahoney, Woodside, New York

Know the facts

Books often paint a rosy picture of nursing, but in the beginning it isn't easy, and it can take a toll on you physically. Within a few weeks, though, things fall into place, and breastfeeding is definitely worth any initial discomfort it creates. Nonetheless, I wish I had known that the ambivalence that I felt at first—because of sore nipples, sleepless nights and being constantly attached to my infant—was not unusual.

Sue Paul, Parma, Ohio

Get information *now*

Because my baby and I took well to nursing, the hospital staff assumed I knew what I was doing. But once I was home and my milk came in, Kayla had a hard time latching on to my engorged breasts. One night she got really irritable and I called the hospital for help. I was referred to a lactation consultant, who had an answering machine and didn't get back to me until the next day. By that time I had given her a bottle, which was the beginning of the end of nursing. I'll try again with my next baby, but I'll be sure to ask my doctor or the La Leche League for a breastfeeding hotline that's available around the clock.

Helena Falco, Chatsworth, California

Keep supplies nearby

I keep a basket filled with things I often need while I am breastfeeding my daughter: a cloth diaper for burping her, the TV remote control, a portable radio and phone, mail, baby-care books and my

Recommended Reading on Breastfeeding

The Working Woman's Guide to Breastfeeding, by Nancy Dana and Anne Price (Meadowbrook). Practical advice for working women—from planning for a leave of absence to selecting the right breast pump.

The Complete Book of Breastfeeding, by Marvin S. Eiger, M.D., and Sally Wenkos Olds (Workman). This new version of an old standby has all the up-to-date information you'll need in a format that's attractive and easy to follow.

The Parents Book of Breastfeeding, by Susan Flamholtz Trien (Ballantine). A reassuring and down-to-earth guide to the breastfeeding experience.

The Nursing Mother's Companion, by Kathleen Huggins, R.N. (Harvard Common Press). This book offers survival guides for the first week, the first two months and on.

Breastfeeding Your Baby, by Sheila Kitzinger (Knopf). Scientific, emotional and practical support for nursing mothers, though not very supportive if you plan to supplement breastfeeding with formula feeding.

eyeglasses. When my daughter gets hungry, I just grab the basket and I'm ready. She doesn't have to wait for me to get organized, and I don't have to jump up once we're comfortable.

Cathy Campbell, Harrisburg, Pennsylvania

Which breast is next?

While nursing, I found that I often forgot on which breast I last began. To remind myself, I bought an inexpensive ring that I switch from hand to hand each time I changed sides. It was an easy and discreet way to keep track.

Kalynne Pudner, Fredericksburg, Virginia

Hot packs work

While breastfeeding my second child, I developed a blocked milk duct. To unclog it, the nurse recommended frequent nursing on that side, massage and hot compresses. I didn't have a lot of time, so instead I bought the hot packs that are designed to keep your hands warm in ski gloves. They worked perfectly. I tucked one in my bra, and the heat lasted for hours. If the pack is too hot initially, try wrapping it in cloth.

Gail Knowles, Bellevue, Washington

Bottle-Feeding Basics

There are many good reasons to choose bottle-feeding. For some moms, bottle-feeding is a personal preference; for others it's a necessity. It allows you to share feeding time with your spouse and with others. It's also a choice of many parents of on-the-go toddlers. Most formulas are made of a mixture of cow's milk, water and sugar; some substitute soy for cow's milk.

ASK THE EXPERTS
What Are the Nursing Bra Basics?

A good nursing bra is a must. If you're shopping during pregnancy, shop between the 29th and 36th week for the best fit. "After that, your rib cage will have expanded to the point where you won't be able to obtain a true measurement," says Sarah Coulter Danner, M.S.N., a certified nurse midwife and a member of the Playtex advisory board. Many moms wait to buy nursing bras until after the baby's birth, of course. When you're shopping, try on a few until you find the style that offers the comfort and support you need.

Some contain added iron and/or vitamins. What are some of the best ways to make bottle-feeding a safe and healthy means of feeding?

Be confident

I couldn't believe it when I was bottle-feeding my infant son in public and perfect strangers would tell me that it would be much better to breastfeed him. I finally got tired of just pretending to go along with them and told anyone who made a comment that he is adopted (which he is) and that the agency was unable to provide a milk-filled breast in the deal. That usually quiets them down fast.

Ellie Shapiro-Markem, Whitestone, New York

Keep baby's bottle cool

When my son switched from formula to milk, I was having trouble keeping the milk cold while we were out. Putting gel-filled, reusable ice balls (the kind made to keep adult drinks from getting diluted) in his bottles solved the problem for me. Ice balls are easy to use and won't water down baby's milk.

Peggy McAllister, Dover, New Hampshire

Keep baby's hands warm

Slip a tube sock on your child's bottle to keep her hands warm. The sock also absorbs moisture from the outside of the bottle, keeping clothing and furniture dry, and makes the bottle less slippery in baby's hands.

Julie Dietz, Lafayette, Indiana

Safe dishwashing

Do you wash your child's bottle and cup accessories by hand? If you have a dishwasher, you can easily reduce the time that you spend on this task by creating a separate dishwasher compartment for just these items. Take two empty plastic berry baskets and hinge them together with a twist tie. Fill one of the baskets with bottle caps, nipples, cup spouts or caps and use the other basket as a lid, closing it with another twist tie. You won't have to worry about all those small pieces flying around during the wash and you'll gain a little extra time for yourself during the day.

Jane Krasley, Emmaus, Pennsylvania

Bottle-cleaning breakthrough

Cleaning baby bottles thoroughly can be a difficult task. No matter how curved

How Clean Do Feeding Supplies Need to Be?

Many parents believe that everything and anything that their baby puts into his or her mouth needs to be sterilized, either in boiling water or in an electric sterilizer. Not so. Bottles, nipples and bottle rings that hold breast milk or formula *should* be sterilized because milk is the perfect breeding ground for bacteria. Tap water used to make formula, too, should be boiled, either before mixing or as part of boiling formula-filled bottles before feeding. To keep bacteria from growing, keep bottles and formula refrigerated until heating and feeding time.

Once your child reaches one year of age, however, bottles, nipples and rings can be hand- or machine-washed with detergent and water, but needn't be sterilized unless your water supply is tainted. Dishes, spoons and pacifiers need only hot water and detergent washing, either by hand or in the dishwasher. Toys should be washed in soap and water before their first use and periodically after that.

a bottle brush is, it doesn't quite reach the bottom. I solved this problem by putting some uncooked rice, along with a small amount of water, in the bottle and shaking it for a few seconds before discarding the contents. It works like magic.

Judy Hey, Rapid City, South Dakota

Feeding Schedules: When to Eat and How Much?

As one four-year-old reported to a visitor who was meeting his newborn baby sister, "She's pretty boring. She just eats and eats and sometimes she poops. She's kind of like an eating and pooping machine." He had his new sibling summed up pretty well. Babies eat often throughout the day, skillfully sounding their own dinner bells whenever hunger strikes. As your baby grows, you'll learn to differentiate a call for a meal from a call for another kind of attention. A healthy infant will take in what she needs and will turn away when she's full. As long as your baby is growing at a rate her healthcare provider deems appropriate, she's eating enough. As for when a baby needs to eat . . .

Baby's the boss

Forget any ideas about a schedule and feed your baby when he cries. Before you listen to nurses or friends, or your mother, listen to your baby.

Joy Hannan-Copanezos, Atlanta

Is baby really hungry?

Whenever my baby cried, I rushed to feed her, but often found that she wasn't

Measuring Breast-Milk Intake

Because a nursing mother cannot determine if her infant is getting enough milk by simply counting ounces as she could with a bottle, she must rely on other guidelines: A breastfed baby should have six to eight wet diapers in a 24-hour period and two to five bowel movements a day.

hungry because she'd just suck for a few seconds or not at all. A friend suggested that instead of assuming that she was hungry, I should just pick her up and talk to her and wait to see if she moved toward my breast. I found that about half the time I had been trying to feed her, all she wanted was a little conversation! Now that I let her tell me when it's time to eat, I'm much less worried because she eats with real gusto, rather than halfheartedly like before.

Eleanor Campbell, Flushing, New York

Limit water intake

Because I knew that it was good for me to drink lots of water, I wrongly assumed that it was good for my infant son, Malcolm, too, and I supplemented his formula bottles with about four eight-ounce bottles of water a day. But when he wasn't gaining enough weight, the pediatrician asked me about his diet. He told me to limit water bottles to one a day because Malcolm needed more formula than he

was getting. Since the water filled him up, he wasn't as hungry for nutrients as he normally would have been.

Chelsea Capps, Arlington, Virginia

Allow frequent feedings

Since my eight-month-old was a newborn, and only until pretty recently, she ate as many as 12 times a day. I was exhausted, but Margaret's pediatrician told me that her appetite for lots of short feedings was one of the many types of normal schedules that some babies preferred. Knowing it was normal helped me give in to her needs. I'm happy to report that about a month ago, Margaret changed her schedule to about eight longer nursing sessions a day.

Ellen Johnson-Tate, Kansas City, Missouri

Wean from midnight meals

By the time my son was nine months old, he still wasn't sleeping through the night because he'd wake up for his bottle.

When to Try Skipping the 2:00 A.M. Feeding

Once a baby weighs about nine pounds and is over one month old, you can try to substitute a pacifier or a water bottle for a middle-of-the-night feeding. You may also want to let your baby fuss for a few minutes before rushing in to feed him or her to see if the baby is ready to go back to sleep on his or her own.

ASK THE EXPERTS

What's a Recommended Time Line for Table Food?

Babies can begin eating table food between four and six months as long as it's healthful and the right consistency. It's important to let your baby decide if he or she wants to begin early or to wait until another month or two has passed. There's nothing gained by rushing the baby if he or she is uninterested in solids early on. And if the baby's family has a history of allergies, waiting may be better.

Introduce solids gradually—just a few spoonfuls a day—giving your baby time to get used to this new experience. (Of course, for those babies who like solid foods immediately, let them dig in right away.) While there's no set rules about which foods to introduce first, pediatri-cians usually recommend beginning with infant cereal and then moving on to fruits and vegetables a few weeks later, then grains and, finally, meats. Whatever the choices, this texture guide will help you see what's best for your baby at each age.

4 to 6 months	Liquids and strained foods
6 to 8 months	Strained or mashed foods
8 to 10 months	Mashed or finely minced foods
10 to 12 months	Minced or chopped foods
12 to 36 months	Chopped foods or regular table foods

Over the course of a week, I gradually cut down on the formula and added water, which he didn't like nearly as much. Within a few days of getting a water-only bottle, he stopped waking up for his 4:00 A.M. feeding.

Ricki Mendolez, Jersey City, New Jersey

Try feeding substitutes

When my son used to wake during the night, first I'd try singing softly, letting him suck on a pacifier, or rocking his crib for a few minutes before I'd feed him. More often than not, he'd go back to sleep. Finally, he broke his 3:00 A.M. drinking habit.

Nancy Moore, Camden, Maine

Late-Night Feeding Made Easier

No infant has ever been known to wake up hungry and say to herself, "Mom really needs her sleep, so I'll just hold out until morning." Though your personal all-night diner will eventually close for business as your baby grows, it can sometimes seem that an uninterrupted night's sleep is the stuff that dreams are made of. Until that day comes, here are some ideas to help make those late-night encounters more manageable.

Have a working nightstand

Want to save yourself trips to the kitchen in the middle of the night? Keep a small cooler with a milk bottle inside it and a wide-mouthed Thermos filled a third of the way with boiling water on your night table. Then, when it's time for your baby's midnight feeding, you can have the luxury of warming up his bottle from bed. Just place the milk bottle in the hot water until it's the right temperature.

Coral Ropple, Derry, New Hampshire

Try softer lighting

To make 3:00 A.M. feedings less stressful, I replaced the light bulb in my baby's room with a blue one. It creates a peaceful mood.

Ram Degant, Dallas

Keep water handy

When I nursed my daughter in the middle of the night, I found that I was often thirsty but I didn't have the energy to get myself a drink. To remedy this problem I filled a large sports bottle with ice and placed it next to my daughter's crib before I went to sleep. By the time she was ready for her feeding, I had refreshing cold water waiting for me.

Jenny Gleber, Charlotte, North Carolina

Take a diapering break

Until recently, whenever I breastfed my son and changed his diaper in the middle of the night, I faced a dilemma: If I changed his diaper first, he would cry hysterically because he was so hungry. But if I fed him first, he would fall asleep before finishing and would wake a short time later, hungry again and still wet. Now, however, I have found an easy solution: I give him one breast first and then change him. Now my son is calmer during changing and more alert when I resume breastfeeding him.

Elisa Mitschow, New Preston, Connecticut

Wake up to music

My daughter always awoke at exactly midnight and at 4:00 A.M., and her cries never failed to startle me. I found that I was so groggy that I would be halfway through her feedings before I woke up and felt the least bit loving. So I started to set my clock radio to a classical station for five minutes before her wake-up call. Getting up to the soothing music gave me a much calmer start to the nighttime meals.

Margaret Keeler, New York City

PARENTS' ALERT

No Microwave Warm-Ups

Never warm up baby food or bottles in the microwave. This method can create hot spots of scalding food that can seriously burn your child.

Weaning: From Breast to Bottle or Cup

It's a bittersweet moment when you realize that your baby is ready to move on. On the one hand, you're delighted to discover that she's grown and is now capable of making her first foray into the larger world; on the other hand, there's a part of you that wants to hold on to the closeness of nursing forever. Be assured that though she may now take nourishment from another source, she'll still be turning to you for her nurturance.

Go slow

I gradually weaned my daughter by taking away one nursing session at a time and substituting it with a formula bottle. I took away her morning nursing session last. It was her favorite.

Martha Boldin, Knoxville, Tennessee

Offer familiar milk

Pump breast milk into a bottle. Giving your baby the milk she likes may make it easier to wean her. Then gradually mix formula with breast milk until she's getting just formula.

Tanya Smith, Hawkesbury, Ontario, Canada

Sample the choices

Give your baby a taste test of formulas to see which one she likes best. Some doctors will give out free samples so that you can experiment without spending a lot of money.

Donna Lattin, Graham, Washington

PARENTS' ALERT
Say No to Honey

Honey contains bacteria that can be harmful to young children. It should not be given to any child under the age of 18 months.

Try an orthodontic nipple

My sons liked this kind because the rubber around the nipple pressed against their mouth and chin. Apparently the sensation is similar to breastfeeding.

Elizabeth Buffenmeyer, Barto, Pennsylvania

Share feeding time

Let someone else give your baby her bottle once a day while you leave the room. You can breastfeed her during her other feedings. A mother's presence and scent will initially make weaning more difficult.

Gale Speer, Rowlett, Texas

Try a new taste

Offer your child a juice bottle once a day. My pediatrician okayed it once my son was six months old, and my son loved the taste. A different liquid might help your baby get used to a bottle. Check with your baby's doctor, because children with a family history of allergies may benefit from postponing having juice until age one.

Renee Emma, Geneva, Illinois

Be persistent

I felt guilty when I wanted to wean my daughter. I realized, though, that I would only hurt my relationship with my daughter if I continued breastfeeding and resented it. Don't worry. Your baby will take to the bottle eventually.

Stephanie Testa, Edmond, Oklahoma

Go outside

At home, I found it impossible to interest my daughter in a bottle. I discovered

10 Tips for Healthier Eating

1. Whenever possible, involve the children in food selection and meal preparation.

2. Small, whole vegetables and florets and most fruits are almost always appealing to kids. Now and again, encourage your picky eater to try a new fruit or vegetable by arranging a platter in fun shapes or pictures.

3. Serve vegetables on, in or with something your child really likes (as part of a pizza topping or stirred into macaroni and cheese). Be warned that at certain points in the preschool years, sneaking in good foods can backfire because many kids will, at some point, balk at eating one food that has touched another.

4. Remember that bribes and rewards for eating (or punishments for not eating) can lead to problems later on. Be patient and try to remember how awful you once thought lima beans and cauliflower tasted.

5. Be satisfied with a taste test. If she doesn't like it, she doesn't like it.

6. Don't insist that a child join "the clean plate club." The long-term goal of helping a child regulate his food intake can be undermined when a child is told to eat even when he is full.

7. A tired or upset child is not likely to eat much of anything. This is not the time to experiment with new foods.

8. Create an interest in good foods at the supermarket, helping toddlers identify colors and shapes, preschoolers compare sizes and kindergartners find veggies that begin with each letter of the alphabet.

9. Include some fun as you encourage healthful eating. For example, pretend that broccoli stalks are trees, that peas are magic pebbles or that orange slices are smiles.

10. Eat nutritiously yourself. Be more than a role model. Be healthy.

that by taking her outside while I was wearing a jacket, she'd be more willing to try the bottle because she could neither smell me nor get at my breasts. After a few days of eating midday meals outside this way, she switched to the bottle.

Marilyn Michaelson, Hope, Pennsylvania

Go straight to a cup

To avoid a two-stage weaning process (from breast to bottle and then from bottle to cup), I weaned my son Clarke right from breastfeeding to a toddler cup when he was 10 months old. He's now three, and unlike many of his playmates, he's not

having any trouble giving up a bottle now because he's never had one.

Daphne Walker, Montreal

Making the Switch to a Cup

Some are ready for the big move at 9 months or 10 months. Others want to hold on to their "bots" until age two or longer. There's no right time for the transition, so relax. Help your child make the move, but don't force her. And remember that no one's ever been known to go off to college still clutching their bottle.

Use a straw

Weaning my daughter from her bottle was easy because instead of just taking it away, I offered it to her a different way. I cut the tip off the bottle nipple, inverted it, and then inserted a straw through the hole. My daughter still enjoyed the familiar feel of her bottle, but she quickly learned to use it like a cup.

Heidrun Rebenstorff, Santa Clara, California

Offer a flavor

My 22-month-old son, Matty, drank from a cup during the day, so I knew that his nighttime bottle was a breakable habit.

After many attempts at weaning him that resulted in screaming fits, I decided to let him make the decision. I simultaneously offered him a water bottle in one hand and a cup with juice in the other. The first night was hilarious because he tried to drink from both at the same time. Eventually, after a few nights, it was clear that the juice was more important than the bottle. Letting him take control made weaning easy.

Michele Campbell, Waukesha, Wisconsin

Enlist help

A friend and I helped each other wean our youngest children. When my second child was born, my friend's two-year-old daughter gave her old bottles to my baby as a gift. Two years later, when my friend had a new baby, my two-year-old gave her bottles to my friend's new baby. Saying a formal farewell to their bottles helped our toddlers feel good about growing up.

Theresa Kump Leghorn, New Rochelle, New York

Introducing Solid Foods

Imagine the delight, the awe, the utter confusion your baby experiences the first time she discovers that food can be chewed.

FROM THE FOOD EDITOR'S KITCHEN

Vegetable Cupcakes

This recipe is a great example of how vegetables can be added in where kids least expect to find (or taste) them.

Preparation time: 20 minutes
Bake time: 25 minutes
Yield: 18 cupcakes

Ingredients

2 packages (10 ounces each) frozen chopped spinach, thawed and squeezed dry
1 jar (16 ounces) beets, drained
1 package (18¼ ounces) devil's-food cake mix
Ready-to-spread vanilla or chocolate frosting

Directions

1. Preheat oven to 350°F.
2. Lightly grease 18 muffin-pan cups.
3. In food processor or blender, puree one package of spinach and the beets until smooth. Chop the remaining package of spinach firmly. Keep chopped spinach separate from pureed mix.
4. Prepare cake mix according to package directions, using four eggs instead of three.
5. Stir in pureed spinach and beets, then add the finely chopped spinach.
6. Spoon batter into muffin cups, filling to the tops.
7. Bake 22 to 25 minutes or until a toothpick inserted in the center comes out clean.
8. Cool completely on wire racks before frosting.

Nutrition per serving: 219 calories; 4 grams protein; 12 grams fat; 25 grams carbohydrate; 317 milligrams sodium; 47 grams cholesterol

---

Have a camera handy to catch your baby's expression the first time you introduce spoon-feeding. What should your baby eat? How do you serve it? These moms have some great ideas.

Offer homemade goodies

To save myself time in the kitchen, I prepare a dozen portions of pureed fresh vegetables and fruits by freezing servings in ice-cube trays. When the food cubes are completely frozen, I pop them out, seal them in a plastic bag and store them in the freezer. All I have to do is defrost or heat and serve when my baby is ready to eat.

Jane Parkinson, Clemson, South Carolina

Mix in the familiar

One of my twin sons always balked at any new food. I learned to add things he knew to anything different. For instance, I put strained peaches over peas the first time he tried peas. He's not at all troubled by these unusual combinations.

Valerie Marksman, Elks Grove, Illinois

Start with greens

With my first son, I introduced sweet things like custards and pureed fruits before green peas or squash. As a result, he spit out all the vegetables and ate only fruits. With my second son, I introduced pureed greens and orange vegetables before he learned to prefer sweets. He ate them with gusto. He also liked the fruits when I gave them to him a month later.

Rachel Chu, Fort Worth, Texas

Don't pass the salt

Because I found my daughter's food so bland, I wanted to add sweeteners or salt to it, but Sara's pediatrician recommended against it. He explained that liking these flavorings is a learned behavior and that Sara didn't find her food too plain. Now, at age four, she's much less interested in sweets or in salting her foods than I am. I'm glad that I took her doctor's advice.

Harriet Lovell, Tulsa, Oklahoma

Allow handling

I thought that my daughter didn't like solid foods until I realized that she didn't like *me* putting the spoon in *her* mouth. When I allowed her to try to feed herself, either with the spoon or with her fingers, she dived right into the solid-food experience! Sure, it was messy at first, but eventually she became somewhat neater.

John McDermott, Anchorage, Alaska

Handling High-Chair High Jinks

This particular throne sometimes encourages little lords and ladies to act the part. These parents have found some ways to use their babies' high chairs without too much trouble.

Create a no-skid seat

My one-year-old was constantly sliding around in her wooden high chair even though she was harnessed in. To keep her safe and comfortable, I cut a small rubber bath mat into quarters and suctioned a piece onto her chair. It's easy to clean and it fits into my diaper bag.

Sandi Chaddwick, West Chester, Pennsylvania

Attach toys

My 13-month-old son loves to play in his high chair when I'm working in the kitchen, but constantly picking up his tossed toys was tiring. I invested in some suction-cup toys that stick to the tray and attached other toys, such as his favorite plastic truck, with plastic links that he can't get tangled in and that allow him to pull up the toy that he's tossed by himself.

Carol Ann Hurley, Hanover, New Hampshire

Skip the plate

Because Ellie, my nine-month-old, liked to toss her plate or bowl from her high chair, I began to put the food directly onto the high-chair tray. I know this sounds messy, but it's a lot less work washing off the tray than repeatedly picking up and replacing all the tossed food from her dishes.

Maryanne Cummins, New York City

High-Chair Use and Safety

At around six months of age or when they can comfortably sit up by themselves, babies can start to get their meals in high chairs or hook-on seats. Earlier than this, even the most safely constructed high chair is a potential hazard because the baby could tip over or slide out. Make sure the high chair you use is certified by the Juvenile Products Manufacturers Association and bears their seal. When placing your baby or toddler in a high chair, always remember to:

- Be sure that the baby's fingers are out of the way when sliding in or snapping on the tray. Get in the habit of saying, "Hands up," whenever you adjust the tray.

- Position the chair far enough from the table or counter so that the baby cannot pull himself out or reach for items he should not touch. If possible, also position the chair in a quiet corner of the kitchen so that older children or pets will not knock into it.
- Use the safety belt correctly when you put your child in the chair. The tray is not designed as a restraining device and isn't a substitute for the belt.
- Store folding high chairs in places where babies and toddlers cannot get at them. A child can easily pull a collapsed chair over onto herself.
- Do not leave a child unattended in the high chair.

Try bathtub feedings

I never know when my 14-month-old son will splatter his food or spit it out. I solved the clean-up problem by serving messy foods in the bathtub where I can easily wash him and the area up after meals. I reserve the high chair for eating finger foods like Cheerios and for socializing with me and my husband during our dinners. When he's not eating, I give him some quiet toys to play with in his chair.

Odie Fenwick, Boston

Encouraging Nutritious Choices

Believe it or not, your child is not the first one to declare that everything green is yucky or that rice cakes are gross. (As one preschooler announced to a playmate's mom who had just given her a rice cake, "This is not cake.")

Should you insist that a child never eat a candy bar or that he finish the spinach on his plate? While doing so might get some short-term results, in the long term, joining the food police puts you at odds with your child's many other needs, such as the need for autonomy and the need to learn to make choices.

Your job is simply to provide healthful foods so that when your child does eat, he's assured of getting something wholesome. And give him enough latitude in choosing what and when he will eat so that mealtime doesn't become battle time.

Offer choices

My children refused to eat vegetables. Finally, I made a deal with them: They only had to eat half the amount of vegetables on their plate, and they could eat them any way that they pleased—dipped in brown sugar, ketchup or barbecue sauce. I think this approach is working because they feel more in control. Of course, I dish out double portions.

Michele Russell, Bethesda, Maryland

Dress it up

The best secret to getting kids to eat vegetables is ranch dressing. As long as my kids have that for dipping they'll eat any vegetable: broccoli, cauliflower, even radishes.

Susan Szuberla, Address withheld

Don't force the issue

When I was a child, I had to eat everything on my plate and I think that's one of the reasons I developed eating problems in my teens. I let my kids stop eating when they're full and I never make them finish their dinner before they can have dessert. In fact, I put dessert—things like Jell-O, a piece of carrot cake or sliced banana—right on their plate with their din-

ner. My two girls usually eat a little bit of everything.

Mariela Martinez, Bronx, New York

Allow sampling

The only rule for dinner that I have found that works is that everyone has to take at least one bite of everything. If they don't like it, they don't have to eat it. Because I never forced them to eat a bunch of broccoli, all of my children learned to like it by the time they were in school.

Anne Balliford, Chicago

Let kids decide

My three-year-old daughter really liked sweets, including junk like soda and candy, which she learned about from going to birthday parties. She was always begging me to buy some. I told her that I would let her buy some candy and other sweets if she could show me that she wouldn't eat it all at once. I also told her how foods helped her body get strong but that junk food didn't. Once she was in on the decision-making and understood a little about nutrition, she cut down on her demands for sweets. Last week she even went to a party and chose a second slice of pizza over a second helping of cake.

Laura Farrell, St. Louis

Offer nutritious snacks

I put frozen peas (unthawed), green beans or little carrots into small bowls and hand them to my six-year-old when she is watching TV, and she just starts eating them. Sometimes I put a bowl on a table without saying a word. After about 20 minutes, it's always empty.

Annie Bailey, Address withheld

ASK THE EXPERTS

How Can I Spot an Eating Disorder?

Preoccupation with weight has become almost epidemic among American youngsters. Children as young as seven or eight are dieting, often without a doctor's supervision and sometimes even when they are within the normal weight for their height.

For some, fears of being fat lead to anorexia nervosa, a condition in which victims starve themselves into illness and even death. Others develop bulimia, characterized by binge eating followed by purging.

Parents need to be alert to the signs of a developing or already established eating disorder in their children, particularly their preteens and teens. If you answer yes to any of these questions, talk with your child *and* his or her physician. Do not wait for the problem to go away on its own.

- Is he preoccupied with the calorie and/or fat content of all or most of the food he consumes?
- Does she continue dieting even after having achieved her original weight goal?
- Does he weigh less than 80 percent of his ideal weight?
- Has your daughter stopped menstruating?
- Is he wearing baggy clothes and covering up a thin appearance?
- Is she a perfectionist who views taking control of all aspects of one's life the most important goal?
- Does he eat secretly, hiding food wrappings or eating in the middle of the night as others sleep? Does she retreat to the bathroom after eating?
- Does your child eat far more or far less than you consider normal?

Schedule snacks

Don't give children a snack too close to dinner. You want them to come to the meal good and hungry. And I set a good example by eating all my vegetables.

Leah Soltas, Address withheld

Make food fun

I purchased an inexpensive gumball machine that I fill with nuts, cereal, yogurt-covered raisins and other healthy treats. My kids think it's fun to help themselves, and it saves me trips to the cupboard when they make requests for seconds and thirds.

Soraya Peeters, Van Nuys, California

Keep snacks handy

To encourage my child to eat healthy snacks, I leave a bowl of cut fruit in the refrigerator. It sits within reach on the lowest shelf, a tempting assortment for a between-meal treat.

Ellen Hoeft-Edenfield, Alameda, California

Five Bright Ideas for Kids' Breakfasts

Everyone needs a good breakfast to start the day off right. Beyond the traditional cereal with milk, introduce these tasty alternatives. You might want to try them yourself.

1. Toast a whole-grain English muffin and top with tomato sauce and shredded cheese for a breakfast pizza.
2. Spread a microwave pancake with a thin layer of peanut butter and/or apple butter, roll up and serve with a glass of milk.
3. Slice a ripe banana and freeze the slices overnight. In the morning, toss the slices into the blender, add low-fat milk and a few drops of vanilla extract. Blend until smooth. Serve with a corn muffin.
4. Fill an ice cream cone halfway with yogurt. Add crushed whole-grain cereal and diced fruit.
5. Warm a soft pretzel, served with a piece of fruit and milk.

Serve in stages

To make sure that my child is hungry at dinner time, I stop serving snacks after 4:00 P.M. Sometimes, I bring out dinner in stages. For example, rice or vegetables first and the main dish last. If I put less food on the plate, my child is more willing to sit still and eat it.

Noeleen Mitchell, Norma, New Jersey

Dress up leftovers

Whenever my refrigerator becomes cluttered with leftovers, I place them cafeteria-style in small dishes around the kitchen table. My children eat a balanced meal and have a little fun at the same time.

C. M. Wegner, Minneapolis

Solving Mealtime Dilemmas

Your child is not alone in wanting to have nothing to eat but tuna salad sandwiches for breakfast, lunch and dinner— every day. Children's natural aversion to certain foods, their extremely conservative approach to expanding their culinary horizons ("Something new? No, thank you!"), and their horror at seeing one food touch another can lead parents of toddlers and preschoolers to wonder if their child will ever be fit for civilization. Fortunately, despite kids' picky eating styles, most get all the nutrition they need over the course of a few days.

Limit creative service

I followed the recipes for all sorts of cute foods—things like pancakes with faces—thinking that this would help my son learn to like eating. But when he had to spend a weekend with my mother, she wouldn't give in to his demand to make "smiling soup." I then realized that Joshua would have to learn to eat food that looked like food. It took a while to wean him from funny-face foods, but with my next child, due in two months, I'm not

FROM THE FOOD EDITOR'S KITCHEN

20 Smart Snacks

It's okay for kids to snack on a sweet treat once in a while. Just don't let a snack substitute for an entire meal. Here are some smart snacking ideas.

1. Toaster or microwave pancakes and waffles
2. Fruit, including fresh, canned and dried, plus juices
3. A small bowl of soup topped with little crackers
4. Fruit and cookies stirred into yogurt or cottage cheese
5. Rice cakes
6. Ready-to-eat cereal or instant hot cereal
7. Toasted minibagel with cheese spread
8. Blended frozen fruit
9. Frozen soft Dutch pretzels, freshly baked
10. Chopped vegetables, mixed with kidney or garbanzo beans and salad dressing
11. Plain popcorn (for older children)
12. Flat breads or Norwegian crisp breads topped with peanut butter and fruit spread or with mustard and then topped with sardines and lettuce
13. English muffins, pita bread or mini-bagel with cream cheese and fruit or with cubes of cheese or sliced cheese melted over a slice of tomato
14. Sliced, hard-cooked egg served on wheat crackers
15. A glass of milk, chocolate milk or a milk shake
16. Pizza
17. Tortillas
18. Frozen nonfat desserts or frozen low-fat yogurt topped with syrup and chopped fruits
19. Ham-and-cheese roll-ups
20. Gelatin and yogurt sundaes

going to try to pretend that food is anything but food—except maybe on special occasions.

Abby Brown, Brooklyn, New York

Try separate plates

My four-year-old daughter got hysterical every time one food, such as the meatloaf on her plate, touched another, such as the green beans. Serving casseroles or stews became impossible because Sarah had to be able to identify each food clearly before she would eat it. After talking to my older sister and finding out that my niece, who's now nine and has perfectly ordinary eating habits, went through the same crazy stage, I got less worried. My sister suggested that I serve Sarah each food in a separate bowl and to let this stage pass on its own. It did. Once I let Sarah know that I wasn't going to try to force the issue, her obsession with food touching disappeared within a few weeks.

Kathleen Holsteider, Cape May, New Jersey

FROM THE FOOD EDITOR'S KITCHEN
Fun Lunch Ideas

Crazy cutouts: To make sandwiches more visually appealing, use cookie cutters to give bread, luncheon meat and cheese new shapes. Animals, numbers and letters are always popular, and you and your child can have fun spelling out names, the abbreviation of the month or the days of the week. Younger children will find learning to count more fun using sandwich number cutouts.

Going crackers: For a super-fast treat, sandwich together animal-shaped cookies (like the large dinosaur-shaped grahams) with peanut butter mixed with minced dried fruits. Or try crackers with cheese spreads mixed with minced raw vegetables.

Whale-wich: With a notch cut for a mouth, a sandwich made on rye or pumpernickel bread looks like a whale. Just add a slice of pimento-stuffed olive for an eye, two wedge-shaped pieces of carrot for a tail, and let the whale spout off with a celery leaf tucked into the sandwich above the eye.

A better butterfly: Cut one slice of sandwich bread diagonally in half. Arrange the two triangles on a plate with the cut sides facing out, to make wings. Place a piece of string cheese between the wings to represent the body. Cut square slices of luncheon meat or cheese on the diagonal and place on the wings. Decorate the wings and body with bits of vegetables and mustard designs. Add two chives for antennae.

Try TV trays

Although putting foods on separate plates is a good idea for children who hate it when their foods touch, I have found an easier solution. I serve my four- and five-year-olds their meals on plastic TV-dinner trays. Now each of the foods has its own compartment and I only have two plates to wash.

Bonnie Lapierre, Grand Isle, Vermont

Include a favorite food

I was really concerned when my four-year-old son would eat only peanut butter and jelly sandwiches. His pediatrician told me to serve him a quarter sandwich at every meal along with something else. When Matthew saw that he could always have at least some of his favorite food, he began eating a better variety.

Marilyn Hunt, Syracuse, New York

Add a multivitamin

The only thing my child will eat is hard-boiled eggs, spaghetti (with no sauce) and hot dogs. His doctor told me not to worry because he was getting most of the things he needed with this limited diet. He also suggested that I give Charlie a multivitamin every day until his appetite expanded.

Leona Simpak, New York City

Hide the heels

Picture this: You finally get your pre-schooler to agree to eat something for lunch. (Of course, he chooses peanut butter and jelly.) You take out the bread, only to discover that you're down to the last two end pieces. Don't panic: Simply flip the end pieces over, and spread the peanut butter and jelly on the outside. Your child will never know that he's eating the "yucky" bread.

Lori Griffin, Conyers, Georgia

Cut down on juice

My three-year-old daughter, Katelyn, ate only about enough to keep a canary alive. I swear that her entire day's food intake would fit into a small bowl. I was really worried that she was starving. I talked to her pediatrician who also asked me how much Katelyn was drinking every-day. I realized that she consumed about eight glasses of apple juice and two or three glasses of milk each day. "That's the problem!" the doctor told me. So I cut her back to just four glasses of milk or juice a day, and her appetite for food went up.

Margo Kempsey, Flushing, New York

Shop together

I have a way to get my son—a notoriously picky eater—to eat better. I let him help me do the food shopping. He's responsible for selecting two healthy snacks (such as bananas or rice cakes) and one treat (usually cookies) for himself. He knows that he's allowed to eat the healthy snacks anytime, and the cookies are a special dessert. Including my son in shopping decisions helps him learn about making proper food choices, and cuts down on

the number of times I hear *yuck* and *no* at mealtime.

Linda Orrego, Franklin Park, New Jersey

When Kids Put Nonfood Items in Their Mouths

For some parents, the source of concern is not getting their kids to eat but keeping them from putting everything in their mouths. If that's the case in your home, try these ideas.

Explain your reasons

Explain why you don't want your children to put things that aren't food in their mouths. Tell them there could be germs on the objects that could make them sick.

Cynthia Bethune, Fairbanks, Alaska

Ask your child

Try asking your child why he puts things that aren't food in his mouth. When I asked my son, he told me that he saw his younger sister put objects in her mouth and he did it, too, to get my attention. I explained to him that this is something only babies do and that he's a big boy now, not a baby. That helped a lot.

Rhonda Lee Fortin, Warren, Rhode Island

Make a food book

Look through magazines with your child and have her point to food items and then to nonfood items. Together, cut out the pictures and put them on a poster. Put the food items opposite nonfood

Choking Hazards

Because a small child doesn't have molars or teeth that can grind food, he doesn't always chew his food sufficiently and is at risk of choking on anything that goes into his mouth. Avoid giving a child under four years any round, firm foods unless you have chopped them up into very small pieces. In particular, these foods present the greatest risk.

- **Hot dogs:** Before serving, cut lengthwise into quarters, then cut each quarter into quarter-inch segments. Also, remove the skin from thick-skinned franks.
- **Chunks of meat:** Any piece that's too large to be swallowed whole safely is too large.
- **Grapes:** Peel and cut into tiny pieces before serving.
- **Hard candies**
- **Popcorn**
- **Peanut butter:** Spread very thinly before serving since a spoon-size portion could stick in a child's throat.
- **Raw vegetables or fruits:** Including carrot sticks, celery stalks and hard apples.

items. Be sure to include several pictures of items she puts in her mouth. Then label each side in large letters—Food and Not Food.

Verna Villella, Minneapolis

Be vigilant

My son, who's now three, was constantly putting things like keys and coins and even bath soap into his mouth until he was about two. To keep him from hurting himself, I was always on the lookout for little items in our house and on our outings that might have enticed him and I warned baby-sitters and others who were ever in charge of him of this habit. Eventually it passed, thankfully with no harm done.

Anne Sherman, Lincoln, Nebraska

Helping the Overeater

Chubby-cheeked children invite extra helpings of hugs—something everyone can use. But it's extra helpings of another sort that can work against a youngster. When a child becomes heavier than is healthy, parents, understandably, want to help trim food intake. That can be a difficult task and carries the risk of making food a major issue in a child's life. Some alternatives to cutting back on food include increasing the child's activity level and substituting healthful choices for fatty, high-calorie meals and snacks.

Cut down on fat

Without disrupting our family's eating style too much, we're helping our 11-year-old eat less, particularly less fatty food.

We've switched to 1 percent low-fat milk and low-fat cheeses. I've stopped serving creamed anything and use more tomato sauce as a substitute. And instead of cakes and cookies for dessert, I now serve fruit, sorbet or gelatin.

Lenore Elsasser, Richmond, Virginia

Get moving

I followed my daughter's pediatrician's advice when she began to get overweight. I enrolled her in a gymnastics class one day a week, in swimming another day and in ballet on a third day. I also began walking with her instead of using the car for short trips. Within a year, even though she never really cut down on food, her weight and her height were in proportion.

Marge Levy, Alberta, Ontario

Limit television snacking

Because the whole family decided to try to lose weight together, my chubby nine-year-old isn't alone in her struggle. We all found that we did our worst nibbling during television viewing and we now snack only on cut-up veggies or plain popcorn. We've all lost weight without any other serious changes in our diet.

Michael Levinson, Chicago

Clean the cupboards

It was too difficult for my son to keep from snacking on junk foods when we kept so many in our pantry. So we cleaned them out and substituted lots of healthful snacks. Jeremy has a much easier time choosing to eat something like a banana or an apple now that there are no potato chips nearby.

Alison Joy, Montgomery, Alabama

Work with your child

I knew it would be a mistake to get too involved in my daughter Suzanne's eating habits. I also knew that she was getting too plump and needed guidance about food. I took her to a pediatric nutritionist who, with Suzanne, worked out a meal and snack plan that she could live with. At age 12, she needed to have control of the situation and this plan seems to be working.

Cynthia Desmond, New York City

Enlist others' help

When my preschooler began to put on too much weight, I realized that it was because her babysitter often gave her treats of ice cream, cookies and other fattening foods. I explained how important it was to limit Chelsea's snacks to nutritious foods, and the babysitter agreed to work with us on this issue. Slowly, Chelsea's excess chubbiness is going away.

Linda Spivak, Key Biscayne, Florida

Kids in the Kitchen

Sure, it's easier to prepare dinner without the kids underfoot and on many occasions this probably is the best course of action. But there are also many times when having a toddler or preschooler lend a hand has a number of benefits—a chance to learn about food and to experiment with it and an added incentive to try new foods. The child who proudly announces "I helped make that!" is likely to heartily dig in when that food is put on the table.

(continued on page 64)

FROM THE FOOD EDITOR'S KITCHEN

40 Palate Pleasers

1. Make a healthy fruit sundae by topping frozen yogurt with cut-up fruit or berries.

2. Put dinner courses in little containers labeled No. 1, No. 2, No. 3 and so on. Let kids open them in order, eating what's in each before moving on to the next.

3. Scatter a variety of cut-up vegetables on top of a pizza.

4. Make exotic sandwiches using bagel chips, waffles or peeled apple slices instead of bread.

5. Experiment with different kinds of breads. Don't overlook cocktail breads—they're perfect for pint-size hands.

6. Add shredded vegetables such as carrots or zucchini to ground beef and make into patties for burgers.

7. Make tasting platters sampling small portions of your child's favorite foods mixed together with new foods.

8. Create friendly names for foods: broccoli trees, bunny salads, mashed-potato sandcastles, applesauce soup.

9. Let your child choose the vegetables he wants to add to homemade soups.

10. Have breakfast for dinner or vice versa. There are no rules as to what foods should be eaten when. Serve waffles with fruit for dinner; pizza or potatoes can be healthy morning meals.

11. Talk about different countries with your child, then try a new food from those lands.

12. Stuff celery sticks with shredded vegetables mixed into cottage cheese, peanut butter, tuna salad or any other food your child loves.

13. Make a meal with foods that all share the same basic shape. For example, at one meal, serve meatballs, pasta circles and peas.

14. Make vegetables into fun, creative shapes using a parer, small cookie cutters, a spiral cutter or a ripple cutter.

15. Make a rainbow-colored meal for your child with foods of different colors.

16. Make a meal with a theme that's based on your child's favorite story. For *Goldilocks and the Three Bears,* for example, try three pieces of meat in different sizes, three piles of peas and three portions of potatoes.

17. Serve sauces in small pitchers that are kept on the side of your child's plate so that she can pour them over the food herself.

18. Make a shish-kebab meal by arranging bite-size pieces of meat and cut-up vegetables on skewers.

19. Sweeten vegetables such as carrots, winter squash or cabbage with a drizzle of maple syrup or a splash of orange juice.

20. Sprinkle vanilla yogurt with granola, raisins or cold cereal for an instant sundae.

21. Puree vegetables in a blender, then add the batter to soups, stews, sauces or baked products such as muffins, quick breads or brownies.

22. Stir a bit of ground tumeric into a rice, bean or vegetable mixture to make it an appealing yellow color.

23. Let your child bring her favorite stuffed animal to the dinner table so it can watch her eat food.

24. Melt a favorite cheese over vegetables, such as Cheddar cheese over broccoli or cauliflower.

25. Puree two packages of frozen spinach, thawed and squeezed dry and one 16-ounce jar of beets, drained; add to devil's-food cake batter; bake as directed. (We've tried this and it really works! Your child will never know he's eating veggies.)

26. Add vegetables such as tomatoes or chopped cooked broccoli to a grilled-cheese sandwich.

27. Wrap foods in tortillas for an easy, quick pick-up meal.

28. Add shredded zucchini or carrot to potato-pancake batter.

29. Plant a vegetable garden with your child. Homegrown foods are often more enticing than the store-bought ones.

30. Serve food in miniature forms: mini-meatloaves, mini-waffles, mini-muffins—they're more kid-friendly.

31. Cut up sandwiches into playful shapes such as stars and hearts.

32. Serve vegetable juice one night instead of vegetables.

33. If your child is fussy about drinking milk, try serving it with a fun straw.

34. Wrap vegetables in biscuit dough. Bake and serve.

35. Make a menu. Cut pictures out of a magazine with foods for each course. Paste them on a piece of paper. Let your child choose what she wants to eat.

36. Change the setting. Dine picnic-style in the living room.

37. If your child won't drink milk, add nonfat dry milk to such foods as tomato sauce, eggs and soups.

38. Pour juice into cups and then freeze them to make juice pops. Add sticks for handles when juice just begins to freeze.

39. Serve foods in amusing dishes shaped like animals, fruit or clowns. Serve drinks and foods in unexpected dishes, such as vegetables in tea cups. Use special plates with pictures on the bottom; your child will want to see the image underneath.

40. Freeze cubes of chicken broth to cool down and enhance the taste of too-hot soups or stews.

Play school

I've learned to use meal preparation time as the time of day to help my five-year-old practice all that he has learned at kindergarten that day. It's a great time to talk about colors and shapes. He helps me measure and count out ingredients. And now he even wants me to read the recipes to him, even though most of them are written on a macaroni box.

Lilly Walker, San Francisco

Have kid-made menus

I got tired of arguing with my children (a boy and a girl, ages five and seven) about what I was serving for dinner. So now I let each of them take turns planning the meal. The only rules are that the menu can include only those foods that we have in the house and that at least one part of the meal be a vegetable. Once in a while, we wind up with things like pizza and mashed potatoes but, for the most part, they actually do a pretty decent job of planning well-balanced meals.

Matt Preston, Highland, New York

Serve up some play

I couldn't keep my eye on my toddler and cook at the same time—until I bought him his own plastic food to play with and a toy stove. Now he prepares dinner by my side. It's fun watching him decide what to make.

Angelo Lacy, Plano, Texas

Welcome little chefs

Let your child help you prepare dinner. My son loves to fold napkins, bring his own plastic dishes to the table and help take food out of the refrigerator. In fact, he gets upset when I don't let him help! I think your child will be more likely to sit down and enjoy the meal if you involve him in the process of getting it ready.

Beverly Lusso, Bethpage, New York

Make kid-size treats

Whenever I make a cake for a special occasion, my two children don't understand why they can't have a piece as soon as it has cooled off. I solve this problem by using some of the cake batter to make two cupcakes (the small amount of batter I use doesn't ruin the recipe). My children get to enjoy an immediate treat and can forget about my cake.

Priscilla Bohrer, Augusta, West Virginia

Choose cool tools

When I bake cupcakes, I give my kids a Popsicle stick to use for frosting. The stick is a good size for preschoolers to handle, and it's safe for them to use to lick off the leftover frosting when they're done.

Mary Lachat, Sobieski, Wisconsin

Notes on Neatness

Because they just can't help themselves, and experimenting with food is more compelling than actually eating it, kids and food can be a messy combination. But there is help, as these parents found.

Measure out neatness

My daughter, Lauren, has discovered how to feed herself, but she often gets more food on her face and on the floor than in her mouth. To help her, I give her a plastic measuring spoon instead of a baby spoon. Not only does a measuring spoon hold her food much better, but the handle is easier to grasp and there is less for me to clean up afterward.

Karen Samuhel, Conway, Arkansas

Catch messes with wristbands

We all know how sticky children can get when they're eating fruits like oranges, plums or watermelons. To minimize the mess that my daughter makes, I put terry-cloth wristbands on her to absorb the juice that would normally drip down her arms.

Jeng Hsu, Gaithersburg, Maryland

Make big-kid bibs

My two kids are four and eight and are too big to wear bibs when eating. But they don't object to having a napkin pinned to them with two clothespins to protect their party clothes and favorite outfits.

Marybeth Rudzinski, Sterling Heights, Michigan

Teach tricks

For some reason my son, Chris, had a hard time mastering the use of a straw. He felt frustrated until one day I simply told him, "Just kiss it." Lo and behold, it did the trick.

Jean Coggan, Woodland Hills, California

Catch drips

Try this trick if your children love ice cream as much as mine do. Before they eat a popsicle, slide the ice-cream stick through the lid of a fast-food soft-drink container. The rim will catch the ice-cream drips (most of them) before there's a chance of making a big mess.

Janet Swanson, Fridley, Minnesota

Dab away mustaches

To get rid of the bright-colored mustache that children wear after drinking fruit drinks, use a dab of toothpaste on a damp washcloth instead of soap and water. It works and tastes much better. Be sure to rinse well after the gentle scrubbing. Toothpaste also works well to remove spots on clothing caused by other foods that stain, such as tomato sauce and ice pops.

Kristen Heeringa, Minneapolis

Dad's Corner

It's no longer unusual for dad to preside over meal preparations. These dads share their favorite mealtime strategies.

Perfect pizza

I like making pizza for my family, but each one of us likes a different topping. So I put out little cups of chopped olives, pepperoni, mushrooms and garlic powder. Then I mark the pizza with strips of cheese to show each slice and ask everyone to put his or her favorite topping on before I put it into the oven.

Peter Winston, Elmira, New York

Breakfast to go

The Saturday- and Sunday-morning breakfasts are my job. I buy fresh bagels and make my wife and each of our two kids a meal that fits neatly on top of a bagel—scrambled eggs, grilled cheese, peanut butter and jelly, for instance—and I serve it in individual plastic baskets. Everyone gets a kick out of these bagel specials.

Mike O'Farrell, Boston

Take a course

My wife gave me a gift certificate to cooking classes at our local adult-education center. (I took the hint.) Surprisingly, I really got into it. I find that the most important ingredients you need to cook properly are the right tools, including sharp knives, stainless steel mixing bowls and large pots. With the rights tools and a cookbook, you can't go wrong.

Robert Greenspan, Atlanta

Get a good cookbook

Because my wife and I have an agreement—whoever does the cooking doesn't do the cleanup—I really wanted to learn how to cook more than the spaghetti I knew how to make. I started widening my repertoire by making things suggested on the sides of pasta boxes. Seeing things turn out pretty well gave me the confidence to tackle a real cookbook. Now I actually enjoy reading the cooking pages of the newspaper, too.

Nick Trabor, Athens, Georgia

Enjoy the basics

I've discovered that you can't go wrong by making a meal out of a fresh salad, soup and some good bakery-quality bread. It's simple, healthful and quick.

Tim Johnston, Auburn, Massachusetts

Teaching Table Manners

None of us want our dinnertime to resemble a scene out of Animal House. *Nor do we expect our kids to eat with the dignity and grace of a charm-school graduate—at least not at every meal.*

Instilling table manners does more for a child than helping him get down a meal without having to be corrected regularly—in itself a good thing. Having manners gives a child social standing that will serve him throughout his life. It's never too late to begin teaching manners. Nor too early. Here's how.

Rely on rituals

As the mother of four-year-old triplets, I know how hard it is to keep kids from running around at the dinner table. I've established some rituals to make the dinner hour calmer and more pleasant. I turn off the TV, turn on the answering machine and play mellow music. I also clear the dining-room table of books, puzzles and other toys that are likely to sidetrack my children during our meal.

Sandy Yadaie, Douglaston, New York

Talk

If my daughter gets restless, it usually means she feels left out. My husband and I try to include her in the mealtime discussion by asking questions about her day and telling her stories about ours.

Jill Scales, St. Augustine, Florida

Address one rule at a time

I decided to work on one rule of manners at a time because covering all the rules at once, I knew, would be too much to handle and would leave me correcting my son all the time. This was my system: First, "Chew with your mouth closed." That took about two weeks. Next, "Don't slurp your drink." A week later, "Elbows off the table." I kept going until Georgie was reasonably well mannered. Now I can honestly say that he never embarrasses himself or me whenever we eat out.

Cindy Huron, Silver Spring, Maryland

Prepare for parties

I'd always been so happy that Charlene, my six-year-old picky eater, would just eat that I didn't pay much attention to the fact that her manners were terrible. I'd let her do things like eat with her fingers and blow bubbles in her milk. Then one day, after a birthday party at a friend's house, she came home crying because all the kids made fun of her terrible manners. I felt awful and so did she. So we got a book out of the library on manners for kids. I guess if there's a book about it, we weren't the only ones who had something to learn. She practiced using her utensils correctly, swallowing quietly and everything else. It was a hard way to learn that manners are important, but at least she's better now.

Name withheld, Nutley, New Jersey

Enforce the rules

Although it might seem drastic, I use time-outs when my daughter won't sit still at the dinner table. When she gets completely out of hand during dinner, I set the timer on the microwave and she sits on the stairs right by the kitchen. After a few minutes, she's usually calm and ready to rejoin us at the table.

Ann Symonds, Arlington, Virginia

Be tolerant

A young child shouldn't be expected to sit still and be quiet through an entire dinner hour. As children get older and learn to be more patient, you can raise your expectations for their behavior.

Tammy Hoyer, Woodland, California

Work off energy

If your child can not sit still at dinner, try arranging late-afternoon playdates so that he has an outlet for his energy and doesn't need to act up during dinner. Or perhaps he's ready for a gymnastics class or other sport. If you and your husband work, set aside time before dinner to roughhouse with your child. Sometimes children are so excited to see their parents after a whole day apart, it's difficult for them to contain themselves at the dinner table.

Molly Smith, Sacramento, California

Eating Out with Kids

The decor is different. The menu is likely to be more varied than it is at home. There's people watching, sugar-bowl exploring and fork fiddling to be done. Some kids enjoy the restaurant experience immensely. Others hate it.

Most kids can learn to be great guests at a restaurant. Success usually involves choosing a child-friendly restaurant, planning for quiet distractions and being willing to cut short the experience if necessary. Here are some ideas to help your child win smiles from the staff and an extra mint on the way out.

Invite kid companions

We often arrange a dinner date with another couple who have a child around the same age. This way the children can keep each other entertained for a little while. Also, board books are good to take along because they can be wiped off if any food gets on them.

Lydia Antoniou, Chevy Chase, Maryland

Shorten sitting time

I avoid putting my daughter in the high chair until the food is almost ready to be served. That way, she's more likely to sit still once it's time to eat. If she's confined for too long, she gets restless and cranky.

Pamela Goerss, Morton, Illinois

Bring a stroller

If there's a wait to be seated, my husband and I can take a walk with our son without causing too much chaos.

April Herbster, Columbus, Ohio

Have a few plans

I make sure my daughter has taken a nap and is hungry by the time we get to the restaurant. Whenever possible, I invite her grandparents to come along with us— they never mind taking walks with her in the middle of a meal if she gets fussy.

Fara Sax, Miami

Play table games

When we go out to eat and my one-year-old starts to get restless, we play a game called "What's missing?" I'll put a few things in the center of the table, like a fork, salt and pepper shakers and a napkin. Then I ask her to close her eyes while I remove one of the items. Then I ask, "What's missing?"

Grace Kelly, East Norwich, New York

Feed kids first

I ask the waitress for some "emergency fries" right away to buy some time for me and my husband to peruse the menu.

Mary Mayrose, Shelbyville, Kentucky

Choose the right table

I try to grab a table that is a bit out of the way but has a good view of the action. I position my daughter, Emma, so she can people watch; my husband or I take the seat facing the boring wall.

Kathryn Brown, Columbia, Missouri

Check for high chairs

Before I choose a restaurant to eat at with our four-month- and four-year-old sons, I check to make sure that they have high chairs. A restaurant that has high chairs is used to kids and tends to be more understanding.

Patricia O'Henry, Plattsburgh, New York

Review the rules

I always explain what she can expect before we enter a restaurant. I also remind her that I expect her to use her best "restaurant manners" during the meal. When she does, which is almost all of the time now, she gets to pay the bill herself, which makes her feel very grown-up.

Sandra Scarpy, Bronx, New York

Start simple

I introduced my kids to eating out in stages. First we tried fast-food places, then diners and family-style restaurants before we worked our way up to places with tablecloths. When we go out to nice restaurants now, I always dress my kids up so that they're aware that this is a special occasion and that they're expected to act the part.

Alison Laurrine, Springfield, Missouri

Help the staff

When my kids make a mess in a restaurant, I help clean up instead of waiting for the staff to do it. I think it's important to be a good guest myself if I want to feel comfortable bringing my kids back to the same place again. I've been told by more than one waitress that she really appreciates my help.

Tina Pellicano, Oswego, New York

Making Meals a Family Affair

Do you and the other members of the family eat your sit-down meals while the baby is sleeping? Do you prop the baby nearby—or even on your lap—while you eat your own meals? As you begin to work out the system that works for you, keep in mind that your goal is to help make mealtime a pleasant time for all family members and that serving up a sense of humor may be your best course of action for a while. As one Pennsylvania mother of three says, "After saying grace, I say a special prayer to thank whomever invented paper towels, since we never get through a meal without using plenty of them."

As the kids get older, the dinner table is likely to become the focus of family time. It's an important occasion, especially for today's busy families. The menu doesn't have to be fancy; neither does the table setting. What is important, however, is that the dinner table be a place where everyone can hear about one another's day, where the focus can be as much on each other as on the food.

Snack and relax

When I got home from work, I was often too tired to give my kids (ages seven and three) the attention they needed and to get dinner together all at once. We have recently started a new routine to get us past this hungry and grumpy stage. In the morning, I make a platter of cheese, crackers and fruit and put aside drinks we all like—chocolate milk for them and iced tea for me. Now instead of trying to make dinner right away, I take out the appetizers and we sit together for about 20 minutes. The snacks take the edge off the hunger. Now we eat a smaller dinner a little later in the evening. I wish I'd figured this out long ago.

Edwina Chomsky, Seattle

Get fancy

Before the baby was born, my husband and I rarely ate at home, opting instead for meals in restaurants. That became too difficult—and too expensive—after Cecily was born. To feel less deprived, I make a point of setting the table with a tablecloth, using the good china and even lighting candles—even though dinner is likely to be something quick and easy like hamburgers or macaroni. Not only do Steven and I like the ambiance, but Cecily is so fascinated by the candlelight and so relaxed during these fancy meals that none of us feel deprived at all.

Rebecca Lawsen-Schultz, Larchmont, New York

Invite guests

I'm a single parent. To make dinnertime more lively, I invite another family over at least once a week for a potluck or for an easy spaghetti dinner. I love having other people to talk with and so does my daughter.

Margaret Rosetti, Mt. Holyoke, New York

Add a surprise

Make a place setting for your child's favorite doll. Eat outside. Have a picnic in the living room. Put a sticker under his dinner plate. Light candles. Do something special.

Laura Schaefer, Lemon Grove, California

Have picnics

As soon as the weather gets nice, we plan family picnics at least once a week instead of sit-down dinners. It's a nice break after school and work.

Leslie Tauge, Concord, New Hampshire

Why Is the Family Meal So Important?

Besides the readily apparent emotional benefit to all family members, the family meal offers a surprising bonus: Educational researchers have found that the students whose families share at least four family sit-down meals a week achieve better grades in school than their counterparts whose families skip this ritual. The family meal was found to be more indicative of high achievement than economic, social and even intellectual factors.

Take turns

To make sure everyone, even our three-year-old twins, takes part in the dinner conversation, we take turns telling the funniest thing that happened that day.

Michael O'Rouke, Tenafly, New Jersey

CHAPTER THREE

Bathtime and Grooming

*C*hildren *are supposed to be messy. Dirty hands and* smudged faces serve as proof that they've had a good, child-friendly kind of day. One six-year-old put it well as she balked about scrubbing clean: "I can see my whole great day disappearing down the drain."

Nevertheless, clean them we must—and tend to their hair, brush their teeth and help them dress reasonably and seasonably well. These everyday routines do more than just make your children presentable. They lead children to develop a sense of well-being and form the basis of a child's self-esteem.

Baby Bathtime Basics

Your delicate baby is likely to feel quite at home in a bath of warm water. For you, baby's bath will require some dexterity and a bit of planning. Bathtime also offers you and your baby a chance to learn about your child's body and about the wonderful pleasures of touch.

Get a grip

When my daughters were babies, I wore a pair of white sports socks on my hands when I bathed them so that their bodies wouldn't feel so slippery. The socks made good washcloths, too.

Sara Gensler, Rockfield, Kentucky

Add a towel

I found that putting a towel inside my daughter's baby bathtub kept her from slipping.

Margaret Quinton, Flushing, New York

Clear the area

Keep things that the baby shouldn't have away from the bathtub or sink. I couldn't believe it when my four-month-old son pulled down a box of dishwasher detergent into the kitchen sink while I was bathing him. Now I keep anything that doesn't belong in the bath an arm's length away.

Susan Solomon, Tucson, Arizona

Cover faucets

Faucets can be too hot or too cold to touch your baby. Until my son was seven months old, when I bathed him in the sink, I turned the faucet toward the wall. Now that he's in the big tub, I bought a foam rubber cap that covers the metal but still allows water to flow.

Irene German, Nova Scotia, Canada

Wear a coverall

My daughter loves to splash in her little tub. Until I started wearing a plastic apron, I'd be soaked to the skin after each of her baths. Now I roll up my sleeves, put on my cover and let her splash away.

Barbara J. Henderson, Ames, Iowa

Bathe in tandem

As long as someone else is nearby in case you need some help and who can also hand you the baby as you get in and out of the tub, consider taking a bath with your infant. Put a towel on your chest to keep from becoming too slippery.

Andrea Strabinski, Oklahoma City, Oklahoma

Use a floor mat

I advise every parent to make sure that he or she has a bath mat near wherever you are bathing your baby. I didn't and because the floor got so wet and slippery, I took a fall while holding my child. Fortunately, neither of us was seriously hurt, but the moment was terrifying.

George Kurtz, Morristown, New Jersey

Add toys

I was delighted that my daughter, Erica, loved her bath. What surprised me was that even at four months of age, she loved bath toys. Her favorites were little plastic floating ducks. She clearly learned a lot by kicking them and watching me hold them under and let go so that they'd pop up again. It even made her laugh.

Roselyn Vitale, Brooklyn, New York

Remove your jewelry

Before bathing my son, I always remove my rings so that he doesn't get scratched. I also take off my gold chain because if he pulled at it after the plug was pulled, it would easily go down the drain.

Charlotte Embers-Twitty, Raleigh, North Carolina

Bathtime Fun

By the time children are ready to move from the sink or infant tub into the family tub, most are ready to turn tubtime into fun time. These parents have found ways to make bathtime a real splash.

Have theme nights

Theme baths can make bathtime more appealing to reluctant bathers. When it is "fishermen's night" at our house, my kids take a toy fishing pole and rubber fish into the tub with them. For "hunter" baths, they play with plastic crocodiles, birds and bears; and when it is "silly kids' night," I give them a bubble bath and bubbles for blowing.

Jennifer Fraase, Buffalo, North Dakota

Make bath cutouts

Use cookie cutters or stencils to trace shapes on a colorful rubber place mat. Then cut out the shapes and let your children play with them during bathtime. When wet, the shapes will float and stick to the sides of the tub and tiles.

Diane Jacobs, Charlotte, North Carolina

Tubtime Tips for Infants

- Before you put your baby into the tub, fill it with two inches of water.
- Have everything you'll need—soap, washcloth, shampoo, towel and robe—close at hand.
- To prevent scalding, install an anti-scald device on your water heater, which will keep the water temperature set below 120°F.
- Never leave your baby unattended, not even for a second. A baby can drown in less than two inches of water.
- Drain the tub after you remove the baby. The sounds and sight of an open drain may frighten him.
- Make sure that there's a bath mat or floor covering that will keep *you* from slipping if water should get on the floor.

Use kitchen toys

There's no need to buy expensive bath toys since many common household objects give hours of fun. My daughter loves to play with plastic ladles, colanders and juice containers from the kitchen, her beach ball and other rubber balls from her toy box and even plastic flowers from the living room during her bath.

Marleen Monohan, Highland, New York

Try foam soap

I buy foam soap at the drugstore. It comes in pump bottles in a variety of colors. My kids love to spray pictures on the tile and make necklaces and bracelets on their toy clowns and bears. Best of all, they voluntarily soap themselves.

Tarry A. Majewski, De Pere, Wisconsin

Wash dolly, too

When my seven-year-old takes a bath, I let her take her doll into the tub with her. First she shampoos her own hair and then she washes her doll's.

Lela Haddad, Las Vegas

Enjoy a Popsicle

As the mother of nine children, I've found ways to make bathtime fun. During the summer, when the kids really need to take a bath every day, I let them take a Popsicle into the tub. It's a fast way to get them in there, and the drips get washed away.

Cathy Frisby, Orem, Utah

Create an island

Out of a piece of floating foam rubber, I made an island for my two children to play with at bathtime. My son uses it along with his toy pirate figures and my daughter uses it with her mermaid dolls. Each one also has a shell collection that he or she places along the shore of the island. The only problem is that they find it very hard to end their play.

Jill Henson, Madison, Wisconsin

Avoiding Bathtime Battles

Let's face it. When you're a kid, you may have better things to do than take a bath. Some children balk at bathtime simply because they're busy with another activity but once in the tub, settle down for some serious play. Other children resist bathtime because they have trouble with transitions and going from all dressed up and dry to naked and wet is a pretty big transition to make. If your child resists hopping into the tub, try some of these ideas.

Buy special linens

My four-year-old son, who was a real bathtime battler, loved anything that had The Lion King on it. I made a deal with him: I would buy him a Mufasa towel set if he took his bath every night for a week without a fuss. It worked. A month later, just to reward him for keeping up his end of the deal, I bought him a Simba bath toy. Now I can't get him out of the tub.

Stephanie Stern, Milwaukee

Follow up with fun

In my family, I always make the hours after bathtime special, when all of us cuddle up together and read a story. Parents

PARENTS' ALERT
Bathtime Safety

- Always have a bath mat or adhesive-backed appliqués on the bathtub floor to prevent slips.
- Cover the spout with a soft sponge-like or inflatable cover to prevent burns from hot faucets and injuries caused by bumping into these protrusions.
- Teach your child never to touch the spigots to avoid accidentally turning on the hot water.
- Keep all adult bathing items—shampoo, shaving cream, razors and so forth—out of your child's reach.
- Never have an appliance, such as a hair dryer, radio or electric razor, plugged in when your child is in the bathroom.
- Clean up any spills and dry your child's feet thoroughly immediately after a bath to prevent slips.
- Never leave a child under the age of six unattended in the tub. Don't make older siblings who are bathing with younger ones responsible for their little brothers or sisters.

do this naturally with their younger children, but they sometimes forget that their older children might like it, too. Since the kids know that an enjoyable activity will follow, they are more likely to cooperate.

Janis Barrett Graham, Pleasant Grove, Utah

Make a puppet washcloth

My son, age three, really balked at having his face washed in the tub until I created washcloth puppets. Letting the puppet do the dirty work makes him laugh instead of cry.

Gina DiVinci, Miami

Cut down on baths

After struggling nightly with my eight-year-old about her bath, I finally said that she could skip every other night if she wanted as long as she didn't put up a fuss on the nights that she was still taking a

bath. And she agreed. I don't know why I didn't think of this sooner!

Theresa Antonetz, New York City

Take summer sprinkler showers

I tell my children that the idea is to freshen up and get rid of the dirt. They don't have to use soap if they don't want to. In the summer, bathtime can be accomplished with a garden hose or a run through the sprinkler. During the winter, I tell my kids that they only have to take a bath twice a week.

Linda Wong, Rio Rancho, New Mexico

Enlist your older child's help

I let my older daughter help me bathe her younger sister by letting the little one get into the tub with her. It makes her feel important and she gets clean in the process.

Nancy Duecker, Hurricane, West Virginia

Handling Bathtime Fears

For some children, the resistance to baths is really based on fear. Some of their concerns are common and developmentally appropriate. Will I go down the drain? Is the water too hot or too cold? Will I slip? Rather than showing a lack of cooperation, these concerns really show that your child has learned enough about the world to be asking some thoughtful questions. Other children's fears are based on specific incidents. A child whose bathtub had been invaded by a spider one night is likely to develop an aversion to the tub for a while. Sometimes the fears are harder to understand, but they are no less real to the child who is experiencing them. Be patient. In the meantime, these ideas can help.

Try a new toy

Introduce a new toy to distract a child who's afraid of the bathtub. Look for one that attaches to the tub to keep him sitting while you wash him.

Wendy Finley, Myersville, Maryland

Be patient

When my two-year-old daughter developed a fear of the bath, I decided to sponge-bathe her by the sink every night. After about two weeks of this, she was ready to try the bathtub again.

Evelyn Rosen, Montgomery, Alabama

Soap Operas

Tips for Keeping Suds Out of Kids' Eyes

- Experiment to see which shampoo-rinsing strategy works best for your child—leaning her head way back, covering her eyes with a wet washcloth or wearing a soap-catching headband as you spray or pour water.
- Remind children to rinse their hands before touching their faces when they're bathing.
- Use "tearless" shampoos and soaps.
- Keep a dry towel or washcloth nearby, where your child can find it with her eyes closed and without having to jump up in a panic.
- If a child has a particular fear of getting soap in his eyes, let him take some baths without soap.

Show problem-solving

My seven-year-old daughter freaks out if she sees any hairs floating in the tub when it's time for her bath. No matter how much I rinsed out the tub, there was always some left. We tried bailing out the hair, but some always remained. I finally hit upon the solution: I lay a dry towel on top of the water for a second and pull it out before it sinks. The hairs always stick to the towel. It's a bit of a nuisance, but her feelings of being grossed out are real so I'm glad to help.

Cherlyn Martlie, Hoboken, New Jersey

Bathe a doll first

My daughter had loved baths as a toddler, but at age three she suddenly became very fearful. After a whole week of no baths and just using a washcloth to clean her up, I bought her a doll in its own tub. After practicing bathing her doll for a few days, she wanted a bath, too.

Dana Fair Moon, Oklahoma City, Oklahoma

Give children control

Involve a fearful child in preparing for the bath. You could let him put the plug in the tub and if you have a handheld shower head, let him hold it as the tub fills with water. This way he will feel more in control of the situation and get used to the tub filling up slowly.

Maya Matulio, Jersey City, New Jersey

Bathe standing up

Let your child stand up in the bathtub while you carefully hold her and wash her if she's afraid to sit in the tub. (Make sure you have a nonskid mat under her so that she doesn't slip.) She'll sit down when she's ready.

Kelly Petrou, Ramsey, Illinois

Bathe together

Bathe with your child if she's afraid to get into the tub. Ask your husband to take a bath with your son, or, if you are comfortable with the idea, you can take one with him. Children feel more relaxed about taking a bath if they know that bathtime is something that they can share with a parent and not something that is being forced on them.

Missy Kennedy, Geneva, New York

Uncover the fear

When a child is frightened of the bathtub, try to find out what is scaring her. If the sound of rushing water is the culprit, muffle the noise by keeping the bathroom door closed while you run the water. If sitting in the water is scary, try not to overfill the tub; the feeling of buoyancy frightens some children.

Maryann Zihala, Chiefland, Florida

Give kids responsibility

Let a bath-phobic child help you at bathtime by getting his own pajamas, diaper, towel, soap, bubbles and a special toy ready for his bath. Giving him responsibility and control may help him overcome his resistance to taking a bath.

Stephanie Wadsworth, Elk Grove Village, Illinois

Conduct experiments

When my son developed a fear of going down the drain, I made of point of telling him that I was once afraid of that, too. Then we played together, experimenting to see what would and what would not go down the drain. When he saw that a big boy like himself was way too big to fit into the drain, his fears vanished.

Kendra Brown, Oakland, California

Bathtime Comfort Tricks

Like every other regular routine, bathtime brings with it some discomforts—and these great solutions.

Protect your knees

Bathing children can be pretty tough on parents' knees. I solved the problem by buying a gardener's pad at the hardware store. I'm so much more comfortable now that I encourage my one-year-old to splash around a little longer.

Valerie Cognetto, Buffalo

Warm lotions in the bath

While I run the water for my daughter's bath, I let the bottles containing her baby soap, shampoo and lotion float in the tub for a few minutes in order to heat them up. My daughter loves the feel of the warm liquids against her sensitive skin.

Janet Mans, Wichita, Kansas

Stick soap in socks

If your child wants to wash himself but has trouble handling a large bar of soap, stuff a sock with small soap pieces and knot the open end. When the sock is wet, he'll be able to work up a lather because holding the sock is much easier than holding slippery soap.

C. Gibson, Fontana, Wisconsin

Steam the room

I bathe my son after I have taken a shower, to prevent him from catching a chill. The steam keeps him nice and toasty during and after his bath.

Jean Heum, New Berlin, Wisconsin

Make toasty towels

If your child hates to get out of the bathtub because he feels chilly, warm his towel in the dryer for a few minutes before he gets into the tub. When it's time to dry your child off, he will love the towel's toasty feel.

Elizabeth Sharo, Cornwall, New York

Bathtime Cleanup

Having to clean up after a bath is further proof that life can be illogical. Nevertheless, bathtime cleanup is a fact of life. These ideas can make it easier. Always remember that bathtubs have a slick surface. Use a bath mat and tell children to be very careful getting in and out of the tub.

Use kitchen organizers

A great place to put my daughter's bath toys is in a three-tiered vegetable-and-fruit basket. I hang the basket from the towel rack inside the bath. Whenever company comes, her toys are conveniently out of sight.

Lori Wastlick, Plano, Texas

Personalize towels

I couldn't stand the pile of towels that my two children, ages 8 and 11, left on the floor after each bath. They each claimed the other had made the mess. I finally gave them each one towel with their names embroidered on it, and I've made it clear that they can use only their own towels. No more mess!

Christina Moran, New York City

Offer disincentives

After their bath or shower, I give each of my children a spray bottle of tub cleaner to clean up after themselves. The deal is that if one forgets to clean up after himself, he has to clean up after his brother, too.

Harriet Crow, Albany, New York

Line soap dishes

I've found that the best way to keep soap from melting into the soap dishes is to line them with wax paper. Now I just throw away the liner every week instead of trying to wash away built-up soap suds.

Margo Chaim, Englewood Cliffs, New Jersey

Spray vinegar

Once a week or so, I spray vinegar and water on the shower curtain, bathtub and tile walls. This really keeps soap scum from building up, and I don't worry about any chemical residue from commercial cleansers.

Berry Williamson, Pueblo, Colorado

Sort clothes now

Put two hampers in the bathroom— one for colors and one for whites. Teach your children to put their clothes directly into the appropriate container as they undress for their baths. It will save you lots of trouble. By doing this, I feel I'm training my sons for futures as good husbands by teaching them that they are responsible for doing their share.

Blair Nelson, Indianapolis

Hair-Washing Pointers

Few things in life are as delectable as the smell of a child who's just been bathed from head to toe—including a good hair washing. Gaining your child's cooperation in the hair-washing department can take a bit of creativity, as these parents demonstrate.

Enjoy ceiling art

Whenever I washed my son's hair, he would scream and cry because he was afraid of getting water and soap in his eyes. To solve this problem, I taped pictures to the ceiling right above the bathtub. Now when I rinse out the shampoo from his hair, I say, "Look up at the picture of the moon (or the stars, flowers or Big Bird)," and he keeps his head tilted back until I'm done.

Karen Ziemlak, Reading, Massachusetts

Do a coyote imitation

Rinsing shampoo from my daughter's hair always drove both of us to tears, until I thought of a trick to keep the soap and water out of her eyes: coyote calls! She raises her chin and howls, which keeps her head tilted back long enough for me to rinse the shampoo from her hair.

Becky Knight, Houston

Encourage independence

My six-year-old daughter and I were having real battles about washing and rinsing her hair. Finally, before her bath one evening I asked her if she thought she was big enough to wash and rinse it herself. With a very grown-up smile on her face, she answered yes. She agreed to let me check the rinse and when I saw that there was still soap in her hair, I held her a mirror so she could see, instead of insisting on finishing the job myself. It took her a while, but she got all the shampoo out. After a few times, she learned to do it herself and do it very well.

Rose Keniston, Scranton, Pennsylvania

Take a shower

Hair washing became much easier when my four-year-old son decided that showering was better than bathing in the tub.

Alyse Drew, Kingston, New York

Imagine rain

I use a handheld shower head to wash my daughter's hair, and I tell her the water will feel soft like rain. I give her a washcloth to hold over her eyes. Sometimes, I let her pour the water over her head with a cup.

Ruth Solomon, Harrisburg, Pennsylvania

Swim suds away

My five-year-old was learning how to swim at the local YMCA. One day, while he was demonstrating his technique to me in the tub, it occurred to me that this was a perfect way to get around the hairwashing hassles we'd been having. Now he swims the suds away, and I only have to use a cup or two of clear water to finish the job.

Abigail Farhoodi, Alexandria, Virginia

Hand Washing and Other Good Habits

Children are great believers in the unseen and readily accept visits from the Tooth Fairy and other mythical creatures who slip in while they sleep. Yet, many insist that unseen germs on their hands don't exist. "My hands are clean," they say whenever the dirt is less than obvious. Helping children to learn to wash their hands routinely is one of the best good-health habits you can teach your child and can greatly reduce the number of colds and other bugs kids pick up.

Carry baby wipes

Baby wipes are not just for babies. Because my children like to snack when we're at the park where there are no washing facilities, I always carry some wipes in my handbag so we can do a quick washup whenever necessary.

Eleanor Gravis, Hastings-on-Hudson, New York

Use liquid soap

My two children are much more agreeable about washing their hands when they can use liquid soap from a dispenser, since they don't like the slimy feel of a bar of soap.

Kendra Johnston, Tahoe, New Mexico

Buy silly soaps

My mother-in-law recently bought my sons soaps shaped like starfish and dolphins, and now they love washing their hands. I've already purchased six more little soaps for when these are gone.

Marilyn Evers, Keene, New Hampshire

Give them toys to wash

I always ask my son to wash one of his little plastic toys before a meal and after he uses the bathroom. This gets him washing his hands without any battles about it.

Nicki Weiss, Houston

Make a bubble bath

My two-year-old daughter made hand washing a nightmare until I started making her own bubble bath for hands. I simply put a drop of antibacterial soap in a mixing bowl, add warm water until it foams up and put it on the floor for her to splash and play in. Her hands get clean and so does the floor, and I don't have to endure a tantrum! By the way, since we started washing her hands this way, she hasn't had as many colds. Plus, she actually asks to wash.

Jennifer Fowler, Address withheld

Get sand off

To clean off your child's wet and sandy hands before lunchtime at the beach, gently rub them with a soft cloth sprinkled with cornstarch; you'll be surprised how easily the sand comes off. And to make the ride back home more comfortable, do the same over her body and feet.

Laura Parks, Gardnerville, Nevada

Haircutting Shortcuts

Early on, you might resist cutting off your son's curls for fear they'll never grow quite so coiled again. Later, you'll consider trimming your daughter's long and lovely hair for no other reason than to cut down on tangles.

Before letting haircutting become a hair-raising experience, remember these two things. First, hair grows back. Second, someday not so far away, your child will want a haircut that you'll find appalling, so you might as well enjoy your involvement in his or her tresses now. These shortcuts may help.

Be the chair

I put my little boy in my lap and hold him while the barber cuts his hair. I'm able to help move him from side to side when necessary, and then I have him sit facing me so that the barber can trim his hair in the back.

Cynthia Montgomery, Sommerville, New Jersey

Find a child-friendly barber

I always take my children with me when I'm getting my hair cut. This way they can see that it doesn't hurt and that I'm comfortable sitting still. It also helps to have a child-friendly hairdresser. My children really enjoy sitting on a rocking-horse-style barber chair.

Maggie Hall, Dunedin, Florida

Pack diversions

Take along a coloring book or some type of lap game to keep your child occupied during the haircut.

Cyndi Rafus, Loganville, Georgia

Trim in the tub

When my children were little, I cut their hair while they were in the bathtub. That way their hair was already wet and they were already sitting down. It was easy to distract them with toys and water games and then quickly give their hair a trim.

Kim LaBrecque, Roanoke, Virginia

Role play

I try to prepare my son for a trip to the barber by playing haircut at home. This way he can learn how to sit still for the 10 minutes it takes to cut his hair.

Linda Lierman, Phoenix

ASK THE EXPERTS

How Do I Treat Head Lice?

Head lice are not a sign of poor grooming. They are contracted by contact and no one is immune. You can cut down on the chances of contracting these speck-size insects by never sharing hats or hair accessories and by thoroughly delousing the house and clothing items that have been in contact with the person or pet who has lice.

Just about everyone can be treated at home for head lice, according to the National Pediculosis Association in Newton, Massachusetts. Here's what to do.

Offer reassurance. Approach the problem calmly so that your child doesn't panic or feel ashamed. Explain what lice are and how you're going to get rid of them. Assure your child that you don't blame her for getting lice.

Buy an OTC head-lice product. You can banish the invaders with many over-the-counter products such as RID, A-200, R & C and NIX, pharmacists say.

Consider a trim. Although it's not necessary to cut a child's hair because he has lice, shorter hair is easier to deal with. Remember, don't take a child with lice to a barber or hairdresser.

Wash hair over the sink. This way you can confine treatment to the scalp. You don't want to use lice products in the shower, where the rinsed-off solution can cascade over the body or in the tub where the diluted products would come in contact with the entire body. Remember, these products are pesticides and should be used with caution.

Be a nitpicker. The lice product will kill the lice, but not all the nits (eggs). The more nits you can remove, the less likelihood there is of a recurrence. For nit removal, use a fine-tooth comb.

Treat everyone at once. It only takes one little louse to infest a child (they lay up to 10 eggs a day) and lice easily spread from one person to another. Examine everyone in the house for lice.

Make a clean sweep. Once you've detected the lice and treated your children, you need to tend to the household. Wash everything, including hats, scarves, hooded coats, hairbands and any clothing your child may have worn in the past few days. Don't forget sheets, pillowcases and towels. Wash all items in hot water and dry in a hot dryer. Vacuum sofas, sofa pillows, mattresses and rugs (especially around the beds) and then put the vacuum cleaner bag in a plastic bag and throw it away.

Always check with your doctor before using a home lice treatment on:
- Children under two
- People with allergies or asthma
- Pregnant or nursing women

The doctor may prescribe a different medication or want to supervise the treatment for these people. Ask your doctor's advice for how to cope with lice and nits in the eyebrows and eyelashes. Also, if *you* are pregnant or nursing and need to use a lice treatment on someone else, contact your doctor first.

What to Do If (When) Your Child Cuts His or Her Own Hair

There's a good chace that somewhere between the ages of 3 and 10, your child will experiment with cutting his or her own hair. The youngest ones will be surprised that they can't simply put back the hair they cut off. Many children will invent creative explanations about how their hair happened to disappear. Some will hide the evidence and insist that their hair looks funny because the wind blew it that way. Most older children will be surprised that their attempts at haircutting didn't have the desired results. If your child has been overcome with an urge to practice amateur barbering, try these responses.

• Realize that no child ever planned on giving herself a dreadful cut. If she makes up a wild tale about what happened, don't demand the truth right away. She's upset enough. Try saying, "I know you wish that your stuffed tiger bit off your hair, but since the tiger can't put your hair back on your head, you and I will have to find a way of making your hair look right."

• Even if you don't regularly take your child to a stylist, now's the time to enlist the aid of a professional. Even a close-to-the-scalp cut can be fashioned into a reasonably good look.

• Keep your sense of humor. While you don't want to laugh at your child whose sense of self is threatened right now, store the incident up for the future. In time, your child will laugh along with you and the outrageous thing he did back when he was little.

Let Dad do it

My husband takes our son, Robert, to the barber whenever he goes. By the time it's Robert's turn to get his cut, he can't wait.

Melanie Roman, Tulsa, Oklahoma

Get the tools

As the mother of three sons, I decided I could save a fortune by learning to cut their hair myself. I bought professional clippers and practiced on my two-year-old who wouldn't have to face the taunts of classmates in case I made too many mistakes. Actually I was pretty good at it, even the first time. Now I do my husband's haircuts, too.

Beth Evers, Butte, Montana

Preview the big day

My middle daughter, Megan, generally needed lots of warm-up time before she'd try anything new. To get her used to the idea that she'd soon be getting a haircut, I said to her a few times over a two-week period, "I think you're almost old enough for a real haircut." Since she was also at a stage where she wanted to feel grown-up, she finally begged me to take her for a haircut.

Deirdre Farrell-Simonti, Des Moines, Iowa

Hair Combing Made Easier

Kids' fine hair can get into a fine mess, but help is at hand. Begin by choosing a good hairbrush, comb or pick. Wide-toothed, flexible combs or brushes with rub-ber-tipped bristles are best for detangling. And these suggestions should help, too.

Use a satin pillowcase

Try using a satin pillowcase if your child wakes up with lots of tangles. The hair just slides around on the pillow instead of bunching up, which prevents snarls. I had the same problems, and it worked for me.

Susan Heath, Meriden, Connecticut

Braid it

Every morning used to be a battle when I tried to brush the tangles out of my six-year-old daughter's long hair. I solved the problem by braiding Jennifer's hair at bedtime. Now our mornings are tear- and tangle-free.

Brenda Fitzgerald, LaPorte, Indiana

Choose short styles

Four of my five daughters have short hair because I can't take the daily battles. Try to make a short haircut appealing by looking through magazines together to find a style that your child likes. Some short styles would still allow a girl to wear barrettes and headbands, which she could pick out to go with the new hairstyle.

O.J. Scott, Charlotte, North Carolina

Start at the bottom

To get out tangles, start from the bottom and work in sections. That way you're not pulling on your child's scalp, which can be painful.

Robin Becroft, Wallingford, Connecticut

Let kids do it

Let children comb the snarls out of their hair themselves. Watch how they do it. Sometimes kids have fresh ideas.

Pam Polis, Lancaster, California

Remove gum with ice

A neighbor taught me this trick for removing gum from my daughter's hair and saved her from having to get a haircut she didn't want. Hold ice cubes around the gum until it freezes and then the frozen gum will break off.

Adelaide Curran, Cincinnati

Use conditioner

When you wash your child's hair, be sure to use conditioner. The snarls will be easier to comb out. Also make sure you use a large, wide-toothed comb.

Deirdre Masi, Boynton Beach, Florida

Brush Up on Brushing Techniques

Helping your children take care of their teeth starts when their first teeth erupt and continues until your children are old

When a Tooth is Knocked Out

If your child knocks out a tooth, place it back in the socket immediately, if at all possible, and hold it in place as you head to the dentist. If the dentist can work on the tooth within 30 minutes, this procedure gives you about a 90 percent chance of saving the tooth. If you cannot hold the tooth in place, put it in lukewarm milk until you reach the dentist.

enough to have developed independent self-care habits. Here are some tips to help you bring out your child's best smile.

Brush each other's teeth

When it was time to brush her teeth, my 18-month-old daughter, Samantha, used to turn her head, clench her teeth and cry if I tried to help her. I was afraid I would turn her off brushing forever! Finally I figured out a solution: I let her brush my teeth while I simultaneously brushed hers. She gets a big kick out of it, and it seems to have taken away her fear. Although I still have to remind her to brush, I find that I'm wiping off toothpaste from her face instead of tears.

Susanna Perrin, Long Beach, California

Position a mirror at kid's level

Getting my toddlers to brush their teeth used to be a very difficult task until I attached a mirror to the wall above our

Tooth Time Line

Infants: Primary teeth begin developing in the womb. At around 6 months, most babies start to teethe, usually getting their bottom front teeth first. At around 8 months, upper front teeth emerge. At 12 months, the four lateral incisors appear, and the first molars begin to come in. Between 15 and 21 months, the canines (pointed teeth) usually appear, and by 21 months, all four first molars are in place.

Toddlers: Between 2½ and 3 years of age, four second molars emerge, giving your toddler a full set of 21 baby teeth.

5 and 6 years: At this age, a child's first permanent teeth—the first molars—emerge in a space next to the baby molars.

6 and 7 years: This is when most children begin to lose their primary teeth, usually starting with the lower front teeth. The process of losing their baby teeth continues through age 11 or 12.

Between 11 and 14 years: A second set of permanent molars emerges, giving your adolescent 28 teeth.

Age 15 and up: One to four wisdom teeth emerge.

bathroom sink—at their eye level. Now that they can see themselves, they are much more enthusiastic and actually do a better job.

G. Blaha, St. Paul, Minnesota

Tooth-Fairy Fun

To a child, losing a baby tooth is a mark of maturity, a visible sign of growing up. Children may begin to lose their primary teeth at any time between four and eight years, usually beginning at age five. Help make the occasion even more momentous with these tips from the Tooth Fairy.

- Before putting the tooth under the pillow, place it securely in a little box (such as a jewelry box) or specially made tooth box so that it doesn't get lost during the night.
- Sprinkle a little glitter on the windowsill of your child's room as evidence that the Tooth Fairy's been there.
- If a child is frightened of the Tooth Fairy visiting her room as she sleeps, suggest that instead of leaving her tooth under her pillow that she leave it on the kitchen table. Assure her that the fairy knows where to find it.
- In addition to leaving a coin under your child's pillow, leave a special sticker, a note from the Tooth Fairy or even a brand new fancy toothbrush.

Brush to music

To remind my son, age four, to brush long enough, I put a music tape in his portable cassette player and ask him to brush until one song is completely over.

PEDIATRICKS
Baby's Teeth

To keep your baby's gums healthy, gently clean and massage them each night with a moist gauze pad or washcloth. As teeth begin to emerge, clean them gently with a soft-bristled infant toothbrush; no toothpaste is necessary. Never let your baby fall asleep with a formula, milk or juice bottle in his mouth. Milk can pool around the teeth and cause decay. If you're breast-feeding or if your local water supply doesn't contain fluoride, check with your pediatrician to see if a fluoride supplement is recommended since fluoride has been proven effective in helping growing children to develop harder tooth enamel, thus preventing cavities.

Since most of the songs last about two minutes, he brushes thoroughly.

Everett Jackson, Bristol, Connecticut

Brush before dressing

I recommend reminding children to brush before they're dressed in the morning to avoid having to wash toothpaste off their outdoor clothes.

Barbara Morgan, Annapolis, Maryland

Dressing Babies and Toddlers

There's nothing quite like trying to get a squirming infant into a stretchie—except, perhaps, trying to get a sleeping infant into

Helping Your Child Enjoy a Visit to the Dentist

When teeth first erupt and twice a year after age three, children should be seen by a dentist. How can you help make these visits go smoothly? Here are some ideas for preschoolers and young grade-schoolers.

• Prepare your child in advance. Explain common procedures such as tooth counting, x-rays and cleaning so that your child knows what to expect.

• Let your child see you enjoy a dental visit. Do not have your child sit in on any uncomfortable procedures you're undergoing.

• Never threaten a child with a dental visit, saying, for instance, "If you eat that candy I'll have to take you to the dentist."

• Bring along a diversion, such as a story cassette and player, in case you have to wait.

• Most important, choose a dentist who is understanding of young children's needs and who will put your child at ease.

one. In some ways, dressing your child will never be easier than it is now, before your little squirmer develops clothing preferences. For now, try these ideas to make dressing a bit less frustrating.

Bag those shoes

Winter in Minnesota means a constant struggle with snowsuits. We found that if you place a large plastic bag over your toddler's shoe, the snowsuit pant leg will slip right on. Be sure to put the bag away after using for safety against suffocation.

Lisa Mills, Montrose, Minnesota

Use your lap

Here's a dressing idea that I think other parents of infants can use. Dress your baby in your lap instead of on the changing table, where she's more apt to roll around. My daughter put up a real fuss about dressing until I learned that she probably was getting a chill lying naked on the table.

Marietta Waterhouse, Denver

Dress in one-piece undies

Onesies are great. They really beat regular undershirts that leave a baby's tummy hanging out. They're also smooth against baby's skin and keep any stitching outside the outfit from chafing your baby.

Linda Moor, San Diego

Pin sleeves

Keeping the long sleeves on her shirt from riding up while I put on my daughter's jacket was difficult until I discovered a new use for old diaper pins. I now pin the cuff of her sleeve to the cuff of the jacket as I put the jacket on. I remove the pins once she's dressed.

Lenore Martinez, New York City

Choose basic colors

Keep your baby's wardrobe as color-coordinated as possible. That way, when you have to change the bottom of the outfit because it's become wet, you can leave on the same shirt. Likewise, if the top gets soiled during mealtimes you only have to change one piece.

Joanna Katz, Poughkeepsie, New York

Smart Ideas for Smart Dressing

While clothing designs have improved greatly over the years, some items still need your personal touch to stay on comfortably and securely in order to look just right.

Clasp jumper straps

If the straps on your child's jumpers or overalls keep falling off her shoulders, try snapping on a child's barrette. The barrette will keep the straps securely in place.

Barbara Cason, Evansville, Indiana

Opt for tights

My two-year-old son was always pulling off his socks and I was afraid of his feet being cold. So now I put tights on him under his sweats or jeans.

Jean Boscovi, Huntington, New York

Make no-slide slippers

My three-year-old daughter loves to wear her Minnie Mouse slippers. Unfortunately, some of the rooms in our house have slippery hardwood floors. To prevent her from falling, I purchased bathtub decals and stuck them on the bottoms of her slippers. They work like a charm.

Mae Trefrey, Newport, Rhode Island

Make a hat strap

I love the way my daughter looks in little hats, but sometimes she flings them off while we're out. We lost two of them because I never saw it happen and another wound up in a muddy puddle. She hates chin straps so tying the hats under her chin was not a solution. I finally sewed short ribbons (about three inches) to the back of each bonnet and I pin each hat to her collar. Now when she flings her hat off, it doesn't go far.

Julliette Mahoney, Jacksonville, Florida

Turn tights inside out

If your child's tights are full of runs, turn them inside out and they'll look as good as new.

Name and address withheld

Cut and snap

Though I buy only shirts and sweaters that have snaps on the shoulders to make

the neck holes big, my son has received a number of gifts that have smaller neck holes. He hates getting into these. I solved the problem by cutting a slit down the back of each top and adding a button. By making the cut on the back instead of on the shoulders, I don't have to worry too much if my sewing isn't great.

Jane Morris-Pomander, Redwood City, California

Replace buttons with bows

I'm always worried that the buttons on my daughter's sweaters and fronts of dresses would wind up in her mouth. So I replace the buttons with four-inch pieces of coordinating ribbons. I sew on the ribbons to where the buttons were and I pull one two-inch piece through the button hole and then tie a bow. The clothes stay closed and I can relax.

Karen Kennedy, Salinas, Kansas

Sew with floss

I'm always concerned about the potential choking hazard from loose buttons or bows on my children's clothing. To eliminate my worry, I reinforce each of these adornments with clear dental floss, which is much stronger than regular sewing thread. (Note that there should be no buttons or bows on infant clothing or sleepwear.)

Marily Gross, Santa Ana, California

Kids Won't Get Dressed? Try This . . .

Naked is nice; so is wearing the same outfit for four days in a row—at least from some kids' points of view. If your kids resist getting dressed, here are some ideas to help them ease on in to clothing.

Sleep in clothes

My son hated getting dressed in the morning for day care. A friend made the suggestion that I put him to bed in the sweatsuit that he'd be wearing the next day. What a difference this has made in our mornings!

Priscilla Casey, Indianapolis

Go out in jammies

I made my life a lot easier when I started letting my four-month-old son wear his cotton pajamas as his outfit for the next day.

Ginnie Lawrence, Skokie, Illinois

Forget the frills

During the warmer weather I don't even try to get my 10-month-old dressed up. I just put her in diapers and a T-shirt. It makes life easier for both of us.

Madelaine Brevot, Kent, Ohio

Make it a game

If you line up your child's underwear, socks, shirt, pants and shoes on the floor, he can pretend he is a choo-choo train as he dresses himself. My son used to love to go down the line putting on his clothes while making choo-choo noises.

Annette DeMaio, West Springfield, Massachusetts

Make up stories

Try and make up silly stories to capture your child's attention. I tell my daughter something like, "Did you hear about the little kitty who was driving a car?" Often she doesn't even notice that I've finished dressing her because she's listening so intently.

Tori O'Halloran, San Jose, California

Let dolly play

I ask my daughter to select her clothes and dress her baby so that she can come out with us, too. This usually motivates her to cooperate and get dressed.

Jana Tucker, Montevallo, Alabama

Encourage independence

I offer my daughter two outfits and let her decide which one she wants to wear. It makes her feel important and seems to take her mind off the fact that she didn't want to get dressed in the first place.

Sherri Starr, Plainview, New York

Cuddle and dress

Try to combine dressing time with cuddling time. My son usually calms down when I put him on my lap, cuddle him and talk about our plans for the day.

Nancy L. Knettel, San Antonio, Texas

Be firm

My son usually gets the message to get dressed when I tell him, "You will have to stay home cooped up with Mama if you wear pajamas, or you can go outside and play if you get dressed."

Donna G. Chuley, Clovis, New Mexico

Don't overreact

I have two-year-old triplets and a four-year-old son, and I've learned to take their fun out of pushing my buttons. If I don't argue with them over what to wear, they get dressed faster. When my daughter

wanted to wear three dresses, I let her. Sooner or later she took two of them off herself. As long as my children are safe and warm, I'm happy.

Deborah Walter, Summit, New Jersey

Encouraging Independent Dressing

Helping children learn to dress by themselves is one of those investments in the future that really pays off. The extra time taken to teach how to dress when your child is young, assures that you won't have to spend the time later.

Have a contest

I made up a game with my three-year-old daughter to get her to dress herself. We have a contest to see who can be faster. She dresses herself and I dress one of her dolls. She usually wins and so do I.

Aretha Black, Milwaukee

Find role models

The best way I found to encourage a preschooler to get himself dressed is to expose him to other, slightly older kids who can do it. My son decided that he was old enough to get himself dressed when we were at a pool in our community and he saw the big boys themselves dressing.

Caryn Karpovitch, Tarrytown, New York

Work in stages

Take self-dressing in stages. When my daughter was younger, I'd put on one sock and then she'd put on the other. I'd help her into one sleeve of her shirt and then

Making Self-Dressing Easier

Until they're about two, most children are far more interested in taking clothing off than putting it on. In the preschool years, however, "I can do it!" takes over. Try these ideas to make getting dressed child's play.

- Buy clothes that won't present too much of a challenge: tube socks, elastic-waist pants, shirts with ample neck openings, jackets with large-size zippers.
- Tops with appliqués, monograms or other decorative touches will help a preschooler distinguish back from front. Teach the child that the inside labels usually go in the back; if there's no label, mark the back of the garment with a laundry pencil.
- Have your child always button from the bottom up. That way, the buttons and holes are more likely to match up. And to make the buttons easier to fasten, sew them on with elastic thread.
- Teach your child to put on his jacket by laying it on the floor, lining side up, with the collar end at his feet, putting his hands into the sleeves and then flipping the jacket over his head.
- To be sure shoes go on the correct feet, make a mark on the inside edge of each. Your child will know he's got it right when the marks meet.
- Invest in a doll that offers practice in the fine art of fastening.
- Limit choices. A general "What do you want to wear?" is overwhelming. Instead take out two shirts and let your child pick one. Be sure to praise the choice.
- Remember that children choose clothing for emotional as well as practical reasons and that an outgrown or unseasonable favorite may offer special comfort. As much as possible, allow your child's preferences, letting him wear a summer T-shirt as an undershirt in winter, for instance.

she'd do the other. Knowing that she didn't have to struggle with the whole job of getting dressed, I think, gave her the confidence to try and also kept getting dressed from taking all day.

Melinda Day-Lennon, Selma, Alabama

Don't criticize

When I criticized my daughter for making mistakes while dressing, she'd get so discouraged. So I followed the lead of her preschool teacher and learned to accept the results of any attempts. It's sometimes hard to let her go out with her underpants or T-shirt on backwards or with mittens on the wrong hands, but by keeping quiet, she does it herself.

Grace McGovern, Mayfield, Pennsylvania

Coordinate the wardrobe

It's hard to let kids pick out an outfit when it's possible that they'll pick plaid

PARENTS' ALERT

Clothing Hazards

Certain clothing elements can pre-sent hazards to young children and should be avoided. These include:

- Drawstring hoods and scarves that can become entangled around a child's neck.
- Slippery winter pants, which can fail to stop a child from sliding on snowy hills.
- Loose buttons and tiny hair bows or barrettes that young children may ingest.
- Nonskid shoe soles, especially on wet walking surfaces.
- Jewelry, including dangling earrings, bracelets, necklaces and rings.

pants to go with polka-dot shirts. I limit my three children's wardrobes to coordi-nating colors (navy, khaki and green) and buy patterns (that contain one or more of the chosen colors) only for tops. This way, just about anything they choose makes a presentable outfit.

Cecilia Oppenheimer, Las Vegas

Putting Their Best Foot Forward

Unlike most other items of clothing, in which a little big or a little small is okay, shoes need to fit just right. Getting shoes on and keeping them on is also a challenge for

most parents. These parents are really on their toes about their children's footwear.

Wet laces

Are your children's laces always coming undone? To help keep my child's shoelaces tied, I wet them slightly before I tie them.

Joie Baker, San Francisco

Buy wild shoelaces

To encourage my son to learn to tie his own shoelaces, I let him pick out a few pair of really cool shoelaces in neon colors and replaced the boring laces the shoes came with.

Mimi Ortega, Bronx, New York

Make a match

So my daughter, Caroline, could tell which shoe went on which foot, I paint her right big toenail red with nail polish and I mark each of her right shoes on the inside with a red marker.

Sally Morgan, Oswego, New York

Avoid hightops

Hightop sneakers may be fashionable for kids, but getting them on and off is a real pain. After going through the experi-ence, I now buy only low sneakers, which my son and daughter can each put on and take off on their own.

Molly Dwyer, Northampton, Massachusetts

Tell boots to take a hike

Here's a warning to parents. Avoid hik-ing boots that have metal ice-skate-like loops for shoelaces. The lace from one shoe can easily snag in the other shoe, causing your child to fall. This happened to my son and one of his friends. The other child broke his arm in a fall caused by this design.

Lisa Downs, Nashua, New Hampshire

Go for soft shoes

Here's an idea for parents of toddlers. Avoid putting those heavy leather shoes on your child. I was playing with my two-year-old, holding him high above my head, when he kicked his feet in fun and accidentally knocked out my front tooth. My dentist told me that I wasn't the first person who'd been inadvertently harmed by her child's hard shoes.

Imogene Battaglia, New York City

Double the lifespan of boots

I always buy winter boots that have removable liners inside. That way they fit as winter boots one year and, when the liners are removed, as rain boots the next.

Marge Quinn, New York City

When Clothing Tastes Clash

You don't have to wait until your child is a preteen to discover just how different your idea of well-dressed and your child's can be. From the preschool years onward, children commonly have strong feelings about their clothing. Some want to wear their superhero outfits or their ballet costumes day in and day out. Others have an aversion to anything with elastic in it. How much should you give in to your child's fashion statements? When should you intervene? These parents offer pointers.

Dress up dolls

For no apparent reason my three-year-old daughter, Samantha, refused to wear certain outfits, and it drove me *crazy*. One morning her attitude changed when she awoke to find her dolls wearing the clothes that she said she hated. Naturally, they had on exactly what she wanted to wear.

Patricia Paglinco, Denville, New Jersey

Set aside a dress-herself day

My six-year-old daughter often chooses wild combinations of clothing to wear to kindergarten. To put an end to our morning hassles, I declared Thursday an Anything Goes Day. My daughter knows that on Thursdays, she can wear anything she wants—provided that it matches the weather conditions.

Patty Grasty, Middletown, Ohio

Pick your battles

I'm proud that my five-year-old wants to get himself dressed, but I can't stand the choices he makes—things like striped long-sleeve shirts with plaid trousers. While I'm planning to buy only things that can be mixed-and-matched in the future, I've come up with a plan that works for now. He's allowed to choose what he wears to preschool as long as it's for the right season. I get to pick out what he wears for church and other dressier occasions.

Anna Lepoltz, Bay Ridge, New York

Compromise

My seven-year-old daughter really wanted some clothing that I consider very inappropriate for young girls. She particularly wanted a lacy dress similar to ones

Getting the Right Fit

- Have your child's feet measured at a shoe store each time you buy shoes. (For children three-years-old and younger, shoe size is likely to increase every two months. Four- to six-year-olds outgrow a size every four to six months; six- to nine-year-olds, about every three to four months.)
- Buy a shoe with room for growth. There should be about a half inch between the end of your child's longest toe and the tip of his shoe. The heel should not feel pinched or move around inside the shoe.
- Avoid shoes that have pointed toes, which can prevent feet from elongating and spreading out comfortably. "Pick the occasions when you let your little girl wear 'cute' shoes," says Tom Brunick, director of The Athlete's Foot Wear Test Center at North Central College, in Naperville, Illinois. "The rest of the time, she should wear shoes that are roomy enough for her to wiggle her toes."
- Look for laces or midfoot support straps, which offer more ankle support and are less likely to fall off while running.
- Choose all-purpose sneakers, not those designed for running. The all-purpose variety will provide good cushioning as well as side-to-side support.
- Don't wait until a pair of shoes are totally worn before you replace them. When wear-and-tear are apparent or when the wearer's toe touches the front of the shoe, it's time for a new pair.

her friends have. At a yard sale, we found a dress that she really wanted and I agreed to buy it for her if she promised that she'd wear it only in the house. Now she puts it on when her friends are playing here and seems satisfied with that.

Coleen Briman-Deacon, Flushing, New York

Get a teacher's help

What's with five-year-old girls and dresses? I can't believe that every girl in my daughter's kindergarten insisted on wearing dresses only, even in colder weather and even though they find it harder to play with their dresses on. A number of us mothers wanted our girls to wear pants and we approached the teacher who agreed to help us. She decreed that Fridays would be pants days, as an experiment to see if the girls would get used to wearing pants. Within a few weeks, more and more of them, my daughter included, began to opt for pants on other days of the week, too.

Crystal Taylor, St. Joseph, Missouri

Store clothes in sets

To help my four-year-old pick matching clothes, I put them away in sets only, with shorts or pants, socks and T-shirts together in his dresser drawers instead of putting each type of item in a separate place. He can pick out any set he likes.

Raye Jimenez, Miami

Work with teens

Frankly, I hate the way my two teenagers dress. But instead of battling with them over every outfit, I've made just two rules and they've agreed to abide by them. My rules: No T-shirts with obscene or otherwise inappropriate statements printed on them and when we visit relatives or when the relatives visit us, I have veto power over their choices. I've also vetoed weird hair dying, body piercing and tattoos. By the way, when my kids were little, I never thought that these things would ever be an issue in our home.

Jolene Davidson, Tallahassee, Florida

Don't overshop

My daughter's taste in clothing changes from week to week, depending on what the other kids in school are wearing. I've learned that instead of buying a lot of new school clothes in September, I buy her just one or two new outfits. Then as the school year progresses, she can pick out things that she needs, one outfit or so a month. I don't buy more this way and what we buy, she actually likes.

Danielle Cole, Maplewood, New Jersey

Shop with kids

I take both of my children (a boy, eight, and a girl, five) with me when it's time to buy them any new clothing. I insist that they try things on to find out ahead of time if something is scratchy or feels funny. I find that if they pick out their own clothing, they don't later decide that an outfit is *hideous*, a favorite word of my son's.

Nicole Swedman, Huntington, New York

CHAPTER FOUR

Bedtime from A to Zzz

To sleep, perchance to dream." Shakespeare may have written this line for Hamlet, but in the intervening centuries, parents have claimed it for their very own. Helping your child learn to sleep through the night is essential for him and for you. Your children need more sleep than you do, but Mother Nature can't lull your daughter into a sleeping pattern that follows *your* schedule, at least not in the early months. Eventually, your child's need for sleep will resemble your own. In the meantime, the tips in this chapter will help you both rest easier.

Hush, Little Baby

Watching your baby sleep is one of those grand paybacks. During the first few months, mom, dad and baby's alarm clocks are not likely to be synchronized—and you're apt to be exhausted. While nothing can make a baby sleep "like a baby," these ideas can help give you and your infant some needed peace.

Hold her close

My daughter was born a little early and had a particularly difficult time sleeping in her cradle. Out of desperation, I put her into one of those front carriers that kept her close to my chest. She fell asleep almost instantly and slept peacefully. Until she was three months old, I kept her in the carrier about eight hours a day and she slept. Keeping her close in those early weeks and months was a lifesaver.

Meaghan Montgomery, Ypsilanti, Michigan

Reset baby's clock

I found that each of my three sons had a very different infant sleeping pattern.

FUN FACT

According to sleep experts, once a baby has reached 12 to 13 pounds and is about four months old, he or she is ready to develop a regular sleep-wake cycle and sleep for a 9- to 10-hour stretch.

The first was an easy sleeper right from the start. The second liked to sleep all day and stay awake all night. For a few weeks, to help him reset his internal clock, I put bright lights in his bedroom at night while keeping the house dark during the day, gradually changing the light and dark phases until they matched the real day and night. For my third son, who slept well at naptime but awakened every two hours during the night, I put his crib in the living room and the noise from the other boys during the day shortened his naptimes. When he awoke at night, he didn't disturb his brothers as easily.

Mercedes Macky, Pueblo, Colorado

Find a favorite tune

To help my baby fall asleep, I sang "Mockingbird," every time I carried her to her crib. Though she surely didn't understand the words, she got the message that this particular tune meant bedtime.

Leona Mercy, Lawrence, Kansas

Get fresh air

My son, Ben, slept much better outdoors than indoors and being cooped up indoors during the day was making me nuts. We started a routine of taking long walks and going to a local outdoor café. There I read and had some tea and conversation while Ben slept peacefully. I went home before lunch and did what needed to be done. In the afternoons, I went out again. I also found that opening his bedroom window and letting in fresh air helped him sleep better at night.

Maryanne Farrell, New York City

Share a room

Keep your baby in your room during the first few months so that when she does wake up during the night, you don't have to stumble into another room in the dark. Besides, with her there, it is also more likely that your husband will wake up and help feed her a bottle or give her to you to be breastfed.

Gwen Swenson, Minnetonka, Minnesota

Warm baby's bedding

I warm up the sheets with a hair dryer before I put Amanda to bed. The warmth combined with the sound of a nearby ticking clock calms her.

Hu Kim, Flushing, New York

Read regularly

Even when your child is an infant, read him to sleep. From the time my son was born, I've always read to him before putting him in his crib. The rhythmic speech that comes with reading puts him right to sleep.

Natalie Marchanski, Maplewood, New Jersey

Avoiding Bedtime Battles

From a child's point of view, bedtime represents an end of the fun, so it's no wonder that many kids look for ways to procrastinate. Having firmly established routines is the surest way to avoid battles at bedtime, as these parents have found.

Have a set bedtime

Consistency and control are two of the most important aspects of my child's bed-

PEDIATRICKS

Bedtime Safety Checks for Babies

- To make sure that your baby hasn't squirreled away food or a foreign object that she could choke on while sleeping, check her mouth before putting her to bed. Wash your hands and then gently sweep your finger along the inside of her cheeks and around her teeth and gums.
- Before bed, check your baby's hands and feet to uncover any loose, single strands of adult hair that can tightly wrap around an infant's fingers or toes and cut off their circulation.
- Keep your infant's crib free of clutter. Quilts and stuffed animals pose a suffocation hazard.
- Post a note by your child's crib to remind yourself and all caregivers to lift and lock the side of the crib.
- Don't let a baby sleep in an adult bed or in a water bed.
- To reduce the risk of SIDS, have babies sleep on their backs.

time routine. His bedtime is 8:00 P.M. and we stick to it, getting him ready around 7:00 P.M. I let him pick out his pajamas, a stuffed animal and a story for me to read to him. I tell him how proud I am when he gets into bed and stays there without a fuss.

Sommer Hahn, Portsmouth, Virginia

Give bedtime choices

I wish I'd set up a regular routine when my son was younger because by the time he was four, bedtime battles had become our routine. It took a lot of work to undo the inconsistencies of his toddler years, but now things are much better. I let him decide on three things he would like to do before bed (from a list of appropriate activities) and I tell him three things he must do: Brush his teeth, go to the bathroom and get into his pajamas. He usually picks hearing a story, having a small snack and turning on an audiotape as he drifts off.

Peter McNichols, Menlo Park, New Jersey

Make a map

My four-year-old daughter and I drew a bedtime map, to show visually what bedtime routines had to be followed. On the portion that shows the bathroom, we marked the toilet and sink to remind her to go to the bathroom, wash her hands and face and brush her teeth. On the bookshelf shown on the map, we put a big star to show that the treasure of a bedtime story comes next. Then we look at the map to find the bed, where we say our prayers and kiss good night.

Venessa Brown, Brooklyn, New York

Beat the clock

In our family, we set a 60-minute timer at 7:00 P.M., so it's easy for the children to determine how much time is left to get into pajamas and into bed by 8:00 P.M. We let the kids decide in what order they'll follow their routine. The only rule is that toothbrushing and face washing must be done before the buzzer goes off. It's comical to watch them scramble through the routine at 5 minutes to 8:00, but they've learned to beat the clock.

Anne Perry-Crichton, Tampa, Florida

Have a reward system

We keep a bedtime chart on each of my children's doors. After they accumulate 10 stars for going to bed without too much fuss, they earn an extra bedtime story.

Kathy Fenton, Hartford, Connecticut

Calm down first

I find that the more stressful the day has been, the earlier the bedtime routine has to start. Neither of my two children can sleep properly if they're angry or upset about anything. On more difficult days I have them take their baths right after dinner and try to arrange something pleasant to do, like watching a short tape together or playing a board game, to calm them down.

Finola Day, Quebec

Quench nighttime thirst

If your child doesn't have a table near his bed, a drink holder (the kind hung on car windows) hooked onto the headboard can hold a cup of water for quenching a nighttime thirst.

Randy and Deborah Gremmer, Britt, Iowa

Put toys to sleep

When my 22-month-old son balks at the idea of putting away his toys before bedtime and isn't ready to call it a night, I tell him the toys have played with him all day and are just as tired as he is. As I start the cleanup process myself, I encourage him to join in by saying good night to his

PARENTS' BOOKSHELF
Bedtime Favorites

Toddlers

Goodnight Moon, by Margaret Wise Brown

Jamberry, by Bruce Degen

Wheels on the Bus, adapted by Paul Zelinsky

Polar Bear, Polar Bear, What Do You Hear? by Bill Martin, Jr.

Sheep in a Shop, by Nancy Shaw

Where's Spot? by Eric Hill

First Words for Babies and Toddlers, by Jane Salt

You Go Away, by Dorothy Corey

When You Were a Baby, by Ann Jonas

A Very Hungry Caterpillar, by Eric Carle

Preschoolers

The Runaway Bunny, by Margaret Wise Brown

The Tale of Peter Rabbit, by Beatrix Potter

The Little Engine That Could, by Watty Piper

Curious George, by H. A. Rey

Caps for Sale, by Esphyr Slobodkina

Millions of Cats, by Wanda Gag

Ask Mr. Bear, by Marjorie Flack

A Snowy Day, by Ezra Jack Keats

The Nutshell Library, by Maurice Sendak

Make Way for Ducklings, by Robert McCloskey

Parents

Solve Your Child's Sleep Problems, by Richard Ferber, M.D. (Fireside/Simon & Schuster)

---

toys and by putting them in a nice safe place so that they are ready to go in the morning.

Liz German, Somerville, New Jersey

Beyond the Basics: Special Bedtime Routines

Beyond the basic bedtime routines, these parents have discovered some special night-time magic to help their children enjoy bedtime.

Set up an aquarium

An aquarium is the perfect night-light. The company of the fish, the glow of the light and that rhythmic sound of the heater help my two-year-old son fall asleep without a fuss.

Kristine Morris, Monroe, Ohio

Whisper

Sometimes after a hectic day of running and playing, my children, ages four and two, can't calm down and go to bed. My answer? Whisper. Every night, about an hour before their bedtime, my husband and I whisper to the children and to each other, too. We find that it puts our kids in a sleepy mood.

Sandy Coady, East Boston, Massachusetts

Install red lights

When you look in on your baby at night, are you afraid you'll wake her when you turn on the light? Here's an easy solution my husband came up with: Put a red bulb in the lamp instead. A red bulb also helps my son, who gets scared if he wakes up in a dark room in the middle of the night. For him, we sometimes keep the light on all night; it casts a calming glow, without being so bright that he can't fall asleep. (Red bulbs are available at hardware stores and supermarkets.)

Candace A. Goff, Lowell, Massachusetts

Keep a diary

When my son was a newborn, I used to write in his baby book every night, but as he got a bit older, I somehow dropped this wonderful record-keeping. Recently, now that Todd is four, I've begun helping him keep his own records. Each night at bedtime he dictates a story or a reminder of the day to me, which I write down in his special journal. I know I'll treasure this book and future volumes for years to come.

Molly Anderson, Kalamazoo, Michigan

Weave dreams together

Ever since my daughter Caitlin was three, we've finished up the bedtime routine by making up the dream she'll have. Usually I work in something pleasant that's happened during the day or something that she's anticipating in the near future. For instance, after her bed-

PARENTS' ALERT

How Much Sleep Does My Child Need Each Day?

Newborns	16 to 22 hours
6 to 12 months	14 to 16 hours
1 to 2 years	8 to 13 hours
3 to 4 years	8 to 12 hours
5 to 6 years	8 to 10 hours
7 to 10 years	8 to 10 hours
11 to 13 years	8 hours

time story, I'll tell her that once upon a time there was a fairy princess (named Caitlin, of course) who went to the playground and found a magic rock. Then she'll add something about what the magic rock can do. Once she's decided that there's enough of a plot, she rolls over and says, "Okay, that's what I'll dream about."

Margaret Casey, Cambridge, Massachusetts

Camp in

My daughter was a real bedtime balker until she received a pup tent and sleeping bag for Christmas. Now she can't wait to climb into her private space. I'd like to give a medal to whomever invented this combo.

Kathleen Hofer, Pottersville, New Jersey

Sleepwear Solutions

Those adorable nighties and other sleepers are just right for some children. Others need creatively altered bedwear, as these parents have found.

Keep child covered

My one-year-old son is fascinated with taking off his clothes at bedtime. To keep him from taking off his one-piece sleeper, I cut the feet off and put the pajamas on backward. Now that he can't reach the zipper, he stays dressed and warm all night.

Pamela Fink, Elyria, Ohio

Put wristbands on drooping pajamas

I put elastic wristbands around my toddler's ankles when he wears all-in-one pajamas with feet. The bands keep the pajama feet in place so my son won't trip when he's walking.

Kristi Stevens, Beulah, North Dakota

Add leg warmers

My daughter, Emma, loves to sleep in fancy nightgowns which ride up and don't keep her warm enough. I bought some leg warmers and leggings for her to wear under her gowns. Now we're both happy.

Dianne Carlucci-O'Donnell, Forest Hills, New York

From Crib to Bed

Once a child is agile enough to climb the bars of her crib, it's time to make the transition to a bed. Will she adjust to her new closer-to-the-floor sleeping place? You can make the change easier on both of you by trying some of these ideas.

Limit transitions

Give your child a familiar toy to take to bed and cover him with his old blanket—even if it's too small. Keep his bed on the same side of the room and in the same position that his crib was in. If you're worried that he might fall out, put a bar up by his bed and a cushion on the floor. Also, don't take his bottle or pacifier away while he's getting used to his bed; that may be too much at once. These ideas worked in my family.

Shauna Norman, West Point, Utah

Start on the floor

To ease your child's transition from crib to bed, place the mattress on the floor. (Make sure your child's room isn't drafty.) I liked the idea because if my son fell out of bed in the middle of the night, he fell only a few inches onto a pillow that I had placed on the floor. After a few weeks we added a box spring and, later, a bed frame.

Liza Judd, Kelowna, British Columbia

Alter crib bedding

To help my 16-month-old son, Alex, make the transition from crib to bed we took his favorite Mickey Mouse crib sheets and had them made into pillowcases for his new bed. With the leftover material we

Checking Bunk-Bed Safety

Bunk beds do not generally pose a great risk to children over the age of six, but no matter what your child's age, follow these guidelines to determine if the bed is safe.

Guardrails: Be sure that the top guardrails are at least five inches above the mattress and are secured properly to the frame. A loose rail can trap a child or allow him to fall. Also be sure that both sides, including the side that faces the wall, have guardrails. Kids can get trapped between the bed and wall. If you need a second rail, call the store where you purchased the bed or the manufacturer and request the addition.

Mattresses: Use the correct size. Bunk-bed mattresses and frames come in two sizes—regular and extra long. Placing a regular mattress on an extra-long frame creates gaps that a child can fall through.

Mattress slats: Place each mattress on wooden slats placed five to six inches apart or on another supporting structure to keep it from becoming dislodged if pushed or kicked.

Joints: Check that the top and bottom bedposts fasten together, otherwise they must be lifted at least 1¼ inches in order to separate them.

Ladder: Make sure the ladder is anchored to the bed frame. If it's not, secure the ladder to the frame of the top bunk with screws or carriage bolts. Replace loose or missing rungs immediately.

Footboard, headboard and guardrail spacing: Spaces between rails or between the bottom guardrail and bed frame should be no more than 3½ inches. If the spaces are larger, screw a board in place to cover dangerous gaps.

Metal frames: Regularly check that the welds on the eight corner brackets that hold the top bunk in place have no cracks or fissures. If structural problems develop, stop using the beds until the affected pieces have been replaced.

To find out if the bunk beds you are using are considered safe, call the Consumer Products Safety Commission hotline at 800-638-2772.

---

made several smaller pillows. He found the look and feel of his familiar sheets comforting.

Kim Batson, St. Joseph, Michigan

Keep bumper pads

When my daughter made the leap from crib to toddler bed, I moved the bumper

pads along with her to help her cope with the big change. I simply tied the bumper pads along her bed frame.

Pam Repko, Logan, Utah

Use a toddler-transition bed

With my older daughter, we made the transition from crib to big bed abruptly and she had some sleepless nights as a result. With my second daughter we bought a toddler bed, which allowed her to have the same mattress and sheets that she was used to. It worked like a charm. She hardly noticed the change.

Queena Muffurty, Brooklyn, New York

Choose bedding together

Even though my son was only two when we bought him a big-boy bed, I took him with me to the store to pick out his own sheets. He loved the Barney sheets and couldn't wait to sleep on them.

Barbara Stout, Madison, Wisconsin

Staying in (Their Own) Bed

Getting your child to adjust to his new bed solves one problem but can create another: Keeping him in his own bed now that getting out of it is so easy. These parents share what worked for them.

Let them camp out

If your child has gotten into the habit of coming into your bed, try this: Let him in your bed (without a fight) for a few more nights. Then introduce the idea of camping out with his pillow and blanket on your floor. After a few nights or weeks of this, lead him back to his bed when he gets sleepy. Always reassure him, however, that he is free to come in and camp out with you. In time, he'll choose the comfort of his own bed.

Sheri Miller, Grandview, Missouri

Help kids see the light

In our family, we worked out a compromise. We designated sunrise as the time when our son is permitted to cuddle or sleep with us. We're clear that he must stay in his bed until he sees that it is starting to get light outside. If my son wants to get into my bed in the middle of the night, I just keep marching him back into his room.

Victoria Witt, Carpinteria, California

Reserve rituals for child's bed

Establishing loving rituals at bedtime, but only in your child's bed, will help associate the room with closeness. Make up a story about falling asleep on a big fluffy cloud, rub your child's back, cuddle with her, sing to her, do anything that will lull her back to sleep. When she comes into your room in the middle of the night, calmly take her back to her bed and repeat your routine. Keep your bed off limits.

Dana Laquidara, Upton, Massachusetts

Stick to a plan

If your child keeps coming to your room at night, delay his bedtime so that he is especially sleepy by the time he gets into bed and stay in his room until he falls asleep. Tell him, "If you stay in your bed, I'll stay in the room, but you must stay in your bed and be quiet." If he is not quiet, walk out of the room for 10 to 15 seconds and then come back in. Repeat this process as many times as you need to. By doing so, you will show your son that there is no advantage to his acting up and coming into your bedroom.

Michele Lipman, Bayside, New York

Have a sleepover

I invited my niece, age six, to spend the night with our family. I let her know that I needed her help in convincing my four-year-old daughter to stay in her own bed. The two girls slept together and when mine woke up and started toward my room, her cousin said, "I'll help you stay here," and she did. From that night on, I was able to remind my daughter that she was able to stay in her room all night.

Lynn Leiberman, Merrimack, New Hampshire

Beating the Bogeyman

Nighttime can be scary for children. Shadows on the wall can take on ominous shapes. Sounds that go unheeded during the day can rattle young nerves. And after the socialness of daytime, the night can seem especially lonely. Here are some sure-fire monster busters to help you and your child take control of the night.

Make up monster stories

Monsters are scary because they're unknown. You can make monsters less frightening by giving your child some experience with them. Make up monster stories together. What are their names? Where do they live? What do they like to eat? What games do monsters like to play? Make sure you create a happy ending to the story, one that your child feels comfortable with. Even if it doesn't make sense to you, it will make him feel better and in control of his fears.

Nikki L. Rowell, Wildomar, California

Go for glow-in-the-dark

To ease nighttime fears, buy a glow-in-the-dark toy that your child can take to bed and install a night-light. This gives children the extra feeling of security that they need.

Marlene A. Parr, Van Horne, Iowa

Save scary talk for daytime

Establish calming rituals before bedtime to ease the transition to sleep. Read a happy story, listen to a soothing cassette, scratch backs or give a massage until sleep takes over. When you talk to children about fears, try to do it during the early evening when everything is a little less scary than it is at night.

Lisa Chipkin, Rego Park, New York

Help kids relax

Divert your child's attention to happy thoughts when she feels frightened. Lie down next to her, hug her and remind her of a special memory, like Christmas or Hannukah or a birthday party. Once she relaxes, she'll forget about the monsters and fall fast asleep.

Lisa Ropella, New Berlin, Wisconsin

Stargaze

My daughters share a bedroom and are afraid of the dark. But when I left their light on, they'd talk for hours. Finally, I found a solution: glow-in-the-dark stick-on stars. Since I made their ceiling a celestial treat, my girls love to lie in the dark and stargaze.

Dana Coleman, Newark, Delaware

Chase monsters away

Chase the monsters out of your child's room with a broomstick and demand that they get out of the house. Then let your child do the same. This should help bring on the feeling of being protected.

Paula Santry, Inola, Oklahoma

Monitor TV

If monster's invade your child's sleep, monitor TV viewing and limit it, especially before bedtime. A child (or adult) who mulls over something scary or troubling that he has seen before bed will most likely have a hard time falling asleep.

Rose Huston, Muldraugh, Kentucky

Choose special books

Read storybooks that confront children's fears, such as *There's a Nightmare in My Closet* by Mercer Mayer.

Maureen Milne, Ballston Lake, New York

Show them the light

Turn on the lights and show them that everything is the same in the light. Then

Ideas to Scare Away Monsters

- Keep the lights on low or use a night-light.
- Play a tape of soothing music.
- Put a stuffed animal at the bedroom door or on your child's bed to act as guard.
- With your child, create and decorate a "No Monsters Allowed" sign for your child's door.

shut off the lights and show them with a flashlight that even though the room is darker, everything is still the same.

Bev Sumpter, Sterling Heights, Michigan

Spray away monsters

I purchased a spray bottle for water and told my daughter that the bottle contained anti-monster spray. Now when she is frightened at night, she just sprays a fine mist of water to chase away whatever is scaring her.

Valerie Dinetti, Hot Springs, Maryland

Help for Early Risers

If your child has rooster-like urges to crow at the first sign of dawn, you can steal more sleep by borrowing this advice from parents who no longer get out of bed with the sun.

Set up activities

My son, Ben, enjoys a special picnic on my bed in the morning, with as many activities as possible—puzzles, favorite toys, crayons and coloring books. He can play, and I don't have to keep getting up. I don't mind being awakened as long as I can stay in bed.

Lyra Blumenthal, Address withheld

Have toys nearby

I hang a small plastic pail on each of my twins' cribs and put in some toys. In the morning, they entertain themselves, giving me a few extra minutes of sleep. I change the toys every few days to hold their interest.

Carol Silvi, Fairport Harbor, Ohio

Set up breakfast the night before

On Saturdays I want nothing more than to sleep late. Since my four- and five-year-olds are early risers, I set out a bowl of dry cereal for each of them on the kitchen table on Friday nights. I put a plastic glass of milk in the refrigerator for each of them to pour onto their cereal. I also set the table with an activity for them to do after they eat, such as coloring books and crayons or a newly rented tape for the older one to put into the VCR. So far, it's working. Last Saturday, they let me and my husband sleep until nearly 9:00 A.M. I remind them, of course, that they may wake me if there's an emergency.

Victoria Stapleton, Akron, Ohio

Use blackout shades

I bought blackout shades for my son's room so that the sun does not shine in there at all, until I roll up the shades.

Marjorie Rollens, Bridgehampton, New York

Naptime Made Easier

Watching toddlers or preschoolers on the run, it's easy to see why they need to stop and recharge their batteries at least once during the day. Preschool teachers are expert at getting children to lie down quietly for an hour or so each morning or afternoon. Part of their success is due to the simple fact that the naptime routine is firmly entrenched in the day and all other distractions are off limits for a time. At home, however, naptime must often be worked in around other, equally compelling activities and parents' busy schedules that can change from day to day.

Make naptime special

Here's an idea to help a younger child take a nap when her older siblings who don't nap are home. Get the older children involved in another activity (preferably in the backyard). Then tell the younger child, "It's our time to be together," and begin a quiet activity with her, such as reading. This way the quiet time is a reward of special attention from you. She'll slow down and be ready for a nap.

Karen Kierpaul, Warren, Michigan

Do some bird-watching

Getting my children, ages two and four, calm enough to take an afternoon nap has been easier since I put birdfeeders in our backyard. Now, not only do they love to stock the feeder and watch for the birds, the birds capture their attention long enough to slow them down and prepare them to go to sleep.

Mary Zumstez, Sunnyvale, California

ASK THE EXPERTS

What Causes My Child's Nightmares? What Can I Do to Help?

Nightmares and night terrors visit almost every child's sleep now and then, especially between the ages of two and six. Nightmares, explains Lawrence Kutner, Ph.D., of the Harvard University Medical School, are simply dreams gone bad and most often occur in the early morning. Children who are having nightmares usually calm down quickly when their parents offer comfort. Night terrors, Dr. Kutner notes, are very different from nightmares and occur most often in the first few hours of a child's sleep. A child who is experiencing night terrors may scream, sit upright in bed with his eyes wide open, and, though he may be calling for his parents, may react to their attempts to soothe him by pushing them away. While he appears to be awake, he is, in fact, in the deepest stage of sleep.

"Nightmares are a result of the child's processing of his daily emotional experiences," says Susan E. Gottlieb, M.D., chief of developmental medicine at Brooklyn Hospital in New York City and the author of *Keys to Children's Sleep Problems* (Barron's). A two-year-old's unpleasant dreams are often about becoming separated from a parent. A three-year-old's are likely to contain scary monsters that symbolize the emotions that he is trying to control.

The most common trigger of a child's bad dreams is witnessing violence—either parents' loud arguments, frightening events in the neighborhood or scenes on television.

Nightmares are not just the result of negative experiences but also an effect of positive growth. "Nightmares," notes Stanley L. Greenspan, M.D., child psychiatrist and professor at George Washington University Medical School, "mark a milestone in development. They coincide with a burst of highly imaginative, if

Time rest periods

My three-year-old son had stopped sleeping during his naptime, but he still couldn't get through the day without taking a break. To help him get the rest that he needs, I put a clock radio in his room and set the sleep feature for 60 minutes every afternoon. He doesn't come out of his room every 5 minutes anymore to ask

"Can I get up now?" because he knows that his rest is over when the music stops.

Linda Crawford, Phoenix

Wake them gently

I hate to wake my four-year-old son up from a nap before he's ready, but sometimes I have to. To make it as painless as possible for him, I sit by his bedside and

not quite logical, thinking and with a child's growing ability to create his own mental images of the world."

The causes of night terrors are something of a mystery, says Dr. Kutner, though he notes that they do tend to run in families and may have a genetic basis. "Sometimes they occur in children who are overtired, have recently given up naptime or have experienced changes in their sleep schedule," he says.

Help for nightmares

- Reassure your child that the nightmare was only a dream and was not real.
- Offer a hug and, if she wants, a glass of water or milk.
- Leave on the night-light if she asks you to.
- There's no need to talk too much about the dream during the night.

- The next morning, suggest that your child draw a picture of what frightened her, or help her draw it. It won't seem as frightening to her once she sees it on paper.
- Don't attempt to analyze the dream for your child. This is likely to confuse her.

Help for night terrors

- Don't try to wake up the child. It seldom works and may prolong the incident. (He'll probably return to an undisturbed sleep within a few minutes.)
- Stay calm and make sure that he doesn't hurt himself.
- If he wakes up, calmly tell him to go back to sleep. If you show concern and reassure him that everything is okay, it may upset him because he won't understand why he might have cause to be concerned.

start to read him a story. It doesn't take long before he begins to stir, eager to look at the pictures.

Sandra Wolf, Oswego, Illinois

Quiet the family

It works to have a house rule that naptime is a quiet time for everyone, not just the child who needs the nap. The older

children can play quietly, reading or drawing, while the youngest one goes to sleep.

Sharon C. Jackson, Washington, D.C.

Don't fret about schedules

When my son, who is now five, was an infant, I was religious about making sure to be home so he could nap in his familiar surroundings at exactly the same time

PEDIATRICKS
Shorter Naps for Longer Sleep

To encourage your baby to sleep for longer periods during the night, gradually reduce the length of his daytime naps starting at 9 months to 12 months. If he usually takes a 4-hour nap, wake him after 3½ hours, then 3, then 2. To make up for lost sleep, he should snooze longer at night. If he doesn't, it may mean he isn't ready to sleep through the night just yet.

every morning and afternoon. But with my daughter, who's two, I began right from the start to fit her into our regular routine. This meant that even though her naptime had been 2:00 P.M. every afternoon, it had to change when her brother began preschool and I had to pick him up at 2:30 P.M. I started to put her down for her nap in her car seat and I carried her and it to the car when it was time to go. Eventually, she learned on her own to nap earlier in the day. Now she gets all the sleep she needs but not always at the same time or in the same place each day. It doesn't seem to make any difference to her.

Natalya Horracibi, Jersey City, New Jersey

Sing to stuffed animals

My son isn't too interested in his own need for sleep, but he likes to take good care of his many stuffed animals. So every afternoon, I remind him that it's time to sing little songs to his collection to help

them take *their* naps. He lies down next to them, begins to sing and drifts off to sleep himself.

Sonny Crishen, Address withheld

Big Kids and Bedtime

There comes a time when children can start to make their own bedtime decisions. In your family that might mean letting your 8-year-old decide how late she may stay up on a Friday night. Or your 12-year-old may need to stay up late on a school night to finish a book report. By the teen years, your child will likely be staying up later than you do. Here are some tips from parents who've helped their children develop independence in making their own nighttime schedules.

Let kids be responsible

I gave up trying to get my 12-year-old son to get to sleep early enough on school nights. Instead of fighting about it, I made a deal. I bought him an alarm clock and told him to set it for his normal 7:00 A.M. wake up. I agreed to make no bedtime rules as long as he got himself up and out for school the next morning. For about a week, he stayed up past midnight. He was so tired in school that he could barely stay awake. One afternoon, he had to skip soccer practice because he was too tired to play. After that, he set his own bedtime back to 9:00 P.M., which was actually 30 minutes sooner than I'd been setting it.

Teresa Jones, Wappingers Falls, New York

Do homework early

Getting my seven-year-old to bed had been a struggle since she began school. She

Sleepovers
10 Ideas to Make It through the Night

1. Keep the guest list short. Parents who have hosted slumber parties recommend no more than six children over the age of eight and no more than four children at age six or seven. In general, children under six are too young for sleepovers.

2. Keep the menu healthy. While you'll want to serve some kid-pleasing favorites like pepperoni pizza, too much party food will lead to sick tummies late at night, something you'd rather avoid. Offer favorites such as tuna, pasta, homemade pizza and peanut butter and jelly.

3. Rent some fun tapes, but no horror films. Kids may squeal with delight while watching them but be fearful for the rest of the night. It's also a good idea to check with other parents before showing any movie that does not have a G rating.

4. Have each child bring his or her own quilt, pillow and towels. This will save you a pile of laundry the next day.

5. Fun party treats for overnight guests include new toothbrushes, hair decorations for girls and T-shirts for decorating and/or sleeping in.

6. Have every child's home phone number handy in case parents need to be notified of overwhelming homesickness or other maladies. Make sure you have a number where parents can be reached if they're not planning to be home.

7. Prepare to be kept awake past your own bedtime. There's usually at least one child who'll need your attention.

8. Plan on an easy breakfast, served buffet style.

9. Be sure that all other parents are aware of the morning pick-up time.

10. Throughout the event, be available, but let the kids make their own fun.

needed to be in bed no later than 8:30 P.M. on school nights, but wasn't settled down until nearly 10:00 P.M. on most nights, largely because homework was taking an hour or more to do after dinner. I started a new rule that homework had to be done immediately after school. Since she's less tired then, it now takes only 15 minutes. Another new rule is that she has to stay in her bedroom after 8:00 P.M. She can play or read but must be in the room. She gets bored after a short time and falls asleep.

Renee Marcucci, South Ozone Park, New York

Tape favorite shows

My 10- and 13-year-olds like many of the TV programs that come on at 9:30 P.M. or 10:00 P.M. I tape the programs that are on at those hours and let them watch them on Saturdays.

Adrianne McAdams, Elk Grove, Illinois

Try the lights-out rule

Instead of setting bedtimes for my 10-year-old son, I have a lights-out time. He can stay awake as long as he likes, provided he's in bed with no lights on by 9:30 P.M. on weeknights and 10:30 P.M. on weekends.

Matthew Davidson, Springfield, Illinois

Don't give up reading

I thought that by the time my son was seven, he'd be able to put himself to bed without much fuss. That hasn't been the case. I've found that if I read him a bed-time story, even though he can read himself, that he'll get into bed readily.

Martha Link, Barre, Vermont

Set a goal

Our eight-year-old daughter and a friend's eight-year-old daughter both had trouble getting to bed on time on school nights. They also each wanted a very fancy doll from a collection that is very popular. Together my friend and I made deals with our girls that if they went to bed on time for two whole months, they would each earn their dolls. For each month of school that they continued to go to bed on time, they would each earn an outfit for their dolls.

Gina D'Angelo and Marlene Edmonston,
South Falls, Indiana

CHAPTER FIVE

Potty Time

There isn't a parent who hasn't looked forward to the day when the diaper bag could be put away. Sure, we may miss the wonderful baby and toddler years. But miss the diapers? Not likely. Parents recognize that the transition from diapers to big-girl or big-boy underpants is a monumental one for their kids to make. From the child's point of view, it's even bigger.

Even if they are initially resistant, most children do arrive at daytime dryness by age three or so, with girls generally preceding boys by a few months. Nighttime dryness may take another six months to accomplish and for some children, through no fault of yours or theirs, the process may take years. But it will happen.

Detecting Daytime Readiness

One child might step up to the toilet one day and announce that she wants to use it. Another might consider the toilet a terrific receptacle for the TV remote control, but shows absolutely no interest in using it for its intended purpose. Toilet-teaching readiness cannot be forced, but it can be encouraged—if your child is ready to absorb the instruction and if his or her body has matured enough to control the bladder and the muscles that control bowel movements.

Go slow

Don't push a child to give up diapers before she's developmentally ready; it can hurt her self-esteem. Don't let her think it's the most important thing in the world to you that she use the toilet properly. If a toddler thinks she can't please you, it may feel like the end of the world to her.

Judith Solomon, Glen Head, New York

Help kids anticipate

My husband and I always let my son be in the bathroom with us if he chose to be. His natural curiosity led him to want to know what the toilet was for. We never pushed him, but we gave him direct answers to his questions. I told him that when he was a little bit bigger that he could use the toilet, too. He couldn't wait. A few weeks after he first expressed interest, I asked him if he wanted to try using a big-boy toilet, and I took him with me to the store so he could pick out his own potty. He couldn't wait to get home to use it.

Marilee Best, Salinas, Kansas

Let her play

I bought my daughter a potty book and a doll that came with her own little potty. I took the potty seat out of the closet and told Bridget that this was her own potty—just like her doll's. For about two weeks, she did everything with the potty—fill it with little toys, wear it on her head—before showing any interest in sitting on it. I think taking it gradually helped her get over any anxiety she had about using it. Except for occasional accidents, she pretty much trained herself in a month or so.

Linda Scott-DeGreco, Englewood, New Jersey

Know if Your Child Is Ready

Watch for a combination of any of the following behaviors to signal your child's readiness for toilet teaching.

- Indicates a dislike of being in a wet or soiled diaper.
- Announces when he is about to urinate or have a bowel movement.
- Understands the purpose of a potty and/or a toilet.
- Knows the words that your family uses for going to the bathroom.
- Can pull her pants up and down by herself.
- Stays dry for a couple of hours between diaper changes, or wakes up dry after he has had a nap.
- Demonstrates curiosity about how her parents and siblings use the bathroom.

Get Kids Motivated

A child's conscious and successful effort to use the potty is an important milestone and signals a new level of physical, intellectual and emotional maturity. Children reach this milestone at different ages, and there is no benefit in trying to rush them. For toilet teaching to be successful, your child must join in the process willingly—and that will happen, if you just let your child tell you when he is ready. Here are some ideas for smoothing the process.

- Shop for a potty seat and big-kid underwear together.

- Resolve to focus only on your own child and to pay no attention to how your child's readiness compares with other children's.
- Realize that toilet teaching is a collaborative effort and that you can never have the upper hand.
- Understand that the process takes a while and that one or two successful attempts does not indicate that toilet teaching has been accomplished. Expect accidents and respond to them very matter-of-factly, not punitively.

Respect individual differences

There's no way to tell when a child is ready; he'll just surprise you one day. With my first son, I read all the book and magazine articles and did everything that was suggested. He wasn't interested, so I gave up, but not before driving both of us a little crazy. By the age of 3, however, he was getting uncomfortable with dirty diapers. He also wanted to join a playgroup program, which required that he be out of diapers, so he finally succeeded. With my second son, I decided to wait and not even attempt to teach him until he was at least 2½ years old. About a week after his second birthday, he announced that he was too big for diapers (something his big brother had told him) and wanted his own potty.

Phyllis Scharr, Wayne, Indiana

Choose models carefully

I read that using a doll to demonstrate using the toilet was a good idea, so I tried it. It worked almost too well. My son plopped his fuzzy teddy bear into a just-used potty. Now I keep only washable, plastic dolls in the bathroom in case he tries to toilet train any more of his toys!

Karen Horn-Magdola, San Jose, California

Let kids be comfortable

My son always preferred walking around the house naked and would run off as soon as I'd remove his diaper. I thought this was a problem—until it came time to try to toilet teach him. I told him he didn't have to wear his diaper if he would try to sit for one minute (the length of time measured by a wind-up music box (continued on page 118)

Constipation Is a Caution Flag

Constipation can be a red flag for several serious physical or emotional conditions, pediatric experts warn. When it occurs in infants, constipation *always* warrants checking by the doctor because it can be a symptom of intestinal blockage.

Also, if your breastfed baby goes two or more days without a bowel movement, you should definitely contact your physician. For an older child, you should contact your physician for the following:

- Your child is in a lot of pain, his stomach is distended and he is not eating well. (This could be a blockage or another intestinal problem.)
- There is blood in your child's stool.
- Your child seems to be withholding stools for emotional purposes, especially during toilet teaching.
- Your child has accidental bowel movements when he's not on the toilet. Withholding stools can, over time, lead to encopresis, a condition in which the child's intestines become so impacted that he loses sphincter control and some feces leak out.

Before trying any home remedy for treating your child's constipation, consult with your child's doctor.

For infants

A slick solution: Younger children and babies can be given glycerin suppositories, doctors say. These are very thin, bullet-shaped waxy substances that melt when they are inserted in the rectum. "They relieve constipation in two ways: stimulating the rectum and 'greasing the skids' for smooth elimination. But only occasional use is recommended. Regular use will make children dependent and then they won't be able to have a bowel movement without them. Glycerin suppositories for a child or infant can be purchased at any pharmacy and directions are on the package.

A thermometer: Once your infant's constipation is diagnosed by a physician, you can use a rectal thermometer approved for infant use to help her release stool. Thoroughly lubricate the thermometer with petroleum jelly. Then stick it in the baby's rectum no farther than 1½ inches and pull it out. Sometimes you'll get a "present" along with the thermometer, doctors say.

For older children

Give an over-the-counter laxative sparingly: If a child age 10 and older already has constipation, there are several over-the-counter medications that can provide relief temporarily. For an older child it's okay to use over-the-counter laxatives such as milk of magnesia or mineral oil, say pediatric experts. But only use them as advised by a physician. Mineral oil, in particular, shouldn't be used regularly because it interferes with the body's absorption of fat-soluble vitamins. Other laxatives, too, can cause problems if taken regularly. A child can become so dependent on them, she loses the natural urge to move her bowels.

Keep a daily food record: Write down everything your child eats and drinks each day, doctors advise. This may allow you to pinpoint precisely what in your child's diet is causing bouts of constipation. If your child has been drinking a quart of milk a day, for example, you may be able to make the connection quickly. Consuming too many dairy products can be constipating. Other constipating foods frequently found in children's diets include applesauce, bananas and white rice.

Make some high-fiber muffins: Dietary fiber helps keep stools soft, doctors say. But, unfortnately, Americans take in far too few fiber-rich foods like fruit, vegetables, whole wheat breads and bran cereals. You can introduce your child to fiber sources that are fun to eat. There's no reason why a child can't eat a bran muffin every day, for instance. To make these muffins more appealing, add lots of raisins—which most kids love to eat.

Serve snacks fit for a rabbit: When your child is hungry between meals, try giving him some raw vegetables, such as carrots and celery. These foods carry plenty of kid appeal because they're crunchy. To make these snacks even more appealing, spruce them up with some add-ons. A piece of celery spread with a bit of peanut butter is great for preventing constipation for instance.

Work in vegetables: Maybe it's tough to get your child to eat cauliflower or broccoli—high-fiber vegetables that help the constipation situation. But you can camouflage those helpful veggies to make them more palatable, say pediatric experts. All it takes is a little creativity. Try cutting them into different shapes. Tell him broccoli florets are little trees. Or chop up vegetables and hide them in meat loaf.

Take advantage of fruits: Kids who won't eat vegetables usually will eat fruits, and many kinds of fruit are effective at getting bowels moving. Offer lots of apples, pears and peaches. But hold back on bananas and applesauce, which tend to be constipating, doctors say.

Offer liquids galore: Make sure your child is drinking plenty of fluids, including fruit juices, because they, can help prevent constipation, pediatricians say. This is especially important if you're

(continued)

Constipation Is a Caution Flag—Continued

introducing more bran and other high-fiber foods into your child's diet. Liquids help bulk up fiber in the gut to form soft, easy-to-pass stools.

Don't start toilet teaching too soon: Kids who aren't ready to use the potty may withhold stools as a way to assert control over their own bodies, doctors warn.

For example, a two-year-old may want to be in control so desperately that if you tell him, 'You've got to go to the potty,' he'll actually try *not* to go—just to show you who's in charge. Instead of forcing the issue, wait and watch for signs of readiness on the child's part. Most kids really don't express much interest in toilet teaching until they're

close to three. That's when it's developmentally appropriate to begin, doctors say.

Turn over some control: Children who are engaged in a stool-withholding power struggle with their parents may need to be given the freedom to make some decisions for themselves, pediatricians suggest.

Look at other control issues in the child's life—what clothes he wears or what kind of sandwich he eats for lunch, for instance. If you let him have more say in these matters, he'll feel like you're starting to let go—and that's important to him. Your youngster may be able to relax and pass stools more freely.

song) on the potty. He liked this idea. One time, he had to make a bowel movement when he was on the potty and he jumped up and wanted his diaper. He was amazed when I told him that it was okay to poop into the potty. After that, he'd try to know when it was time to use the potty so that he could try this great experiment again. It wound up actually being fun.

Charlotte Kessler, Winston-Salem, North Carolina

Choose one change at a time

Don't introduce toilet teaching when another big event is going on in your

child's life—such as a move or the birth of a new sibling. Young kids can't deal with too many big changes at once.

Frederica Moren, Santa Fe, New Mexico

Test the toilet

My son, Matthew, wouldn't use his potty seat and I thought it was a resistance to toilet training. It turned out that he only wanted to use the real toilet. I recommend that all parents ask their children where they want to go to the bathroom because some may not like their potty seats.

Eleanor Edelman, Forest Hills, New York

Toileting Tricks

For you, the object of the toilet teaching process is to get your child to use the toilet somewhat skillfully. Your child may have other priorities right now—like demonstrating her competence with crayons or learning to ride a tricycle. That's when some creative distractions can work, as these parents found.

Retain diapering routines

Keep some of your diapering routines when you're toilet training. For instance, use baby wipes instead of toilet paper, which can be too rough. Smooth on some lotion if your child likes it. Play with him or her—reading or something—just as you did when you diapered your child. I think the biggest mistake parents can make is to leave a child on the potty while

you go about your business because the child will learn that the potty is no fun.

Alan Tomas, Chester, Pennsylvania

Find fun distractions

At first my two-year-old daughter was afraid of using the toilet. But I found a fun way to help her relax: blowing bubbles. It helped distract her and she learned to use the potty in no time.

Stacy Turner, Lindstrom, Minnesota

Have a big kid help

At nearly three, my daughter was showing no interest in using the toilet and I was a bit desperate. So with the permission of another child's mom, I invited her four-year-old playmate to come by and show my daughter how to use the toilet. Though Rosie wouldn't sit on the potty for me, she did so right away when her big-girl friend Adrianne (whom she really admired) told her that she was too big for diapers. Adrianne was a great teacher. She even said things like "I know it's hard to get used to but if you want to go to nursery school like me, you have to." That's all Rosie needed to hear. Now Rosie feels very proud of herself for using the toilet.

Ashley O'Connor, Sioux City, Nevada

Try reverse psychology

I used a bit of reverse psychology to toilet train my son. When another boy who's about four months older than Nicholas told him that he was a baby for wearing a diaper, I said to the boy (so that Nicholas could overhear me), "Nicholas is still too little to use the toilet." Nicholas immediately wanted to prove that we were both wrong, so he went home and sat on the toilet. He wasn't sure what he was supposed to do, so I said, "Some bigger kids like to wee-wee or poop into the toilet." I asked him if he'd like to try that, too. He wasn't able to that first time and we agreed that he could try again later, before his nap. That time (after he'd had a lot to drink) he was successful. The next day, we bought underpants together. He was so proud of having them that at the park he stripped off his outside shorts to show them to the kid who had called him a baby. We had a few accidents over the next few weeks, but within a month he was dry during the day.

Beatrice Moore, Seattle

Offer a reward

Though I'm generally not in favor of bribing my 30-month-old daughter, I made an exception when it came to toilet training. We had had a great time visiting an amusement park about an hour away from home and she was begging to go back. I told her that if she tried to use the toilet and went a whole day (not counting naptime) dry that we would go back. The very next day, she stayed dry. To keep my end of the bargain, we went to the park, as promised, the day after that. She's been dry every day since.

Alison Henry, Scottsdale, Arizona

Ready, aim . . .

My son was having a bit of trouble with his aim and as a result the bathroom was pretty much soaked with urine. So I started putting one square of tissue paper into the toilet and asking him to shoot it. It worked!

Isabel Jervitz, Massapequa, New York

PARENTS' ALERT
Preventing Injuries

Potty seats that include a urine-catching device for boys can save you lots of cleanup, but be careful that the protruding part does not catch and scratch a child's penis as he sits down or gets up. Look for a seat that has a smooth design or remove the urine guard before your child uses the seat. Then teach him to hold his penis down while he urinates.

Keep track of progress

Every time my daughter used her potty, she put a sticker on a Potty Poster I'd made for her. Every time she had a row of ten stickers, we went out for an ice cream or other treat. This not only encouraged her to use her potty but helped her learn to count.

Yolanda Chambers, Kissimmee, Florida

Practice with a doll

I used my daughter's wetting baby doll to help teach her about using the potty. We'd give the doll a bottle of water and then rush it to the potty. Katie thought this was a riot and would do it over and over again. One day I told Katie that she could do the same thing. She drank a big glass of water and then ran to the potty.

Janine Pfizer, Allendale, Pennsylvania

Single moms can help boys

I'm a single mom and I wasn't quite sure how I was going to teach my three-year-old son to stand up and urinate since I had no male role-model around. Rather than wait to find a man I trusted enough to show him, I decided to enroll him in a program at the YMCA, where he'd see lots of other little boys standing up in the bathroom. He came home so excited one day and had to show me what he'd learned.

Cherlynn Oberman, Milwaukee

Use pull-up diapers

I let my son wear pull-up diapers. (They are like underwear but offer a diaper's protection.) After this was successful for a few weeks, he graduated to regular underwear.

Karri Gyorkos, Pensacola, Florida

Success on the Road

At home, it's far easier to develop consistent toileting routines and respond to the inevitable accidents. But no family needs to be housebound for the weeks or months that toilet teaching takes. Here are some ideas for handling toileting away from home.

Carry a port-a-potty

Bring a fold-up potty cover wherever you go to make your child feel secure on a public toilet. It fits easily in a diaper bag.

Annette Melendez, Bronx, New York

Pack extra clothes

Always bring a spare diaper, clean underwear and some extra clothes once you start toilet teaching your child, in case of accidents. (And bring an extra pair of shoes, especially for boys, who often pee on them by mistake.)

Karen Holt, Clifton Park, New York

Ask about Day Care Policies

What are the diaper-time and potty-time routines in your child's preschool or day care center? To assure that hygienic and respectful practices are followed, check that:

- Child care workers wash their hands with an antibacterial soap *before* and *after* changing a diaper or helping a potty-taught child wipe.
- Children are taught to wash their hands after using the toilet.
- Potty accidents are treated very nonchalantly, without shame or punishment, for a child who wets or soils himself.
- Children who prefer some privacy during toilet time are given it.

Be prepared

Have your child go to the bathroom before you leave the house. While you are out, ask her every half hour or so if she has to go and be prepared to find a public bathroom fast.

Stevina Ugbah, Dublin, California

Consider the season

Because my daughter indicated a readiness to use the toilet in February, I had a dilemma. Should I encourage her or wait until the snowsuit season was over? (I really didn't want her to want to go inside to use the potty since getting her in and out of her snowsuit was a big job.) I told her

Dad's Corner

Toilet teaching can provide dads with some particular dilemmas. Here are some questions and solutions provided by other dads.

Robert's question

What do you do when you're out with your daughter and she has to use the bathroom? Do you take her with you into the men's room or do you let her go into the ladies' room by herself?

Matt's answer

Until my daughter was about four, I took her into the men's room with me. I admit that I walked her past the urinals quickly and into a private stall. It always unnerved me a bit, but often, we had no choice. Now that Lin is six, I wait at the ladies' room door and ask the first mom I see to keep an eye on Lin while she's in there.

Peter's question

I'm not comfortable using the bathroom when my daughter is in the room, but my wife says I'm being a prude, especially since I don't care if our son is in the bathroom with me. Should I let Sari see me urinating?

Nick's answer

You should do what you're comfortable doing. I think it's okay to have different ways of doing things with sons and daughters. After all, when you go to a restaurant or store, they have different bathrooms for men and women. I don't think it will hurt your daughter at all to learn to respect your privacy.

Robert's answer

At the same time, I wouldn't get too worried if your daughter walked in on you. It happens. Just don't make a big deal out of it. If she has a brother, especially, she's already figured out that boys' bodies and girls' bodies are different.

Matt's answer

I guess we're a bit loose in my house because Lin has seen me urinate. Once she tried to do it standing up, too, but I explained that boys and girls are made differently and that she is supposed to sit down just like her mother.

---

that during the winter the potty was for indoor use only and that outside she could still wear her diapers. By late spring, when she was really good at knowing when she needed to use the toilet, I was ready to let her.

Heather Loughlin, South Burlington, Vermont

Practice on the toilet

Let your child practice using the regular toilet in your home and not just the potty seat because when you're out and he has to use the bathroom, you want him to be comfortable on the big toilet.

Sally Melendez, Houston

Add lessons in wiping

When a friend of my daughter's was here without his mom present, I learned something about toilet training. A child needs to know how to wipe him or herself. I was really taken aback when this four-year-old wanted me to help him. I told him to do the best job he could on his own. That night, I made sure my own daughter knew how to wipe herself and to take care of the entire toileting routine on her own so that she wouldn't ask another parent or a teacher to do this for her.

Margot Hue, Pleasantville, New York

Keeping the Potty Clean

These parents have found some creative ways to make the potty seat a more desirable piece of equipment for themselves and their children.

Line it with a coffee filter

I found a way to keep my child's potty chair clean with the help of disposable coffee filters. Line your child's potty with one. It makes clean up of bowel movements quick and easy.

Kristina Brew, Bayside, New York

Add water

To make potty cleanup easier, I always keep about one inch of tap water inside the pot.

Dr. Anna Neber, San Pedro, Colorado

Find inspiration

Changing the paper in our bird's cage gave me an idea about my son's potty. I thought, why not put cut-up old newspapers on the bottom of his potty just as I do the cage? It's cost-free and really works.

Tina Pellicano, Cambridge, Massachusetts

Use a floor mat

My daughter often got very excited when she first learned to use her potty and would jump up midstream to see what she'd accomplished so far. I put a plastic mat under the chair to make cleanups easier.

Florence Greene, Honolulu

Handling Accidents

Accidents are a fact of life—particularly with a newly toilet-taught child. There are limited measures you can take to avoid them. Our real power comes with how we learn to respond to them. Just remember that your child is already distressed by the accident. What she needs now is your reassurance that wetting or soiling herself is not a big deal.

Empathize

On my daughter's second day of first grade, she wet herself because she was too uncomfortable to ask to use the girls' room. She was devastated until I told her that I'd done the exact same thing in second grade. I think that having empathy for her plight instead of adding to her embarrassment really helped her get over it. I also suggested that if any other child made reference to the accident that instead of crying she might try laughing and saying, "I was so embarrassed. I sure don't want that to happen again." In that way, she wouldn't allow anyone else to make her feel bad.

Finola Reilly, Bridgehampton, Massachusetts

Wait for re-teaching

Because my son never seemed to care when he had an accident, I realized that I'd probably been assuming he was toilet-taught even though he really wasn't. I casually went back to diapers and a few months later tried again to let him wear underpants. The second time around he really wanted to stay dry himself.

Polly Blacke, Erie, Pennsylvania

Use pull-ons

I run a day care center from my home and I've seen about a thousand accidents over the last few years. I really encourage parents not to jump to the conclusion that their two-year-olds are potty-trained. Most are not or will be potty-trained at home but not when there are a lot of distractions around. I ask the parents who use my center to use those pull-up dia-pers/underpants so that neither the children nor I have to deal with too many changes of clothes a day.

Delia Santoro, Whitestone, New York

Offer reminders

My 30-month-old daughter Amanda never tells me if she has to wet if she is busy playing. Almost every day, she was wetting herself rather than interrupting a game with a playmate. I've learned to say every hour or so, "Okay, kids, let's all take a potty break." Because everyone stops playing for the time it takes, Amanda doesn't mind.

Sophie Birmbaum, Indianapolis

Ask for child's suggestions

Kids need to know that accidents do happen and to feel that you'll help them—not embarrass them—for wetting themselves. Always have a change of clothes handy. You might also want to ask, non-judgmentally, what the child can do next time to avoid wetting himself.

Erica Carr, Boise, Idaho

Nighttime Routines

Remember those months when you'd give anything if only your child would sleep through the night? Now your sound sleeper rouses only to announce "Mom, I dreamed I was swimming," as one sheet-changing mom recalls. Nighttime dryness, even more than daytime, requires a degree of physical maturity—a large-enough bladder—to accomplish. Also unlike daytime dryness, the sleeping child is incapable of making a decision to use the toilet.

Easing Toileting Fears

Seeing part of yourself disappear in a swoosh of water can unnerve some children. Similar to bathtub fears of being swept down the drain, fears of being flushed away are relatively common in toddlers. Try these ideas to ease your child's worries.

- Instead of automatically flushing the toilet, ask her if she'd like you to do it now or later or if she'd like to try it herself.
- Some children feel better placing a familiar diaper inside the potty seat, which makes the transition less dramatic for them.
- For some, using small toilets, such as those in nursery schools, eases their fears.
- Occasionally, children might agree to use the toilet for urination but insist on having bowel movements in their diapers. This behavior often coincides with their growing realization that they are separate from their parents and are able to make decisions about their bodies on their own. To counteract the problem, try to treat this behavior with as little fuss as possible. You may want to visit your child's health care provider to discuss medical treatment for constipation (a common result of holding stools). In the meantime, provide diapers and assure your child that he or she will use the toilet when ready.

Use diapers at night

I put diapers on my daughter every night for about six months after she was daytime toilet-taught. After she'd gone about two weeks with dry diapers, I finally switched to underpants at night, too. She only had a few nighttime accidents after that.

Barbara DiCordia, Winston-Salem, North Carolina

Protect the mattress

Once you make the commitment to try nights without diapers, make sure you've got a rubber mattress pad in place. I didn't, and as a result, my son's mattress was ruined and had to be replaced. It was an expensive lesson.

Andrea Meltzer, Annapolis, Maryland

Skip nighttime drinks

After my daughter goes to the bathroom right before bed, I don't allow her to have any more drinks. It's impossible for her (or any young child) to stay dry when they go to bed with a full bladder.

Barb Economos, Princeton, New Jersey

Have dry clothes ready

Before I go to bed, I make sure that clean sheets and pajamas are stacked on my daughter's dresser. I've found that there's nothing worse than having to trek to the laundry room in the middle of the night to get the clean clothes. It's so much easier when anything I need is already in her room. Fortunately, changing her and (continued on page 130)

What the Experts Say about Bed-Wetting

About one in seven children wets the bed regularly past the age of three. More often than not, enuresis (as bed-wetting is clinically called) runs in families. If both parents were bed wetters as children, the chances are three in four that their children will suffer from this condition, too. If one parent had the problem, the child's chances are about one in two.

If your child is over age two and shows no sign of bladder control, you should bring this to the attention of your doctor. Some children take longer than others to begin potty training, but your pediatrician should be aware of your child's progress at this age. Also see your child's pediatrician if your child has any of the following symptoms to rule out such conditions as a urinary tract infection, diabetes or a physical abnormality.

- Complains of abdominal pain, backache or fever
- Wakes up at night regularly with an intense thirst
- Wets during the day as well as at night
- Has pain during urination
- Has urine with an unpleasant odor
- Is suddenly wetting again after months of staying dry

Say no to guilt

Once you have established that there is no health problem causing your child to wet the bed, relax.

Realize that you're not a bad parent because your child is not yet ready to achieve nighttime dryness, and make it clear to your child that he isn't a bad child because he wets.

Bed-wetting is a biological problem, specialists say. It occurs in a child who, during sleep, has not learned bladder-control skills.

Rarely is it a psychological problem. Some very good parents burden themselves with guilt unnecessarily because they see themselves as being to blame somehow.

What are the best tactics for helping bed wetters?

Usually bed-wetting can be cured without medical intervention, given enough time, along with a healthy dose of patience. Here are the techniques the experts recommend.

Ban punishments: One study found that nearly three-fourths of parents punished their children for bed-wetting. Never punish or scold your child, for a wet bed, pediatricians advise. Punishment is not going to help your child, and no child wants to wet the bed.

Protect with plastic: A zip-up plastic mattress cover should be standard equipment on any bed wetter's bed. It protects the mattress, of course. But also it means there's less of a crisis when the child wets the bed. Both the parents and the kids will stay a lot calmer if they know that there's not much cleanup to worry about.

Encourage cleanup duties: Parents should matter-of-factly tell the child he is expected to clean up the wet bed or at least help. Even a four- or five-year-old can take the sheets off the bed and put them in the laundry room. Don't make the task punitive, though—just an acknowledgment that this is the child's responsibility. This technique also helps you. You don't feel the child is doing this to you.

Check out your child's motivation: Before taking active steps to cure bed-wetting, make sure your child wants to stop, pediatricians advise. Ask yourself, "Does my child want to be dry?" If the answer is say "no," all of your efforts will probably be for naught. If a child wants to stop, she'll not only cooperate, but her conscious mind will also work on her subconscious to help her awaken at night.

Recognize the signs of readiness: A child often becomes motivated to stop wetting when it begins to interfere with his social options, doctors say. When the child starts to refuse invitations to spend the night away from home, or doesn't go to camp because of bed-wetting fears, you can point out the benefits of being able to do these things.

Then suggest some ways your child can help himself get through the night with a dry bed.

Pick a good time: Before starting, choose a relatively peaceful period—not, for example, just before an exciting holiday or vacation, specialists advise.

And pick a time when you are not having multiple stressors at work and in the home.

Keep bedtimes calm: Lots of roughhousing or even an exciting television program close to bedtime can increase the risk of bed-wetting, one psychiatric expert points out. When kids are excited, they tend to produce more urine. So instead of letting your child watch television before bedtime, give him a book to read, have a quiet conversation or read a story to him.

Put the child in charge: You want your child to understand from the outset that staying dry at night is her responsibility. That means don't wake your child at night to take her to the bathroom. That doesn't teach her anything about bladder control, and it's probably counterproductive, doctors say. If the child goes to bed thinking her parent is going to wake her up at night, that's teaching the child that the parent is going to take care of her bladder and that she doesn't have to worry about it.

To stay dry, your child has to go to
(continued)

What the Experts Say about Bed-Wetting—Continued

bed just a little bit worried.

Reward dry nights: Consistently reward or congratulate your child when she has made it through the night with a dry bed. Positive psychological support such as hugs and warm congratulations will go a long way, doctors note.

Some kids might like happy faces drawn on a calendar or special stickers. Whatever reinforcement you use, do it first thing in the morning.

Mum's the word: If your child wakes up with wet sheets, be careful not to grimace or say something like, "Oh, no, your bed is wet this morning." Instead, say nothing, doctors advise. Focus on success. If you give as much attention to failure as success, you're defeating the purpose.

Make getting up easy: Some kids are reluctant to leave their beds, and others have been ordered by parents never to get up after they've been tucked in, doctors note. Give your kids permission to get up to go to the bathroom. Provide them with a flashlight or a night-light, and ask if they want a potty chair next to their bed. Some kids who don't want to go into the bathroom are perfectly willing to use the potty chair and go back to sleep.

Give your child an alarm clock: If the child has a regular pattern of wetting the bed at the same time every night, furnish an alarm clock and explain how

it works, says one pediatrician. The child can set the alarm to wake him in 20 minutes to half an hour before he usually wets the bed so he can get up and go to the bathroom.

Encourage a dry run: One pediatrician recommends a dress-rehearsal technique your school-age child can do during the day.

Have the child lie in bed, close his eyes, pretend it's the middle of the night and give himself a pep talk. It could go something like, "I'm in a deep, deep sleep, my bladder is full, my bladder is starting to feel pressure and is trying to wake me up. It's saying, 'Get up before it's too late.' "

The child should then practice getting up, walking to the bathroom and going to the toilet. Have him actually walk from the bedroom to the bathroom, so that he knows exactly how many paces it is.

Avoid caffeine: Caffeine is a diuretic, a substance that encourages urination. It's in many sodas and in chocolate as well as in coffee and tea. Avoiding these foods and drinks may help your child avoid wetting.

Encourage daily bladder-control practice: Explain to your child that she can help train her bladder by practicing during the day. Have your child drink a lot, and then wait as long as she can to go to the bathroom. Have her try to wait a little bit longer each time, doctors say. Train a child to associate the feeling of having a full bladder with having to go to the bathroom.

Stream-interruption exercises can also help. Have your child begin to urinate and then stop briefly before starting up again. She should try to do this several times each time that she urinates. These exercises will build up the bladder sphincter.

Buy a bed alarm: Most experts agree that moisture-activated bed alarms are the most effective treatment for bed-wetting. When moisture hits the pad, an alarm goes off and wakes the child. This conditions the child to recognize the sensation and wake up before he has to urinate.

Alarms are battery-operated, cost around $40 and are available without a prescription. Ask your pediatrician to recommend a brand or type. Use the alarm until your child is dry every night for one month.

In most alarms, wetting triggers a loud sound that awakens the child. A silent, vibrating alarm is also available for children who don't respond to sound. Portable, transistorized alarms can be worn on the body rather than the bell and pad devices.

However, don't insist on using the alarm if the child is opposed to it.

Stick with it: Be understanding and patient with your child and stick with your efforts to stop the bed-wetting. Remember, conditioning requires time, doctors say.

Learning bladder control is something like taking piano lessons. Children might not get any results in the first month or two, but if they continue to practice, they'll be able to improve.

Are there any medications that can help?

Recently, drugs have come onto the market that can help older children stay dry during the night. Tofranil (imipramine), which is taken orally, is often prescribed.

Its side effects include potentially dangerous changes in a child's heart rate. DDAVP (also known as desmopressin acetate) is given via a nasal spray. Its side effects include nasal irritation, headaches, disorientation and, in rare cases, seizures.

Many doctors are hesitant to prescribe these drugs because it's not clear what their long-term side effects are, medical experts say.

But if a child wants to go on a sleepover, he or she may be able to take one as a short-term solution. Remember, however, that the problem may recur once the child stops taking the medication.

the bedding is not an every-night event, but it still helps to be prepared.

Georgia Ruth Halpern, Dallas

Beating Bed-Wetting

Beyond the age of three or so, bed-wetting can begin to affect a child's self-image. Older bed wetters need lots of reassurance that you will help them learn to stay dry and that your love and care for them is not diminished by their inability to stay dry.

Be understanding

My eight-year-old daughter still wets the bed and I've assured her that eventually she will outgrow the problem. I know, because I, too, wet the bed until I was about nine. In the meantime, she wears a large pull-up diaper to bed. So that her brother and younger sister don't make fun of her, we don't let the other children know that she wears diapers at night. She's terribly anxious about sleepovers. For the few that she's agreed to attend, I talk to the host mom before the party and ask that she awaken my daughter early to take her to the bathroom so she can change into underpants before the other children wake up. So far this has worked.

Name withheld, Chappaqua, New York

Get more sleep

My five-year-old's pediatrician said that bed wetters often don't get enough sleep at night. I began to put Jason to bed an hour earlier every night. Within a week, he was dry.

Natalie Epstein, Key West, Florida

Offer lots of daytime fluids

To help my son stretch his bladder so that he could stay dry during the night, I began offering him lots of drinks during the day. I also suggested that he try to hold his urine for five or ten minutes, also as a bladder-stretching exercise. These were suggestions that my sister's son's pediatrician made for him years ago. It worked then for my nephew and now for my son.

Eloise Dunn, Maplewood, New Jersey

Give rewards

I kept a calendar on my daughter's wall, putting a sticker on each dry-night date. Every time she earned 10 stickers, we went to a movie. This reward system really has made my daughter more alert to the problem and more interested in working on it.

Alison Freeston-Halbert, Mt. Kisco, New York

Check for allergies

When nothing else worked, I took my son to an allergist who suggested that Matthew, my seven-year-old, systematically eliminate different foods from his diet to see if he might be allergic and if the allergy might be causing sleep disturbances (which, in turn, cause bedwetting.) The allergist pointed out that Matt's sleeping habits—snoring and breathing from his mouth—indicated a possible allergy. On the week that we eliminated colas and chocolate, which both contain caffeine, he stopped bedwetting. When we reintroduced those items, the bed-wetting resumed, which was the indication we needed that caffeine was the culprit. Now Matt strictly avoids caffeinated beverages and foods and sleeps—dry—through the night.

Terry Nostrom, Denver

Invest in an alarm

I bought a moisture sensor to attach to my son's underpants that sets off a beeper when he began to urinate during the night. At age nine, Nick was desperate for a cure and was willing to try anything. The beep woke him and he went to the bathroom. After using this device for just a week, he learned to wake himself when he had to urinate. I just wish I'd discovered this tool earlier.

Naomi Choinski, Lakewood, Illinois

CHAPTER SIX

Health and Safety

*K*eeping *children safe and instilling healthy habits that* will serve them throughout their lives are parents' top priorities. Though we can't protect our children from every hazard, we can take thorough steps to assure ourselves and them that we are doing all we can to help them grow until they are equipped to take care of themselves. Here's how to protect your children, whether they're on the road, visiting Grandma or "safe" at home. We'll also review first-aid procedures for those inevitable boo-boos.

Home, Safe Home

Children's curiosity adds many levels of joy to our lives as we watch them explore the world. That same curiosity leads children to open bathroom cabinets, put small objects in their mouths and peer precariously from windowsills. Childproofing your home is a must.

Double-check

Are you concerned that you may have overlooked an area in your home to childproof? Although my girlfriend and I are vigilant about our children's safety, we doubled-checked each other by doing a room-by-room inspection of both of our homes. It was very helpful to have another parent's perspective, especially because our daughters, who are friends, have different interests.

Cindy Henry, Denton, Texas

See their point of view

To see what your child sees, crawl around the floor to look for anything that a toddler might find interesting. My extremely curious son gashed himself on a protruding screw as he explored the underside of the kitchen table. After this happened, I decided to look at the world from his vantage point and found many things that I couldn't see from above five feet.

Julia Stone-Andres, Santa Monica, California

Remember windows

In the city, we had window guards on all of our apartment windows. It never occurred to me to install guards on our two-story suburban home when we moved in

PARENTS' ALERT

Beware of Buckets

Do not use large buckets when cleaning the house. Toddlers who fall into these untippable containers can drown quickly.

until my daughter nearly fell out her bedroom window lunging after a toy. Thank goodness I was there to catch her. That same day, we locked all the windows at the bottom and the next day, we put in metal guards. (To make them look less ugly, we also put in window boxes to hide them.)

Bonita Chavez, Englewood, New Jersey

Invest in safety devices

One of the best shower gifts I received was a home-safety kit that included things like outlet covers, electrical cord wrappers and cabinet locks. Having these things available before I needed them made it easy to do a safety check without waiting for disaster to strike. If you haven't received these items, they're the best gifts you can give yourself.

Tina Aubausan, Tenafly, New Jersey

Remove temptations

Safety-proofing my house allows me to stop telling my two-year-old son, Trevor, no all the time. I notice that in some of the homes we visit, the kids need to be supervised too closely and corrected too often because so many things are dangerous.

Samantha Ethers, Shaker Heights, Ohio

(continued on page 136)

Home-Safety Checklist

In the kitchen

- Keep toddlers out of the kitchen with a safety gate when you're cooking or otherwise distracted. Turn pot handles away from the front of the stove so your child cannot grab them. Use only the back burners when possible.
- Unplug appliances when they're not in use. Make sure that appliance cords do not dangle over the edges of counters where curious children may tug at them.
- Store all cleansers, toothpicks, plastic bags and other hazardous items high above a child's reach in a locked cabinet.
- Store knives, scissors and other sharp utensils in locked drawers or cabinets. Store glassware out of children's reach.
- Hang a working fire extinguisher within your reach, but high enough to be out of young children's reach.
- Remove stove dials or cover them with childproof caps.
- Keep children away from uninsulated oven doors.
- Install safety locks on drawers, especially if they contain dangerous objects.
- Place a lock on your microwave to prevent young children from using it. Never allow children under the age of eight to use the microwave.

- Keep hot foods and liquids away from the edges of tables. Do not use tablecloths or place mats around babies and toddlers to reduce the risk of a child pulling hot foods and beverages down on himself.

In the bathroom

- Never leave a young child unattended in the bath, not even for a few moments.
- Place nonskid decals or a mat inside the tub to prevent slipping.
- Keep the bathroom tile floor dry and use a rubber-backed cloth mat so that feet are thoroughly dry before walking on bare floors.
- Install an anti-scald valve on the hot-water heater to keep the temperature below 120°F.
- Put a lid lock on the toilet to prevent toddler drownings.
- Store razors, medicines, soaps and cleaning products high in a locked cabinet. Medicines, in general, should not be stored in the bathroom because the heat and humidity may affect their potency; store them in a locked cabinet in the linen closet or other room. (For additional bathtime safety suggestions, see pages 72 and 75 in Chapter 3.)

Throughout the house

- Have at least one working smoke detector on each level of the house and at least one carbon-monoxide detector.

- Keep matches and lighters out of children's reach.
- Place houseplants on high shelves.
- Cover *all* electrical outlets with outlet covers, including those outlets in use. A snap-on cover allows parents easy access to plugs while keeping little hands away. (These covers are available nationally from Gerber Products and from Tots World Company in Blue Bell, Pennsylvania.)
- To keep small fingers safe, keep front-loading VCRs out of children's reach or secure the machines with a commercially available VCR lock.
- Install window guards on all windows. Do not rely on screens to keep children in. Never, however, nail windows shut or partially open because the windows may be needed for exit in the event of fire.
- Wrap window shade and other cords high above a child's reach (including her reach from the sofa, crib or other potential climbing position) to avoid entanglement.
- Place nonskid mats beneath area rugs.
- To keep children from accidentally locking themselves in rooms, remove the door locks (and replace them, if you wish, with simple hinge locks at the level of your reach) or place a towel over the tops of doors to pre-

vent doors from closing completely.
- Replace glass, if possible, with sturdier plexiglass in high-traffic areas that your child regularly uses, such as patio doors and doors with glass panes. Or cover the glass with clear contact paper, which reduces, but does not eliminate, the risks.
- Install child-safety gates at the top and bottom of each staircase.
- Place a cover over radiators to avoid burns.
- Use extension cords wisely. Unplug them and put away when not in use. Stop using a frayed cord or one that is hot or warm to the touch. Never file an appliance plug to make it fit the extension; never use an indoor cord outdoors or use any cord under a rug, near a wet surface or near a heat source.
- Install an air-pressure device to slow down any fast-closing heavy doors, such as screen doors, which can slam on children's arms or legs.
- Perform routine maintenance on schedule, including chimney sweeping, checking heating devices to assure safe operations and discarding unused chemicals throughout the house.
- Remove and/or replace small drawer knobs or electronic equipment knobs (such as stereo dials) that curious

(continued)

Home-Safety Checklist—Continued

young children may remove and ingest.

In the garage, laundry room, garden and backyard

- Replace your current automatic garage door with one that contains a sensing device that will not close if blocked by a child.
- Do not allow your child to play in the front seat of your car, where he may accidentally disengage the brake. Keep trunk doors locked when not loading or unloading your car.
- Keep garden and barbecue supplies in a locked bin out of your child's reach.
- Keep children away from barbecues. Put a fence around the barbecue area and keep children a safe distance away while you cook and for the hours that it may take for coals to cool.
- Never leave children unattended near a pool, even a wading pool. Make sure your pool is securely fenced in so that children cannot have access without your knowledge and supervision. Do not rely solely on pool alarms or pool covers to keep your children safe.
- Remove the doors from old, unused appliances such as refrigerators and freezers. Lock any out-of-the way freezers, coolers and trunks securely because these things are intriguing hiding places for young children who may suffocate inside them.
- Secure the doors of clothes dryers, so that children cannot open them.

Use detectors

A home carbon-monoxide detector probably saved my family's lives. Two months ago, while we were sleeping, the alarm went off. My husband and I got our three children out to the sidewalk. They were really dazed and we both felt ill. The fire department found that our newly installed water heater was incorrectly hooked up. My youngest son spent two days in the hospital recovering. We still have trouble feeling safe in the house, but at least we're alive.

Iris Campbell, Brooklyn, New York

Schedule a safety day

Every six months, when the clocks have to be changed, I schedule a safety day. In addition to changing the smoke-detector batteries, I check to see if the fire extinguishers and flashlights are in working order. We also conduct a family fire drill. It's a good way to start off a new season.

Hani Skutch, Cherry Hill, New Jersey

Safety Away from Home

Childproofing your own home is something you can control. But your child is likely to spend time at other people's homes, too, especially grandparents' and baby-sitters' homes. While you can't completely oversee the childproofing of another's space, you can take reasonable precautions.

Carry pipe cleaners

When visiting someone else's home with your toddler, bring along a few pipe cleaners. If the house isn't childproofed, pipe cleaners wrapped around knobs work well as temporary locks for cabinets that are off-limits to little ones.

Julie Harrington, Chicago

Explain your concerns

If a family member refuses to take childproofing her home a priority, I would limit my visits to her home and ask her to come to yours. If she asked me why I stopped bringing the children over, I would explain to her my anxiety about their safety and the possibility of breaking something valuable.

Ronna Park, West Jordan, Utah

Do a safety check

Take the attitude that others are just as concerned about your children's safety as you are. Enlist their support in protecting your children rather than making the issue a point of contention. Remind the homeowner that accidents can seriously harm children, even kill them. When you arrive at someone else's home, look around and indicate safety hazards and fragile objects that children may break. Explain how terrible you would feel if your children did break some cherished possession. Bring rubber bands along to keep cup-

board doors closed. Most important, watch your children very carefully when you are visiting.

Kathy Matheny, Culver City, California

Stock the diaper bag

I always keep a couple of extra padlock safety latches in my son's diaper bag. This way I can easily attach one to a closet or cupboard whenever I visit friends or family who don't have small children. It keeps my son out of danger and makes me feel better.

Heidi Holmes Tagg, Coopersville, Michigan

Supervise kids

We can't expect others to childproof their homes if they don't have young children themselves. When visiting in another's home, follow your kids around, keep them out of rooms with valuables and out-of-doors as much as possible. It is up to the parents to supervise their children. If a grandparent or neighbor is watching your children for you, then it's up to them to follow them closely around their house.

Jill Crowley-Wahler, Pleasanton, California

Make a travel kit

My husband and I like to travel a lot with our three-year-old. I have a travel safety kit for hotel rooms and friends' homes that we visit. It contains a working smoke detector, outlet covers, a working flashlight and masking tape (to lock cabinets and hotel refrigerators, which really intrigue our son).

Michelle Mercy , Little Neck, New York

What You Need to Know about Poisons

Every year, at least 620,000 children under the age of five are exposed to poisons. To keep you and your kids safe:

Childproofing measures

- Post your local poison-control center phone number next to every phone in your house.
- Keep all household chemicals and medicines in a locked cabinet out of the reach of children and avoid using them when children are present.
- Buy containers with child-resistant closures when possible and close them properly after each use.
- Keep all potentially harmful products in their original containers. Never store chemicals in food containers.
- When visiting others or when others, especially grandparents, visit your home, check to make sure that appropriate precautions have been taken to keep harmful products, particularly medicines, out of children's

reach. Babies and toddlers love to explore purse contents, which may contain things that are poisonous, such as perfumes, nasal sprays or aspirin. To be on the safe side, store your guests' handbags with yours on a closet shelf or otherwise out of children's reach.

- Discard any old medicines, which can become toxic after their expiration date. Flush them down the toilet—do not put them into the garbage where children might find them.
- Keep syrup of ipecac on hand, but do not administer until you have checked with a poison-control specialist since some poisons do additional harm if thrown up. If syrup of ipecac is unavailable, use a clear dishwashing liquid to induce vomiting, again, checking first with a specialist.
- Keep harmful houseplants out of children's reach. For a brochure that

Plan public outings

Plan short visits, fully supervised, or bring your own childproofing equipment with you when you visit someone else's non-childproofed home. Or, instead of visiting at their house, perhaps you can all go out to the zoo or some other public place for your get-togethers.

Jeanne Eckel, Columbus, Ohio

Preventing Home Accidents

In spite of your best planning, certain home hazards can often be overlooked. Other dangers are more of the momentary variety. Together with your vigilance, these following tips can help you keep your children safe.

contains detailed descriptions of the toxicity of various common house-plants, send $1 to The Children's Hospital of Pittsburgh, 3705 Fifth Avenue, Pittsburgh, PA 15213. Request "Common Harmful Plants."

• Be aware of common household items that are not poisonous to adults or in limited doses to children but which can harm or kill a child. Following are a few.

Vitamins

Ingesting just 15 tablets of chewable children's vitamins with iron can sicken or even kill a 25-pound child. Adult iron supplements are deadly in even smaller doses.

Salt

Just 1 to 2 *teaspoons* ingested by a child of 25 pounds can cause irritability, lethargy and possibly seizures. More than 1½ *tablespoons* can cause death.

Nicotine

Eating one cigarette, three butts, a small handful of chewing tobacco or half a piece of nicotine gum can cause vomiting, high blood pressure, increased heart rate, breathing difficulties, cardiac arrhythmias and seizures in children.

Nutmeg

One to three whole nutmegs or 5 to 30 grams (about ¾ of a tablespoon to 4 tablespoons) of ground nutmeg can produce redness of the face, increased heart rate, dry mouth, confusion, hallucinations, drowsiness, upset stomach and vomiting. Symptoms usually occur three to eight hours after ingestion.

Mouthwash, aftershave lotion and perfumes

Three mouthfuls of cologne containing 90 percent alcohol can cause vomiting, drowsiness or even induce a coma in a 25-pound child.

Make glass doors visible

With three small children in the house, I used to worry about them accidentally running into our sliding glass doors. But I found an easy solution. Putting vinyl play-set stickers at a child's eye level on the doors lets my kids know the glass is there.

Jane Ray, Sanford, North Carolina

Turn pot handles inward

It took my four-year-old only an instant to reach up from her high chair for a pot of soup cooking on the stove. The extended handle of the pot made it easy for her to reach. She tipped the hot soup all over herself, fortunately missing her face and neck, but giving herself second-degree burns on her arms and chest. It

The Family First-Aid Kit

Every family should keep a first-aid kit at home and in their car. Use a tackle box secured with a childproof lock and stock up on the following necessities.

- One or two rolls of adhesive tape
- One roll of gauze
- Adhesive strips in various sizes
- One or two elastic bandages
- Bar of plain, unscented or antibacterial soap and/or hydrogen peroxide
- Cotton balls and cotton swabs
- Antiseptic cream
- Petroleum jelly
- Calamine lotion
- Acetaminophen (liquid for infants and young children; chewable for older children; full-strength tablets for teens and adults)
- One bottle of syrup of ipecac
- Thermometer
- Scissors
- Tweezers with ridged edges (and alcohol wipes for sterilizing them)
- Flashlight with extra batteries
- Chemical ice pack

- Sunscreen
- Meat tenderizer (for treating insect bites)
- Zinc oxide (for treating rashes)
- Emergency phone numbers (doctor, hospital, local poison-control center)

If you are going on an extended trip or are traveling in a remote area, a more fully stocked first-aid kit is advised. Include in addition to the above:
- Snakebite kit
- Bee-sting kit
- Tongue depressors (to use as splints for injured fingers and/or toes)
- Anaphylaxis kit for severe allergic reaction
- Backup supply of prescription medication
- Change and/or phone card for making emergency phone calls

was a preventable nightmare and took weeks for her to recover. I now cook only on the back burners whenever the children are anywhere near the kitchen.

Annie Scippoliano, Augusta, Georgia

Watch out for electric eyes

My six-year-old daughter was recently injured by the elevator door in our apartment building. It operates on an electric eye, which didn't register her because she is much shorter than where the beam shines. A similar accident occurred to a neighbor's son in the supermarket. He was caught in a closing door that couldn't see him. It's so important to walk alongside young children in and out of doors that are designed to respond only to people who are taller.

Cathy Duffy, New York City

First-Aid for Burns

Serious burns require immediate medical attention. (As a rule of thumb, if a burn is larger than a quarter on a child, if a burn is on the face or if the victim is under age one, you should seek medical help.) Minor household burns can be safely handled at home. The sooner first aid is applied, the better the chance that the skin will heal properly. Here's what to do.

- **Soak the area in cool, not cold, water.**

Do not run tap water directly onto the burn. The force from the water can irritate the delicate skin of the burn area. Also, do not apply ice, which can further damage skin.

- **Do not break any blisters.**
- **Keep the burn clean.**

After initial cool-down, wash the area with hydrogen peroxide, pat dry and cover with sterile gauze. After 24 hours, wash the area gently with soap and water or a mild Betadine solution. Repeat washing daily until the skin has healed.

- **Do not apply butter or lotion.**

They can retain the heat and cause deeper burning and infection. However, over-the-counter topical antiseptic creams designed for minor burns can help, particularly those containing polymyxin B sulfate or bacitracin.

- **Elevate the burn area.**

Elevation will help prevent swelling.

- **Be alert to infection.**

If there's an increase in swelling or redness to the burn area or if the area starts to smell or ooze, the burn may have become infected and need to be treated with antibiotics. See your doctor.

Tie back long hair

My four-year-old daughter and I were baking when a preventable accident occurred. Her hair got caught in the electric mixer. She was standing next to me on a step stool pouring the ingredients into a mixing bowl. When I turned on the machine, her hair swung into the bowl and in a second it was wrapped around both beaters. She screamed in pain until I unplugged the machine. A patch of her hair was pulled out, and two months later it still hasn't grown back. I implore parents: Tie or clip back your children's hair when they are in the kitchen with you.

Susan Westerfield, Reynoldsburg, Ohio

Keep drawers closed

Recently, my daughter left open the bottom drawer of her tall dresser. Our 18-pound cat jumped in and the dresser tipped over, breaking the cat's leg. Thank God, Julia, my eight-year-old, was able to
(continued on page 144)

First-Aid

Splinter removal

If your child has a splinter in his fingertip, locate it more easily by taking him into a darkened room and shining a penlight through his finger. Before attempting to remove it, soak it in warm water first, which may cause the splinter to ease itself out.

If it doesn't come out on its own, wash the area with hydrogen peroxide or antiseptic soap, and ease the pain by applying a teething-pain reliever to the area. Wait briefly. The topical anesthetic will minimize the pain of extracting the splinter. (If teething pain relievers are not available, numb the area with ice.) If part of the splinter protrudes above the skin, grasp it with ridge-edged tweezers, which should first be wiped with alcohol. Pull it out at the same angle at which it entered the skin. Use a magnifying glass if possible. Also work in good light.

If no part of the splinter is graspable, do not pursue it with tweezers or a needle. If it remains lodged or if it is a metal fragment, glass, is under a fingernail or is from a used (and therefore bacteria-laden) toothpick, get medical assistance.

Removing a foreign object from the eye

Flush the eye with cool, clean water. Do not force open the eyelid. Instead, use an eyedropper and put the drops into the tear-duct area; the drops will wash over the eyeball when your child blinks. If the object comes out and there is a possibility that the eyeball has been scratched, cover the eye with a sterile patch for 24 hours and check again. If the object remains, if redness appears or if discomfort continues for more than a few hours, see an ophthalmologist. If any large object pierces a child's eye, take her to an emergency room immediately and insist on seeing an ophthalmologist.

Cuts, scrapes and scratches

Use a clean cloth or gauze pad and apply pressure directly to the wound. If you don't have a cloth handy, use your hand alone. Apply the pressure for about 60 seconds, releasing it as soon as the bleeding slows. Then elevate the wound above the level of your child's heart to slow blood flow. If you can't stop the bleeding, get emergency medical care. Do not apply a tourniquet, which can cut off circulation and ultimately cause more problems than it solves.

Once the bleeding is controlled, apply an ice pack wrapped in a towel. Leave the cold pack on for only 15 minutes or until the area is numb to restrict blood flow.

Cleanse the cut or scrape thoroughly with soap and water, hydrogen peroxide or even a saline contact-lens cleanser and cover it with antibacterial cream. It's important to remove any grit to prevent infection and/or scarring. Some children will be more cooperative washing the wound in a sudsy bath rather than focusing on washing only the wound.

Bandage scrapes with a gauze pad placed tent-like over the wound. Bandage minor cuts with a butterfly bandage to close the wound. These butterfly-shaped bandages are sticky all over and keep the edges of the skin together so that the wound heals with a nice, straight scar.

As the wound heals, wash it daily and reapply antibacterial ointment until it has completely healed. After the first day, remove the bandage from a scrape and let it heal in the air, provided that the wound won't be exposed to infectious elements. (If your child will be playing in dirt, cover the wound loosely and wash it again after playtime.) In the case of a cut, leave the butterfly bandage in place for 24 to 48 hours for the skin to knit together and heal.

Make sure that tetanus shots are up-to-date, especially if your child has been scratched by an animal or cut by a dirty implement such as a nail. If the shots aren't up-to-date, see your child's doctor for a booster. Also see the doctor if the healing wound contains blood or pus or there is redness that is traveling away from the site, which indicates that it has become infected and needs to be treated with a course of oral antibiotics, says Samuel Wentworth, M.D., a pediatrician in private practice in Danville, Indiana.

Black eyes and bruises

Wrap some ice in a clean dish towel or washcloth or use an ice-pack or bag of frozen vegetables rather than applying ice directly to the bruised area. Ice the area for 20 minute periods with short breaks between sessions when the bruise first occurs, to minimize swelling.

If a bruised arm or leg is swelling after applying ice, elevate the arm or leg above the heart. After 24 to 48 hours, apply warm compresses rather than ice or cold cloths. The warmth encourages blood flow and speeds up healing. If a child is complaining of pain, you can give an appropriate dose of children's acetaminophen. However, if the bruise is to the child's head or stomach, consult your child's doctor before administering any medications.

Seek medical help if the child's eye or head is bruised; the blow is to the side of the head above the ear, an area at high risk for fracturing; your child has trouble walking, talking or seeing, becomes drowsy or unresponsive or has one pupil (the black part of the eye) that is larger than the other after receiving a blow; swelling occurs at a joint, particularly an elbow; a blunt or hard object, such as a bicycle handle-bar, has struck your child's abdomen with significant force; a fever accompanies the bruising; or if bruising appears with no apparent cause, a minor blow results in a large bruise, or bruises appear in abnormal places, such as the back, calves or backs of the arms.

(continued)

First-Aid—continued

Antiseptic Applications

Apply antiseptic ointment directly onto a bandage instead of onto the cut, since putting medication on cuts frightens some children.

Bloody cuts

Keep a red or dark-colored washcloth in your bathroom or kitchen to cleanse bloody cuts. The blood won't show and your child will be less frightened.

Fat lips

When a child won't let you hold an ice pack on a bruised lip, offer a frozen fruit bar to calm her and reduce swelling.

Canker sores

Soak a cool black tea bag in sugar water and offer that to a child with canker sores. Black tea contains tannin, an astringent that relieves pain.

Hiccups

Make sure a child doesn't eat during a bout with hiccups to avoid choking. To stop a hiccup attack, try these methods.

- Drink out of the opposite side of a glass of water. Looking down at the glass, sip from the top side instead of the bottom.
- Swallow a teaspoon of sugar. (Place it on the back of the tongue.)
- Gargle.
- Drink water through a paper towel.
- Drink pineapple juice. Actually, drinking any liquid helps.
- Lie on her back across a bed with her head hanging toward the floor and

jump out of the way in time or the heavy dresser could have killed her. This incident was a scary reminder that childproofing and reviewing home-safety rules is still important even when children pass the preschool years.

Sonia Williams, Northampton, Massachusetts

Wrap cords

My daughter was nearly killed when she was eight months old because she'd gotten entangled in the Venetian blind cord that hung next to her crib. After finding her with the cord around her neck be-

fore it choked her, I tied all the cords high above. The inconvenience is a small price to pay for her life.

Donna Umberto, College Point, New York

Check picture hooks

A heavy picture hanging in our living room came crashing down on our couch. I had hung it up years ago, but somehow the nail came loose. If any of us had been sitting there at the time, I can't imagine what might have happened since the glass shattered everywhere. I rechecked all the other pictures and mirrors and found two

while her arms are stretched over her head. Then have her take a deep breath and then hold it for as long as possible.
- Plug her ears with her fingers for about 20 seconds.
- Breathe into a paper bag.
- Stick out his tongue.
- Tickle the roof of his mouth with a cotton swab.
- Pull her tongue gently.

If your child hiccups for more than a day, call the doctor.

Removing a bug from the ear

Don't go after it with tweezers, which may push it further inward. In a dark room, shine a flashlight into the child's ear. If the bug is alive, it may be at-

tracted to the light and fly out. If not, try to kill it with a drop of rubbing alcohol, then add a few drops of peroxide to bubble it out. Or, using an eyedropper, flood the ear with mineral oil. If the bug does not come out, have your child's pediatrician remove it.

Getting a child's head unstuck

Instead of trying to pull out your child's head from the same direction that it got stuck between fence posts, railings or other slats (using the logic that if it went in that way it should come out the same way), get the help of another adult and try doing this: Gently lift the child's body and then turn him so that his shoulders are parallel to the opening and pull him out from the other side.

others that were also at risk of falling because the plaster wall behind them had become soft (probably due to a leak over a year ago that dampened the wall behind the pictures).

Piper Ramsey, Address withheld

Hide houseplant soil

To prevent my children and pets from exploring or eating the soil from our houseplants, I wrapped each pot with netting and tied it tightly with a ribbon at the base of the plant. I can still water the plants through the netting.

Louisa Meyer, Dallas

Enhancing Home Safety

Beyond the by-the-book home-safety rules most parents follow, these parents have come up with new ways to make their lives easier, too.

Install handrails

To help my three-year-old son, Matthew, climb the stairs in our home safely, I put in a lower handrail at his level, approximately 8½ inches below the regular rail. It was simple to install: I bought a 1½-inch-thick handrail rod at the lumberyard and secured it along the wall on brackets. Now my son climbs up and down the stairs with ease, and I worry less.

Michelle Lorenz, Appleton, Wisconsin

Holiday Home Safety

A cozy home decorated for the holidays makes everyone in the family feel safe. But the lovely decorations can also pose a hazard, unless certain precautions are taken.

- Don't use lighted candles on or near a tree, near curtains or upholstered fabrics or where children and others are likely to pass.
- Use only lights that have been tested for safety by an independent testing lab. Look for a label to indicate that your lights have passed the test. Discard any lights that have broken or cracked sockets, frayed or cracked wires or loose connections, all of which are fire hazards.
- Avoid bubbling lights around young children, because these breakable lights contain toxic chemicals.
- Use no more than three sets of lights per extension cord.
- Turn off the tree lights and other electrical decorations when going to bed or leaving the house.
- If you have small children, avoid decorations that are sharp or breakable, have small parts or that resemble food or candy.

Make an easy alarm

My three-year-old was always climbing onto the built-in bookshelves, which run eight feet high. He has some developmental problems and really can't be made to understand why doing something dangerous is a no-no. Since I couldn't watch him every second, I placed a row of dinner-type bells on each shelf to alert me. As soon as he touched a shelf, he'd knock over a bell, my signal to come and get him.

Ruth Davison, Ridgeton, Kentucky

Put the Christmas tree in the playpen

To keep my twin toddlers away from the Christmas tree, I put the tree inside their playpen for the season. We can all still enjoy it, but it's now impossible for them to pull it down.

Lilli Dolentz, New York City

Keep doors from slamming

When my son discovered the joy of slamming doors, I discovered a really easy solution: I drape a thick towel over the top of the door. Now his fingers can't get trapped and any noise is muffled.

Rita Winer, Oak Park, Michigan

Making Boo-Boos Better

Bumps and bruises are the badges of growing up. After the hugs and kisses that really make boo-boos all better, these tips can take the ouch out of your child's hurts a little sooner.

Never Bandage Baby

Never put adhesive bandages on infants or small children's fingers. When they naturally put their hands into their mouths, they may inhale the bandage and choke.

Take teethers out of retirement

Instead of throwing out those old teething rings—the kind you put in the refrigerator to cool—move them to the freezer and when your child hurts herself, give her the frozen teething ring to put on the boo-boo instead of ice. She can hold it herself, it doesn't sting (as ice often does) and there is no drip or mess to mop up.

Deborah West, Westfield, New Jersey

Oil bandages before removing

A painless way to remove an adhesive bandage is to saturate it with a cotton ball dipped in baby oil or vegetable oil. It peels off without pulling on sensitive skin.

Alison Mahoney, West Palm Beach, Florida

Check the freezer

No ice packs available to soothe the pain of bumps and bruises? Try using a bag of frozen peas or other frozen bags of food. The plastic-wrapped bag works wonders and wraps around a hurt knee, arm or forehead very well.

Elizabeth Banks, Tarrytown, New York

Make a bandage handle

Here's a slightly less painful way to remove an adhesive bandage. Make a small fold in the corner of the bandage before applying it so that you have something to grab on to when you remove it. My daughter, Claire, and I agree that it beats the nuisance of trying to get it started.

Hillary Morgan, Bloomfield Hills, Michigan

Remove bandages in the bath

I let my six-year-old daughter remove Band-Aids in the bath by herself. She soaps the area around the adhesive, which makes removal a lot easier.

Marge Miller, Kalamazoo, Michigan

Create a story

My daughter Catherine, age five, hates it when washing a scrape or putting ointment on it causes the bruise to burn. I tell her that the pain is there because the bad germs are fighting with the good soap or medicine and that although every battle hurts, it's the only way for the good guys to win. She's much more stoic when she can picture this heroic fight between good and bad going on in her skin. Once the hurting stops, she announces, "the good

Never Give Aspirin to Children

Over age two, children's aches and fevers can be treated with children's acetaminophen. Never give children aspirin, which can cause Reye's syndrome, a potentially fatal disease.

guys have won!" I congratulate her for helping them.

Emma Lipton-Seitz, Staten Island, New York

Count on kisses

Whenever my son or daughter gets a minor boo-boo, I ask how many kisses it will take to make it better. They carefully consider how bad the injury hurts and announce anywhere from 1 to 10 kisses, a prescription that I then apply.

Sarah Templeton, Grosse Point, Michigan

Decorate plain bandages

Instead of buying fancy children's plastic bandages, I have my daughter make her own. I buy the plain type and when she gets a cut, she can put her favorite stickers on the bandage we use to cover it. She says that the decorating is fun and helps make boo-boos all better.

Vicki Camadine, Rexford, New York

Dealing with Doctor Visits

It's difficult for a child to understand why a parent—who at all other times works so hard to shield him from discomfort—cooperates with a physician who's poking and prodding him. These parents have found ways to let their children know that they really are still on their child's side and that the doctor is part of the same team.

Role-play

I encourage my four-year-old daughter, Heather, to play with her doctor kit before she has a checkup. She loves to give me and her dolls shots. Sometimes she even takes the kit with her into the examination room and gives the doctor a few injections first. Acting out her fears and aggressions seems to work. She's never thrilled about getting a shot, but she's amazingly cooperative.

Sherri Starr, Plainview, New York

Get the worst out of the way

Sometimes my five-year-old son needs a shot and a blood test during a visit to the

PARENTS' ALERT

When to Call the Doctor about a Fever

- If your child is under three months of age, any fever should be reported. For a child over three months and under one year, a temperature of 101°F warrants a call. For children over one, a doctor should be called if the fever reaches 102°F.
- If the fever is accompanied by other symptoms, such as vomiting or convulsions, or if the child has a headache.
- If the fever lingers for more than 24 hours.
- If the child suffers from any other chronic medical condition, such as cystic fibrosis or diabetes.
- If the child also has a rash, stiff neck, confusion, back pain or painful urination.

Getting the Most from Your Doctor Visits

Whether the visit is a scheduled routine checkup or an unplanned sick-child visit, here's how to make the most of your time.

Before the visit

- Write down any questions you have. In the course of the visit, it's easy to forget to address some of your concerns.
- Bring along any medications your child is currently taking, especially if they have been prescribed by another physician.
- If you know that you need to discuss something that may take some time, tell the doctor or the receptionist ahead of time, when you schedule the appointment, so that no one will feel rushed by the need for extra time.

During the visit

- Be sure you understand what the doctor is saying. Don't hesitate to ask your pediatrician to slow down, explain and restate anything that confuses you. Repeat the instructions to the doctor to be sure that you understand what is being said.
- Write down important information, including the names and dosages of any medicine being prescribed so that you can double check that you're getting the correct medication at the pharmacy.
- Refer to the list of questions you wrote earlier.

---

doctor. After learning the hard way, I now ask the doctor or nurse if one is more painful than the other. Then I make sure my son is given the less painful one first.

Linda Mowry, Florence, Alabama

Prepare your child

I find that at age six, my son is considerably more fearful of getting a shot than he was at three or four. I need to talk to him about it in advance now that he has some experience under his belt—and a better memory.

Pam Abrams, Brooklyn, New York

Be honest

When my daughter asks me if something the doctor is going to do will hurt, I answer her honestly. I also ask her what I can do to help her deal with the pain. Sometimes she wants me to hold her while she gets her shot instead of sitting on the examining table. One time, I suggested that she sing her favorite song really loud and that by the time she got to the end of the song, the shots would be over. I also tell her that it's perfectly all right to cry, scream or feel afraid. I'm also comfortable rewarding her with a special

Choosing a Pediatrician

Being organized can help you interview a potential health care provider with confidence. Here are some questions you may wish to ask.

- What is your philosophy about_____? (Choose the topics that matter to you, such as breastfeeding vs. bottle feeding, allowing your child to sleep in Mom and Dad's bed, children in day care, thumb sucking, teenager's privacy in medical matters and so forth.)
- What fees do you charge for an average visit? What managed health care plans do you participate in? When must payment be made—at the time of visit or when billed? Will the doctor accept direct payments from your insurance company?
- What are your hospital affiliations? Are you board certified?
- What is your call-in policy? How do you handle evening or nighttime emergencies?
- Do you have evening and weekend office hours?
- What is the average waiting time for an appointment and in the waiting room?
- Who covers for you when you are on vacation?

You'll also want to feel comfortable in the office and with the doctor's demeanor. Ask yourself if the pediatrician takes your concerns seriously and answers your questions to your satisfaction and if his or her office staff also treats you and your child in a satisfactory manner.

---

outing or treat after the visit so that she has something to look forward to.

Eleanor Abernathy, Oswego, New York

Read about it

My son and daughter both love a book we have that shows what the inside of human bodies look like. I use the book to help them see what part of their bodies need to have the doctor's attention, how the medicine travels through them and why it's important to take care of ourselves.

Janie Lee, Niagara Falls, New York

Let kids express themselves

I always ask Todd, my four-year-old, to draw a picture to take with him to the doctor to show what a good artist he is. (The doctor always makes a big deal about the picture and hangs it up in the office.) Knowing that his work is met with such fanfare makes Todd eager to go to the doctor.

Linda Jacobs, Annapolis, Maryland

Take a huggy along

Jennifer, my five-year-old, came up with a good solution to calming her fears of going to the doctor. She takes Ralph, a stuffed dog that she's had since birth and that is her special comfort pal, to the office with her. We ask the doctor to demonstrate anything he's going to do on Ralph first. So after Ralph gets his ears checked, for instance, so does Jennifer. It really helps her.

Tina Anastacio, Houston

Treating the Big Three: Earaches, Sore Throats and Colds

Treating ear infections tops the list of children's unscheduled doctor visits, followed by scratchy throats and colds. These parents have found ways to assess their children's conditions and to soothe their children's aches and pains while waiting for the doctors' prescribed treatments to take effect.

Try hot and cold compresses

Each time my son has an ear infection, it takes about two days for the medicine to begin to make him feel better. I've found that for some infections, putting a warm compress on his ear works. Other times, a cold one works better. With each new infection, we try either a cold or hot compress to see which one works.

Christina Manchild, New York City

Drop in mineral oil

My daughter's frequent earaches hurt less when I put a few drops of warm (not hot) mineral oil in her ear. I heat it by placing the bottle in a saucepan of warm

Preventing Ear Infections

Frequent ear infections are not only uncomfortable, they can often lead to hearing loss and delays in language development. Regularly treating ear infections with antibiotics can lead to the development of antibiotic resistant strains of infection. Here are recommended ways to prevent ear infections.

- Do not allow a child to sleep with a bottle.
- Do not smoke or allow others to smoke around your child.
- Have your child drink plenty of liquids, especially when she has a fever or a cold.
- Do not use cotton swabs or any other tool to poke or prod the ear.

water. Then she tilts her head and I use an eyedropper to put it in.

Linda Corsak, Jeffersonville, Missouri

Make a warm-water pillow

To help my son, Griffin, feel less achy when he has an earache, I make a warm pillow for him. Hot-water bottles wrapped in a towel work well. So do warmed gel-filled teething rings.

Jessica Montgomery-Link, Silver Spring, Maryland

Get crazy straws

To help my daughter drink as much as she should when she's under the weather,

I keep a collection of crazy straws—plastic straws that have weird shapes—to encourage her to drink lots of fluids. She loves watching juice, water or soda zip around the straw.

Emma Harding, Larchmont, New York

Offer gum

Whenever we ride an elevator, take a plane or ride on certain amusement park rides, my son gets an immediate earache from the change in air pressure. I've learned that if I give him a stick of gum to chew, his ears won't hurt on elevators or planes. On amusement park rides, when chewing gum might present a choking hazard, I remind him to swallow a lot during the ride if he wants to go on one that's likely to hurt his ears.

Cliff Downs, New York City

Yawn and say, "Ahh"

When my six-year-old son, Jonathan, complains of a sore throat, I can never see anything when he sticks out his tongue and says, "Ahh." There's a better way—yawning. Now, I ask him to yawn and

with the help of a flashlight, I can see his swollen, red tonsils beautifully.

Debra Levey Larson, Urbana, Illinoi

Serve chicken soup

Never underestimate the value of a bowl of chicken soup. That, along with Jell-O and ice pops, really soothes a sore throat. And for upset tummies, try serving flat cola (no bubbles) or ginger ale.

Antoinette Kahn, Kingston, New York

Rub their chests

Because I remember how good it made me feel when my mom did it to me as a child, I rub my daughter's chest with vaporizing cream whenever she has a cold. She, too, loves the feel of a sticky massage and the vapor seems to clear her nose.

Peggy McHenry, Montreal

Give baths

Whenever my son or daughter gets stuffy from a cold, I fill up the bathroom with steam, then I draw a warm bath. Sitting in the warm water in a steamy room really clears them up in no time.

Angela Everson, Duluth, Minnesota

Go for C

Regular orange juice burns my son's throat whenever he has a cold or sore throat. Since I want to make sure that he gets extra vitamin C during these times, I switch to flavored punches that are fortified with vitamin C. These go down easier and still provide the extra vitamins.

Nathalie Jaminez, Bethesda, Maryland

Wear hats

To cut down on colds, I always insist that my children wear hats in the cold.

FROM THE FOOD EDITOR'S KITCHEN
Simple Chicken Soup

Ingredients
½ chicken breast, boiled and cubed
1 can (13 ounces) chicken broth
1 cup chicken stock
2 carrots, diced
2 celery stalks, diced
1 small onion, diced
1 medium zucchini, quartered lengthwise and cut into ½-inch pieces
3 small potatoes, peeled and cut into quarters
table salt and/or garlic salt to taste (optional)

Directions
1. Wash and remove skin from chicken and prepare vegetables.
2. Place all in 3-quart saucepan with water.
3. Boil chicken breast on bone along with the cut-up vegetables for 20 minutes.
4. Pour off stock, saving 1 cup.*
5. Remove chicken from pot, cut meat into cubes and discard bone.
6. Return 1 cup of stock, chicken cubes and add canned chicken broth to saucepan. Add salt to taste.
7. Let simmer on medium heat for 10 minutes.

Makes two to three servings.

*Instead of discarding this stock, pour into ice-cube trays, freeze and use to cool down too-hot soup or pasta on another day.

I've also found that wearing hats that cover the ears keeps them from getting earaches, particularly on windy days.

F. D. Acton, Stockbridge, Massachusetts

Get fresh air
I'm a great believer in the outdoor cure. Whenever any of my four kids is stuffy or has a cold, I bundle him or her up and take a walk. Being in the fresh air always makes them (and me) feel better.

Rebeccah Lindser, Crown Heights, New York

Sleep propped up
Whenever my children get stuffy noses, I find that they sleep better with lots of

pillows so that they're nearly in a sitting position.

Anne Elizabeth Duncan, Mobile, Alabama

Cut down on dairy

I find that by eliminating milk, cheese and ice cream when my kids are stuffy really cuts down on the length of their colds. To make sure they get enough calcium, I serve leafy green vegetables.

Lorna Creighton, Redwood City, California

Help for Chickenpox

While chickenpox can be a dangerous condition for teens and adults, it's rarely more than an itchy nuisance to children. Symptoms usually begin with a slight fever and drowsiness, followed—a day or two later—with the characteristic spots. Here's how to help your child cope during the six days or so that he's cooped up.

Spot a friend

When my daughter, Nariana, was 2½, she broke out with a bad case of chickenpox. When she looked at her spotted face in the mirror, she was terrified. That night while she was asleep, I took her favorite doll (with a plastic face) and dotted her with washable paint.

When my daughter woke the next morning, she was thrilled to see that she wasn't the only one who had the chickenpox. What a difference it made in getting her through a tough time!

Margaret L. Martell, Columbus, Nebraska

Paint on medicine

When my son had the chickenpox, he was very cranky and wouldn't allow me to

PARENTS' ALERT

Limit Exposure

While a family member infected with chicken pox will most likely pass the virus on to those who haven't previously been exposed, limiting contact with the contagious child can result in a milder case for the others. More frequent, close contact at the early stages of the disease brings on a more serious case to those who contract it.

put any calamine lotion on him.

To make him more comfortable, I pretended the lotion was like paint, poured it into a dish and dabbed his pox with a paintbrush. My son loved the idea because he thought it was like face and body paint, not medicine. Instead of squirming away from me, he was sure to point out every single spot.

Teri Nelson, Hamel, Minnesota

Make oatmeal sponges

I gave my three- and four-year-olds oatmeal baths when they were cooped up at the same time with chickenpox. Why? Oatmeal is a great remedy for itching. To contain the mess (at least at first), I made oatmeal sponges by cutting nylon stockings just above the ankles and filling them with uncooked oatmeal. I tied the nylon with a ribbon. The kids thought it was a riot and rubbed themselves down in the bathtub for hours. Eventually, they were smearing oatmeal all over their bodies and making oatmeal pies. It was a big mess,

What Works to Relieve Itches?

Here are two home remedies that doctors recommend for relieving the itching from chickenpox. Mix 1 cup of white kitchen vinegar, ½ cup of baking soda and one to two capfuls of Alpha Keri body oil in a bath. Soak for 15 to 20 minutes, leave the bathtub and then apply Dyprotex cream, an over-the-counter product that is sold as pads or in lotion. This relieves itching better than some anti-itch formulas, and because it doesn't crust like drying agents, there's less chance of scarring.

Also effective is a bath in colloidal oatmeal, which is a raw oatmeal that's been ground into a powder, such as Aveeno.

To keep kids from scratching at the scabs, file their nails daily rather than simply cutting them, which doesn't leave as smooth an edge. Make sure that you keep your child's hands and nails clean to prevent secondary infections.

Also, keep your child cool during her bout with the chickenpox. English researchers reported in the *British Medical Journal* that keeping patients cooler than usual might result in milder cases with fewer pockmarks.

---

but I didn't care—the kids had fun while they soothed their itches.

Lytton Zwemer, Tallahassee, Florida

Get a new bath toy

Because Maryanne, my four-year-old daughter, was spending so much time in the bath during her chickenpox, I bought her a few new bathtub toys and gave her one each day. Having something new to play with lessened her resistance to taking so many baths.

Leslie Ogden, Nashua, New Hampshire

Get artistic

Zackery, my seven-year-old, recently suffered from chickenpox. He quickly got tired of sick-bed activities such as drawing and watching TV. To relieve his boredom, I suggested that he make dot-to-dot drawings on himself (with wash-able, nontoxic markers). He had a ball and created some amazing pictures on himself. I photographed his tattoos and he brought the picture to school to show off to his friends.

Deidre Cunningham, Hannibal, Missouri

Medicines Made Easier

Mary Poppins relied on a spoonful of sugar to help the medicine go down. Thanks to these parents, you have a few other options.

Give medicines friendly names

From an early age, my son has had to take six medications a day for a heart condition. I'm very firm about it—it's just

Cures for the Medicine Blues

The nose knows

If your child resists swallowing her medicine, explain that if she can't smell it, she won't taste it very much. Have her hold her nose and sip the medicine through a straw. Or simply ask the child to hold her nose until the spoon is in her mouth.

Less is more

If your child is fussy about taking liquid medicine, here's a tip: Many antibiotics come in two strengths—125 milligrams (mg) per 5 milliliters (ml), which equals about a teaspoon, and 250 mg per 5 ml. The next time your physician prescribes an antibiotic, ask for the more concentrated dose. Then you'll only have to get your child to swallow a half-teaspoon instead of a whole teaspoon of the less concentrated type.

A cookie

Some children find it easier to swallow a pill that is mixed with a crunchier food, such as a cookie, instead of mixing it with a soft food such as applesauce or swallowing it with a beverage. For some kids, a bite of banana is a good pill-swallowing aid.

Ice is nice

Let a child age five or older first suck on ice chips to numb the taste buds before taking medicine.

Give a choice

Find out if the medicine is available in a variety of flavors or if a liquid medicine also comes in pill form, which older children may prefer.

Chill out

Many liquid medicines can be chilled, which reduces their bitter taste. Note, however, that storing some medicines in frost-free refrigerators can cause the medicine to evaporate too quickly, leaving you a few doses short. Check with your pharmacist about the proper storage temperature for each prescription or over-the-counter medicine you use. Also: To prevent accidental overdosing, do not store medicines in the refrigerator if your children have easy access to the fridge.

Easier eyedrops

Feeling the cold eyedrops is unpleasant for most children. Try letting your child sit up while you gently pull his lower eyelid and place the drops in the pocket. Wait a few seconds to let the drop warm up before releasing the lid. When your child blinks, the drops will coat his eye correctly. If your child prefers to cuddle, try having him lean his head back with his eyes closed and put the drops where the upper and lower lid meet, near the nose. When he opens his eyes, the drops will go into his eyes easily.

something he has had to adapt to. But I find it helps to give the medicines user-friendly names like Monster Soup and Giraffe Juice instead of just saying, "Take your medicine."

Judy Grey, Upper Montclair, New Jersey

Let kids handle it

If your child resists taking medicine that you are giving him, give him the spoon and let him give himself the medicine.

Linda Kaeser, Bricktown, New Jersey

Use a bottle nipple

My 1½-year-old daughter really resisted taking liquid medicine from a medicine dropper until I discovered this trick. I remove the nipple from one of her bottles, which she is happy to place in her mouth. I then deliver the medicine through the dropper placed inside the nipple.

Peter de Costa, New York City

Mix with food

Try mixing medicine with food that is sweet or has a strong flavor, such as grape jelly or applesauce. Check with your doctor or pharmacist first to make sure the medicine and the food are compatible.

Annie Casey, Maywood, Illinois

You go first

I pretend to take the medicine first. Then I tell my child, "Now you do it just like Mommy."

Thelma Osbey, New Orleans, Louisiana

Skip the spoon

I use a medicine dropper instead of a spoon to administer liquid medicine. Putting it in the side of my child's mouth

Tip-Offs to Vision Problems

Because most children think that everyone sees the way *they* do, most don't know when they have a vision problem. So in addition to having a physician give a screening at six months and a full eye exam by age three, parents can be alert to these warning signs of impaired vision.

- Short attention span during reading
- The need to hold objects close to eyes or the avoidance of tasks involving small objects
- Tilting head or covering one eye
- Occasionally crossing eyes
- Recurring eyelid infections, such as blempharitis
- Frequent tripping or bumping into things
- Rapid movement of eyes from side to side
- Recurring headaches or dizziness, especially with any of the above symptoms
- Double vision
- Frequent blinking or rubbing of eyes
- Red, itchy or sore eyes
- Excessive tearing
- Extreme light sensitivity
- Frequent squinting or frowning

and gently squeezing is an easier method for a young child to handle.

Laurie Lee, Palo Alto, California

PARENTS' ALERT

Prescription Know-How

- Always double-check with your doctor about the name, strength and dosage of any prescription medicines rather than relying only on the doctor's prescription, which can be misunderstood by the pharmacist. Also, double check with the pharmacist that you are receiving the correct medicine.
- Don't overuse antibiotics. Taking antibiotics too frequently can lead to antibiotic-resistant strains of infection.
- Discard outdated medicines. All medicines lose their effectiveness over time; some may become toxic after their expiration dates. To help keep track of expiration dates, circle the dates in red each time you bring home a medicine.
- Measure doses accurately. Teaspoons are like snowflakes—they are not all alike. In fact, they can vary in size from 3 ml to 9 ml, which makes household teaspoons unreliable measures for medicine taking. To be sure you're giving the correct dosage, buy a standard (5 cc or 5 ml) teaspoon from your pharmacy.

Serve a follow-up treat

My daughter, Kathleen, age eight, has to take an ill-tasting inhaled medicine for asthma. I make sure that she has something tasty—usually a drink like chocolate milk or even soda, if that's what she wants—available so that she can take frequent sips during the 15 minutes or so that the inhaler treatment takes. Knowing that she can stop the machine to take a drink whenever she needs to gives her more control. She doesn't mind that interrupting the medicine taking makes it take a little longer as long as she can reduce the bad taste during her treatments.

April Corday, Wheeling, West Virginia

Use cream cheese for pills

We learned this pill-swallowing trick from—of all people—our veterinarian.

When our cat had to take pills, the vet told us to hide it in a little piece of cream cheese, which would make the pill glide down. A few months later, my 11-year-old, who has never been able to swallow a pill, needed to take a medicine in pill form. Luckily this was a medicine that he was able to take with dairy products. We tried the cream-cheese trick (he, of course, was in on the trick) and it worked.

Lauren Cole, Juneau, Alaska

Test the timing

To give my daughter a sense of control about her medicine taking, I always ask, "Do you want to take it now or in five minutes?" She usually opts to get it over with and takes it immediately, though sometimes she chooses to wait.

Abigail Lewishown, Miami

Treating Asthma and Other Allergies

There's really no getting used to a chronic allergic condition. But wise parents can help their children cope and remain in the mainstream despite their allergies.

Bake up backups

I am the mother of two severely food-allergic daughters, ages five and three. When my girls are invited to a birthday party, I bake a batch of approved cupcakes and send them along so they don't feel left out at cake time. You can get recipes for milk- and egg-free cakes and other great desserts through *The Newsletter for People with Lactose Intolerance and Milk Allergy.* For information, write to Commercial Writing and Design, P.O. Box 3129, Ann Arbor, MI 48106-3129, or call 313-572-9134.

Denise Boneau, Chicago

Check out alternative treatments

My seven-year-old daughter Ruthanne was diagnosed with asthma two years

---

Keeping Your Home Free of Allergens

Many allergy sufferers can be helped by some relatively simple routines.

- Periodically spray carpets and rugs with tannic acid, available in allergy-supply catalogs and stores. It keeps dust mites (a major culprit in many allergies) at bay for up to two months.
- Keep plush toys out of children's beds. Spray them periodically with tannic acid or, every few weeks, place favorite stuffed animals or dolls in a plastic bag in the freezer overnight. The cold temperature kills the mites.
- Encase mattresses and pillows in special dust-proof covers. Launder the bedding once a week and the covers three times a year in hot water. Use polyester blend sheets and blankets instead of cotton or wool, which attract more dust mites.
- Use washable throw rugs instead of carpeting in the allergic child's bedroom. Also replace dust-catching curtains with simple window shades.
- Damp mop the floors and wash other surfaces frequently.
- Limit household pets access to an allergic child's room. Once every two weeks or so, wash the pet. (Damp sponge or sink spray a cat; wash a dog in a tub.)
- Use a high-efficiency particulate air (HEPA) filter, which traps dust particles, in rooms where the child spends time.
- Limit your child's exposure to cigarette, fireplace and other smoke.

ago. When she first began her nebulizer treatments, she never resisted. But now she's not willing to let her friends see her use the equipment. We went to the allergist who taught her how to use a hand-held inhaler instead. Since she feels that this is a big kid treatment, she's no longer embarrassed about it. This method also allows us to travel more easily without hauling the eight-pound machine with us and makes it easier for her to go to after-school activities without having to stop home first for her treatment.

Rosemary McIntyre, Middleton, New York

Provide portable snacks

Teach your children to say no to restricted foods with confidence. Also make sure that the allergic child's backpack always contains snacks that are approved. When my five-year-old son goes to other people's houses, they often offer him foods that contain peanuts, which could kill him. So many things contain peanut oil that all outside foods are off limits. My son knows that with the exception of milk, cheese and fruits, all other foods are to be avoided unless I read the label first. Having his own snacks eliminates his need to eat unchecked foods.

Essie Hicks, Tupelo, Mississippi

Note food restrictions

I urge all parents to check with their children's friends' parents about any food allergies or other restrictions before a child spends time at their house. I once nearly cajoled a child to eat a slice of pizza only to find out later that this child is highly allergic to tomatoes. I shiver to

PEDIATRICKS

Pointers on Shots

To lessen the pain of a shot, have your child exhale repeatedly through her mouth as though blowing soap bubbles. Researchers at Ohio State University found that children who do this are less likely to cry, say ouch or need comforting. "Blowing helps distract children and gives them a measure of control," says researcher Gina M. French, M.D.

To take the sting out of shots, let the rubbing alcohol that's applied before the shot dry completely before the doctor inserts the needle. When rubbing alcohol that's swabbed on the site doesn't thoroughly dry, it gets pushed under the skin by the needle and causes stinging.

think of what might have happened if I'd kept insisting he try some. Fortunately, the child refused.

Alison Freehold, New Haven, Connecticut

Find support

Our sons, ages 11 and 8, both have severe asthma. About two years ago, we joined a parent support group for parents of kids with respiratory problems and I learned a lot about new forms of treatment. Even better, the boys joined the child peer group and were happy to find that there were other kids with their condition who led active lives.

Scott and Melinda Dewey, Pasadena, California

Find the right tools

My son's asthma attacks always seemed to come upon him suddenly until he and I learned about a device called a peak-flow meter. This is a wonderful tool that measures his lung capacity by seeing how high he can blow a needle up a tube. Long before any symptoms appear, the meter will register that his lung capacity is compromised and we can begin medication to offset an attack. Since using the meter, he has never been sick.

Dianna Ferlick, Arlington, Virginia

Invite friends to your allergen-free home

Both of my sons are very allergic to cats and cannot visit anyone who has a cat. This has kept them from some parties and overnights. I make a real point of inviting lots of kids into our home so that my boys don't feel left out of the social scene. Hardly a day goes by when I don't have a houseful of kids, but the noise and mess are worth it to help my sons be part of the gang.

Peggy Merlin, Philadelphia

Enabling Disabled Children

Having a physical, intellectual or emotional disability does not mean that a child cannot enjoy social and school interactions, as these parents have found.

Share your experience

My four-year-old was born with spina bifida and uses a walker. I was afraid that the other children in her nursery school might make fun of her, so we came up with a plan. With the teacher's and other parents' permission, I rented a half-dozen walkers for a day so that all of the children could have some experience using a walker. It really opened up their eyes to all that my Casey *could* do with this aid.

Evelyn Casey-Minton, Jamaica Estates, New York

Provide exposure

Since my son must use a wheelchair, I take him to all sorts of special sports events like wheelchair marathons and wheelchair basketball games so that he can see that many other sports enthusiasts like himself can be terrific athletes, too.

Michael Harrington, Evanston, Illinois

Foster talents

I think it's important to let every child develop one special talent. My nine-year-old son has limited use of his legs due to a car accident when he was two. But he loves chess. I bought him chess books and computer chess programs and even got him a chance to meet a master chess player who taught him some strategies. Knowing he's the best nine-year-old chess player in his community really makes Luke feel good about himself and his talents.

Mrs. Peter Donovan, Elmhurst, New York

Help educate others

Education is the key to helping your child learn to live with other, able-bodied youngsters. Make it a point to let other children understand your child's
(continued on page 164)

PARENTS' RESOURCE

For Parents of Children with Disabilities

Publications

The Disability Bookshop Catalog stocks publications on caring for children with vision and hearing impairments, physical and mental limitations and general health problems as well as a resource director for parents. To receive a catalog, send $3 to The Disability Bookshop, P.O. Box 129, Vancouver, WA 98666-0129.

The Children With Special Needs Collection features a wide selection of books addressing the needs of families whose children have developmental or physical disabilities. Look for it at national bookstore chains such as Barnes & Noble or B. Dalton.

The Special Education Handbook (Teachers College Press) by Kenneth Shore, Ph.D., is a comprehensive guide to help parents through the special-education process. There's information on referrals, testing, diagnosis and on warning signs that suggest an educational disability.

A Place for Me (National Association for the Education of Young Children), by Phyllis A. Chandler, advises caregivers on helping disabled children achieve independence. Send a check or money order to NAEYC, 1509 16th Street NW, Washington, DC 20036-1426.

Richard Simmons' Reach for Fitness (Warner Books/Karl Lorimar Video) is a book and a video that outline an exercise and nutrition plan for children with any of 43 disabilities. (In addition to the benefit these products provide for the purchaser, all profits go to a foundation that provides exercise programs for the disabled.)

Products

The Jesana Ltd. Catalog contains special furniture, toys and games geared to disabled children. To receive a free catalog, call 800-443-4728.

Exceptionally Yours manufactures clothing for children with disabilities. Items are moderately priced, machine washable, with Velcro closures or zippers with large rings. For a free brochure, write to 22 Prescott Street, Newtonville, MA 02160.

Hal's Pals are cheery, soft-sculptured dolls, each with a different disability. Made by a nonprofit division of Mattel, they can be ordered by calling 800-524-8697.

Funtastic Therapy catalog offers toys, games, books and educational aids for children who have learning disabilities. For a free catalog, write to RD#4, Box 14, Cranberry, NJ 08512.

Information and services

The Sibling Information Network offers help in explaining the disability of a sibling. Contact the network at the A. J. Papanikou Center/UAP, 991 Main Street, Suite 3A, East Hartford, CT 06108.

The National Lekotek Center, based in Evanston, Illinois, works to integrate children with disabilities into family activities and early childhood programs. Fifty centers nationwide are equipped with toy libraries, adaptive equipment, play materials and books for families to borrow. For more information, call 847-328-0001.

Camps for Children with Disabilities is a brochure that guides families on choosing an appropriate summer camp. Send a self-addressed, stamped envelope to the National Easter Seal Society, 2023 West Ogden Avenue, Chicago, IL 60612.

Parents of Chronically Ill Children (PCIC) offers resources and referrals on many types of disabilities. Write to PCIC at 1527 Maryland Avenue, Springfield, IL 62702.

The National Information Center for Children and Youth with Disabilities provides information about any type of disability. Write to NICHY at 7926 Jones Branch Drive, Suite 1100, McLean, VA 22102, or call 800-999-5599.

The Council for Exceptional Children runs the ERIC Clearinghouse on Handicapped and Gifted Children, specializing in services and information for families of children with disabilities. Write to the Council at 1920 Association Drive, Reston, VA 22091, or call 703-264-9474.

The National Information Clearinghouse for Infants with Disabilities and Life-Threatening Conditions helps parents of children with disabilities from birth through age three identify services available both nationwide and locally. Call 800-922-9234.

The Association for Retarded Citizens offers support for parents of children with mental delays. Check the white pages of your phone book for your local chapter.

The Shriners Hospitals for Crippled Children is a network of 22 free pediatric-specialty hospitals for children with orthopedic and burn conditions. Call 800-237-5055; in Florida, call 800-282-9161.

The Social Security Administration offers a Supplemental Security Income Program. To ascertain your child's eligibility, call 800-772-1213.

condition so that it doesn't scare them. Many children think that a disease is contagious even when it is not, or they think that a child is ill as a punishment for something that he has done. All kids need to understand the real nature of a disability.

Harlee Mitchell, Matawan, New Jersey

Find the right school

My daughter has been blind since birth. Finding the right school for her was a priority from the time she was an infant. Quality of programs varies widely and it's up to us parents to get the best for our children. While I first wanted nothing more than to mainstream Samantha, I found that a school that was especially established to help visually impaired children was really the best place for her. Look around. Move if you have to in order to get the best education for your child. The rewards are definitely worth it.

Madelaine Tucci, Yonkers, New York

Give yourself breaks

I have a seven-year-old son with autism. I urge anyone with a disabled child to get outside help so that you can have some time off. I've used such breaks to go to meetings, shop, spend time with my husband, read and even sleep. Try contacting your local American Red Cross, Muscular Dystrophy Association, the March of Dimes, Department of Social Services, state university or church or synagogue. Even if these groups can not help you directly, they may know someone else who can.

Cindy Raivio, Dixon, California

Educate yourself

My two-year-old son, Paul, has cystic fibrosis. I would highly recommend the book *Whole Parent, Whole Child: A Parents' Guide to Raising a Child with a Chronic Illness,* by Broatch Haig and Patricia Moynihan (DCI Publishing) for any parent dealing with an illness. To order, call 800-848-2793.

Janet Brandel, Seicksley, Pennsylvania

Find support

Our eight-month-old son, Ryan, was born with VATER syndrome, which includes severe cardiac defects and orthopedic problems. He has already had the first of many open-heart surgeries. Please remember that nurturing yourself has to be one of your highest priorities. Our local early-intervention program has provided me with the social support of parents who share my feelings of anxiety, sadness, fear and loneliness, as well as hope and immense love.

Evon Buckley, Livonia, Michigan

Seasonal Health: Keeping Warm in Winter

Each season brings with it special challenges. What are some of the best ways to deal with the year's cycle of health concerns?

When a chill is in the air, children playing outdoors need to be bundled up a bit more than they might like to be. Here are some great ideas to help kids stay warm and dry.

Winter Safety Wrap-Up

- Teach a child never to walk on frozen ponds and to avoid walking on ice whenever possible.
- Prepare children for participating in any winter sport by carefully reviewing safety rules. Invest in lessons whenever possible.

- Do not allow children to ride sleds in a prone position, to throw snowballs at others nor to engage in reckless behavior when snowboarding, sledding, skiing or playing.
- Review the signs of frostbite with your children.

Opt for sweatshirts

If your child doesn't like wearing a jacket, he'll probably take it off and leave it somewhere, so buy him heavyweight sweatshirts instead. Boys, especially, seem to prefer them. The kind with hoods are good for fall weather.

Kimberlee Huson, Bremerton, Washington

Let experience teach

Let a child who refuses to bundle up play outside without wearing a jacket or coat. Have a cup of hot chocolate waiting for him when he comes back inside because he's cold. This way you show him that even when he makes mistakes, you'll be there to pick him back up.

Julie Holla, Ulm, Montana

Practice indoors

If your child resists wearing a hat in winter, let him get comfortable with one indoors before he goes outside. Have him try on his hat and then look in the mirror to see what he looks like in it. Tell him how good he looks. Then pretend to try on the hat to show him that mommies wear hats, too. Also tell your son that just like adults, he must wear his hat outside to keep warm and to keep from getting sick.

Julia Bowers, Dublin, Ohio

Model hat wearing

My three-year-old son wants to do whatever I do, so when I want him to wear a hat, I wear one myself. Then I say, "See, even daddies and mommies wear hats."

William-Paul Thomas, Houston

PEDIATRICKS

Prevent Chapping

Outdoor play in the winter can cause your child's face to chap, especially if she has a runny nose or has been drooling. To prevent chapping, apply a thin layer of petroleum jelly or gentle moisturizing cream or sunblock to the exposed area of her face before she goes out.

Frostbite Do's and Don'ts

Prolonged exposure to cold, wind and moisture can increase the risk of frostbite—when skin and underlying tissues freeze, turning skin pale, numb, glossy and hard to the touch, says Carl Milks, M.D., a pediatrician and advisor to the Upper Delaware Nordic Ski Patrol. Frostbite primarily affects the cheeks, hands, feet, nose and ears.

To prevent frostbite

- DON'T let your child play outdoors if the temperature approaches 5°F and 0°F windchill.
- DO dress your child warmly in layers of natural fibers, making sure especially that hands, ears, feet and faces are covered in cold, windy weather.

Choose waterproof mittens over warm gloves if your child is playing in the snow. Place plastic bags over socks and under shoes or boots to keep feet dry.

- DO give a child plenty of fluids and a hearty meal or snack before she goes outside. This helps blood distribute heat to the body's extremities.
- DO teach your child to learn the warning signs of frostbite and to come indoors if they get wet or at the first sign of numbness.

Go for comfort

I let my daughter pick out her winter hat from the store and I make sure that the fabric is soft, not scratchy.

Dori Ann Waile, Levittown, New York

Make wearing a hat into a game

Have a contest to see who gets to the car first with his or her hat on. Another idea is to wait to put the hat on until you're outside because putting it on inside may make a child too hot.

Martha Baty, Lake Oswego, Oregon

Choose earmuffs and hoods

My son won't wear a hat, but he will wear earmuffs. I also buy coats with hoods so that when the earmuffs aren't keeping him warm enough, he'll choose on his own to put up his hood.

Salena Moreno, Tarrytown, New York

Wear winter helmets

To keep my son, age eight, and my daughters, ages seven and four, safe while sleigh riding, I insist that they wear their bike helmets over their woolen

- DO bring a child indoors for a change of clothes immediately if she gets at all wet.

Warning signs of frostbite
- Ice crystals form on the skin.
- Sufferer feels pain and burning sensation as skin begins to thaw.
- Skin turns red, pale or white.
- Skin blisters and/or dark patches form under the skin.

To treat frostbite
- DO bring your child indoors at once.
- DO cover the affected areas with extra clothing, a warm, wet washcloth or blankets. As rewarming occurs, your child should feel a tingling and burning sensation and the skin should turn red.
- DO seek medical attention if the skin blisters, if you see dark blue or black areas under the skin or if the skin remains numb and/or painful after 15 minutes of warming.
- DO dry the affected areas. Wrap in sterile dry dressings, separating fingers and toes if you can't see a doctor right away.
- DON'T apply heat from heating pads, which could burn numb skin.
- DON'T rub sensitive frostbitten skin, which can cause further damage.

caps. Because the helmets are made to fit snugly without hats underneath, I switch helmets for the winter. My son wears my larger helmet, my seven-year-old wears his helmet and my younger daughter wears her big sister's helmet. To keep the straps from hurting (which they do when they're frozen), I knitted small tubes that I pull the straps through.

Justine Tremont, Montreal

Prepare for changing weather

Because temperatures can change so much during the day, I always pack sweaters, gloves and hats inside my children's backpacks. That way, if the afternoon is chillier than the morning or if they're going to stay out after school be-fore coming home, they always have additional clothes to put on.

Veronica Sales, Pueblo, Colorado

Provide refueling breaks

My children's favorite winter activity is snow sculpting. I don't want to discourage this creative play but I worry about frostbite. Now I have a rule that they must come indoors for a warm-up hot chocolate or other snack every half hour. I invite any kids who happen to be in our yard in, too, so that everyone gets a chance to refuel.

Terri Nordstrom, Minneapolis

Bring snow indoors

My two-year-old son, Christopher, loves to play in the snow but he gets cold very quickly. I bring a bucket of snow into the house and let him play (still wearing his boots and mittens) with the snow in the bathtub. There's no mess and he stays warm.

Arlene Cassiano, Whitestone, New York

Teach safety skills

The most important thing you can teach a child who's learning a winter sport like sledding, skating or skiing is how to fall (in the case of sledding, how to fall off a fast-moving sled). Until each of my children could show me that they could stop quickly by falling correctly, I didn't let them participate in these sports unsupervised.

Ursella Brompkin, Ithaca, New York

Play together

Make participating in winter sports a family affair, not just something for the kids to do. By playing outdoors together, you not only get to supervise, but you get a good workout yourself. Because my daughter wanted to learn to ice skate, for instance, I took up the sport, too, and now we enjoy it together. We're also planning to learn to ski.

Margaret Hanlon, Poughkeepsie, New York

Summertime Safety

Summer offers its own pleasures—and its own discomforts. Here are some great ideas to help make the living easy.

Summer Do's and Don'ts

Picnics

- DO keep hands and utensils very clean when preparing food.
- DO keep foods in a cooler, even for short trips.
- DO refrigerate cooked vegetables and hard-cooked eggs as well as meat and poultry.
- DON'T rely on appearance and odor alone to make sure food is safe.

Heat protection

- DO make sure your child drinks lots of liquid, preferably cold water, before, during and after activities.
- DO schedule cooling off periods when it's very hot.

- DO limit outdoor playtime during the peak heat hours of 11:00 A.M. to 3:00 P.M.
- DON'T ever leave a child (or a pet) unattended in a car, even with the windows open, for even a minute.

Sun protection

- DO keep babies under one year of age out of the sun as much as possible.
- DO make sure that you and your children use sunscreen even if you're outdoors for only short periods of time.
- DON'T think that there's no risk of sun overexposure on a cloudy, overcast day.

Choose the right bathing suit

If your daughter is toilet-training, buy two-piece bathing suits instead, which are a lot easier to remove (especially when wet). If you're afraid of too much exposure to her tummy, put a T-shirt on over the bathing-suit top.

Millicent Casey-O'Brien, New York City

Keep toes covered

Sandals are great as a fashion item, but they're terrible play shoes. After bandaging hurt toes and skinned knees and elbows from the many falls my daughter took while wearing toeless shoes, I now make a point of buying only sneakers.

Tracy Powell, Address withheld

Choose long pants

If your son, like mine, is learning to ride a bike (or Rollerblade) in the summer, encourage him to wear jeans with reinforced knees instead of shorts, to cut down on scrapes. It's a good alternative to wearing knee pads, which my son finds too uncomfortable. He readily wears his helmet and wrist braces so I don't argue about the knee pads as long as he wears long pants.

Colleen Hunter, Cape May, New Jersey

Cover shoulders with a tank suit

My son Tim burns easily. But he hates wearing a T-shirt while swimming. So, in a catalog, I found a great one-piece tank

Water safety

- DO supervise kids closely when they're in or near the water.
- DO learn to swim and to perform CPR.
- DON'T take kids swimming where there are no lifeguards.
- DON'T assume that inflatable toys or swimming lessons will keep kids safe from drowning.

Insect bites

- DO apply insect repellent liberally to clothing.
- DO plan activities to avoid the times and places where insects are most active.

- DO eliminate insect breeding grounds around your house.
- DO see a doctor if you think you or your child are allergic to stings or have been exposed to tick-borne diseases.

Summer poison control

- DO store pesticides (including spray containers of insect repel-lents) and barbecue lighter fluids in locked containers, out of child's reach.
- DO teach children to avoid eating berries, seeds, mushrooms and any other growing items that he or she finds outdoors.

What to Do about Deer Ticks

Deer ticks, which thrive in wooded and grassy areas, carry bacteria and viruses that can lead to Lyme disease, Rocky Mountain spotted fever, Colorado tick fever, and deer fly fever.

To avoid getting bitten

- Dress defensively. Wear long pants tucked into socks and long-sleeve shirts.
- Consider applying a repellent such as Deet to clothing before taking entering tick-infested areas. Use it sparingly, and do not apply it directly to children's skin.
- After walking in an area that is likely to harbor ticks, remove and wash clothes immediately. Check your body and children's bodies immediately for ticks, especially around the hairline.

If you find a tick

- A tick that has not yet burrowed into the skin can simply be removed. Use a tissue and catch it between your fingers. Dispose of it immediately.

- If a tick has burrowed into the skin, use a tweezer, not your fingernails, to remove it. Grab the tick as close to the skin as possible and pull it straight out slowly, without twisting it. If this method doesn't work, use a heated matchstick to urge it to let go. (Light and then blow out a match and apply the hot tip to the tick's back, being careful not to burn the skin.)
- Wash the bite area thoroughly with soap and water after removing the tick.
- Apply iodine or another antiseptic to prevent infection.
- Be alert for signs of infection, which may show up from a day or so to a month later. Redness around the bite area, a bull's-eye rash with a clear center and inflamed red circles anywhere on the body, flulike symptoms (headache, fever, swollen glands, stiff neck and fatigue) suggest Lyme disease, which must be treated with prescribed antibiotics.

suit that looks like diving gear. I also bought one for his cousin, in the hopes that Tim would wear the unusual suit more readily if Ben also had one. Fortunately, they both like their suits and I can relax a bit instead of worrying about Tim's back and shoulders getting too much sun.

Karyn Sanderson-Sparks, Otis, Massachusetts

Use your head

My twins hated wearing their sun hats when they were toddlers. To make wearing a hat cool, I took out books from the library with hat themes. *Whose Hat Was That,* by Brian and Rebecca Wildsmith (HarBrace), *My Hats,* by Sia Aryai (Price Stern Sloan) and two of my childhood favorites *Caps for Sale,* by Esphyr Slobednika

(HarperCollins) and *The Cat in the Hat*, by Dr. Seuss (Random House). The stories helped me build a strong case for wearing a hat. Now I don't even have to ask.

Kate Vander Sluis, Santa Rosa, California

Give choices in sun hats

Because my two-year-old son often refused to wear a sun hat, I hung hats in a variety of styles on a hat rack for him. He doesn't fight me now that he's in control and can choose a hat of the day.

Linda Adams, Ames, Iowa

Open an umbrella

My 18-month-old daughter hates to wear a sun hat, so I attached a sun umbrella to her stroller for our walks to and from the playground. At the playground, I find a shaded area to play. Of course, I also apply sunscreen and have her wear long sleeves and pants whenever it's not too hot.

Jennifer Pogrin, San Diego

Smooth on the sunscreen

To encourage my daughter, Lillie, to wear sunscreen, I let her put some on me and then I put it on her.

Caroline Yolenz, Selma, Alabama

Pitch a tent

While waiting for our shade trees to grow, we've installed an outdoor tent to provide sun protection in our backyard.

Kimberly Tell, Bridgeton, Missouri

Cool the pool

To keep the temperature in my children's wading pool cold on a hot summer day, I make blocks of ice by freezing water in a variety of containers, such as empty

PARENTS' RESOURCE

Backyard Safety

- For information about minimizing exposure to pesticides, call the National Pesticide Telecommunications Network at 800-858-PEST.
- For a free brochure about safety precautions to take when using power tools and equipment, write to the Outdoor Power Equipment Institute, 341 S. Patrick Street, Alexandria, VA 22314 and request "Make Your Day with Safety."
- For expert advice on pool safety and maintenance, all the Pool Care hotline at 800-222-2348.

milk cartons and plastic soda bottles. Then I cut out the frozen blocks and drop them into the pool. It's a built-in cooling system, and a great way to recycle.

Marianne Crane, South Bend, Indianapolis

Cover car seats

Always cover the car seat with a blanket if you're parking in a sunny spot. The vinyl seats and the seatbelt buckles can get extremely hot and can burn a child.

Paul Liptook, Englewood, New Jersey

Start a cap collection

I'm sure that the sunscreen I put on my seven-year-old wears off at day camp, so I bought her an array of neat baseball caps to wear to shade her face. I also never buy sleeveless tops.

Michaela Spachek, Houston

PARENTS' ALERT

Poison Ivy, Oak and Sumac

Teach your child what to look for to avoid exposure to poison ivy, oak and sumac by learning to recognize their leaves. Poison ivy and oak each have 3 leaves per cluster; sumac has 7 to 13 leaves per cluster. Poison ivy has white berries. Poison oak has yellow, hairy berries and sumac has cream-colored berries. If your child is playing where poison ivy may be growing, dress her in protective clothing—long pants and sleeves, socks and gloves. Consider applying a product such as Ivy Shield, which is sold in most drugstores, to exposed skin areas. In a pinch, you can substitute spray-on deodorant, which can prevent the oils in the plants from penetrating the skin.

If you come into contact

- Wash with soap and water within 15 minutes to avoid a rash. Also wash any clothing and tools that have touched the plants.

To relieve itching, try one or more of these

- Make a compress of ice-cold whole milk. Simply soak gauze or other clean cloth in the milk and apply the compress to the rash. Rinse well with clear water.
- Apply calamine lotion or milk of magnesia.
- Take an oatmeal bath, using a product such as Aveeno.
- Apply ice for about one minute; if you don't have ice available, run cold water over the rash.
- Apply zinc oxide.
- For blistering rashes, make a paste of water and baking soda and apply it to the rash.

To destroy the plants

- Dig them up, roots and all, and dispose of them in a sealed container. Thoroughly wash yourself, clothing and tools immediately.
- Never burn them. This releases the toxins into the air where they can be inhaled and cause serious lung damage.

Review pool rules

As the owner of an in-ground pool, I find that we have many more friends in the summer. I make a point of talking to the parents of every child who uses the pool about safety rules. I also have a huge sign to remind kids of the rules. And I never let the children younger than about age 12 play anywhere near the pool if I or another adult is not there to supervise. With my teenage son and his friends, I insist that there be a least three kids (one to help a friend in trouble and another to run for more help if needed) before they can swim unsupervised. Any child who disobeys a rule is kept out for a day for his or her first offense and a week for a second offense.

Name withheld, Montclair, New Jersey

Provide safety vests

We often have pool parties where lots of children are present. I insist that every child wear a safety vest—even over dress clothes—when poolside.

Tamara Schultz, Hampton Bays, New York

Dress to ward off ticks

We live in the town for which Lyme disease was named, so I'm always looking for ways to cut down on my children's exposure to ticks. Whenever they play in the woods or on the grass, I put them in long, light-colored clothing and tuck their socks over the pants legs. I also treat their clothing with tick spray and I insist that they wear hats.

Lenore Greene, Lyme, Connecticut

Serve snow

If you know that your children should be drinking more water, especially on hot summer days, serve them water over crushed ice. My kids love to crunch the snow, and I'm glad they're getting more water.

Sybil Johnson, Thermopolis, Wyoming

Keep drinks handy

I always keep small sports bottles filled with water or juice in the refrigerator for

PEDIATRICKS

For Beach Boo-Boos

Insect bite itches

If your kids are itchy from insect bites, take them swimming. The cold water from the pool or ocean will soothe their skin. If you can't get to water, let them soak in a cool bathtub with a half cup of cornstarch mixed into the water.

Sand in the eyes

Pull the upper eyelid slightly away from the cornea by gently tugging on the lashes. If the sand doesn't fall out, irrigate the eye with tap water or, if possible, with a balanced salt solution, sold in most pharmacies in a sterile squeeze bottle. Squeeze a thin stream into the corners of the affected eye and have your child blink. Gently wipe the sand out with a damp cotton swab.

each of my children. I find that they drink more because they can help themselves at any time.

Faith Stroka, Parma, Ohio

Teach swimming

There is nothing you can teach your children that is more important than swimming. The YMCA offers excellent programs that include not only swimming skills but water safety in general. My two sons have each become good swimmers because of these courses.

Linda Brown, Cincinnati

Family Fun on Wheels

Bike riding and skating are among those wonderful lifelong pursuits that parents and children can enjoy together. Here are some ideas to make early learning more fun.

Get a good fit

When my daughter was first learning to ride a bike, we used an old bike that really was a bit too small for her, even with the seat and handlebars adjusted as much as possible. I didn't want to invest in a new bike until I was sure she would be able to ride, but the small bike, we found, was much more difficult to learn on. With a good-fitting bike, she learned much more quickly.

Evelyn Nyes, Vancouver, Washington

Skip training wheels

My older son had a lot of trouble learning to balance when we took the training wheels off his two-wheeler. But since my second son learned to ride without ever using training wheels, the process was much quicker. I encouraged my sister not to put training wheels on my nephew's bike and she, too, found that he learned faster without them.

Kathleen Horvath, Brooklyn, New York

Helmet How-To's

Young rollerskaters, skateboarders and cyclists—including babies in safety seats—all need to wear helmets to protect themselves from head injuries. For all-around protection, choose a bicycle helmet with a seal of approval from the American Society for Testing and Materials (ASTM), the American National Standards Institute (ANSI), or the Snell Memorial Foundation.

But being well-made is not enough: A helmet also has to fit well. The front should be less than an inch above the eyebrows, the sides should cover the ears and the back should cover the little bump at the base of the skull. The helmet should be snug enough not to slip off when you tug on it, but it should allow enough movement for comfort. "You don't want your child to feel pinched or choked or she might not keep it on," says Dave Halstead, chairman of the headgear committee at ASTM.

Here are other features.

• Opt for a hard-shell helmet for children older than two. Made of hard plastic, this type of helmet resists penetration by sharp objects such as rocks or by a bike pedal. For kids who won't

Let go

I learned to ride a bike with my father holding on and running alongside me, so I thought that's how my son would want to learn. But he preferred that I just stay nearby while he balanced himself.

Mike Dawson, Toronto

Sample different bikes

Before buying a buy based on which one looked coolest, I had my daughter try out a few different models in different sizes to have her see which one felt best to her. To my surprise, she was better able to handle hand brakes than coaster brakes.

Madalaine Crew, Ames, Iowa

Start on grass

My daughter discovered the best place to learn to ride—on a flat grassy area near our home. The grass provided a nice safe landing in case of a fall. It prevented her bike from going faster than she felt comfortable. And it provided good traction. A few hours on the grass did more for her skills than weeks on concrete had done.

Marilee Stodhouser, Hannibal, Missouri

Find a good spot

Teaching my twin sons to ride their bikes in the playground resulted in too many near-misses with pedestrians. So we went to a corporate parking lot on a week-

wear hard-shell helmets, try a lighter, microshell helmet. Choose a foam helmet for kids two and under—hard-shell helmets are too heavy for young children's neck muscles to support—but make sure that it has a fabric covering. In the event of an accident, foam can stick to the road's surface, causing neck injuries. Fabric allows the helmet to slide.

- Look for an easy-to-use clasp. Most children under eight will need help manipulating the clasp. Older kids should be able to work it on their own: If it's too difficult for them, they

won't wear the helmet.
- Look for reflective material so that if your child cannot make it home before dusk, she will be visible.
- Check the helmet regularly to make sure that it still fits properly on your child's head and that it has not been damaged. "Most helmets are for one-accident use only," says Halstead, "and they can be damaged even if left sitting at the bottom of a toy box." If you spot defects, such as cracks, large dents, flat surfaces, missing foam or torn fabric, buy a new helmet.

end, which proved to be a perfect spot. The asphalt was smooth and the area had no pedestrians or cars to worry about.

Nicholas Vermer, San Diego

Add no-slip pedals

To keep my two-year-old son's feet from slipping off the pedals of his tricycle, I applied bathtub decals around the pedals. Now he has no trouble at all.

Terri Barnhill, Address withheld

Safety, Not Showing Off

Showing off new skills is a way to boost kids' confidence. It's important, however, to help kids work within their skill level and not to push those limits by being unnecessarily competitive.

Find new activities

If your child is doing too much showing off in a particular sport, find other activities in his interest range; gather his friends together and go to the skating rink, the swimming pool or a movie. This should give the kids something to do and help to alleviate the tension that arises from conflicts over safety.

Carrie Triggs, Cheyenne, Wyoming

Educate kids to hazards

To bring home the message about why safety is important when a child is rollerblading, biking or engaged in any sport, make an appointment, if possible, with an emergency-room doctor who can tell your child exactly what can happen when children hurt themselves. After your

son or daughter has learned about what it is like to be comatose or confined to a wheelchair for life, he or she will probably be more careful. An outside authority figure like an experienced doctor may have more influence on your child's behavior than Mom and Dad's constant reminders.

Vicki Surges, Carson City, Nevada

Praise responsibility

Complement your children on their generally responsible attitude and the fact that they *are* careful. Then, ask them to take responsibility for their own safety. Tell them how such a step is part of becoming an adult. Since independence is what children really want, this point of view may prove to be very appealing.

Debbie Daugherty, Walnut Creek, California

Take away privileges

I told my son that whenever he acts irresponsibly on his bike, skateboard or rollerblades, I'll simply put the equipment off limits for three days. He only tested my resolve once and did without his bike for three days. After that, he's been much more willing to obey the rules rather than risk loosing his wheels.

Janice Rodriquez-Stein, Riverdale, New York

Teaching Street Smarts

Eventually, every child must learn to negotiate the world on his or her own. The knowledge that's needed to stay safe outside doesn't come suddenly when a child reaches the teenage years. Instead, it's taught step-by-step.

Street-Smart Kids: An Age-by-Age Guide

Here are the safety rules that kids in each age group need to be taught.

Four and under

Always hold the child's hand when walking in streets or parking lots.

Teach children these rules.

- The street is dangerous and off limits.
- Watch out for cars. Even though you can see cars, the drivers can't see you.
- Stop, look and listen before stepping off the curb.
- Tell a grown-up if a toy rolls into the street. Do not get it yourself, even from the curbside.

Five to nine

Children should not be crossing the street unattended under the age of 10. Because most children this age no longer hold your hand as you walk, instruct them as follows:

- Never dart out into a street, driveway or parking lot.
- If you must cross the street alone, seek out help from a school crossing guard or other trusted adult.
- Even when we have the light, look both ways before crossing. Pay particular attention to sirens and flashing lights because emergency vehicles may not stop at red lights.
- Walk, don't run, across the street.

Before allowing an older child to walk unescorted, conduct a few trial runs to make sure that she has absorbed and follows the rules.

Put up a barrier

When my four-year-old twins play ball or color with chalk on the driveway, I automatically put a large trash can or the lawn chair at the end of the driveway. It stops passing motorists from using our driveway to make a U-turn or visitors from pulling in too quickly.

Elizabeth Carlson, North Andover, Massachusetts

Lend a hand

After countless power struggles with my three-year-old son over holding my hand when we cross the street, I needed to find a new approach. So one day I asked him if he would please hold my hand to keep me safe. This seemed to do the trick. Now he feels like a big shot watching out for me.

Betty Hunt, San Leandro, California

Mark safe areas

Are you worried that your child might run into the street when he plays on the driveway? Do what I did: Dip the sole of an adult shoe in white paint and design a trail of prints along the driveway. My son knows to yell stop when he gets to the end of the path. Of course, this is not a replacement for supervision, but it provides a good lesson in safety and limits.

Theresa Benedict, Chester, New York

Explain the rules

When my daughter was about four, I realized that she had no idea why we stopped at red lights and looked both ways before crossing even at a green light. I began to verbalize everything that I was doing automatically, saying things like, "We're stopping now because the light is red," or "The light has turned green and that means we can cross. But we always look both ways first to make sure that no car is coming." Once I started saying what I was doing, she began to understand a lot better.

Irene Proloff, New York City

Playground Safety

The playground is a place to have fun. Too often, however, it's the scene of injuries. Though all mishaps can't be prevented, some can. Here's how.

Check for hot spots

Before your child uses any metal playground equipment that's exposed to the hot sun, check it with your hands first. I wish I'd done that before my two-year-old son, Matthew, slid down a hot slide in his shorts in July. He screamed and I realized how hot the surface had become.

ASK THE EXPERTS

Is My Playground Safe?

Every year, more than 250,000 children are injured in playground equipment–related incidents. A check on (and improvements in) the conditions in your child's playground can reduce that number.

Equipment

- To prevent dangerous falls, the height of slides and other climbing equipment should not exceed six feet above the ground for preschoolers and seven feet for school-age children.
- To prevent head entrapment and strangulation, no opening into which a child could place his head (ladders, handrails, bars) should be less than 3½ by 9 inches.

- To prevent crashes, swings should be placed no more than two per bay, with at least two feet between each swing and 30 inches between a swing and a support post. Toddler swings should always have leg dividers to prevent children from slipping out and should not be in the same bay as big-kid swings.
- All equipment must be in good repair—no splinters, loose or missing pieces or sharp edges. Tire swings should contain drainage holes to prevent water accumulation.

Surfaces

- Safe surfaces offer some give when a child falls. Wood chips and pea

He got a burn and has since refused to use the slide.

Jennifer Pissaro, Cheyenne, Wyoming

Lobby for improvements

I often wonder if playground designers have children. The slide in our new playground is made of tubular metal. The underside, which children frequently run under, contains protruding metal bands where the tubes of the slide are attached to one another. Two children cracked their heads on these pieces before a group of us parents got together and went to the park commissioner with a request that rubber safety covers be placed over the metal. It took us almost a year to get it down, but now the playground is much safer. I urge all parents to take their child's playground safety seriously enough to do something to improve the safety for all.

Eloise Parker-Katz, New York City

Check it out

Every time my child uses park equipment, I check it out to make sure that nothing has broken since our last use. Once I found that a swing seat was about to come unhinged. I tied the swing to the

gravel are excellent materials if kept at a depth of 9 to 12 inches. Sand, too, is a forgiving surface. Concrete, grass and hard-packed dirt are unacceptable ground covers.

General maintenance

- The playground area should be free of broken glass, trash and animal droppings. Trash barrels should be accessible and regularly emptied.
- The sandbox should be thoroughly cleaned and sand replaced several times a season. Only pure sand, containing no chemical byproducts should be used. If animals have access to the sandbox, declare it off limits to your children.

Playground behavior

- Make sure that your children use the playground equipment only as it was intended and use the handrails and other safety features of the equipment.
- Teach your children the rules that apply to each kind of play. For instance, their partner's feet must be on the ground before a child gets off a see-saw. No jumping off moving swings or from high places such as the top of slides. No pushing, running in crowded areas, standing too close to the swing area or riding a bike in pedestrian-only areas.

post so that neither my child nor anyone else's would be the one to fall off when the seat came apart.

Mickey Tandoro, Edgewater, New Jersey

Teach safety rules

It's important to remind your own child—and other children, if necessary—of playground safety rules. I've had to tell my own and others to step back from the swing area, not to jump off the tops of climbing structures and not to climb up slides. If all parents would get involved with all the kids at the playground, there would be far fewer injuries.

Diane Jakowski, Milwaukee

Lost and Found

It's terrifying. One minute your child is right next to you in the supermarket aisle and the next, you can't find her. These ideas can help you keep these all-too-common dramas from becoming part of your or your child's experience.

Have a clear rule

My rule for my four-year-old daughter whenever we're anywhere that I feel we could accidentally get separated is very simple: *You* stay put and I will find you. A few times at playgrounds and once at a supermarket, we did get separated, but Annie remembered to stay still and not to make the problem worse with each of us running in different directions to find each other.

Marjorie Hammil, Scranton, Pennsylvania

Pin on tickets

When my family goes to a baseball game or to a play, I always pin my children's ticket stubs to their shirts or jackets. This way if we ever get separated, the usher or security guard can steer the kids back to us.

Carol Maurer, South Pasadena, California

Dress for visibility

I always dress my three children in the same bright colored shirts or baseball caps whenever we go anyplace where there's a crowd—like the beach, the mall or an amusement park. This way, they're much easier to keep track of.

Sinead Molloy, Bayside, New York

Use a harness

I always put a walking harness on my daughter when we're in stores. (She hates to sit in her stroller when she's awake.) One day, someone who happened to be walking a dog said, "I think it's terrible to put a leash on a child." I simply told her that I cared as much about my daughter as she did about her dog and I was just making sure she didn't wander off. That kept her quiet.

Mary Ann Lowe, Flushing, New York

Carry a recent photo

What would you do if your child wandered away from you at a crowded beach? It can happen to the most cautious parent, so be prepared to make a scary situation less frantic. Carry a recent photograph of your child in your beach bag; that way anyone who offers to help find your child will know exactly what he or she looks like.

Lorraine Lindbult,
Huntington Valley, Pennsylvania

Pick a spot

Every time I enter a store with my children, I point to a cash register or other easy-to-find location and say, "If you get lost, go to this spot and tell the cash-register lady to call me." I state very strongly that they are never, ever to leave the store without me. As we walk around the aisles, I ask them to repeat the rule. It's only been needed once, but it only takes one incident to lead to a tragedy.

Ellen Lubin, Jamaica Estates, New York

Stranger Danger

Few things are as terrifying as the thought that a stranger might abduct your child. Though the actual number of stranger abductions is very low, one incident is one too many. Here are some ways parents have dealt with the issue of teaching their children caution without unnecessarily scaring them.

Teach manners

I don't want my daughter, who's seven, to be fearful of everyone she meets. I also want her to respond positively to adults who say, hello to her. I've always taught her that while she is with me, it's always okay—in fact, it's the polite thing to do—to respond to a person who says hi with a smile of her own.

May Eriksen, Minneapolis

Be vigilant

Watch your children like a hawk because you can't assume that they've learned the lessons you've taught them.

Nearly two years ago, my little boy, then age six, went off with a friend's dad who invited him for a movie. He failed to tell me that he was leaving the playground and the father never bothered to come to my house to get my okay. When I went to the playground, which is just down the block, to get David for lunch, I was horrified to find that he was not there. I called the police and we had an all-out search planned when another child told us where David had gone. For more than a year, my son no longer went out to play unescorted. Because David knew the man, he'd assumed that it was all right to go off with him. What the man's excuse is I'll never know because I'm still too angry and upset to talk to him.

Beverly Burton, Cincinnati

Instill a sense of safety

My son's preschool went a little overboard teaching the children to fear strangers. He was developing a fear of everyone. I told him that most people were very good and were not out to hurt him. I also told him that it was my job and his teacher's job to watch him and keep him safe and that we were doing our job so he could relax. It helped to take the burden of watching out for bad guys off his shoulders and back where it belonged—with the grown-ups who love him.

Monica Arbuette, Columbia, South Carolina

Get involved

I, like so many parents, often observe an adult hauling a screaming child down the street. We always assume that the adult is the child's parent and that they're

What Every Child Should Know

Before sending your child out on a solo venture, make sure that he or she:

- Knows his address and telephone number.
- Knows how to dial 911 and has change to make a call from a pay phone.
- Understands that adults don't naturally ask children for any kind of help—whether for directions or to find a lost dog. Tell your child to suspect any adult—including a woman or an elderly person—who approaches him offering anything or asking for help. Also teach your child to alert another trusted adult to these encounters.
- Stays far away if a car slows down and someone asks for directions. It's also a good idea for parents to never ask a child for directions; it serves as a bad example to your child who knows that you are a safe adult and it reinforces to other children that they can safely assist a lost driver. The next time, that child is more likely to get too close.
- Travels with at least one friend.
- Always walks on well-traveled sidewalks, avoiding shortcuts on deserted streets, alleys or fields.
- Knows safe places to go along her route—businesses and homes of friends. (If your community is part of the Safe Place or Safe Haven system, teach her to note businesses that display these yellow decals in their windows, indicating that children can go inside and get help if needed.)
- Ducks into any store and asks someone to call for help if he thinks someone is following him. If there are no stores and only private houses, teach him to ring the bell and ask the owner to call for help but *never* to go inside a house or car. Children also need to learn to trust their instincts and common sense, making a reasonable choice, for instance, to get into a police car or to enter the home of someone who's offering protection from an immediate danger.
- Yells "This person is not my parent," if someone is harassing him. The last thing an abductor wants is to call attention to him or herself. Also teach your child that hitting, biting, kicking and any other act is allowable to protect himself, but that, by far, the best option is to run and get help.
- Tells you of any adult who asks him to keep a secret from you, who makes him feel uncomfortable in any way, or who offers him gifts or inappropriate attention.

just having a really bad day. But it occurred to me that if a child was screaming about being pulled down the sidewalk, he or she might be in trouble. Although I feel somewhat uncomfortable about it, I've begun to ask each child I see in this kind of situation if he or she is okay and if the adult is his or her parent. Fortunately, the answer has always been yes. No one's ever been insulted about my interference. In the meantime, I've taught my own daughters to yell "This is not my mom," or "This is not my dad," if anyone ever tries to abduct them. I realize how easy it is to ignore a child's screaming because kids yell for so many reasons.

Julia Martinez, Prescott, Arizona

Offer visual reminders

To help my five-year-old daughter remember to ask, "Who is it?" before she opens the door, I posted an eye-level picture of an owl on it for her. My daughter knows that owls always say "whooo"—and so should she whenever the doorbell rings.

Maria Koch, Hyattsville, Maryland

Use the buddy system

It's never a good idea to let a child or even a teenager walk or ride his bike in an uncrowded area alone. I've taught my children, who range in age from 7 to 16, that they must be with a buddy whenever they're off the main road.

Elaine Kaufman, Edison, New Jersey

CHAPTER SEVEN

Child Care Solutions

W*hether your child needs to be in another's care for an* evening or for the course of your workday, choosing a caregiver requires thoughtful planning, flexibility and the ability to trust. The process starts with finding the right sitter. As time goes on, it will also include adjusting your situation as your child grows and your family's needs change. And sometimes even when you've found the situation that's just right, you'll have to find a backup sitter to take over when yours can't be there. The time and energy you put in now to find and keep a good caregiver will save you time, energy and, most important, peace of mind later.

Where to Look

First-time parents, especially, can be unsure and unconfident when it comes to finding the arrangement that will work for them. Parents of older children can feel inexperienced all over again when it comes to finding after-school care once their child has outgrown a full-day program. Here are some good ways to begin your search.

Check school bulletins

Look at the bulletin boards of local nursery schools. Many parents advertise to help their former sitters find work when they are no longer using in-home care because their children are old enough for school. These boards are also good places to find notices from parents who want to share a sitter.

Hallie Longhorn, Kansas City, Missouri

Network, network, network

Talk to other parents. I was sure that I was going to put my daughter into a center near our home after I returned to work when she was three months old. But talking to other moms convinced me that a particular small, family day care center was better for us.

Marilyn Rosen, Buffalo

Join a group

I found friends and caregivers by joining a local La Leche League and a babysitting co-op.

Kathy Quinn, Converse, Texas

Post a notice

A church bulletin is one likely way to find a reliable caregiver. Put a notice in the next issue and have the names and numbers of respondents forwarded to you. This is how I found another wonderful mom, who lives nearby, to take care of my son.

Anne P. Kim, Pittsburgh

Call a referral service

As the project director for Child Care Resource & Referral, I welcome parents to call us at 800-424-2246 for the telephone number of their local branch.

Lisa M. Austin, Phoenix

Go to school

Ask school principals. They may know of substitute teachers who want to take care of children. You'll find many qualified applicants.

Barbara Farbanish, Old Forge, Pennsylvania

Invite a college student home

After my divorce, I was left with no choice but to work full-time and find child care for my three school-age children. I knew that our local university had a housing shortage, so I placed an ad in the college newspaper, offering free room and board to a student in exchange for help with my kids and the housework. Now Suzanne, 21, is home with my children when I'm not. It is working out really well for everyone, and best of all, the five of us have formed a lasting friendship.

Margaret M. Sayers, Toledo, Ohio

Inquire at work

Talk to your personnel department even if your company doesn't have a formal referral service. They can put you in

PARENTS' RESOURCE
Finding Child Care

Publications

- *Who to Call: The Parent's Source Book* (Quill/William Morrow), by Daniel Starer, contains brief descriptions of thousands of organizations that deal with child care, health, education and safety. In the child care section, you can look up resource and referral agencies and parent-resource centers. It's available in most bookstores.
- Child Care Inc., an information service in New York City, offers these low-cost guides: *How to Find a Sitter, Live-In vs. Live-Out Care, Interviewing a Sitter, Checking References, What Your Sitter Needs to Know, Separation Anxiety, Evaluating Your Sitter, Caring for Your Caregiver, Keeping a Part-Time Sitter* and *How to Live with an Au Pair.* For more information and to order, call 212-929-7604.

Information services

- The Child Care Action Campaign, a national child care advocacy group, publishes 28 guides, including *Finding Good Child Care—A Checklist* and *Speaking with Your Employer about Child Care Assistance.* You can receive up to 3 guides free by sending a SASE to Child Care Action Campaign, 330 Seventh Avenue, 17th Floor, New York, NY 10001. Members of this organization (annual membership is $25) can receive all of the guides plus a bimonthly newsletter. This organization also publishes *Parent's Guide to School-Age Child Care, Parent's Guide to Summer Child Care* and *Child Care Primer for Parents,* which, in addition to general information about finding quality child care, lists the addresses of licensing offices in all 50 states. To receive a copy of any of these, send a check or money order for $5 each (or all three for $12) to the above address.

Hotlines

- Child Care Aware: 800-424-2246 (for information about local resources)
- National Association of Child Care Resources and Referral Agencies: 202-393-5501

---

touch with other parents at the company who have found solutions to their child care dilemmas.

Meghan Stowe, New York City

Rely on the Y

A YMCA is always a good place to start when you're looking for child care. They can usually tell you what's available in your community.

Madalyn Morris, San Francisco

Consider the Options

Different options abound—family day care, on-site corporate care, individual sit-

ters who come to your home, community-based centers. Which one is right for you? Your search, of course, will begin by looking at those options that are available within your community and within your budget. These parents report on how they've made a variety of successful choices.

Get together with neighbors

My seven-year-old daughter, Irene, and her four-year-old brother, Mikel, have been cared for by the same sitter, a neighbor who watches two other neighborhood children, since they were born. They feel just as at home in her apartment as they do in ours. All the families involved work on vacation schedules together so that when Marianna takes off, we all do, too. The few times she's had to cancel (for illness and for a death in her family), the parents in the three families who depend on her took days off to cover for one another. We all feel very lucky.

Helena Popodopolus, Astoria, New York

Minimize transitions

My son's day care center closed suddenly and left all of us scrambling to find a new center in a hurry. Because the teachers, too, were in search of new jobs, we were lucky. The new center we chose had also hired one of the teachers that Max was used to. Two other children from his old center also made the same switch. It made the transition so much easier to have people he recognized make the move with him. I recommend that any parents faced with this dilemma work together so that the children can transfer from one place to another with as little stress as possible.

Gordon Seltzer, Albany, New York

Visit

If you're considering various forms of child care, visit each and every place a few times. I spent a few hours in two different family centers, at three different day care centers, and had an in-home sitter for a week so that I could compare all the options. What really surprised me was that I chose a family day care center even though this form of care was last on my list when I began looking. Spending time with each arrangement gave me a feel for what was best.

Adri Mandlin, Boston

Be open-minded

Though we really couldn't afford it, my husband and I had chosen to hire an in-home babysitter because we felt that one-on-one care was so important to an infant. Our first babysitter quit to return to her native country just a week after we had hired her. The second babysitter's sister got sick and she had to take care of her children. We finally started checking out local infant care centers and found one near my husband's office that is really great. The stability that the center offers is so much greater than that of a single sitter. It's also less costly.

Hillary and Ted Munsen, Battle Creek, Michigan

Checking Out Centers

Established child care centers can offer a stable environment, and when one worker is out sick or leaves the center, there are others there to take his or her place. Individual workers are supervised by other staff members. They generally also maintain a fixed schedule, which may or may

How Do I Know My Day Care Center Is Safe?

Is your child's day care center clean and safe? Before giving a center its stamp of approval, the National Association for the Education of Young Children checks to see that:

- Running water, soap and paper towels are readily available.
- Baby toys are washed daily and disinfected twice a week.
- Diapering is done at a changing table, never near an area where children play.
- All electrical outlets are covered with protective caps and all potentially dangerous products, including medicines and cleaning supplies, are stored in original, labeled containers in locked cabinets.
- The center has working smoke detectors, and fire extinguishers are easily accessible.
- Daily cleaning includes disinfecting bathroom fixtures, removing trash and cleaning the kitchen area.
- All play equipment is clean and in good repair, with no sharp edges or rusty nails.
- At least one staff person who knows the Heimlich maneuver and is certified in emergency pediatric first-aid and CPR for infants and children is always present.
- Perishable foods are stored in the refrigerator at temperatures low enough to prevent spoilage, other foods are kept in containers on shelves at least six inches above the floor and lunches from home are kept in the refrigerator.

In addition to these guidelines, check to see if:

- The center conducts periodic fire drills.
- Parents are given written procedure guidelines if their child becomes ill or is injured while in day care and instructed about when to keep a sick child home.
- The kitchen area is closed off.
- Stairwells are closed off from children yet are easily accessible for emergency evacuation.
- Windows have guards that prevent them from being opened more than five inches.
- Children and caregivers wash their hands before and after handling food, using the bathroom and changing diapers.
- Small, easy-to-swallow objects are out of reach.
- Toys and play equipment are age-appropriate.
- The diaper-changing area is sanitized after each use, and dirty diapers are stored in sealed, plastic-lined bins.
- Swimming and wading pools, ponds and decorative fountains are fenced off.
- The outside play area is enclosed.
- Certified car seats are used on trips.

not work with your own. Visit a few centers before determining if this option is right for you. Then visit the center of your choice a few times to determine if this one is right for your child.

Shop around

What is the staff-to-child ratio? Does the center smell clean? Are policies about diaper changing, discipline and daily activities posted and enforced? Take the time to shop around. I looked at eight centers before choosing one for my son.

Heidi A. Davis, South Dennis, Massachusetts

Trust your gut

When you're looking at a day care center, ask yourself: Would I want to spend eight hours a day here? If not, don't assume your child will like it either.

Dunlee Hau, South Bend, Indiana

Talk to families

I liked all of the center directors that I spoke with when I was looking for a day care center for my son, Jared. To get beyond the sales pitch that the directors gave, I went straight to parents to get their feelings and thoughts on the different centers. That helped me make a good choice. Other parents not only were willing to talk about the minuses and pluses, but I was able to see where I would find new friends, too.

Marge Kempler, New York City

Ask about aid

I looked at a lot of child care centers in a wide range of prices. The one I liked the most was too costly for our budget, but I found out that we could apply for financial aid, so I applied there. My daughter was accepted and we received enough of a break on the tuition to make the choice possible.

Name withheld, Fort Lee, New Jersey

The Family Day Care Option

Family day care, the most commonly used form of child care in the United States today, offers children the comfort of homey surroundings with a single child care worker who takes care of a few children at a time, usually in her own home. Unlike child care centers, home care usually does not segregate children by age and can be the right setting for parents with children of different ages. On the downside, the providers are not subject to supervision and may need unscheduled time off.

Inspect for safety

Even if your children are in a neighbor's home, check it out as you would a regular center, making sure that the mom in charge follows safety rules that big centers follow.

Emily Wanachik, Tallahassee, Florida

Get to know others

When using a family day center, be sure to meet the other children and parents who share the child care provider with you. It's essential that everyone's kids get along.

Nancy Harbour, Princeton, New Jersey

A Family Day Care Checklist

When looking for a family day care provider, ask yourself if you feel that you can trust her. Observe how the provider relates to children and parents. Is she comfortable? Is she affectionate and caring—particularly when children misbehave? Check that her home follows all the safety features of a larger center. Beyond your gut feelings, here are questions to ask when interviewing perspective family day care providers.

• Are you licensed or registered? Is your license or registration current? Are you accredited by the National Association for Family Day Care (NAFDC)? This accreditation is your best guarantee of quality. For more information about accreditation, contact them at 206 6th Avenue, Suite 900, Des Moines, IA 50309-4018, or call 515-282-8192.

• How many children do you care for? What ages? Requirements will vary from state to state but the ideal ratio for infants should not exceed two-to-one; for toddlers, three-to-one and for preschoolers, four-to-one.

• Who else will my child be in contact with each day? Be sure to meet everyone your child will encounter.

• How long have you been providing child care? How long do you plan to continue? (It's best if she's had at least one year's experience and plans to continue for at least another year.)

• Do the same children come most days or are there different children every day or on alternate days?

• Do you have a written statement on your approach to child care and discipline? If not, ask what the rules are for the children—and put them in writing.

Look for kindness

I used two different family day care centers in my town and they were so different from one another. The first one had a huge backyard with all the right equipment, but the provider so clearly favored her own children in every play situation that I moved my son, Bradley, to another center. This one, though not as well-equipped with things, was run by a woman who was much more nurturing, and, in my book, that's more important than a fancy swing set. My advice is to pay more attention to the emotional support that the setting offers.

Cecelia Brown, Hastings-on-Hudson, New York

Remember, it's a business

As a child care provider, I urge that all parents who use family day care remember that we are providing a real service and running a real business. That means that parents need to show up on time at the end of the day, arrive on time so that we can all begin our activities together and pay on time. I'm in this line of work

- Do you belong to a day care association or network that offers you support?
- What is the daily schedule? Do children enjoy a good balance of structured and free-play activities? Ask her to describe a typical day.
- Do children ever leave the premises to accompany you on outside errands or on outings to parks and playgrounds? Do you have additional help to accompany you? How do you transport them? Do you provide car seats or should parents leave their own car seats with you?
- How many times in the past year have you been ill? Who cares for the children when you can't?
- What first-aid training do you have?
- What is your policy on sick children? Do you allow those with sniffles to join in? What do you consider too sick to attend?
- Do you provide a written contract spelling out the terms of your agreement?
- What is your vacation policy—for both your own vacations and for the children's family's vacations?
- What supplies must I provide? Diapers? Lunches?
- What snacks and meals do you provide? Are you a member of the U.S. Department of Agriculture's Child Care Food Program? Members tend to serve more nutritious meals.
- Can you provide references?
- Do you have an open-door policy, by which I am always welcome to visit and participate?

because I love taking care of children, but I also need the income that my center provides. Sometimes, when parents sit down in my kitchen and share a cup of tea at the end of the day they forget that we're more than friends—we're also doing business.

Name withheld, Raleigh, North Carolina

In-Home Sitters

Sitters who watch your child in your home provide you with the most ease, *freeing you and your child from the early-morning rush to a center and from the evening rush to get to the center by closing time. In-home sitters can also be the perfect solution for after-school hours. This option, however, lacks supervision and, in general, is costly.*

Show respect

From the time my daughter was three months old until she entered an all-day center at three years of age, she was cared for in our home by Carla, who became a very important part of our family. The reason, I think, that the situation worked so well for so long is that I was very careful to treat her respectfully, giving her time off to register for college, for instance, and coming home when I said I would. I also paid her for any overtime either in extra money or in time off.

Leslie Simpson, Philadelphia

Think about taxes

If you hire a sitter, be sure to pay her on the books. We didn't and it resulted in a serious tax problem down the road.

Name withheld, New York City

Check your insurance

If you have a live-in sitter, make sure she has medical insurance. Also make sure that you have homeowner's insurance that will cover her in case she injures herself in your home.

Myrtle Spivak, Indianapolis

Have a written agreement

When you're hiring a full time sitter, establish a written agreement. Include salary, vacations and sick days, rules such as limitations on TV viewing, cleanup, health, safety and visitors.

Mary Selk, Address withheld

Get the picture

Safety concerns, particularly the lack of supervision, almost kept me from having an in-home sitter although I felt it was best to have our son in his own home while we worked. After hiring a sitter whose references we thoroughly checked, I hired a private firm that does hidden camera monitoring of the sitter. Although

we found no actual abuse, we were horrified to see that the sitter—who seemed so caring in front of us—virtually ignored Matthew during the day when she thought we weren't looking. We changed sitters, again hiring the service to monitor her. The next one was terrific even when she thought no one was looking. I urge parents to invest in this method of double-checking on the safety of their kids.

Name withheld, New York City

Focus on the kids

When I hired my in-home sitter for our two children, ages 3 and 11 months, I made it clear that caring for them was much more important than having the house spotless when I returned from work. In the years that I was a stay-at-home mom, I spent a lot of time with sitters and their charges as I took my older girl on playdates. Often I saw sitters spending their time cleaning up instead of interacting with the children. As one sitter told me, "His mom knows I've been working when she sees the floors clean. But if I spent all day putting puzzles together with her son, I'd have nothing to show for my work." I made it very clear that I'd rather our sitter spend time doing puzzles.

Melanie Katz, Seattle

Provide a network

In-home sitters, like in-home moms, can get lonely during the day. Each time we have a new au pair arrive, I make sure that she gets to know other young people in the neighborhood, particularly other sitters and young moms with whom she can spend some time with my sons.

Rita Reilly, Chicago

The Au Pair Solution

If you need child care, hiring an au pair may be more convenient and less costly than having a babysitter come to your home regularly. Au pairs are typically European women between the ages of 21 and 25 who live with a U.S. family for a year and provide care for their children. In return, they receive a private room, board, a stipend (usually between $100 and $200 per week), plane fare, medical insurance and an education allowance. The pros include the flexibility of having your caregiver live in your home and the opportunity to get to know someone from another culture. The cons include a lack of privacy and the possibility that the young person will become homesick. Before signing a contract with an agency, be sure to ask whether it will arrange for a replacement if the first au pair doesn't work out. Here are some of the top au pair agencies nationwide.

- Au Pair in America, 102 Greenwich Avenue, Greenwich, CT 06830 800-727-2437
- EurAuPair, 250 N. Coast Highway, Laguna Beach, CA 92651 800-333-3804
- AuPairCare, 1 Post Street, Suite 700, San Francisco, CA 94104 800-4-AU-PAIR
- E. F. Au Pair, 1 Memorial Drive, Cambridge, MA 02142 800-333-6056

Allow for privacy

I make it clear to my children that Yona, our sitter, gets time to herself in the evening and on weekends. They really love her and so do I. But I feel that she needs to be undisturbed during her off hours. She's told me that she does appreciate my concern about her privacy.

Linda Youngston, Larchmont, New York

Provide an education

If you're planning to have a sitter come to your home for a long-term arrangement, be sure to enroll her in an infant and child CPR class, even if she's received prior training. Updating her lifesaving skills is the best investment you can make. It also shows right from the start that you have a commitment to her and that safety is your first priority.

Kathleen Heenon, Buffalo

Interviewing a Child Care Provider

Whether you are hiring a babysitter for the evening or seeking a long-term provider, these parents have interview tips that can work for you.

Get personal

I always ask a new babysitter about her family and how she was reared, because those patterns may be passed on to my children. I also ask about the last family she worked for. If she is too critical of them, she may end up critical of me and my children, too.

Nancy Pietrafesa, Address withheld

Work with your spouse

Include your husband in the interview process. That way you can compare viewpoints and feel that you've made a joint decision.

Debbie Long, Albany, Oregon

Do your homework

Be extra cautious and ask candidates for Social Security and driver's license numbers, proof of CPR and first-aid training and three or four references from people who are not relatives. Before hiring our caregiver, I interviewed her three times and took my son to her house once a week for a month, for one hour each time, to watch them interact.

Lynn Musick, Tacoma, Washington

Narrow the field before introducing kids

If your child is old enough to understand what's being said, don't have her present for the first interview, if possible. You want to be able to ask direct questions that you may not want your child to overhear. Once you've narrowed the field somewhat, then you want your child to be present at the interview because you want to see how they interact.

Chelsea Sorentino, Bayside, New York

Role play

Ask a lot of "What if . . . ?" questions, such as "What if my child refused to put on his sweater when it was time to go out?" or "What if my child fell and hit his head—how would you react?" to get an idea of how she would react to discipline issues and safety issues.

Linda Chertz, Denver

Ask for best and worst stories

I've found that when I ask a potential sitter to tell me the best and worst things that ever happened to her on the job, I get the best insights into her competence and her attitude.

Ilana Capriano, Joliette, Michigan

Checking References

Your gut feelings are your most important indicator about a potential sitter's qualifications. Nevertheless, checking references is essential. Here are some ideas on learning about a person's background from those who know her.

Make real contact

When you check a reference, communicate as one parent to another. Ask how the caregiver handled a tough situation (such as a fire or medical emergency). What happened if the parents came home late from work? How did it go when there were disagreements between employer and caregiver? Finally, just before you hang up, say, "I'm depending on your opinion for my children. Is there anything else I need to know?"

Ralph Walter, Summit, New Jersey

Take it slow

As a family day care provider, I suggest to my new clients that they reassure themselves about my credentials by checking my references, coming by for surprise visits and, if necessary, starting their child out slowly, one hour the first week and 90

Safety Checks for Your In-Home Sitter

What happens if your child becomes sick or is injured while in a sitter's care? Providing a telephone number where you can be reached as well as a list of important numbers such as doctors, hospitals and the poison-control center, is always a good practice. Also leave the name and number of a trusted neighbor who can be contacted for advice on minor problems. You should also provide the sitter with a form that authorizes her to consent to medical care on behalf of your child.

A babysitter should also know when and how to take your child to the emergency room and be able to determine if an ambulance is necessary. Post your name, address and phone number by each phone since this important information may be forgotten in the middle of a crisis. Review these guidelines on when to take your child to the emergency room with your sitter.

- If there is a cut with significant bleeding, greater than half an inch in length, especially if the wound is on the face or hands
- If there is a puncture wound with bleeding that does not stop within 10 minutes of firm and direct pressure or if the wound was inflicted with a rusty or dirty implement
- If the child falls with a hard bump to the head, especially if accompanied by loss of consciousness, abnormal speech, abnormal walking, vomiting or significantly altered behavior
- If the child has a fever over 102.5°F (101°F for infants over three months and *any* fever in a newborn) that does not subside with acetaminophen or is accompanied by lethargy or vomiting
- If the child may have broken bones (signs include a snapping sound at the time of the accident, inability to move or bear weight on the injured limb, severe pain, numbness and/or tingling, swelling and discoloration)
- If the child has burns—even burns that look minor can be serious

Instruct the sitter to call an ambulance when the child:

- Remains unconscious after a fall
- Has seizures or convulsions (unless the child is epileptic and the sitter is trained to deal with the situation properly)
- Has severe shortness of breath
- Has broken bones with deformity
- Has chest, abdominal or pelvic pain after a fall
- Is choking or may have aspirated food or small objects

The American Red Cross offers standardized health, safety and child-development training for caregivers and parents, including instruction in first-aid and CPR. To sign up, contact the local chapter, listed in your phone book.

minutes the next. If you aren't allowed this much freedom, find another caregiver.

Liz Martz, Rialto, California

Check identification

Ask to see relevant papers—passport, green card, Social Security card and driver's license, for instance. Be wary of anyone who cannot supply proper identification.

Naomi Shultz, Edison, New Jersey

Trust your instincts

Even if you find a caregiver who has excellent credentials, listen to any uneasy feelings that you or your spouse may have about her.

Karen Morgensen, Palm Harbor, Florida

Ask key questions

When calling a parent who has previously hired a sitter I'm planning to use, I always ask, "Would you hire her again?" That usually brings out a good reason why I should—or shouldn't—hire her myself.

Casey O'Malley, Shaker Heights, Illinois

Helping Children Adjust

You want the transition to be smooth for everyone. Here are some ideas worth noting.

Keep your cool

Don't show your anxiety to your children. That will only make it harder for everyone to make a successful adjustment. You can limit your own fears by not getting caught up in the media hype about isolated cases of child abuse. And don't

rent *The Hand That Rocks the Cradle* from the video store.

Madeline Abrams, Saratoga Springs, New York

Stick around at first

Stay in the house with the caregiver for the first couple of days, but keep yourself busy doing other things. This way you can see or hear what problems might arise and be able to give the caregiver specific directions and advice. This will probably make you feel more at ease once you do actually leave them on their own.

Ellen Bilofsky, Brooklyn, New York

Observe

Watch closely to see how a prospective babysitter acts around your child. I never dreamed of hiring a man, but when I saw the fellow who is now our favorite sitter playing with our little boy, I knew he would be perfect.

Dusky Pierce, Address withheld

Allow for extra time

Get to your new center early, not just on time. Give yourself and your child a relaxing start to the new experience.

Justine Manson, Sioux City, Idaho

Give children reminders of home

My son, Max, was very nervous about starting at his new day care center. We made a special picture book of his family and house and pictures of mom and dad at work (with pictures of him on our desks) to show him that everyone was thinking about each other while we were apart. We also made sure that his center teacher would not try to make him give

up his beloved blankie during the transition period.

Beverly Grossman, Tempe, Arizona

Take pictures

To ease the anxiety my son often felt about being left with a sitter, I bought an inexpensive plastic picture cube and asked each of his various sitters if she had an extra snapshot of herself. The next time I was planning to go out, I could prepare my son with a visual image of the sitter. It has made leaving him much easier.

Maggi G. Maxwell, Wilmington, North Carolina

Keeping Kids Healthy

You've checked the safety standards. You've made sure that your child is up-to-date on vaccinations and isn't sniffling too much to send her to day care. But what happens when other children arrive at the center too ill to mingle? These parents have faced that question and have these suggestions.

Have a policy

I was in a situation where one child in the group was frequently arriving ill, and we decided as a group that it wasn't fair to the other families. The mother of the sick child was upset at first, but we made it clear to her that we did not mean to insult her and even made suggestions of babysitters she could use in the future.

Cynthia E. Parker, Chicago Heights, Illinois

Share your concerns

The best solution is for the group leader or one of the members to approach the parents of a child who frequently comes in sick and gently tell them, without making any accusations, that the group would prefer that they keep their child home when he is sick. By approaching them in a sympathetic way they won't feel threatened or feel that they have to leave.

Frederica Mathewes-Green, Woodbridge, Virginia

Be direct

Be up front and explain to any mother who brings a sick child to group care that she can't continue to do so. It's not fair to subject the other children and their families to the risk of illness. And if she can't abide by the rules, then she should find another center to join.

Anne Z. Willoughby, North Madison, Ohio

Stick to the rules

It's up to a day care director to post the rules on sick children and to enforce those rules. When I see a sick child in my son's class, I immediately approach the director and the teacher and ask for that child to be kept away from mine.

Leslie Ann Phillips, Dallas

Boosting Your Backup Care

Your child will sometimes be too sick to go to day care. It's also likely that your sitter may have to cancel at the last minute. Having a backup plan is simply part of your overall plan to assure that your child is always well-cared-for.

Bring kids to work

My children are enrolled in a day care center a half mile from my office. Occasionally, one of them gets sick enough to need mom, but not sick enough to have to go all the way home. So I keep a duffel bag in my office that contains diapers, toys and snacks, plus a thermometer and some over-the-counter children's medicine. My sick-child duffel bag enables me to give my kids TLC and to continue working.

Susan Palsbo, Arlington, Virginia

Team up

Here's a way that I found to avoid making desperate early-morning phone calls in search of an alternate when the babysitter is sick. My 2½-year-old daughter, Kelly, used to stay with a neighbor during the day while I was at work. My friend Melinda Baker also had a similar arrangement for her child. Both babysitters agreed to back each other up in the event that one of them couldn't work that day. Since the backup babysitter would have the other child only for an extra day or two, it wasn't a problem, and the extra income earned was welcome.

Bobbi Velez, Syracuse, New York

Have an on-call helper

I used to rush through my last hour at work each day, desperately trying to meet the 5:30 P.M. deadline for picking up my daughter, Brittany, from day care. I now have a wonderful arrangement with Shannon, the daughter of a family friend. Each day she calls my office at 4:45 P.M. If I can't leave work on time, Shannon picks up Brittany and cares for her until my husband or I arrive home. We pay Shannon an "on-call" fee of $15 a week, regardless of whether she's needed to pick up our daughter. Her help has given me tremendous relief from a stressful situation.

Shirley J. Hilton, Lexington, South Carolina

Bring work home

Always come home with enough work to keep you busy for the day if you have to stay home from the office because your child is sick.

Brett Thompson, Shelbourne, Vermont

Co-op

Our center charges $5 for every 10 minutes that parents are late picking up their children. A group of us parents got together and agreed to give one another permission to pick up each others' kids. This way, any mom who arrives at the 6:00 P.M. deadline also picks up any other kids from the list and waits with all of them across the street at the pizzeria. (We all have the phone number of the pizza store as well as each other's numbers, just in case we have to get in touch with one another.) More than once, each of us has picked up our child from the pizzeria instead of the school. It's worked very well for all of us.

Molly Noble, Brooklyn, New York

Provide a play space

When you don't have a sitter and you're taking a child where there are no other children, such as a school meeting or the office, here's how to keep the occasion pleasant for everyone. (1) Take a small blanket and pillow. My daughter and I pretend that the blanket is an island that she can't leave until I rescue her. (2) Have a few special quiet toys to offer the child when she gets restless—a stuffed animal, puzzles, a box of crayons and paper. (3) Bring along a special lunch bucket filled with finger foods. (4) Before you leave home, explain where you are going and what will be happening. (5) Take your child to the bathroom as soon as you arrive. (6) Periodically praise your child for playing alone and keeping her voice low. On the way home, give your child a small reward for behaving well.

Nancy M. Reed, Bremerton, Washington

Home Again, Home Again

Parting may be sweet sorrow. But reuniting—well, that can bring on the tears, too. After all, no matter how much fun your child has had during the day while you were apart, he's got a storehouse full of emotions to share with you when you pick him up. Chances are that you, too, are stressed at this time. How can you make the transition from the care of others to your care go more smoothly? These moms and dads advise.

De-stress before pick-up

I always stop for a cup of tea on the way between my office and the day care center. I need these 15 minutes or so of private time to relax and be ready to meet my kids. When I'm calmer and more relaxed, I'm better able to handle their moods.

Cynthia Leipzip, New York City

Reserve time for play

I used to try to get dinner ready the minute I came home, but my son really needed my attention then. I've started to serve a snack to him and to sit and play for a half-hour before getting on with the dinner routine. By giving him my full attention when I get home, he's less demanding for the rest of the evening.

Tomi Lentz, South Bend, Indiana

Trade treats

When I meet my son at his center, I always have a snack and a souvenir of my day for him. Sometimes I bring him a mint from the place I had lunch; sometimes it's just a few paper clips. Then he gives me something he's made at school that day. It's a fun way to begin talking about our day.

James Farrell, Greenwich, Connecticut

Brush off rushing

It really helps my daughter, Elisa, age four, when we hang around her center for 10 or 15 minutes after I arrive rather than rushing home or off to run errands. She loves it when I sit with her in her classroom for a while and she shows me the latest thing she's learned.

Pamela Kuntz, St. Paul, Minnesota

Exchanging Information

Establishing a good relationship with your child's caregiver—whether that care comes from a group of nursery-school teachers or an in-home nanny—goes a long way to ensure that your child's needs will be met. The key is communication.

Trade notebooks

To keep lines of communication open with our caregiver, Patti, we exchange a small notebook with her each day. We use it to write messages back and forth. For example, a message from us might say, "We appreciate your extra-loving care yesterday." Messages from our caregiver might include "Bethany had a great day," or "She was grouchy today. Was she up late?" It's also a great way to keep a diary of our daughter's day.

Debra Robinson, Spokane, Washington

Keep a master list

Because I always felt as if I had forgotten to tell the babysitter something, I typed discipline guidelines, food restrictions and phone numbers on a sheet of paper. Then I had it laminated, along with photocopied instructions for CPR and the Heimlich maneuver.

Heather Henderson, Eugene, Oregon

Keep current

Daily notes titled "All about Leah and Kelsey" from my daughters' caregiver help make me feel part of their day. She jots down what they ate for lunch, new words they learned, when they napped and other activities. These updates make me feel better and more connected.

Judy Harms, Whitewater, Wisconsin

Attach your phone number

When I first began taking my son Luke to his babysitter's house, I attached a luggage tag to his diaper bag. On the tag I wrote my name and my husband's name, our addresses and phone numbers at work, the addresses and phone numbers of our doctor and dentist and the number for the local poison-control center. That way when I leave my son with his sitter, I can relax, knowing that she has handy access to important information in case of an emergency.

Ann Amble, Benicia, California

Encourage caregivers to write notes

In my small family day care, I compose a daily note for each mother, chronicling her infant's day. I record the time the baby had a bottle, how long he napped and other daily activities, along with a few lighthearted observations of my own about the baby's moods and responses. The moms enjoy learning what happened while they were away from their kids and use the knowledge to ease the babies' transition from my care to their care. One mom told me she is saving my notes in her daughter's baby book.

Pamela Sheldon, Concord, New Hampshire

When Change Is Needed

It happens. The sitter you've so carefully chosen turns out not to be the right one after all. Or perhaps she's simply not doing all you wish for your child. Here are some ideas for turning a not-so-good situation around—or for moving on.

Note behavior changes

If your child is acting up after being left with a certain sitter, speak to her in general terms about what she and your child do together. Ask her if she has noticed any recent changes in your child's behavior that might help to explain any problems.

Debbie Stewart, Allentown, Pennsylvania

Listen to your child

If my child said he was unhappy with a particular sitter, I would find another babysitter. I think it is very important for a child to be happy with the person who watches him. We went through this with

PARENTS' ALERT

Spotting Signs of Trouble

- Begin with a trial period. When you hire a caregiver, make sure she knows that there will be trial period so that you can evaluate her for a certain period of time, say, two to four weeks.
- Check in. Drop in unannounced and ask friends and family members to do the same.
- Observe your child. Does she seem happy, clean, alert when you reunite? Is she tired and fussy? Is she fearful, overly reserved or aggressive in the sitter's presence? Does she have any unexplained bruises? If she's verbal, has she said anything that indicates a problem?
- Observe your sitter. What's her mood at the end of the day? Does she seem relaxed or harried? Is she anxious to leave or eager to fill you in on the day's events? Has she interacted with any others in your neighborhood during the day?

our son, and he was much happier after we found a new sitter.

Janet Bachanov, Orlando, Florida

Create an activity box

If your child's sitter doesn't interact with your child as much as you'd like, have an activity box ready and waiting when the sitter gets there. Fill it with crayons, scissors, markers and coloring books. Tell your kids that they can play with the items in the box only when the sitter is there.

Nanci Murphy, Ferndale, Michigan

Compare notes with other parents

Contact some of the other parents who also use a babysitter that you're concerned about. Try to find out if their children also have complaints about her. Sometimes children don't know how to express themselves when something is wrong, and your child may be trying to let you know that there really is a problem.

Suzi Birkinshaw, Roseburg, Oregon

Plan projects

Some sitters allow children to watch too much television. If that's the case, tell

ASK THE EXPERTS
Am I a Good Employer?

Many parents find it difficult to manage in-home employees because the relationship between parent and caregiver is such a personal one. "You and your caregiver need to have a clear understanding of what's expected of each other from the beginning, and the best way to do this is to draw up a written agreement," says Kathryn Welsh, author of *How to Find, Screen and Keep a Good Sitter or Nanny* (Nanny Express). The agreement should include a list of all the caregiver's duties, the amount of paid vacation time, compensation for overtime, a policy on taking unscheduled days off and house rules. This agreement should then be signed by both of you. Welsh also offers these tips.

• Provide a pleasant working atmosphere for your caregiver; don't leave the house a mess or the cupboards and refrigerator empty.

• Avoid being late to pick up your youngster or to relieve your caregiver. If the delay can't be avoided, phone ahead to give her an idea of when she can expect you.

• Always pay on schedule and in full.

• Any changes in your caregiver's responsibilities should be discussed in advance and compensated accordingly. Make sure to incorporate the changes in the written agreement.

• Schedule regular private meetings with your caregiver to discuss in a calm atmosphere any problems or concerns that either of you may have. In between meetings, you can each keep track of issues to discuss.

• Recognize and reward your caregiver's efforts (perhaps, take her out to dinner) and, of course, don't forget to say thank you.

Starting Your Own Child Care Service

To order *Tips about Organizing Day Care Programs: Common Day Care Problems* and *100 Ways to Keep Kids Happy*, send $4 and a business-size SASE to: Child Care, P.O. Box 555, Worcester, PA 19490.

your babysitter that you're concerned about the amount of television the kids are watching. Have regular brainstorming sessions about the kinds of projects that would be fun for your children to do, and then make sure that they have the necessary materials on hand.

Chris Hagenwald, Mishawaka, Indiana

Shop around

I had a problem with a sitter who watched TV all day and found it easier to get a new sitter rather than break the one I wasn't happy with of bad habits.

Nancy Wohlfahrt, Queensbury, New York

Set TV limits

Talk to your babysitter about the kinds of activities you would like to see your children engaged in. Set a limit on how much time can be spent watching television.

Victoria Ugincius, Norfolk, Virginia

Low-Cost Options

Keeping costs low has benefits beyond saving money, as these parents have found.

Compare schedules

Another mom and I who are both students worked out our schedules so that we could swap babysitting. I take classes on Tuesdays, Wednesdays and Friday mornings. She's in class on Mondays, Tuesdays and Thursday afternoons. My husband, who's self-employed, watches the girls on the day we both have classes. Before we met, we'd each been paying about $65 a week for child care.

Gloria Lamont-Simpson, Charlotte, North Carolina

Hire a teen

I kept asking my neighbors until I found a responsible teenage girl who lives a few blocks away from my house. She watches my son for a little while before school in the morning so that I can drive my husband to the train station. After school she'll come by so that I can do food shopping, go to the bank, have a cup of coffee and frozen yogurt out or just pick my husband up. Knowing that she lives nearby and can be called during a last-minute pinch—sometimes for just 20 minutes—has alleviated a lot of stress for me.

Lori Gunner, St. Louis

Trade off with other parents

As graduate students, my husband and I can't afford to pay a babysitter, so we've worked out a solution with friends who have the same problem. On Friday night, one spouse stays with his or her own children while the other spouse babysits the other couple's kids at their house. The following weekend we switch. All the children get to sleep in their own beds, and we parents get free child care every other Friday.

Maria K. Thomas, Bloomington, Indiana

Are You Doing Too Much?

You've made the choice to be at home during the day. Some of your friends and neighbors may come to see you as the perfect backup on days when their regular child care situation fails. What to do?

Be firm

Explain to any neighbor who is taking advantage that while she is working, you are working, too, taking care of your own children. You need all the time you have to give to your children and she will have to make other arrangements for her kids.

Debbie Clark, Grants Pass, Oregon

Suggest a hired sitter

It's best to be honest. Tell any parent who's relying on you to help her out too often, "No hard feelings, but hire a babysitter."

Julie Burghy, Bethesda, Ohio

Explain the options

Express your sympathy for the working mother's dilemma, but remind her that there are options, such as day camp or day care.

Ann C. King, Utica, New York

State your fee

I got out of taking care of all the neighborhood drop-by kids by telling parents who ask if I can watch their kids that I charge $3 per hour, per kid. Some are happy to pay; some find other arrangements.

Myrna Elliot, Elmira, New York

Set times

If a mother depends on you too much, perhaps you can arrange one day a week when her children could come over, but explain to her that if she wants you to watch her children every day, she will have to pay you for the service.

Yvonne G. Harney, Falls Church, Virginia

Special-Occasion Sitters

Out of the child care loop? Need a sitter for Saturday night? Here are some suggestions for finding a special-occasion sitter.

Look for a young sitter

Try to find a sitter between the ages of 12 and 14, before his or her social life blooms. After 16, forget it. Groom younger sitters by hiring them to watch your kids while you are home. As they grow older and become familiar with your routines, you will feel more confident leaving them home alone with your children.

Neil Mayer, Address withheld

Network at the park

Full-time sitters that you meet at the park may be free to watch your child on a Saturday night. You can observe a number of sitters and approach one whom you think handles her charges well.

Lenore Cullen-McIntyre, Bay Ridge, New York

Go to high school

I've found that going to the guidance counselor at our local high school is a great way to find teens who can sit for us.

Beth and Gary Hawkins, Indianapolis

Set up a sleepover

Sending my child to a friend's house overnight is the perfect solution when I can't find a sitter. Usually a friend is willing to watch my child along with her own at her house. I, of course, do the same for her when she needs to get out for an evening. The kids think the sleepovers are really cool.

Rachel Rabinowitz, Miami

After-School Care

As children age out of day care and enter the school years, the focus shifts from full-time care to after-school care. Since this is the time that many parents return to work, looking for a child care situation may be a new experience. What are some of your options?

Lobby for after-school programs

My child's school did not have any after-school program. We approached the PTA to organize a program that would take care of our kids from school dismissal through 6:00 p.m. We first conducted a survey to assess the needs and were surprised to find that 60 percent of the parents favored having an after-school program. We then held a fund-raiser, which raised enough to hire a part-time organizer. We then set up miniprograms, which we felt would be easier to manage—things like a chess club, an after-school movie program and a board-game club. We were careful not to include any activities, such as gymnastics, which did not require an expert to run. The actual

PARENTS' RESOURCE

Self-Care Solutions

Project Safe Home, sponsored by the American Home Economics Association and Whirlpool Foundation, offers several free publications that address child care issues for parents of children ages 5 through 13, including *Finding Quality After-School Care for Your Child*, *Matching School-Age Child Care with Your Child's Needs* and *Preparing Your Child for Self-Care*. For more information, write to Appliance Information Service, Whirlpool Corporation, P.O. Box 85, St. Joseph, MI 49085.

care is provided by a rotating group of parent volunteers. Each family pays a minimal fee to participate. It's working well and we'll soon be expanding.

Megan Kennedy, New York City

Hire a mom

When I needed someone to pick up my daughter after school each day, I hired another mom from her class. She likes earning money and I like knowing that my daughter is with a mom she knows. The kids also get to play together every afternoon.

Orly Davidson, Bethpage, New York

Offer lessons

Rather than just put my sons in unfocused after-school programs, I enrolled them in classes they really wanted. One takes karate, and the other is taking computer graphics. Enrolling them in courses for things they really want to learn makes them eager to have after-school care instead of insisting that they're too old for it.

Janet Muier, Cleveland

Seek guidance

The school guidance counselor was able to give me a list of many after-school programs in our neighborhood that I had no idea even existed. Now my nine-year-old daughter is signed up for two clubs at school and gymnastics at the local YWCA. My son, age seven, is also in two school clubs and joined the Scouts, which meets after school one day a week. On the other two days, I either skip lunch and leave work early or set up a playdate with another family.

Karen Speck, Fayettesville, Louisiana

Creative Care Options for Older Kids

Ironically, a child who's old enough to babysit for others' children may still need some supervision herself when it comes to regular after-school care. These parents have found ways to keep their kids safe and happy.

Set them up in a job

My 14-year-old daughter takes care of two little girls, ages 6 and 8, after school in their home. It's a child care solution that works for everyone. Having a job has made her more responsible.

Nick Armond, Naples, Florida

Swap siblings

I used to put my 15-year-old son in charge of his two brothers after school. A neighbor also had her 14-year-old daughter watch her son and daughter. In both cases, the older siblings got bossy with their younger brothers and sister. So we swapped. Now my son watches her children and her daughter watches mine. We pay the kids as we did before, but now they take their jobs more seriously and don't pick on the younger kids.

Carol Pintchik, Annapolis, Maryland

Pay kids

I pay my 13-year-old son to do volunteer work after school. It keeps him busy and I'd rather pay him than a sitter. We both agree that he's too old for a sitter but that having nothing to do after school can be boring. Paying him for work that he could be doing for free is my way of telling him that I value his contributions to his own care.

Emilie Dixon, Boston

Talk to your employer

I work for a small insurance brokerage firm about a mile from my son's high school. At 15, he's too young for real employment, but I didn't want him just hanging around. I approached my boss about allowing him to come to the office after school every day to do things like run errands, make photocopies, file and do anything else that would be helpful. I pay him $2 an hour, which is double what his regular allowance was. It's a good system because everyone benefits. He's learned some valuable work skills, my co-workers and I benefit from his help and I'm happy to know that he's safe and busy.

Name withheld, Scranton, Pennsylvania

CHAPTER EIGHT

Positive Discipline

We want good kids. We want to be good parents. But it's hard sometimes, especially when our children are doing things that drive us crazy.

Disciplining them, teaching them right from wrong, acceptable behaviors from unacceptable ones, is nothing more—and nothing less—than erecting a safe boundary that allows our children to explore freely and grow. Setting limits is a gift—not a denial of our love or our support.

Everyday Discipline

Discipline begins long before you say your first no to your toddler and lasts beyond the rule-setting that you establish with your teen. These parents have incorporated discipline techniques into their everyday routines.

Have fun

I use stuffed animals to act out good behavior and bad behavior with my 10-year-old. It's a way to point out impolite or other unacceptable behavior without criticizing him. He usually finds these little skits hilarious.

Elizabeth Karras, Lubbock, Texas

Cut down on no's

From the time my now six-year-old was a toddler, I child-proofed the house so that I didn't have to be saying no all the time. Then when I did say it, it meant something. Now the issues are different but still I try not to say no unnecessarily, like when she wants to wear dresses out to play or when she asks if she can paint her new bicycle a different color. I try to keep the rules to a minimum, but I'm very serious about them. Rudeness is never tolerated. Homework has to be done before any television, and so on. She's pretty cooperative because she knows what the limits are.

Callie Cochran, Raleigh, North Carolina

Be firm

I don't agree that all children should be given an option if there isn't one. For ex-

ample, if I said to my two-year-old son, "Your lunch is ready. May I put your truck over here until you finish eating?" I would only set myself up for conflict, because his favorite word is no. From my experience, I find that telling him, "It's lunchtime. You may finish playing with your truck after you eat," is far more effective.

Mary E. Taylor, Yokosuka Naval Base, Japan

Put kindness first

If you want your children to be kind, thoughtful people, treat them kindly and thoughtfully. Nothing else matters as much as helping kids learn to consider other people's feelings as well as their own. Disciplining children is not about getting them to follow a list of rules but about helping them be good people.

Harriet Brown, Brooklyn, New York

Risk their anger

I think the job of parenting is one for which you must be willing to have your kids really be angry at you. When parents try to please their kids all the time, they wind up raising kids who grow into sullen, selfish adults. Being in charge is tough work and your kids won't always appreciate your rules, but it's not fair to them, or to anyone they'll ever meet, to let them run the house.

Martina Santiago, Jersey City, New Jersey

Balance responsibilities with privileges

I always help my children see the links between behavior and consequences and between responsibility and privileges. For instance, my son just celebrated his fifth birthday and, as with all my kids on their birthdays, I announce a new set of responsibilities and a new privilege to help them feel good about growing up. I told him that he was now responsible for helping to clear the table. In return, he could now choose what he wanted to drink at dinner every night instead of me choosing for him. Now he chooses chocolate milk instead of plain. I also explained to his three-year-old brother that when he gets old enough to help clear china plates, he too will earn a privilege. In the meantime, he knows that when he puts his dirty clothes in the hamper, he gets to pick out which pajamas he'll wear that night.

Kendra Jackson, Cambria Heights, New York

Use understandable language

I've found that telling my daughter to behave or to be good means little to her. But when I'm very specific, she responds well. For instance, when I say, "Please do your best to stay quiet at church," she does. Before a birthday party, I say, "Remember to say 'please' and 'thank you' and to allow the birthday child to open his own presents and blow out his own candles." Being very specific helps her understand the rules.

Margaret Dulles, Williamsburg, Virginia

Praise good behavior

Be sure to let your child know how pleased you are when he plays nice or acts polite. If you reinforce his good behavior, he will have less reason to act up.

Megan Paine, Kittery Point, Maine

Make rules clear

I make sure that our children understand the family's rules. If one of the kids is rude, for instance, instead of nagging or criticizing, I say, "At our house, we don't..." When the kids' friends are over, the rules apply to them as well.

Shellee Jole, Hillsboro, Oregon

Follow the Golden Rule

I tell my kids that if they treat others as they would like to be treated, people will like them better and they'll also have more friends. Also, when you catch them behaving well, be sure to let them know how pleased you are.

Bonnie Zebrick, Huntingdon Valley, Pennsylvania

Time-Outs and Other Tactics

That kids will test the limits is a given. Fortunately, there are some proven strategies parents can follow to help their children learn to choose appropriate behaviors.

Actions speak louder than words

I think trying to reason with a two-year-old is ludicrous. When my son began grabbing things from other children at our local playground, I learned to scoop him up and head straight home. It was difficult to do since I much preferred the outdoors, but after three times of being picked up and carried home, he learned that his grabbing would not be tolerated.

Melanie Scopes, New York City

Time the time-outs

I use a kitchen timer to time my children's time-outs. They know they can't move from the kitchen chair until the bell goes off. It's been very effective. Yesterday, all I had to do was just take the timer off the shelf and they decided to get along so that the time-out was not needed.

Karen Glenn-Dimetrius, Anaheim, California

Start a good-behavior jar

I followed the example of my son's preschool teacher to show that there were rewards for good behavior and negative consequences for bad behaviors. I got a jar filled with jelly beans and another empty jar. When he misbehaves, I take a jelly bean out of his "Good Behavior" jar and put it in the "Not Good Behavior" jar. At the end of every day, if he has more than three jelly beans in the NG (not good) jar, he loses his extra bedtime story. (I'm not asking that he behave perfectly.) If there are no jelly beans transferred he gets an extra, extra story for a total of three. Last week the funniest thing happened. He ran into the kitchen to check on the status of his jar and saw that there were already two jelly beans in the other jar and said, "I was going to yell at Scott (a visiting playmate) but I better not 'cause that means no extra story tonight."

Lenore Green, Prospect Park, New York

Calm down

Time-outs never worked with my daughter, who's now four. She became hysterical if I banished her to her room or even tried to make her sit on a chair. The time-outs made her feel totally rejected and, more often than not, seemed to be too much punishment for whatever she'd done just because being separated from the action frightened her so much. Now I sit her on my lap when she's misbehaved. I ask her to explain why she's in trouble and what she could do next time in the same situation. This calms her down and I have to admit has pretty much eliminated my need to correct her.

Jennifer Boulet, Cambridge, Massachusetts

Take away privileges

My daughter is eight and time-outs seem silly. She doesn't take them seriously. So when she misbehaves, I take away privileges, like television or having friends over. Just saying something like, "For talking fresh, you've lost a half-hour of TV," usually does the trick. The important thing is to follow through with your threats.

Christine Underwood, Tallahassee, Florida

How Does a Time-Out Work?

Children under the age of three can't really understand the concept of a time-out (a brief time alone to think about a misbehavior), though removing them from a situation in which they're misbehaving is an effective tool. How can you make time-out, work in your family? Developmental psychologist Carolyn Saami, Ph.D., suggests that parents first help their children understand that a time-out isn't a punishment, but a way of helping kids get control of themselves. Here are some additional recommendations.

- Make sure your child knows ahead of time which behaviors (hitting, name-calling) will result in a time-out.
- Use a neutral space, such as the bathroom or laundry room as a time-out area—any place that does not have a lot of distractions.
- As you escort your child to the time-out site, tell her, as calmly as possible, which behavior prompted the time-out and what she could have done instead. ("You can't hit your brother when you get mad at him. You can yell at him or tell me when he's annoyed you.")
- Set a kitchen timer for a brief period—more than one minute, but no more than three. Place the timer where your child can see it.

- Remind your child that if she breaks anything in the room or makes a mess, the kitchen timer will be set for another three minutes.

For older children

Eventually, children over five stop being fazed by time-outs or they become openly defiant and refuse to sit out their allotted time. One solution is to take a parental time-out. Say to your child, "When you scream and cry like this, I can't think clearly. I need to calm down before talking to you." Then go into the bathroom or your bedroom and shut the door. This temporary withdrawal will probably catch the attention of even the most jaded five- and six-year-olds.

Let guilt work for you

Parents today are too afraid to give their kids a dose of old-fashioned guilt. When either of my children does something that I don't feel is right, I simply say, "I'm very disappointed in you." No lectures. No punishment. But since my kids (like most kids) really do want me to think highly of them, they do their best to undo any wrong. Then I tell them that I realize it must have been hard to apologize to a friend or to tell the truth about something. They know then that it matters to me that they behave in ways that are acceptable and that it's what I expect and what I respect.

Myra Ingram, St. Charles, Missouri

Pack it in

I keep a cardboard box in the hallway closet. My two children know that if they fight over any toy, it goes into the box for one whole day. If they fight over the TV, the remote control goes into the box. This way, I don't have to yell or get in the middle of their fights.

Yolanda Grey, Madison, Wisconsin

Discipline without Spanking

Most child-development experts agree that spanking is not an effective discipline technique because it teaches kids to behave out of fear rather than as a matter of conscience. Spanking also undermines a child's feelings of safety and self-esteem. Perhaps one six-year-old summed up the debate when she said, "Spanking makes grown-ups feel better for a while and makes kids feel worse for a long time." These parents have found ways to discipline without spanking.

Spanking breeds aggression

A friend of mine surprised me recently when she told me that she thought I'm spoiling my children because I never hit them. I replied that the reason her eldest daughter is physically aggressive with other children is probably that her mother hits her.

Amy McAuley, Sarnia, Ontario

Teach without fear

I decided never to spank my son because I was frequently spanked as a child. Although I turned out okay, I often felt alienated, angry and lonely when I was punished. I learned to do the right thing out of fear. I also learned how to lie; I justified my lying by calling it self-defense. I believe that every time parents choose to spank their child, they miss an opportunity to teach him a valuable lesson.

Jennifer L. Craig, Chaska, Minnesota

Establish a firm no-hitting policy

My husband and I established a no-hitting policy, and it works. My kids, ages four and seven, know that we will never hit them and they aren't allowed to hit others. As a former middle-school teacher, I find that much of what I learned about disciplining children in the classroom works at home, too. Make clear what behavior is expected of your child. When she misbehaves, remind her that she is a good person who made a bad choice and discuss other solutions. If punishment is necessary, a time-out or the removal of a privilege or a toy is usually effective. And don't forget to praise your child when she is good. I'm confident that a no-hitting policy is a parent's best decision.

Michelle Shenherd, Brampton, Ontario

Change brings results

I used to spank my son for some misbehaviors. It always got his immediate attention, and he'd behave for a while after being spanked. Then one day, when he was four, I leaned over to hug him and he cringed. I realized that he thought I was going to hit him. I promised him right then and there that I was never going to hit him again, and I've kept my word. It's been two years and his behavior—and mine—has improved considerably. I'm not always shouting and trying to make him behave. I've come to realize that he's such a good kid and that misbehaving is often a result of not really knowing the rules or being too tired.

Name and address withheld

Listen to kids

One evening after being spanked, my son sat sullenly at the dinner table and said, "When I'm bigger, I'm going to hit someone, too." My husband and I were really upset that what we'd been calling discipline was clearly seen as violence by our five-year-old. After he went to bed, we talked about what Peter had said and we decided that we'd never spank him again. We haven't, and he's much more easy to manage and much less given to easy anger.

Cynthia Smythe, Pueblo, Colorado

Pray for patience

I've never actually hit my daughter, but at times she makes me so angry that I want to spank her. Instead I tell her to sit still for 10 minutes while I pray for the patience not to spank her. She knows that I'm serious, and she gives me the time-out I need to calm down. Within that time, I can think of a more reasonable punishment—usually taking away a privilege.

JoEllen Baranski, Rutherford, New Jersey

Using Bribes or Rewards

Sure, we want our kids to behave correctly simply because it's the right thing to do. But, like adults, children can learn to put aside their immediate gratification for a just reward. These parents have found effective ways to bargain with their kids without constantly having to up the ante.

Plan an after-work break

My five-year-old daughter often has to accompany me on business-related meetings, and I know that it's hard for her to keep herself occupied for any length of time. We've made a deal that works. Whenever she has to sit still in an office we go for a fun outing afterward—sometimes for dinner at McDonald's or to a bowling alley. It helps her to know that I understand that I'm asking a lot from her and that I'm willing to reward her cooperation.

Beverly Guzman, Riverdale, New York

Choose to cooperate

I like to think of bribes as incentives. I tell my son that if he behaves at the grocery store and doesn't ask for everything in sight that he can choose three items that aren't on my list as long as they're things that the whole family can enjoy.

Cindy Wong, Flushing, New York

Offer homework helpers

Homework has been a real battle in our house. My wife and I finally made a deal with our 7- and 10-year-old sons. If they do their homework without a fuss, we will deposit 25 cents each toward the rental of a movie. Each time they hit the $3 mark (the cost of a rental), we get a film and watch it—even on a school night.

Sam and Edwina Blakely, Toronto

Teach the art of waiting

To help my 4½-year-old daughter learn to delay gratification, I often give her

Chocolates at the Checkout Line and Other "Gimme" Moments

Marketers know their targets and position their kid-appealing products at their eye-level in stores, guaranteeing that children will want to buy what they see. How can you counter these sales pitches? Try these ideas.

- Ask children to help you prepare your shopping list so that they get a clear idea of what purchases are planned.
- Bring a favorite small toy or treat from home to give to your child at the store.
- Discuss the issue beforehand, reminding your child not to ask for any item more than once. For instance, say, "You may ask me to buy something you want, but if I say *no* once, you cannot ask again."
- Allow children to pick out a certain number of items per shopping expedition.
- Give children a certain amount of money to spend and help him or her find a good buy for the money.
- Promise a fun activity at home after a no-whine shopping trip. Be sure to follow through and give the rewarded activity for cooperation (or withhold the reward if the child fails to keep his or her end of the bargain).
- Play checkout-line games such as "I spy" to distract kids from the goods for sale.
- Bring along a book and read to your child while you're in line.

choices such as "Do you want one story now or two stories later?" Or "Do you want to play a game together now or, if I can finish my phone calls without interruptions, would you like to go out to the playground later?" She usually prefers to wait for the bigger payoff.

Shelly Troika, Muncie, Indiana

Keep promises

Every Saturday, my family makes little promises to one another. For instance, I'll promise to rent a tape for each child; my husband will promise me that he'll change the oil in my car and he'll promise our sons that he'll spend an hour with each one doing whatever that child wants. Each son, in turn, promises us something like, "I'll finish my book report by dinnertime" or "I'll clean my room." We each make a point of keeping our deals, and I think this system makes nagging and haggling unnecessary.

Dianne Ringold, Buffalo

Work together

Our preschooler fell into a pattern of acting up in class. So whoever picks him up from school each day gets a report from the teacher. If he's had a time-out in school, he loses privileges that evening, too, such as television viewing. If he's behaved properly in school, he gets a sticker on his calendar for that day. When he accumulates a certain amount of stickers, he gets a reward. For five stickers, for instance, he gets to visit his favorite mega-playground.

Jeff Bradford, Oreland, Pennsylvania

Sharing and Taking Turns

"What's yours is mine" is the credo of most toddlers and many preschoolers. Even older children can have trouble sharing their possessions with others. But learning to share—including taking turns at a game—is a necessary skill that parents can help their growing children learn.

Choose no-share toys

When sharing was a new concept for my two-year-old, she sometimes felt threatened when guests wanted to play with her toys. Before playmates arrived, she and I chose two or three items she did not have to share. This seemed to increase her willingness to share the rest of her playthings.

Lorraine Roscoe, Manheim, Pennsylvania

Initiate a trade-off

It helps if the parent tries to make sharing toys a game between young children. Sit down with them and explain that they will take turns with the toy. First one plays with it, and then the other gets a turn. The act of trading off the toy tends to distract them from feelings of possessiveness.

Sharon Tyler, Nutley, New Jersey

Share with teddies

To help my three-year-old daughter, Ingrid, learn to share her toys, I set up a playdate with all of her teddy bears and helped her figure out how to share her other toys with them. She gave a whistle to one, a puzzle to another and so on. Learning to share first with her teddies made sharing with friends easier.

Noreen Costello, Nashua, New Hampshire

Find a role model

Because my son, Mark, age four, is so impressed by big kids (anyone over five), I asked his cousin, Max, age seven, to teach Mark all about sharing. I asked Max to explain that big kids shared their toys and took turns and that kids who didn't share and take turns didn't have as many friends. After their little lesson, Mark went out of his way to share and take turns and would even tell his nursery-school classmates how much fun it was to share.

Paula Greenbaum, Jericho, New York

Doing from seeing

To help your child learn to share, let her see you sharing. Be very explicit about what you're doing. When we have guests, for example, I say to my daughter, "I'm sharing the cookies with Aunt Ellen." Also play turn-taking games. "It's your turn to put the block on the tower. Now it's my turn. Now it's your turn again." This gives her a chance to practice sharing at home. I've also taught her to offer playmates alternatives such as "I don't want to share my doll carriage now, but you can play with the cradle." She feels much more in charge now that she has a few strategies for dealing with issues of sharing.

Kathleen Allen-Epstein, Morristown, New Jersey

Winning over Whining

Whining is one of those behaviors tried out by most children. These parents have found ways to keep the experimental stage short-lived.

Look for a mouse

Whenever my daughter starts to whine, I say, "There must be a squeaky mouse here somewhere," and I ask her to help me find it. She usually starts laughing instead of whining. One time, she said, "Mommy, I think I must have swallowed the mouse because the squeaking is coming out of me."

Rita Johnson, Elmira, New York

Counterattack with humor

My husband pretends that he's a robot called The Whining Machine when our three-year-old twins start to whine. He says, "The Whining Machine is coming to get the whine out. You'd better hurry!" Then the kids laugh and scream, "It's out, it's out!" It works.

Karen Winchell, Fort Collins, Colorado

Try distractions

When my son was little, I'd first try distraction to stop him from whining. If that

didn't work, I'd tell him that he could whine for one minute only, and set the timer. When his time was up, he either talked to me in a big-boy voice or went to his room and whined alone.

Judi Weaver, Harrisburg, Virginia

Understand their frustration

Usually my kids whine when they've had a long day or are not feeling well. If I can anticipate their moods I give them extra attention or plan quiet activities. If they still whine while I'm doing something important, I take out my trusty stash of POGs or race cars to distract them. When that doesn't work I tell them, "My ears feel so much better when you ask for things in a big-kid voice."

Heather Gallardo, Sumner, Washington

Be direct

With an older child, it works to confront him. Ask him to talk—not whine—making it clear that any requests must be spoken, not whimpered.

Pam Straley, Kendall Park, New Jersey

Plead for mercy

"Cut that out. You're hurting my ears," is my response to whining. Finally, after a few more minutes of whining and stamping, my kids talk to me normally.

Lea Hoffman, North Versailles, Pennsylvania

Keep 'em busy

Often, my youngest child would rather I find her something to do than play by herself—and she begins to whine to get my attention. So I keep her busy and interested in doing things.

Carol Klein, Scarsdale, New York

Make a list

My husband and I have a surefire remedy for when our three kids—ages 11, 9 and 7—whine about being bored. We supply them with a list of activities— cleaning their rooms, taking out the trash, writing to a pen pal, studying. It's amazing how quickly their boredom ends and they find something to do.

Chris Lang, Alburtis, Pennsylvania

Handling Interruptions

They may not hear you when you're asking them to pick up their toys, but kids have uncannily good ears when you have a conversation with someone else. One mom reported that "whenever I'm not sure where my kids are, I just pick up the phone and they come running in with a million things to say."

Make a communication board

I keep a chalkboard by the phone. On it, I've written *Emergency, I'm Bored* and *Hi*. When I'm on a call and my children want to interrupt, I point to the board. They know they have to check off one of the choices. They've learned not to check off *Emergency* unless there really is one. If they check *I'm Bored*, I reach into a bag I've filled with ideas for projects and a list

of chores that need to be done. (They've learned to be careful about checking off that one!) Usually, however, they just check off *Hi*. This gives them a chance to connect and get my attention without actually interrupting.

Elizabeth Horvath, Tulsa, Oklahoma

Give children a project

If you're going to be on a long call, give your kids a project that will keep them busy long enough for you to finish your call without interruptions.

Lucille Lomelino, Staten Island, New York

Make introductions

Whenever I'm with my daughter, Linette, and we meet an adult with whom I want to stop and talk, I say, "Linette, this is Mrs. So-and-So. She and I are going to talk for a minute, so please don't interrupt us. In a moment, you and I can talk again." We do this each time we're out and I run into someone. I know that Linette, at age four, needs reminders that I need her cooperation. After we're on our way again, I always compliment her on her patience.

Christine Farrell, College Point, New York

Teach politeness

Explain to your children that you try not to interrupt them when they're doing something on their own and that they should return the favor.

Tracey Phelps, Watertown, Tennessee

Let an action-figure help out

I always keep one or two of my son's action-figures in my pocket when we're out walking. That way, when I meet some-

Five Ideas for Battling Breakdowns

1. *Anticipate.* Take note of which situations trigger tantrums and be prepared. If supermarket shopping sets off your child's frustration trigger, leave him with your spouse and shop alone or find another way to relieve him of the experience until he's better able to control himself.

If leaving the playground inspires tantrums, give your child plenty of warning before asking that he make the transition.

2. *Keep your cool.* Responding to a child's outburst with one of your own only raises the level of tension. As hard as it may be, try to respond with a calm, reassuring, no-nonsense stance. Ask your child to help you understand what is it that is troubling him.

3. *Ask your child for suggestions.* Even tantrum-throwing kids may have ideas on how to limit their breakdowns. One three-year-old knew to ask for her beloved teddy bear when she felt herself losing control. "If I squeeze her, I don't have to scream so much," she reported.

4. *Talk to others who know your child.* Enlist the help of a nursery school teacher or other adult who has frequent contact with your child to see if you can develop a consistent means of dealing with the behavior.

5. *Leave the room.* Assure your child that you're not abandoning him and assure yourself that he can't hurt himself, then leave the room briefly. Say, "I'm giving you a minute to calm down. I'll be in the kitchen if you need me."

one and want to talk, I have something available to entertain him and to keep him from interrupting me.

Paulette Cole, Chicago

Spend other time talking

Phone interruptions were a problem in our house, and I solved it by offering my child plenty of time to talk to me when I was not on the phone. I made it clear that when I was on the phone, she was not to interrupt me unless there was a real emergency.

Margie Whiteside, Augusta, Georgia

Invite kids in

The reason why kids interrupt is because they feel ignored. I like to give my daughter special attention when I'm about to launch into a discussion with another adult. For instance, when we're shopping and I meet an adult friend, I ask Ashley, who's six, to tell my friend about something she's done lately so that she's had a chance to be part of the conversation. Before I make a long phone call, I ask her if there's anything she wants to talk to me about before I get started. When the phone rings for me, if she interrupts my conversation, I simply ask her, "Is this something that can wait until later?" Usually it is and she agrees to wait to talk to me until later.

Susanne Pomarantz, Binghamton, New York

Cut your conversations short

I finally realized that maybe I was spending too much time talking on the phone when my child needed my attention. When I put a 10-minute time limit on my talks (instead of talking for a half hour or longer), my son was patient. He realized my conversations were no longer endless. I also started making my calls when he was napping or when my husband came home. I also invited friends over to my house more often instead of shooting the breeze on the phone.

Liz Alameda, San Francisco

Have big kids help out

I have two sons, ages two and seven. Whenever possible, I ask the seven-year-old to give his brother extra attention while I'm busy talking to someone. It makes Harry feel very grown up to be able to help me out, and Justin doesn't need my attention when he has Harry's ear to listen.

Theresa DiGreco, Wilkes-Barre, Pennsylvania

Say you're busy

I run a small business from my home, and my son always seems to want my attention just when I get on a business call. Usually he relents when I tell him, "Mommy's doing business," and he has to be quiet. But if he wants something that's within reach of the telephone, I get it for him while I'm talking.

Nancy Snyder, Lakewood, New Jersey

Tantrums and Tirades

They come at the supermarket when you don't agree to buy gum or at the day care center when you arrive to take your child home. Usually they signal that a child is unable to deal with frustration, fatigue or both. But just because tantrums come naturally to some kids under certain circumstances, that doesn't mean you can't help him find better ways to express himself.

Bring a hug to the rescue

My husband came up with an idea for our six-year-old daughter, Christie, that he coined the grouchy-buster. Whenever she has a temper tantrum or just feels lousy, we ask her to rate, on a scale of 1 to 10, how big a grouchy-buster she needs. Then we give her a hug—ranging from a gentle hold to a big squeeze to get out all the grouchiness. Grouchy-busters have had a very positive effect on our daughter when she is feeling out of control. They affirm that we love her and that we're there to help her feel better.

Esther Choe, Monterey Park, California

Get in on the act

The one time my daughter (then three) threw herself on the floor, kicking her heels, I was astounded. It struck me as funny, but I didn't want to laugh or encourage it. I couldn't take it too seriously, either. Without thinking much about it, I flung myself down on the floor next to her and said, "Okay, I'm going to kick and scream, too, so I can see what it feels like." She couldn't believe it and stopped to stare at Mom on the floor. Finally, she said, "Mom, I'll stop if you stop." That was her first and last tantrum and now that she's seven, we laugh about it.

Marge Keeler, New York City

Get moving

When my son was three and four, he went through a period of throwing tantrums. I learned to remove him quickly from the scene in order to calm him down and to make it clear that I would not tolerate this behavior. When he had a tantrum in the park or grocery store, I simply picked him up and carried him home. It was difficult for me to interrupt my own errands this way, but it helped me make

---

Take a Bite Out of Biting

Biting into an apple is a good thing. Biting into a playmate is not. Toddlers, especially when they're frustrated or angry, may dig their teeth into a playmate. Most are confused that their friends don't react calmly—as an apple would. Although the risk of injury from a toddler's bite is small, the habit can be upsetting to all concerned. Keep in mind that children who bite almost never do so to be intentionally nasty. In virtually all cases, the biter feels emotionally overwhelmed and may be acting out his or her stress. Here are some suggestions for dealing with this behavior.

Do	**Don't**
• Tell your child clearly and briefly that biting is not acceptable and will not be tolerated.	• Lecture your child. A long explanation just provides reinforcement in the forms of lots of attention.
• Let her know that you understand she wants to be good and acknowledge the feelings that led her to bite.	• Overreact. This is a tough one. If you act very upset, you could frighten the child who has been bitten and the biter—unnecessarily.
• Substitute something to bite on when she's getting frustrated—a piece of bagel, a teething ring, a wet washcloth.	• Bite your child back or force him to bite himself.
• Help your child formulate better ways of getting attention and give her lots of reinforcement and praise every time she uses such methods.	• Pay too much attention to a child who bites. This is particularly true in group settings, where other kids may imitate the behavior in an attempt to get attention, too.
	• Scare your child or make her feel like a bad person. Address the behavior, not the child.

my point with him. After the fifth or sixth tantrum, he learned to deal with his frustration better because he knew they didn't get him what he wanted.

Elisa Simone, Essex Junction, New York

Short-circuit the bad feelings

My four-year-old son is pretty high-strung and can get frustrated easily, which often results in a tantrum. I've learned to short-circuit his falling-apart episodes by holding him very tightly and talking softly to him. I tell him that I know that he's upset and that I'm going to help him calm down. Sometimes I get so frustrated myself that I want to yell or walk away but experience has taught me that the hug-and-whisper method works much better.

Melinda Santoro, West Hartford, Connecticut

Stopping Aggression in Preschoolers

Young children don't always have the words they need to express themselves. If your child resorts to aggressive nonverbal ways of making his feelings known, read on.

Play more, fight less

If your child is too rough with her playmates, ask yourself, "How often does she get to play with other children?" If not frequently, it may be that she has not been able to develop her social skills yet. More contact with other kids would get her used to sharing and socializing with her peers. The mothers shouldn't hover too much, as it can make the children act negatively at times.

Kris Allen, Pueblo, Colorado

Start disciplining early

When my son would start acting too aggressively with other children, I would remove him from the situation immediately. Then I'd have him sit by himself for a moment to communicate that his behavior wasn't right. If you start disciplining when a child is still a toddler, it makes it easier when the child is older.

Cheryl Cox, Baltimore, Vermont

Write the script

My son would get very frustrated when he was playing with other three-year-olds. His pediatrician suggested that I sit down with the kids before playtime and encourage them to talk. I would ask Jonathan, my son, what he could say if his friend pulled on a toy he wanted and Jonathan would practice saying, "Don't take my toy." Then I'd say to the playmate, "When Jonathan says, 'Don't take my toy,' please ask him if you may have another toy." By letting both children see that talking would get them more than hitting, Jonathan learned to control his urges to hit first and talk later.

Name and address withheld

Let them work it out

Sometimes it helps just to let the children work it out on their own, except if the child begins to hurt someone. Then it's best to remove her for a while.

Carolyn Whittington, Laramie, Wyoming

Keeping Your Cool

Temper tantrums are not just for kids. Most parents, now and again, feel their tempers rising when children aren't as co-operative as we would like them to be. And, like kids, parents are most likely to have an outburst when tired or frustrated. Here are some ideas for controlling your own anger.

Set realistic goals

When you wake up tomorrow tell yourself, "I'm not going to yell before lunchtime." Keep track of your progress, and congratulate yourself for each victory.

Christine Klag, Elizabethtown, Pennsylvania

Carve out separate space

I took a part-time job because I missed working, and enrolled my son in

Choose Your Words Wisely

How parents state their feelings is as important as the content of what they're saying. Nancy Samalin, *Parents'* contributing editor and co-author (with Catherine Whitney) of *Love and Anger: The Parental Dilemma,* suggests that parents substitute overly personalized statements like, "You're so lazy," which attack a child's personality, with neutral, action-oriented statements such as, "When you don't do your homework on time, we don't have time to play cards after dinner." Here are some other suggestions for avoiding red-flag words.

Instead of saying . . .	Try saying . . .
"You're always dawdling."	"I feel angry when you get to school late. Tomorrow, let's get started earlier."
"Why can't you put your clothes away?"	"We hang our jackets up when we come indoors."
"Who started it?"	"Can you two decide whose turn it is next?"
"If you don't get off the phone, I'm going to suspend your telephone privileges for a month."	"I'm going to set the timer for 10 minutes. Then it will be time for you to do your homework."
"You never put your toys away."	"I expect you to help clean up your room after playing."
"Don't you dare go outside without permission."	"Going outside without permission is against the rules."

preschool. We're both happier. I'm not responsible for him all day, I can keep up with my computer skills, I have more time with adults and my son loves school. Now I have more patience when I'm with him.

Karen Willis, San Marino, California

Take time for yourself

I go to the mall, visit my mother, see a movie or anything for me, by myself. I return home feeling like new.

Lisa Montejano, Chicago

Tape yourself

My husband secretly taped one of my yelling sessions. When I heard it played back, I was shocked at how I sounded. Since then I started using a quieter voice, and I can assure you it's far more persuasive.

Roberta Williams, Iowa City, Iowa

Get enough sleep

The only thing that helps me navigate the family rapids in a normal tone of voice is to go to bed by 10:00 sharp.

Tura Campanella Cook, Austin, Texas

Take a childrearing course

I took a parenthood course at a community center. I learned that the more I yelled the less my kids listened to me and the angrier I got. Like me, you can break this vicious cycle.

Kathleen Nalty, Englewood, Colorado

Remember the audience outside your window

Keep a window open and tell yourself that the entire neighborhood can hear you when you explode.

Jean McCarthy, Lethbridge, Alberta

Understand your feelings

Label your emotions. For instance, when I state in a calm but firm voice, "I'm angry with you for putting tape all over your sister." I'm sending a more powerful message than yelling, "*Stop it!*" at the top of my lungs.

Nancy Tuggle, San Diego

Exercise

Are you and your kids getting enough outdoor exercise? When my kids burn off the energy that they normally reserve for the house, I don't have to yell at them as often.

Monica Zachacki, Morton Grove, Illinois

Get your spouse involved

Does your husband do his share around the house? If not, it may be a hidden source of your anger.

Sara Kent, Winterville, North Carolina

Say, "I'm sorry"

When I say, "I'm sorry for yelling, but I get angry when you jump on the bed," it cools me down and teaches my children to say, "I'm sorry," too.

D. Shierk, Morrisville, Pennsylvania

Visualize

During relaxed moments I visualize myself calmly disciplining my son. It helps me keep my composure when he misbehaves.

Valerie James, North Salt Lake, Utah

Admit mistakes

"We made a mistake" is an important lesson for parents to teach their children. Admit to your child when you've made a mistake, and let her know that it happens to everyone.

Joecile Hoerner, Maryland Heights, Missouri

Lighten up

Instead of yelling, sometimes I talk like a big bear and growl. It grabs my kids' attention, gets my point across and turns a trying episode into a comical one.

Sue Sirvinskas, Park Ridge, Illinois

Find witnesses

Whenever I'm afraid I'll lose control, I take my daughter outside for a walk around the neighborhood. When she asks why we're hurriedly heading out the door, I tell her, "to find witnesses." She knows that I'm doing what I need to do to calm down. And getting outdoors always takes the edge off any anger I'm feeling and allows us to regroup and find ways of dealing calmly with a situation.

Rebecca Staunton, Indianapolis

Start over

I see every interaction with my children as a kind of videotape of the memories we're making together. Sometimes, that tape needs to be reshot. When I feel like I'm about to lose my temper, I pretend I'm rewinding the video. I say out loud, "Let's start over." Then I take a deep breath, and this time I lower the volume.

Marjorie Hirsch, New York City

Breaking Bad Habits

Nail biting, nose picking (especially in public), thumb sucking, hair twirling, cuff chewing—these are the common stress-reducers that children use that drive some parents to distraction.

Use code words

I always try to discipline my three children, who are ages eight, seven and four, with respect. To keep from embarrassing them when they indulge in bad habits in public, I use a code word that each child made up himself as a discreet reminder.

Colleen Plakut, Milwaukee

Provide motivation

We promised our two-year-old son that if he stopped sucking his thumb, we'd buy him a video that he wanted. That motivated him to give up the habit.

Cindy Chambers, Whittier, California

Box those memories

At age 3½, my daughter, Annelise, was still hopelessly attached to her pacifier. To help her break the habit, my husband and I threw her a good-bye pacifier party. First, we gave her a magic box (a plain white cardboard box) to decorate. In it she placed mementos of her babyhood such as a bottle, one of her first pairs of underwear and, of course, her pacifiers. She then supervised storing the box in the attic. Afterward, we celebrated by making and decorating a cake together. Annelise has not asked for her pacifier since her good-bye ceremony, and her day care teachers say she acts more mature.

Sandy Davis, Culiowhee, North Carolina

Go after one habit at a time

My daughter, age six, is both a nail biter and a nose picker. After many unsuccessful battles, I gave up trying to change all of her bad habits at once. I started with public nose picking. That took about six months to conquer, doing things like saying *achoo* whenever she put her finger in her nose. I also handed her a tissue whenever the finger went into her nose. I've decided not to make a big deal out of private, at-home nose picking. Now we're working on the nails. I've promised her a favorite doll if she lets her nails grow by Christmas. She's trying hard. I have made it clear, however, that trying alone won't get her the doll. She'll have to stop biting to earn it. To help her, I ask her if she wants to wear gloves at home. And if she's particularly nervous about something, I encourage her to talk about it and I give her extra hugs.

D. McNamara, Evanston, Illinois

Leave her alone

Until I was in college, I was a terrible nail biter. So was my mother. So is my daughter. It must be hereditary. In any case, I've come to realize that all my nagging wasn't making a difference and that Alison would have to decide to give up nail biting on her own, when she's ready.

Lauren Trainer, Albertson, Ontario

Take a picture

My daughter, age seven, was a chronic nose picker and all my comments did nothing to help. One day I took a photo of her in the act. When I showed her the photo, she said, "Gross!" I gave her the photo, which she tore up. With only a few

reminders since that day, she seems to have broken the habit.

Ellen Rafferty, Address withheld

Switch styles

My son developed the habit of chewing on his shirt or sweater cuffs. He actually ate holes in them. Since nagging didn't work, I simply put him in short-sleeve shirts for a few months. (He wore sweaters and coats to school, of course, but inside he wore only the short-sleeve shirts.) It worked.

Nanci Anne Dubrovnik, Milwaukee

Make an exchange

To break our son of his pacifier habit, my wife and I gave him a deadline of his third birthday—and told him that we'd buy him any toy he wanted in exchange for his "nooks." When he turned three, we headed to the store and he picked out a dump truck he had been begging for. We handed the cashier a box of his pacifiers (along with a check). The first night, he went nuts for his nooks. We told him we could exchange the truck in the morning when the store opened, but that he would have to give up the truck. In the morning, he decided to keep the truck, and he never asked for a pacifier again.

B. J. Botas, Fort Lauderdale, Florida

From the Mouths of Babes

The discovery of the power of language is a milestone in development. With it comes the knowledge that certain words are more powerful than others. If your children pick up words that would make a longshoreman blush, consider these tactics to tame their tongues.

Create your own curse words

Make up curse words that you and your husband can use to blow off steam. My husband and I agreed on *dagnabit*. Not only is it a source of comic relief when tensions are high, but it sounds adorable when our daughters mimic us.

Debie Alderman, Thomasville, Georgia

Let kids know you disapprove

Tell your child that you don't like it and don't want to hear the word again—period. Say it in your most serious tone of voice and then drop the subject. Children will probably listen because they are usually sensitive to their parents' approval and disapproval.

Erica Farquhar, Evergreen, Colorado

Explain your feelings calmly

If your child uses words that he shouldn't, take him aside (don't reprimand him in from the others) and calmly explain that it's not a nice word for anyone to use.

Becky Randall, Newark, Ohio

Don't laugh

Try not to laugh, no matter how tempting it may be, when your child uses a curse word. But if you can't help it, walk into another room and have a good laugh out of earshot.

Barbara Gerhardt, Rhododendron, Oregon

Institute a private policy

Let your child say the forbidden word to his teddy bear only. Insist that he use it with the bear in his room, where no one else has to listen. Pretend you can't hear him, and I bet that after a few minutes without attention, he'll want to do something else.

Joan L. Redeen, Plainsboro, New Jersey

Buy a dictionary

New words delight kids no matter what they mean, and children usually can't resist repeating them. When a child begins to use a curse word it might be a great time to buy him or her a picture dictionary and teach a few extra new words each day. It may help the child forget about the curse word.

Carolyn Deming, Miami, Arizona

Find an alternative

Suggest a silly alternate phrase for your children to say such as "elephant ears" instead of curse words. They'll probably get a kick out of this new word or phrase and repeat it all day instead.

Stacey Wilde, Cedar Springs, Michigan

Keep your reactions cool

Don't act shocked when your child curses, because he probably doesn't even know what he's saying. If he sees that he's getting a rise out of you, you'll only enhance the attraction of the word.

Mary Kenyon, Independence, Iowa

Praise good language

Reinforce the positive by rewarding your child for new and good words that she uses. Express your excitement, and let her know how smart you think she is. This worked for me when my daughter mimicked a curse word that I had used in public. I know how embarrassing this situation can be—I was sure that everyone around us thought I was a bad parent.

Katrina Stebbins, Erie, Pennsylvania

Make a house rule

Fortunately my own son has not experimented with using foul language, but some of his friends have. When they're in our house, I say, "That language isn't allowed here." If the child repeatedly curses, I send him home.

Victoria Honning, Chester, Pennsylvania

In Response to Screaming

They may be too small to reach the light switch, but their voices can reach such high decibel levels that you'd swear the noise is coming from giants. How do you help kids learn to keep the volume down? These parents have answers.

Be firm

Firmly say no to your child when he screams. My nine-year-old son used to scream at such a high pitch, I was afraid that all of the glass in the house would shatter. What worked best for me was to crouch down to his level, look him in the eye, and calmly say, "No! Don't scream; it

hurts Mommy's ears. When you talk softly, I'll listen to you." When he saw that I was serious, he stopped.

Mary Kemp, Magalia, California

Tune out

Ignore your screaming child and go about your business, as long as you make sure that there is nothing wrong. When your child realizes that he is not getting your attention, he will probably stop shrieking after a few moments. Although I know it may feel like it takes forever, try to hang in there.

Susie Harrold, Thomasville, North Carolina

Teach them the words they need

Teach children words to express themselves. My son started screaming when he was around 18 months old, probably because his vocabulary was limited and he couldn't speak as quickly as he wanted to. To help him, I took notice of what he was doing when he screamed and then volunteered the words for him to use. If he started screaming when I offered him juice, I would say to him. "You don't want the juice? Then say, 'No, thank you, Mommy.' " Then I would continue whatever I was doing. This helped him to build his vocabulary and to outgrow his screaming habit.

Vicki Caruana, Safety Harbor, Florida

Try a time-out

Our four-year-old son, Nicholas, has been screaming a lot lately, so we use a kitchen timer to enforce a three-minute time-out. As soon as he realizes that screaming won't achieve the results he wants, he usually stops. Try not to give in when your child screams, or he'll think that he can control you by simply making noise.

Joe Heil, Chandler, Arizona

Walk out

Get away from the noise by leaving the room. When your kid finds that she's all alone, she'll stop.

Laura Justice, St. Paris, Ohio

Let them yell

Sometimes my daughter screams because she needs to release tension. I let her blow off steam without making a big deal about it, and she returns to normal in a few minutes or so.

Terry Schauer, Sherman Oaks, California

Distract a screamer

When my daughter does not stop screaming when my husband or I tell her to, we read to her, give her a toy or move into another room together. The distraction usually helps her forget what she was yelling about.

Priscilla Kelly, Kansas City, Kansas

Ignore him

When your child starts shrieking, ignore him. Once he realizes that this kind of behavior will not be rewarded with extra attention, he'll probably cut it out.

Deidra Harvey, Beaumont, Texas

Praise good behavior

When your child shrieks, tell him, "I'll talk to you when you speak to me in a normal tone of voice." But be sure to reinforce his good behavior too. When he expresses his needs appropriately, tell him, "Since you asked me so nicely, I'd be happy to read you a story."

Marcie Cooper, Fair Lawn, New Jersey

Look for an activity to share

Try distracting a screamer with a favorite activity. This is what I did with my daughter when she was three, and it usually worked.

Joyce Jackson, Encino, California

To Tell the Truth

Few children readily admit that they indeed were responsible for putting peanut butter on the dog's tail. But their inexperience with the world ("I didn't know I wasn't supposed to") combined with their vivid imaginations ("Maybe a dragon really did come flying through the window with a jar of peanut butter") and their need to be seen as good in their parents' eyes ("Mom won't like me if she thinks I did it") all combine to make a child's mistake grow into a fib. Here are some ways to help children come to terms with the truth.

Don't focus on the lie

If, for instance, your child spills a bowl of popcorn and denies it, say to him, "Well, even if you didn't do it, it still needs to be picked up. So let's do it together." Remind your child that everyone—including mommies—can make mistakes. That way he may not be afraid to tell you the truth the next time.

Lorraine Rissky, Topeka, Kansas

Value honesty

Tell your child that if he is honest—even if he did something wrong—you can always work it out. My son knows that lying will only get him into more trouble, and that I'm always proud of him for telling me the truth.

Jean Ellen Tomczak, Russellville, Arizona

Keep things in perspective

Don't overreact to a fib, or your child may feel too scared to tell you the truth. When my five-year-old son covers up, I gently coax the truth from him by stating the facts. For example, if I see him take a toy truck away from his brother and he denies it, I'll say in a firm but friendly tone, "I saw you do it. Please don't lie or take your brother's toys again." Then I drop the subject.

Lori Rigney, Vacaville, California

Use humor

When your child denies that he or she did something wrong, try using humor. Say, "Oh, it must be Mr. Messy again who got crayon on the wall, because there's no one in the house except you and me." I bet the child will say, "That's silly," and admit to his misdeed.

Mary McCormick, Bechtelsville, Pennsylvania

Enforce consequences

Reprimand your children if they lie. Tell them that lying is not acceptable behavior. If necessary, take away a privilege such as going to a friend's house. If your children see that there are consequences to lying, they'll be more likely to stop it.

Maryann Borriello, Smithtown, New York

Get to the root

Sometimes a child will lie about petty things when there is something troubling him or her. Maybe the child is having problems in school or didn't get invited to a birthday party. If your child continues to lie, talk to his or her teacher to make sure there's nothing going on in the classroom that you should be aware of.

Heather Sheppared, Clovis, California

Don't be fooled

Kids are always testing parents, and lying is just one way they do it. Make it clear that you won't permit fibbing. Believe it or not, children feel more secure knowing that they can't fool you.

Karen Streator Smith, Cleveland

Debunking Myths of Discipline

Ironically, there are several myths about discipline that actually perpetuate fights between parents.

The united-front myth

It's unrealistic to expect that parents will always agree on discipline issues. In fact, it's important for children to see their parents disagreeing because children develop empathy by being exposed to a variety of points of view. Also, you can model fair fighting in front of your children, which can actually be constructive.

The right-way-to-discipline myth

"Parents who focus on the 'correct' way of disciplining," says psychotherapist Ron Taffel, Ph.D., "are missing the point." In truth, there are many disciplinary methods that work well.

The need-for-consistency myth

Consistency is too often confused with rigidity. It's best when parents have a consistent overall philosophy toward discipline, but that doesn't mean that you have to do the same thing every time, especially if there are extenuating circumstances. Children can accommodate differences between parents' styles.

If your child complains that Dad lets her watch an extra half-hour of television before bed when he's home, you can explain that you and Dad have different feelings and rules about TV. Children understand and accept these differences.

Be a good role model

Do you lie? Sometimes my kids may overhear me say to my husband, "Tell so and so that I'm in the shower and can't talk on the phone." These actions send mixed messages to children. Rightfully, they may think that lying is acceptable. Model the behavior that you expect.

Colleen Singer, Stockbridge, Georgia

Don't tempt lying

If you see your child doing something wrong, don't ask, "Did you_____?" This approach may only encourage lying. Instead say, "I saw you_____. Please don't do it again." I've found that this makes a big difference.

Kris Livingston, New Brighton, Minnesota

Explain the importance of honesty

I make it clear to my six-year-old daughters that I think there would be nothing worse than being unable to trust one another. I remind her that I am always honest with her and that it would break my heart if I couldn't trust her. I also let her know that there's more to honesty than just not telling a lie. For instance, when she hid a jewelry box that she had broken, I explained that this was a kind of dishonesty and that the next time she did something that she didn't want me to know about, she should tell me anyway. I promised I would never, ever punish her for being honest.

Marge Hinton, Paramus, New Jersey

Making Allowances

In some families, receiving an allowance is part of the routine and is not tied to chores or behavior. In other families, allowance earnings reflect behavior. These parents have found ways to incorporate their children's allowances into their discipline techniques.

A no-strings plan

We decided to give our children half of their age. My 8-year-old gets $4 a week, and my 10-year-old gets $5. I don't believe that allowance should be connected to doing chores around the house, because to us that's just part of being in a family.

Channa Eberhart, Falmouth, Maine

Have a penalty clause

I have four children, ages 10, 8, 6 and 4, and they receive a weekly allowance of $1, 75 cents, 50 cents and 25 cents, respectively. For any disciplinary infraction, there's a 5-cent penalty.

Jane Reckart, Tucson, Arizona

Take deductions

I give my eight-year-old 50 cents a week and my seven-year-old 45 cents. They can spend their allowance on one snack a week at the school canteen. On occasion we penalize them if they don't keep their rooms tidy.

Fay Young, Oak Park, Michigan

Make deposits— and withdrawals

My child's allowance is split into two parts. Drew gets $2 every week no matter what. The other $3 of his potential $5 allowance is earned for good behavior. It operates like a negative-deposit bank. He starts with $3 in quarters and has to pay me 25 cents for every misbehavior, fresh remark or item lost from his backpack. Some weeks he gets the entire $3. Some weeks, just 50 cents or $1. Once in a while, he earns nothing, but on the whole, the system works.

Emily Gottlieb, Wappingers Falls, New York

Life with an Adolescent

As the saying goes, "Little children, little problems. Big children, big problems." Certainly not all adolescents are pushing the limits to extremes, but as any parent of a teen knows, pushing the limits now can have major consequences. Here are some ways to guide your child as she or he reaches for independence.

Trade off with your teen

I wanted to make it perfectly clear to my teenage son that if he wanted the rewards of growing up that he'd have to take the responsibilities that go with it. To his great surprise, I told him that he would have to set his own weekday and weekend curfews and live with the consequences, which he would also decide. To my surprise, he set his hours earlier than I would have—8:00 P.M. on school nights and 11:00 P.M. on weekends. And he decided that a fair trade-off for missing his curfew would be to lose his car-driving privileges for the weekend. He's never missed his curfew so he's never lost his driving privileges.

Donna Halpern-Davis, Bayside, New York

Begin early

As the mother of four, I've had lots of trials and errors in raising my kids. The thing that's been most important, I've found, is to begin raising your teens when they are still toddlers. The rules and the attitudes about life are best absorbed early.

Noreen Donovan, Albany, New York

Respect their maturity

I make a point of letting my children, ages 15 and 17, know that I see evidence of their growing up. Whenever they do something that signals their maturity, I make sure I tell them. For instance, last summer my son saw that a serious storm was headed our way while he was home alone. He taped all the windows, took in the lawn furniture and turned off the gas. His actions protected both himself and our property. I let him know how proud I was. Another time, my daughter left a party early because liquor was being served even though her actions caused her embarrassment with her friends. My children have really earned my respect.

Adelaide Rowling-Pearson, Montgomery, Alabama

Practice new experiences

I think being a kid, especially a teenager, is particularly hard today. I let my children know that I can't always be watching and that they'll have to make moral decisions on their own. Whenever I can, I practice "What if . . . ?" games with my three kids, ages 9, 14 and 15. For example, I'll say, "What if a friend offers you a drink?" I give them a variety of possible reactions, such as putting the blame on me for saying no ("My mom would kill me if I had a drink") or saying that they don't like the taste or simply responding, "Not now." Then I pray that they'll live by the standards we've set.

Mark Tyson, Philadelphia

Find the cause

I never knew that a sweet kid could turn into a surly and secretive teenager, but that's what happened in our family. It took a lot of work—including time with a family therapist—to find out that my son had gotten involved with a really bad crowd at school and didn't know how to get out. He felt loyal to kids who were involved in many dangerous and even illegal acts and felt, too, that it was too late to turn back. We let him know that we'd help him. We placed him in a private school and we helped him make restitution for his petty crimes. His behavior changed dramatically within weeks. Once he was able to relax and come clean about his behavior and his fears, he was back on track. I urge parents whose kids seem lost to stick with them. The child you knew is still there underneath all the outward bravado.

Name withheld, Marina del Ray, California

Open your home

Yes, it may be annoying sometimes to have a bunch of teenagers sprawled all over your house, but inviting your teen's friends over and making them feel welcome is far better than pushing them out all the time.

Ruth Cramer, Buffalo

Give teens an alternate parent

When my teenage son and daughter each reached 13, they became very reluctant to talk civilly to me and my husband. Fortunately, each is attached to his and her aunts and uncles. I asked each of these important grown-ups to spend time with our kids so that the children would have a trustworthy adult to turn to even when they wanted nothing to do with their parents. It's made a positive difference in all of our lives.

Name and address withheld

When Spouses Disagree

Kids need rules, that's for sure. And they need parents who agree on the fundamental issues—like being honest and caring. But do they need their parents to agree on every issues, from television watching to *acceptable fashions? These parents have found ways to agree to disagree for their children's benefit.*

What's really important?

My husband comes from a very stern family. When he was growing up, he and his brother were expected to be completely obedient and compliant. I, on the other hand, grew up in a looser household, where rules were discussed and punishments were minimal. Now that we have children our two backgrounds are really apparent. Rather than fighting between ourselves over our children's behavior all the time, we decided to make a list of the three things we each felt were most important to us. He listed that they sit at the dinner table properly, that they pick up their toys from the living room and that they answer when we called them. On my list were that they limit TV watching to one hour a day, that they go to bed without too much fuss and that they spoke kindly to us and to one another. We told the kids that these were the important household rules that they had to follow. We also told them that they could not ask one parent to overrule the other one, and we've agreed to back each other up even when we might disagree. So far, this new approach is working pretty well.

Anna Phelps-Curran, Spokane, Washington

Explain about differences

Because Will, my husband, and I don't always agree on discipline, I tell our children that different people have different rules and that if everyone agreed on everything, life would be dull. In the meantime, they have to follow the rules of whichever one is watching them at the moment. When we're both there and we disagree about a rule, Will and I take a break from the kids and come back to tell them our compromise decision.

Shanade Wilson, Tucson, Arizona

Play poker

Our kids were in a habit of asking one parent for permission for something and then, if he or she didn't like the answer, asking the other parent to intercede. This got to be a problem until we came up with this solution: We put two poker chips—a red one (representing Mom) and a blue one (representing Dad)—in a bag and having the kids close their eyes and pick a chip. Whichever color they got told them who would decide that particular issue.

Nancy Smalley, Chappaqua, New York

Back each other up

When my daughter complains to either me or my husband about a rule the other has made, we simply tell her that we agree with the other. A few times when my husband made a rule I thought was unnecessary, I spoke to him about it privately and we agreed to tell our daughter that we'd changed the rule. He, too, tells me if he disagrees with my rules and we change those, too, when we agree that we should. The one rule we never change is between ourselves and that is not to argue over discipline issues in front of our daughter.

Nancy Zeller, Cape May, New Jersey

Disciplining Other Children

Setting up and enforcing behavior standards for your own children can seem easy when compared to disciplining the children who visit your home—especially when the young visitor's parents look the other way when their children misbehave. Some suggestions for dealing with this sticky issue.

Share your feelings

If you and a friend have a true friendship, talking honestly about her children's behavior won't ruin it. But if you don't express your feelings, it will hurt the friendship because you will resent this family. Sometimes parents just aren't aware that their children's behavior is disturbing, and don't mind when it is pointed out to them.

Deborah McCormack, Jamestown, Rhode Island

Tell kids your rules

I tell all visiting children, "In my home, there are house rules which every child must follow." Most parents, I find, don't seem to mind if you enforce these rules with their kids as long as your children are also expected to follow them.

Kim Ballantyne, Cortland, Ohio

Phone home

I've found the easiest way to handle a seriously misbehaving child in my house is to call the parent and say that it's time for the child to go home. I also make a point of inviting that child back and not mentioning the prior incident so that they are assured that they're welcome here—as long as they behave.

Oona Donovan, Austin, Texas

Be direct

If a friend of my son's does something I consider wrong, I say something like, "Does your mother permit you to talk that way at home?" or, in one case when a child used our phone to make long-distance obscene phone calls, I gave the child the bill and, with his parents' okay, gave him a series of jobs to work off the bill, such as cleaning our garage and mowing the lawn.

Barbara Corsican, Jamestown, Virginia

Talk to the child's parents

When a friend's child misbehaves in your home, tell her that you want to maintain a certain amount of order in the house and you would appreciate it if she could ask her kids to settle down when they are visiting. You might even tell her that you are trying to get your kids to settle down, too, and that if her children are more restrained, they will be setting a good example.

Vest Stump, Hayward, California

CHAPTER NINE

Family Relationships

W hatever roles we play—*mother, father, sister, brother, aunt, uncle, cousin, niece, nephew, grandparent, grandchild*—define our place in the family. Yet these labels tell nothing of how our relationships with one another really work. Parents give children their first understanding of what it means to belong. Siblings give a life-long reflection of one another. Grandparents and grandchildren give a history and a future. Developing these relationships makes and takes a lifetime.

Introducing the New Sibling

Siblings generate a fierce kind of relationship, both loyal and rivalrous, that will likely outlast any other relationship in their lives. These parents have found ways to help their older children welcome their new siblings into the family.

"That one's mine!"

To help the proud new big brother or big sister in the family locate the newest sibling in the hospital nursery, have the nurse tape a photo of the older child on the baby's crib. This will make the baby easier to locate when the older sibling comes to visit.

Andrea Skinner, Norcross, Georgia

Write a letter

Before I gave birth to my second child, I was concerned that my six-year-old son, Gerrod, would feel jealous of the new baby. To make him feel special, I packed a suitcase for him and placed it next to mine, ready to take to the hospital. I filled his suitcase with snacks, juice, little gifts and, most important, a letter about the day he was born and my feelings for him then and now. I reminded him that with each new baby, the love in our family would only grow. He carried that letter around with him for days.

Tari Lynn Jewett, Palmdale, California

Celebrate Big-Sister Day

When my second daughter was born, we decided to have a party in honor of her three-year-old sister, Katie. We called it a Big-Sister Party and invited all her grandparents, aunts, uncles and friends. I asked everyone to bring inexpensive token gifts, such as coloring books. I made Katie a cake and decorated the house. My daughter loved the extra attention during a time when she was feeling a bit left out.

Melissa K. Jacobs, Miami

Create a special memento

When my second child was born, I wanted her three-year-old brother, Conner, to feel special. When he visited me in the hospital, I took a picture of him with his new sister and had my husband develop the film at a one-hour photo store. Then he had the picture transferred onto a T-shirt at a quick-copy center. My son loves wearing his "Big Brother" shirt. It's just one small way that we can help him feel good about his new status in the family.

Kelly King, Oklahoma City, Oklahoma

Go one-on-one

Give your firstborn one-on-one time. Your older child needs dramatic proof that you still love her as much as you did before the baby came along. If you can, arrange a day trip or an overnight alone with her. Treat her to a special Daddy or Mommy breakfast or lunch.

Bill Bercow, Westport, Connecticut

Initiate special moments

Set aside time to read a few extra books at bedtime with your older child. Go out for an ice cream alone with her. And most important, talk about how she's feeling. Once I did this, my son was much calmer and even helped out with the new baby now and then.

Edie Williams, Olathe, Kansas

Acknowledge feelings

Acknowledge your older child's feelings. Psychologists say that when a new baby comes home, the feelings that the older sibling experiences can be as powerful as those you would have if your husband brought home another woman to live with you. Try to understand your older child's jealousy and anger at you. Be sure to give extra hugs and kisses.

Barbara Berman, Bayside, New York

Allow for anger

Explain to your older child that it is okay for her to feel jealous and angry toward her new baby sister, but that it's not okay for her to hurt the baby in any way.

Susan Eberle, Media, Pennsylvania

Encourage involvement

Let your older child help out. Give him special responsibilities during the times when you're busy with the baby so that he feels included and important. Ask him to hand you a fresh diaper; let him rinse out a bottle or wind the music box at bedtime.

Mary Jackson, Smithfield, Utah

Supply creative outlets

To give your older child a way to vent aggression, ask her to show you how angry she is by pounding on clay or drawing a picture. This will let her know that negative feelings are okay.

Michele Lipman, Rego Park, New York

Make the baby a science project

Buy your older child a notebook and label it "My New Baby." Enter your child's observations about how the baby reacts to different colors, shapes and sounds. What kind of music does the baby like? What makes the baby laugh?

Leslie B. Kirzner, Livingston, New Jersey

Find kids in the same boat

See if you can find another child around your older child's age who also has a new sibling. Try to alternate houses for play dates. This way your older child will see that she's not the only one who may be feeling a little left out lately. As a bonus you will get to have some needed one-on-one time with your newborn.

Patrice Gilbert, Enfield, Connecticut

Explain turn-taking

My husband and I explain to our four-year-old son that it his baby sister's turn to be fed, his turn to be read to, Mommy's turn to relax or his turn to get cheeseburgers with Daddy. Most of the time he doesn't seem to feel displaced by the baby because he has learned that his turn for attention will come soon.

Jane Van Order, Corvallis, Oregon

Indulge your eldest

I encouraged my friends and family to make a fuss over my 18-month-old son before they started cooing over the new baby so that he wouldn't feel left out.

Lorraine McGlade, Woodlyn, Pennsylvania

Enlist big kids' help

I involved my two sons, ages three and two, in their new baby sister's routine right away. They gave her a bottle, pushed her stroller and helped wash and feed her. I never said to them, "Don't touch her," or, "Be quiet. The baby's sleeping."

Joanne Nicholas, Amprior, Ontario

Let siblings show off

I bought my son and daughter, then 6 and 2½ years old, respectively, "Big Brother" and "Big Sister" T-shirts as gifts from the baby to them. I figured they'd think that a baby bearing gifts couldn't be all that bad.

Pam Niehaus, Pittsburgh

Foster a generous spirit

My four-year-old son baked cupcakes with his grandmother to bring to the hospital, along with a flower for the new baby.

Cindy Creager, Seattle

Encourage pre-baby bonding

While I was pregnant, I encouraged my three-year-old to talk to the new baby every day. He also helped us select baby names.

Robin Masters, Morgantown, West Virginia

Keep her close

The first week the baby came home, I let my two-year-old stay home from day care. It made her feel special, and she could picture what went on in the house when she wasn't there. By the end of the week, she was happy to go back to day care.

Lisa Bennett, Roswell, Georgia

Build self-esteem

Our family moved right around the time our second child was born. I think that was hard on our five-year-old. I kept up a running dialog with him, always greeted him with hugs and kisses and said, "It's so good to see you!" I complimented him every chance I got—on his imagination, his vocabulary, his mechanical ability, his drawings. Six months later, he has a busy social life and he's forgetting what his old life was even like.

Jeff Bradford, Oreland, Pennsylvania

Resolve Regressive Behavior

Many preschoolers who suddenly get put in the role of big sister or big brother take great pride in showing off their emerging maturity. Others take a different tack and decide that being the baby in the family is too good to give up. These parents have figured out ways to help their displaced older kids feel good about growing up.

Give plenty of hugs

Feeling jealous toward a baby is natural for young children. When you're holding your little one and your older child starts insisting that he be held, too, get down on your knees and give him a hug.

Annmarie Byrnes, Poughkeepsie, New York

Point out the big-kid perks

Describe the privileges that go with being big, such as picking out the tape the family listens to or being able to watch a favorite television program. Emphasize that the baby is too young to do these things.

Caren Schwartz, Southport, Connecticut

Give older kids responsibility

Give your older child a responsibility that she can handle so that she'll feel more grown-up. For example, when you leave the grocery store, give her a small package and say, "I have to hold the baby, so could you help me by carrying this?"

Margie Fair, Elizabethtown, Tennessee

Recall your childhood

When my older daughter said that she was mad at her new baby sister because she took too much of my attention, I told her how I had felt the same way when her uncle, my little brother, was born. She was amazed that I had ever had the same experience. I told her how I, too, wanted to be the baby again but that I eventually learned that it was great to be a big sister. From then on, whenever she's feeling jealous, she says something like, "Mom, when Uncle Jerry was born, did you ever want to drink from his bottle?" as a way of letting me know what she's thinking or feeling. It helps her that I can reassure her that her feelings are normal and okay with me.

Marilee Moore, Salinas, Kansas

Talk about their babyhood

One night, after I put the baby to bed, my almost three-year-old son asked if he could have a bottle again. I could see that he missed his own time as a baby, but I really didn't want to allow him to revert to drinking from a bottle. Instead I took out the picture album of himself at his little

brother's age and we sat together for more than an hour looking over the pictures. He finally said, "I liked being a baby, but I like being a big boy now."

Celeste Holmes, New York City

Help them relate through play

My daughter is very impatient for her baby sister to grow up. In the meantime, I encourage her to talk to her sister while I hold the baby and play her voice: "Hi, Charlotte, I'm too little to play, but I love you!" My daughter follows my lead and makes up her own dialogue with her.

Jennifer E. Hays, Saxonburg, Pennsylvania

Battling Sibling Wars

Brothers and sisters may share the same gene pool, but that doesn't mean they always want to share their bedrooms, toys and (most of all) you. Here are some ideas for calling a truce in the sibling wars.

Keep closet space separate

When two young siblings share a closet, paint each half of the rod a different color to prevent squabbles.

C. M. Wegner, Minneapolis

Share cereal-box prizes

Deciding who gets the prize inside the cereal box is hard with three children, ages six, four and one. To make life easier, I remove the toys and hide them before the kids have a chance to argue. Then, when the kids aren't looking, I tuck the toys inside their lunchboxes as a middle-of-the-day surprise.

Stephanie Sanders, Warren, Michigan

Stagger their bedtimes

When my son and daughter were three and four, they used to fight constantly. It was no wonder. They were in the same classroom at nursery school, came home at the same time and had their dinners, baths and bedtime stories together, too. To cut down on their fighting, I realized I had to cut down on their togetherness. The solution? My husband and I started to stagger their bedtimes by a few minutes and take turns tucking them in. We found that we enjoyed reading bedtime stories and snuggling with our kids one-on-one much more. Best of all, their fighting noticeably decreased.

Ruth Mason, Jerusalem, Israel

Sibling Squabble-Buster

Siblings' fights erupt most often when Mom is watching, less often when Dad is in charge and least of all when both parents are in the room. In a study by Marcia Summers, Ph.D., professor of educational psychology at Ball State University in Muncie, Indiana, children spent almost 30 percent of their time fighting when they were with their mothers—"mainly because they were fighting for her attention," says Dr. Summers. Fighting took up only 20 percent of the children's time when they were with their fathers—"possibly because they see him less and value their time with him more," she adds. When the whole family is together, Dr. Summers found, siblings spend only a few minutes of each hour fighting.

Parents can minimize siblings' conflicts simply by being together in the same room with the children. "Parents don't even have to interact with each other or the kids. They can be reading or paying the bills. It's their presence that makes a difference," says Dr. Summers.

Don't insist on friendship

My two sons, though close in age, are very different. The sibling wars slowed down at our house when I stopped insisting that they each allow the other one to join in his games. Now when one has a playmate visiting, I do something with the other instead of insisting that they all play together.

Wendy Shu, Alexandria, Virginia

Develop kind habits

From the time my children were each about four, I ask each one to say one nice thing about each other at the dinner table. It's a fun way to start dinner and it reminds the children to see the better sides of their siblings.

Elaine Daucher, Salt Lake City

Stick to the rules

I don't ask my two children to be crazy about one another all the time. I just make it clear that hitting, teasing and name calling are not allowed. I also insist that they do their best to settle their differences before coming to me with a problem.

Traci Mullen, Schenectady, New York

Fake favoritism

Whenever one of my three children claims I spoil the other, I say, "Yes, he's my favorite." It always gets the kids laughing and gives them a chance to cool off and it works because I get to use this line on each of them at least 10 times a week.

Kiersten Lochner, Bethlehem, Pennsylvania

Let Each Sibling Shine

Older siblings have an edge in the family dynamics—at least from the younger child's perspective. Naturally, many younger siblings seek to imitate their older, more competent siblings. While a certain amount of big-sib admiration is to be encouraged, overidentification can inhibit the younger child's individuality—and can drive the older sibling nuts. Here are some ideas to help each establish his own identity.

Buy big-boy toys

My three-year-old son, Matthew, likes to pretend that he is like his big brother, Dustin. He acts out taking his lunch box on the bus and going to school. To make him feel grown-up, I bought him his own lunch box. I pack him a sandwich when I make one for Dustin.

Deborah A. Nanney, Temperance, Michigan

It's just a phase

It's quite normal for tagging along and copycat behavior to happen with children close in age, especially since the younger one may feel excluded if she doesn't participate in the activities her older sibling has already established.

Sandra Bendickson, Lake City, Minnesota

Foster friendships

Make an extra effort to help your younger child pursue her *own* friends and activities. Rather than just suggesting that she invite her own friends over or join her own extracurricular groups, ask her specific questions like, "Who would you like to invite over from school tomorrow afternoon?" so that she is more likely to make a date.

Michelle Fee, Severna Park, Maryland

Separate them

When one child is always tagging along with an older sibling, put them in separate bedrooms, if at all possible. Start separating them during activities by having one parent take the older child somewhere, while the other parent takes the younger child to a special class. A certain amount of admiration is quite wonderful, but too much will aggravate the older child.

Arlene Robinson, Lawrenceville, Georgia

Point out uniqueness

When a younger child is frequently copying his or her older sibling, the most important thing is to figure out what the younger child has going for him that makes him special. Emphasize his uniqueness by pointing out that he's *not* his brother or his sister. And be patient; with time, he will develop his own talents.

Joyce Taylor, Westminster, California

Empathize with your older child

If your older child is tired of having a younger sister or brother join in all the big-kid activities, talk to your older child and explain that her sister or brother is having

The Do's and Don'ts for Breaking Up Sibling Battles

Nancy Samalin, contributing editor of *Parents* and author of *Loving Each One Best* (Bantam), suggests these strategies for turning down the volume on sibling battles.

DO give children a chance to vent their negative feelings about each other. Allow them to draw a picture or write a story describing just how angry they are. Or give a child three minutes to say everything he wants to say about his siblings. (The sibling should not be within earshot.) When the timer rings, move on to problem solving.

DO encourage kids to come up with their own solutions. Say something like, "You kids have a problem. You both want to play with the same truck at the same time. How can you work this out?"

DO make suggestions if your children cannot come up with a solution.

DON'T take sides. Unless you were there from beginning to end, you have no way of knowing what really happened. And once you take sides, the child you sided against will have just one thing on her mind: getting even with her sibling.

DON'T take on the job of referee. It's a hard habit to break and your kids will not learn to resolve conflicts on their own.

DON'T allow either physical or verbal abuse. Words *can* hurt and siblings usually know just what to say to hurt the most. If a fight escalates into cruelty, you must step in.

DON'T underestimate the power of your words to stop fights. An often repeated rule such as, "We don't hurt anyone in this family, no matter how we're feeling," will eventually sink in.

---

a difficult time understanding who he or she is right now. Let the older one know that this is a tough period for all of you.

Maggie Ellis, Pittsfield, Massachusetts

Stress respect for privacy

I have two sons, ages four and seven. The four-year-old often wants to join his big brother and his big brother's friends when they're playing at our house. I believe strongly that my older son, Graham, deserves his time away from Gary, his little brother. I simply tell Gary that "Graham and his friends are playing together and the two of them want to play alone." I encourage Gary to do things with me or by himself when Graham has his friends over. I remind him that he has a right to play with his friends in private when they are visiting, too. I also encourage Graham to play with Gary when no friends are visiting. He does so pretty willingly, and I think it's because I've never made him include Gary in his play with his friends.

Anita Pearson-Bates, New York City

Creating Private Time

Family togetherness has its limits. Kids thrive on one-on-one time with each of their parents, as these writers have found.

Find special time each week

I arranged Lily's nursery-school schedule so that she gets out of school a couple of hours earlier than her big sister, Alison, two days a week. That way we have two afternoons to be alone together. I also have a standing date to take Alison home—without any siblings along—one day a week.

Chris Fleming, New York City

Pair up with friends

My friend Molly has two children the same ages as my two. Every Monday, I take both of the older kids and she takes the younger ones. On Wednesdays, we do the opposite. This way we get to be involved in an activity with our kids that is right for each child's age, instead of having to share their time with me with one another, too.

Marge Heenan, Albany, New York

Have one-on-one nights

With four children, finding time for each one used to be a problem. But now my husband and I have worked out a system that works. Each child gets one evening (from after dinner through bedtime) with one of us exclusively. That child gets to choose the menu, gets double dessert, watches TV or plays a game with a parent, takes a walk or does whatever else he or she wants (that doesn't cost any money). None of the kids get jealous because each one knows that his or her time is coming too. As an added bonus, Fridays are parents' night, which means we leave the kids with a sitter and have our own private time with each other.

Karyn Davis, Shaker Heights, Illinois

To each his (or her) own time

Late-night treats are a big hit with our four kids. Once a week, each child can stay up a half-hour extra. You learn a lot about a child when you don't have three others vying for your attention.

Karma Fordis Lindner, Galt, California

Raising More Than One Toddler

Siblings who are close in age present a special challenge. Here are some ideas to make life with more than one under two a little easier.

Buy the right equipment

Purchase a double stroller. First, take it for a test-drive in the store: Load it up with the children, the diaper bag and so on. If it's easy to steer with one hand, then you have a real winner.

Paula Thompson, Waianae, Hawaii

Consider the pluses

Look on the bright side. One, you don't have to find space to store infant clothes and other items. Two, you don't have to lose your postpregnancy weight twice. Three, your older child is much too young to regress. And, best of all, your kids will always have a playmate.

Laurie H. Duhan, Baltimore

Scheduling is crucial

As a mother of quadruplets, I suggest feeding, bathing and putting your children to bed at the same time (as much as possible) to save your sanity. I know it sounds difficult, but with determination, it can be done.

Janey Harton, Indianapolis

Baby your firstborn

Don't always rush to calm your younger child first when both children are crying and in need of attention. Sometimes I soothed my older child first, and I found that he quieted down much faster than if I had made him wait until I had taken care of the baby. The baby wasn't old enough to say, "It's not fair!"

Cari G. Virkus, Portage, Michigan

Indulge your older child

Often on Saturdays, my husband and I take turns caring for our baby daughter for a couple of hours while the other takes our son to the park or for a walk. When I am nursing my daughter, I make sure I keep juice, snacks, books and toys nearby so my son won't feel left out when I can't devote my full attention to him.

Karen Coolidge, Lafayette, Louisiana

Enlist your spouse's help

Talk with your husband about how things have changed. Let him know that you want him to be extra supportive and sensitive to your needs. If you don't have family or friends to depend on for child care, line up reliable help for the times when you will need to get out of the house for a break.

Peg Haan, Wappingers Falls, New York

Double up

A baby backpack was my savior. As soon as my infant son could firmly hold his head up, I carried him in a backpack everywhere I went. With my hands free, I could tend to my older, but still very young, daughter.

Andrea Levesque, Berlin, Vermont

Save steps when diapering

Keep plenty of diaper supplies on hand in different areas of the house—you'll be changing a lot of them.

Nenie Waller, Virginia Beach, Virginia

Get organized

Being organized is key. Every night, I prepare as much as I can for the next day—milk bottles, diaper bag, clothing. I also plan everything on my calendar—from going to the bank to dates with my husband to frozen-yogurt nights out alone for me.

Judy Miller, West Linn, Oregon

Be prepared

If you already have one baby and are expecting another, freeze food now. During the last two months of my pregnancy, I prepared and froze casseroles, soup and muffins. I loved not having to cook for a while after the baby was born. I froze everything in large resealable bags to save space.

Carolyn Doherty, Winston-Salem, North Carolina

Don't sweat the small stuff

With two babies in the house, remember that you don't have to be the perfect homemaker. If your house doesn't get dusted and vacuumed, it won't collapse—but you might if you try to do too much.

And if you have to eat soup and sandwiches a few nights a week, so be it.

Audrey Lewis, New Kensington, Pennsylvania

Enjoy them

I think having two children who are close in age is great. In time, your kids will entertain each other and give you plenty of love and laughter.

K. C. Gallagher, Lakewood, Ohio

The Only Child

The one-child family has become increasingly common. These tips can help you and your one and only enjoy your family configuration.

Help your child enjoy friends and solitude

I was an only child growing up and I never felt that I was missing out on anything except when I broke something and I had no one to blame. I had lots of friends, but I really liked being alone and entertaining myself, too.

Dana Gue, Frederick, Maryland

Realize you're not alone

As a preschool teacher, I can tell you that many parents, for whatever reasons, are choosing to have only one child. I don't think that an only child today feels out of place with his or her peers, the way that I did growing up as an only; it seems to me more normal now.

Tambina Lucas, Erie, Pennsylvania

Create sharing opportunities

I make sure that my son, an only child, has plenty of opportunities to play with other kids—many of whom are onlies, too. When he was 18 months old, I enrolled him in a church-sponsored playgroup that met three times a week and gave him plenty of opportunities to learn to share and take turns, the things that children with siblings learn at home.

Mattie McGovern, Exeter, Rhode Island

Be understanding

For a couple of years, my seven-year-old daughter has been saying that she wants a sister or brother. I let her know that I understand that her desire is reasonable, but that I love our family just as it is. I also make sure that she spends lots of time with her cousins, some of whom are also only children, so that they all enjoy a sense of family.

Evelyn Nyes, Bronx, New York

Offer experience with babies

My four-year-old son wanted a new baby—just like his best friend had. One day, when the friend's mom had to take the older boy to the doctor, she asked me to watch the baby. After spending an afternoon helping me feed, change and comfort the infant, Josh said, "Mom, promise me that you'll never get one of these of our own, okay?" That afternoon's experience seemed to settle the issue forever.

Marjorie Maelstrom, Oshkosh, Wisconsin

Create a strong sense of family

As a single mom of one child, our immediate family is very small. I worried about Catherine growing up without siblings and a father. "Is our family a real family?" she asked one day about two years ago. That startled me into action. To help her feel connected to her large extended family, I went about filling our apartment with pictures of three generations of her family and at least once a week, I call another family member and let her talk to an aunt or cousin. I also make a point of inviting lots of people over to our home for holidays and other occasions so that all family and friend gatherings are not just at larger families' places.

Edwina Moran, Scranton, Pennsylvania

Get a pet

I explained to my five-year-old that Mommy and Daddy wouldn't be having any more children, but I also told him that we could add to our family by getting a pet. We spent a few weeks learning about cats, dogs, hamsters and birds before deciding that a cat would be right for our family. We then went to a nearby shelter and got to know a few kittens before adopting one that Jason has named Pete. Jason and Pete are now constant companions and, I'm happy to add, Jason no longer asks to have a baby brother.

Janet Anne Kucheski, Huntington, New York

Raising a Large Family

If "the more, the merrier," is a slogan that applies to your brood, read on.

Each child is special

We try not to refer to our six children as "the kids," since other people often ask about them as a group rather than by name.

Peg Gannon, Milford, New Jersey

They're not always equal

You'll hear "No fair!" a lot as your kids grow up. I have six children, and they require different discipline at different times. For example, one of my sons may be able to go out to play because he cleaned his room, but his brother may have to wait because his room is a mess. Equal treatment just isn't always possible.

Jill Hoben, Wapello, Iowa

Spend time together

Spend one-on-one time and enjoy the little things with your kids. Every day, I try to set aside time to draw, play games, read aloud, go for walks or talk with my four children, ranging in age from four months to six years.

Laurie McCusker, Wrights Beach, North Carolina

Limit babysitting by older kids

Don't force responsibility on your older children and expect them to babysit for their younger siblings. Let each of your children develop a natural feeling of responsibility toward the others.

Marsha Thompson, Sperryville, Virginia

Let each child star

Designate a star helper once a week. That child can plan the evening menu, say the meal prayer, select a TV show or video for the family to watch or surprise his grandparents with a call.

Tracey Erickson, Willmar, Minnesota

Read all about it

A must-read for mothers of many is *Raising a Large Family* (Collier Books), by Katherine Schlaerth, M.D. The author, a mother of seven, offers wise advice.

Kate D. Kueser, Lubbock, Texas

Take turns with privileges

Rotate privileges, such as answering the phone and door. Our fastest child always used to get the honors, followed by his younger siblings screaming and pushing, followed by me getting in the middle of a big fight. Rotation works.

Judy Thomas, Waukesha, Wisconsin

Respect ownership

Ownership is important to children, especially those in large families. Each of my six kids has his or her own drawers, hooks and boxes for personal belongings.

Darlene Rogers, Piedmont, Oklahoma

To each her own style

As the oldest of seven, I hated to be dressed just like my siblings. Though it may look cute, resist dressing your children in identical or even similar outfits. Let them develop a personal style.

Siobhan Toscano, New York City

Swap clothing

Buying new clothes for each of my five children for the start of school year or for special holidays is impossibly expensive. But I don't want my children only to wear one another's hand-me-downs. I've begun to bring some of the good outgrown clothes from one child or another to a second-hand clothing store and swap them for someone else's hand-me-downs. That way, each child gets new clothes—or at least things a brother or sister hasn't worn before.

Eloise Stein, Forest Hills, New York

The Grandparent Bond

Grandparents and children have so much in common—starting with you. As your child's parent and your parents' child, you are the filter through which your children and your parents relate. With your help, they can also develop an independent relationship all their own.

Stave off jealousy

If your own mother is jealous of your children's other grandmother, remind your mother how lucky your children are to have *two* terrific grandmothers. The next time she is with your children, take a special picture of all of them together and send it to her in a pretty frame.

Charlotte Kirk, Detroit, Michigan

Allow lots of time

To help your children get to know their grandparents better, make an effort to provide more opportunities for your parents or in-laws to be with the children so they feel more comfortable with each other. If possible, start dropping them off for a few hours a week at their homes.

Kathryn Cast, Ronkonkoma, New York

Keep communication going

If one set of your children's grandparents lives far away and can't see the children as much as they see their other grandparents, have the children make tape-recordings and artwork to send to the out-of-town grandparents so that they can be assured of their grandchildren's love.

Beverly Carroll, Chattanooga, Tennessee

Use the mail

My mother sends my children knock-knock jokes, words of wisdom and stories about my own girlhood that they treasure.

Leslie Marcelain, Newark, Ohio

Personalize audiotapes

My mother tape-records herself reading aloud my daughter's favorite storybooks. She even rings a bell to signal to my daughter that it's time to turn the page.

Anne Nock, North Olmsted, Ohio

Work with pictures

I feel bad that my son, age two, lives so far away from his four grandparents. I made up a game that he and I play using large photos of them and a bunch of cutout hat drawings that we made. We take turns taping different hats on different pictures and saying things like "Grandpa Bill is a fireman today," or "Grandma Elaine is wearing a clown hat today." His grandparents have all gotten in on the act and send him silly pictures of hats and a few play hats, too.

Rhoda Lee, Aspen, Colorado

Put aside your differences

I am amazed at how patient and giving my parents are with my children because they were very distant and judgmental of my brothers and me when we were growing up. I recently bought my mother a sweatshirt that sums up what I feel are her feelings. It says, "If I had known having grandchildren was so much fun, I would have had them first." While I still have some grudges from my own growing-up years, letting my mother and father develop a good relationship with my children has been a blessing to all of us.

Monica Mary Clark, Tampa, Florida

Handling Unwanted Advice

They mean well. But let's face it: You have your own way of doing things, and those ways may not be the same as your parents, in-laws or others who are involved in your children's lives.

Have a heart-to-heart talk

When I admitted to my mother-in-law that her suggestions made me feel as if I wasn't a good mother, she was surprised and told me she didn't mean to make me feel that way, nor did she expect me to follow all of her advice. Ever since, she has cut down on her comments, and I'm less defensive. It's still hard sometimes, but getting along is worth it for the people we both love the most: my husband and my daughters.

Jennifer Morrell, Knoxville, Tennessee

Learn from experience

At first I was so intimidated by my mother-in-law and my mother that I let them convince me to stop breastfeeding. Now I am more confident, and instead of agreeing with unwanted advice, I say, "That's an interesting idea. I'll give it some thought."

Name withheld, Simi Valley, California

Ask for suggestions

Make a relative feel needed by asking for her advice *before* she offers it. My mother-in-law acts less controlling when I ask her for advice or ideas such as recipes and sleep tips.

Rebecca Zugg, Bountiful, Utah

Get mad

After my mother-in-law planned my daughter's baptism without our consent and repeatedly warmed her bottle in the microwave after I had asked her not to, I told her that if she wanted to raise another child, she should have one. She backed off.

Name withheld, Watertown, Wisconsin

Bend the truth

I told my mother-in-law, I hate it when *my* mother gives the baby candy or tells me how to raise her (even though she never does that). I was able to get the point across without offending her.

Name withheld, Chicago

Consider professional help

Seeking counseling was the smartest thing my husband and I ever did. He learned that I was not being overly sensitive to his mother's criticisms; I learned that the reason he wasn't speaking up was that he took what his mother said with a grain of salt. The outcome? I cut my husband some slack, and he started to stick up for me.

Name withheld, Ontario

Make your husband your ally

Instead of arguing with his mother, ask him if he will be supportive of your child care methods in front of her. There's a big difference.

Name and address withheld

Call on the experts

"The doctor said . . ." is the perfect out any time your mother or mother-in-law tries to impose her opinions on you.

Joanne Hurst, Dedham, Massachusetts

Be understanding

Try to be gracious. Our parents only want us to benefit from their experience.

Tina Liuzzo, Jamestown, New York

Put it in writing

I wrote a letter to my mother-in-law. She thanked me for being honest and apologized for interfering.

Kellie Pelletier, Lewiston, Maine

Find allies

My sister-in-law and I discussed similar problems we were having with our husbands, and they both agreed (surprisingly) to do something about it. Together, they talked with their mother and so far she's tried to be less intrusive in our lives than she was before.

Name and address withheld

Be direct on disagreements

My mother-in-law behaved badly toward my child at times. I just took her aside and told her in private, "Don't do it." That's it. Otherwise, she would have never understood how I felt.

Joyce Vento, Brooklyn, New York

Suggest some reading

I refer to child care books when I feel rattled by my mother-in-law's comments. Then I feel that I have an authority behind me.

Name withheld, Haines, Alaska

Speak up

My mother tends to make obnoxious comments to my daughter when she misbehaves, and often says she is acting as I did as a child. I think this is offensive to my daughter, although she doesn't seem to take it that way. I think it's important to speak up. Biting one's tongue doesn't always help the situation.

Chris Jones, Eugene, Oregon

Connecting with the Extended Family

Families may be scattered geographically, but emotionally, everyone can stay close. Some ideas . . .

Turn on the video camera

I videotape the everyday moments for my relatives: my son saying new words, singing, dancing, showing off his toys and reading from his favorite books. I've recorded first teeth, trips to the park and visits with Santa. There is even footage of me gardening, en route to work and grocery shopping. By letting our families in on the little moments, we all feel more connected.

Tara Barton, Ellenwood, Georgia

Start a family-gram

First list the names and addresses of everyone who wants to join in. Then each participant shares a bit of news, a joke, a small drawing or a photo, signs and dates his entry and mails it to the next relative on the list. Whoever gets the family-gram last sends a photocopy to everyone.

Reene Granlin, Telkwa, British Columbia

Picture this

I made a "Me book" for my two-year-old daughter. It includes pictures of all of our family and friends. When we went home to my parents for Christmas last year, my daughter shouted out the names of people she had never met as soon as she saw them. It made our relatives feel great.

Suzanne Franklin, Roselle, Illinois

Publish a newsletter

I write a monthly newsletter for my faraway family and run four regular columns: "Milestone Magic" chronicles my 14-month-old son's latest talents; "Dr. Mikey" includes his health reports; "From the Car Seat Window" details family excursions; and "Get-a-Life" is about what my husband and I are up to.

Carla Strong McGrath, Lexington, Virginia

Map the family

I purchased a large map of the United States for my kids and hung it in our playroom. Then I taped small photos of long-distance family members onto their respective states. We always use the map as a reference when we make phone calls, write letters or send gifts.

Susan Hammock, Darnestown, Maryland

Hook up with e-mail

We are computer nuts in my family, and many of us subscribe to Prodigy, an interactive computer service that has an electronic bulletin board and e-mail. The bulletin board lets me share conversations online with my family. At first I thought the price was steep ($14.95 a month), but when I compare it with what we get in return, I feel that it's worth it.

Eva Weitzel, Centreville, Virginia

Design your own stationery

Photocopy pictures of your children on white or colored paper for personalized stationery. It makes a delightful surprise for faraway relatives and friends when you are catching up on correspondence.

Sherry Girvin, Fountain Valley, California

Write to at-home family members, too

Whenever I have my son's picture taken, I always make an 8 × 10 copy and write a letter on the back. I tell him what is happening in our family and funny things he's said or done. Most of all, I tell him how much he's loved. Now his pictures will always be special to both of us.

Melissa McCann, Rocklin, California

Videotape a family storytime

During a recent celebration that brought in most of our family from out of town, I seized the opportunity and got out our video camera. I set it up on a tripod and taped anyone who wished to read my two-year-old son one of his favorite books. He now has a storybook video treasury that includes three grandparents, three aunts, two uncles, four cousins and several family friends. My son delights in following the books along with the video. It's a great way to instill a love of reading and keep him connected to the people who love him.

Hinda C. Bodinger, Bayside, New York

Color my world

Many of our family members live out of state and are anxious for ways to stay in touch with my four-year-old son. I encourage them to buy a coloring book, cut out the pages and mail my son a page from the book once a month. My son loves getting mail and he eagerly colors each picture that he receives. When he's done, I send his artwork back to our delighted relatives.

Tammy Griffith, Oklahoma City, Oklahoma

Break the ice with books

We visit my mother in Florida every Christmas. Before we arrive, I let her know which book is my son's latest favorite. She then either borrows it from the library or buys it so that it's waiting for him when he arrives. My son is thrilled that his grandmother always knows what his favorite book is, and that she just happens to have it on hand to read to him. My mother finds that it's an easy icebreaker after long separations. We like to call it literary bonding.

Beth Lommel, Bridgewater, New Jersey

Send special get well wishes

When a faraway friend of mine who is like a grandmother to my son became ill, I decided to send her a special get-well card. I took a photo of my son, Oliver, holding a big love note and wrote my own message on the back. It was the next best thing to being there.

Shelley Craig, Montreal

Jog memories with photos

My parents, who live out of town, love to talk on the phone with my four-year-old son, Seth. But he often has trouble thinking of things to say. To help keep the conversation going, I post recent photos near the phone of him engaged in his favorite activities. These "cue cards" help him relate everyday and special events to his grandparents, and make talking on the phone a more positive and fun experience.

Gwen Nowak, Great Falls, Montana

Let a puppet do the talking

My four-year-old son is sometimes too shy to talk on the phone when his father calls him from work or his grandma wants to chat. But if I ask him if Her (his brave bunny puppet) would like to say a word, he suddenly becomes very talkative.

Debra Levey Larson, Urbana, Illinois

How to Keep the Family Peace

Every family's dynamics include at least some hot-buttons—the things relatives do that trigger one another's ire or those situations that arise and leave someone's feelings hurt. Here's how some families coped with sticky situations.

Let kids say no to hugs

I don't make my children hug relatives. If the children wanted to hug the relatives after they had been around each other for a while, that would be fine.

Helen Patterson, Central, Indiana

When kids are shy . . .

Explain to the relatives ahead of time that the children are not demonstrative and do not like to be touched, if that is the case.

Loretta Mayer, Los Angeles

Be accepting

My family, like most, contains its share of oddballs, most of whom we see only at holidays. One aunt drinks too much and my brother likes to tell off-color jokes. I explain to my children that though I don't approve of their behavior, I prefer not to make a big deal of it because they're family. Throughout life, kids will be confronted with people who do things differently and they need to learn to be tolerant of other people's shortcomings. No one is perfect. When these relatives visit us, I just make a point of serving non-alcoholic beverages and telling my brother to keep his jokes to himself when the kids are around.

Name and address withheld

Resist the urge to compare

In our family, there are 11 cousins, ranging in age from three to seven! When we're all together every year for our parents' anniversary, my sisters, sister-in-law and I have a pact: We will do everything in our power to try not to compare our children to one another. So what if one walked at 9 months and another didn't until 16 months? We do, however, let the older kids each take a turn telling about the accomplishment that he or she is most proud that has been made in the past year. That way, each child gets a chance to shine and the moms don't feel obliged to brag.

Mara Aarons and Jennifer Briggs,
Naples, Florida, and Chattanooga, Tennessee

Prepare for family gatherings

Before relatives come over, I review some things with my kids—like how to say hello politely, how to handle too many hugs and how to help serve food. By giving them specific things to do, they feel more at ease in these situations.

Marian Hanover, Bensalem, Pennsylvania

Apologize for children's rudeness

If your young child says she doesn't like a gift, you should apologize to the relative and tell her that, at your child's age, he or she is just learning how to cope with social situations. Then explain to your child why what she said was impolite.

Susan Quaintance, Mead, Washington

Help kids learn kindness

I have a five-year-old, and I know that kids this age can make hurtful remarks to relatives without meaning them. I think that parents should take their children aside when this happens and tell them that what they said was not nice. Then have *them* apologize to any relatives whose feelings they have hurt.

Kathy Gray, Parma, Ohio

Teach empathy

When kids are inadvertently rude, *calmly* say, "Would you want someone to say that to you? You might have hurt so-and-so's feelings." Don't get mad or yell, or you will embarrass your child.

Susan Helm, Fredericksburg, Texas

Set a limit on gifts

If relatives are overindulging your child in gifts, speak up and ask them to limit the presents to one per family, rather than each member giving a gift.

Leslie Glick Parsons, Bridgeport, West Virginia

Understand the fun of giving

Relatives lavish children with gifts because it is so much fun to indulge and give people things. I found this out when a friend of mine asked that we not give her a baby shower for her second child. I realized I was looking forward to it more than she was.

Patty Lou Kattner, Bryan, Texas

Withhold some of the gifts

When family members give too many gifts to your child, confront the relatives and explain that if they don't curb their generosity, you will withhold some of the gifts from the child and dole them out over a period of time rather than let the child have them all at once.

Victoria A. Lytle, Conifer, Colorado

When a Family Member Is Ill

The in-between generation often must handle their parents' illness while raising their own children. It's never easy, but these families have given their kids powerful lessons about life while caring for their parents or other gravely ill relatives.

Just be together

It didn't matter what my son or nieces and nephews were doing when their grandmother was sick—as long as they were with her. The four- and six-year-olds would color, play board games or watch videos in her room. I know that seeing their faces and hearing their voices gave my mother joy.

Tricia Skrinak, Indianapolis

Little things count

I encouraged my three-year-old daughter, Lauren, to bring my mother things such as her mail, books and a glass of water. Sometimes Lauren would just sit next to her grandmother on the bed and talk or play quietly.

Dana Webb, Federal Way, Washington

Respect your child's feelings

If your child feels like withdrawing, let him give in to his emotions. It's hard for a young child to see a grandparent, once an active playmate, slow down.

Connie Packard Kamedulski, Wilton, Connecticut

Keep in touch by telephone

Because we lived in different states, my mother read her grandchildren stories over the telephone each week. My kids looked forward to these special calls; it helped them feel close to her until she died.

Laurie McCusker, Wrightsville Beach, North Carolina

Talk openly about death

My mother lived with us while she was dying and during that time I explained to my children, ages two and four, that everything lives and dies—flowers, trees, animals *and* people. I think this explanation helped them see that illness and death are natural.

Cindy Eaton, Mount Vernon, Indiana

Record special memories

With your child's help, keep a journal of your dying parent's impressions of his or her own childhood, and things such as his or her favorite season, colors and foods. Doing this will help keep the memory alive for your family after their grandparent dies.

Janet Schnitzer, Philadelphia

Let an ill person set the tone

Let the person who is ill be the judge of how much time he or she wants to spend with your children. In a weakened condition, someone may not be able to appreciate the children—seeing them might even be depressing. I'm relieved that my son remembers his grandmother as happy and full of life. Also, because I didn't take my son along on visits, and thus didn't have to worry about his reactions, I had time alone with my mother-in-law to say my good-byes.

Ellen K. Bass, Dix Hills, New York

Be honest

Use specific medical terms when you talk to your child when a family member is very ill. When my father was dying, I was very careful not to say, "Grandpa's sick"; instead I would say, "Grandpa has cancer." I think it's important to make this distinction because otherwise your child might be afraid of dying every time he gets sick.

Sharon Rowell, Braintree, Massachusetts

Let kids express themselves

Drawing pictures and singing and talking into a tape recorder was how my three-year-old son, Ryan, expressed his love and concern for his great-grandmother. Because of the severity of her condition, I could not bring him to the hospital. The gifts from him, however, always lifted her spirits.

Brenda Dyer, Fort Collins, Colorado

Let them see you grieve

When my brother was dying, I sometimes couldn't help crying in front of my young children. I let them know that I was sad that their uncle was so sick. I also took this time to explain to my kids how each one of us is important to others and that even though a person's soul may go to Heaven, that doesn't mean that we don't still want them here with us. Although they barely knew my brother, who'd lived in another country and had only met them once, they understood the loss by seeing my loss. They also surprised and delighted me by showing me sympathy, making me feel better by doing things like hugging me and wiping away my tears. As awful as the experience has been, my children learned a lot by it.

Eileen Keeler-Hunt, San Francisco

Helping Kids Deal with Separation and Divorce

Helping children understand adult decisions is never easy and requires particular sensitivity when that decision so profoundly affects their day-to-day lives. These parents have this good advice.

Keep some feelings to yourself

No matter what animosity you may have toward your ex, never share your negative feelings with your children. Since my divorce four years ago, one of the most difficult challenges I've faced is not to dump my feelings on my three kids but instead to show that I'm happy whenever they've had a good day with their dad.

Marilyn Casper, Brooklyn, New York

Limit at-home dating

When I began to date again after my divorce, I made it a point to meet my date at a restaurant or theater instead of allowing him to come to the door. I think my private life should not be part of my children's experience. It's too confusing to them.

Nancy Galdiero, Highland, New York

Share your love

No matter how hard it gets, remind your child at least once a day that you are thrilled to be his mother. Never for a minute let him think that he's a burden to you. And never give kids more responsibility than they can handle or confide in him as you would to a friend. My 10-year-

old son had a hard time after the divorce and started to act bossy with me and act out in other ways that said, "I'm not a kid anymore." It took a lot of work, but I finally convinced him (with the help of his father) that he was still a kid and that his parents were still in charge. He relaxed visibly once the message sank in.

Candece Buchanan, Hamden, Connecticut

Find emotional support for your child

My two children, ages 6 and 11, benefited a lot from an organization at their school called "Banana Splits," which is a support group for children whose parents are divorced. Talking to other kids in the same situation has helped them so much. My older child told me after a few weeks of meetings that she was surprised to find out that she wasn't the only divorced kid in her school.

April Santiago, Fort Lee, New Jersey

Growing Up in Stepfamilies

Creating a family is always a somewhat complicated business. When marriage includes children, it's even more so. These parents have navigated the often choppy waters of living in a stepfamily.

Keep communication going

I feel very lucky in that my stepson's mother is very willing to talk over any issues concerning her son with us, just as we are always willing to listen to anything she has to say about Greg to us. We work hard constantly to let Greg know that he matters to all of us and that we're all in the business of raising him.

Sandra Kemp, Orlando, Florida

Set up rules

When my husband and I married, each with two children from previous marriages, we all sat down together to draw up house rules. We agreed to meet formally each month to smooth out the wrinkles. It's an ongoing process, and even after four years, we're still working the bugs out, but at least we're working at it.

Christi Bolini, Port Chester, New York

Don't overstep

I think it's imperative that the biological parent be the one in charge of the child for the first few years in a stepfamily. It's impossible to step in and become a parent overnight. But gradually, you can assume the rights and responsibilities of parenthood. The important thing is not to try to rush into being what you think a perfect family should be like. Instead give everyone time to adjust.

Donna Epstein, New York City

The Adoption Experience

All parents are deeply grateful for their children. Adoptive parents, perhaps, are even more so. These families have discovered ways to celebrate their special bond.

Reach out

The Adoptive Families of America has been a great resource for my family.

Through this organization, you can find out about local support groups and also order books, toys and even videos and audiotapes related to adoption. They also publish a bimonthly magazine called *Ours,* which has a page for adoptive children seeking pen pals. Our seven-year-old daughter has had great fun writing to several girls her age. For more information write to Adoptive Families of America, 2309 Como Avenue, St. Paul, MN 55108, or call 800-372-3300.

Caroline Warmington, Palo Alto, California

Talk, talk, talk

For me, joining a support group for adoptive parents was extremely helpful. I learned that adoptive children have a wide range of attitudes toward their circumstances—some choose to ask a lot of questions, and some go through a period of not wanting to know anything. Most, however, eventually have questions. Who do I look like? Where are my birth parents? Why didn't they keep me? My support group has helped me to help my child as she struggles with many of these questions.

Christine A. Mezzoni, Shelton, Connecticut

Share the experience

My daughter's favorite book on adoption has been the one I made for her. It starts with a wedding picture of my husband and me and in colorful writing says, "Once upon a time, there was a man named Alan and a woman named Valerie who were happy except for one thing; they couldn't make a baby together." The story continues with our visits to the adoption agency, the preparation of the nursery, the baby shower and finally her homecoming—with pictures of us in front of the house, under a banner with pink balloons that says, "It's a girl!" This book has made telling the story (over and over again!) comfortable and easy for us.

Valerie Jacoby, Waretown, New Jersey

Celebrate the adoption

I have two adopted children: a 6½-year-old son and a 2-year-old daughter. We have a party every year to celebrate the anniversary of their adoptions. The children decide what we will eat for a special dinner and get to select a present from the toy store. After dinner, we talk about how they joined our family and how important they are to us.

Kate J. Hart, Wilton, Connecticut

Begin talking early

I disagree with the idea that a parent should wait until an adopted child asks questions to discuss her adoption further. She may interpret your silence as meaning that there is some terrible secret that you don't want her to know. She may not have an interest in learning about adoption as a concept, but most children want to know about themselves. I like to use quiet, cuddly times to talk with my children about their adoption.

Sally Dodge, St. Louis, Missouri

Keep talking

I have four adopted children, ages nine, eight, six and three. A good technique that I learned at an adoption conference is called dropping pebbles. During a casual conversation with your children, build on something you are discussing. You might say, "Yes, you are really doing well in math. I wonder if one of your birth parents was a math whiz," or, "You have such pretty blond hair. You must wonder if your birth mother had blond hair like yours." The pebble should never require an answer. It's merely food for thought.

Corine J. Reed, Algonquin, Illinois

Accept your child's sense of loss

When my daughter, Krista, first realized that she'd grown inside another woman, she cried and said, "I wanted to grow inside *you*, Mommy!" I cried and told her honestly, "I wish that you could have, too, sweetheart." There is no way to get around the fact that being adopted means facing loss. Each child will need to grieve that loss in his or her own way. I feel that our part, as parents, is to help our children through the process and to let them know that no question they have is ever forbidden.

Larrilyn Lindquist, Snohomish, Washington

Read about child development

I've found it extremely helpful to read up on what is considered normal child development so that I don't automatically attribute problems that our daughters are having to their being adopted.

Nancy Barth, Fresno, California

Gather medical information

As an adoptee, I was concerned during my pregnancy about genetic disorders that my child might be predisposed to. I wished that my mother had been able to get a medical history of my birth parents.

I suggest that all adoptive parents get as much information as possible.

Debbie Kaiser, Houston

Understand their questions

When your adopted child does ask questions about his or her adoption, make sure that you're answering what the child is really asking. Sometimes "Where did I come from?" requires a simple answer like "Baltimore" rather than an explanation of infertility and adoption. I've found that Lois R. Melina's books *Making Sense of Adoption* and *Raising Adopted Children* (HarperPerennial) have good age-appropriate information on when, how and how much to tell your children about their adoption.

Kathy Byrd, Houston

The Family Pet

Pet-owning families know that their beloved furry, feathered or finned friend is really an integral part of the family. Here are some ideas for helping the various species relate.

Teach pet care

We got a kitten when Timothy, my son, was 18 months old. At first, I worried only about keeping Timothy safe from the kitten. But after Timothy pulled the kitten's tail and tossed a plastic bucket at her, I realized that I had to teach him the importance of treating a pet kindly. We practiced on a stuffed animal as I showed him the nice and not nice ways to touch Crissy, the kitten. Whenever Timothy got too rough or didn't pay attention to Crissy's feelings,

I sat down with him and again showed him nice and not nice ways of treating Crissy. Eventually he understood and became very gentle with the kitten.

Rebecca Walters, Winston-Salem, North Carolina

Give kids jobs

I don't expect my 10-year-old son or my 7-year-old daughter to take full responsibility for our dogs, but I do give each one of them a job to do. My daughter is responsible for keeping their water bowls filled and my son is responsible for feeding them. Because they can easily see if the other has done his or her job, they remind each other of their jobs so I don't have to. Of course, I always check to see that the dogs aren't left without food and water.

Carol Ann Sturbentz, Santa Fe, New Mexico

Learn about your pet

Having Buster, our Lab, is a wonderful thing for our family. But beyond being a great companion, the family dog has also been a great teaching tool. My son, age seven, had trouble getting interested in reading and math at school. I used Buster to help him learn. We got library books about dogs, about training and especially about different breeds to get Philip interested in books. We also worked with him to write "Buster's Life Story," to practice his writing. And we made up silly math problems about Buster (such as, "If Buster had 10 bones and gave 3 to the poodle down the street, how many would he have left?") Philip found learning this way much more fun and it gave our family one more thing to be glad about having Buster around.

Naomi Aaronson, Douglaston, New York

Find the right pet

My son has allergies and could not have anything with fur or feathers around. Even fish proved to be a problem because mold, to which he is also allergic, grew in the tank, no matter how well we cleaned it. He wanted a pet so badly that we talked to an allergist who suggested a poodle, which does not affect most people who suffer pet allergies. Now Felix, our poodle, is a treasured friend.

Anne Wexler, Seattle

Encourage a special bond

My daughter is an only child and is a very loving and caring girl. I know she misses having a little sister or brother to take care of but I've done my best to let her know that our kitty needs her, too. For instance, when Sylvester is meowing, I tell her, "I'm not sure what he wants, but I bet you can figure it out." She always does. Also, when she's annoyed with me, I encourage her to tell her troubles to Sylvester and she does.

Jennifer Howland-Cassidy, Omaha, Nebraska

Creating Special Family Times

When the kids are grown, it's likely that their memories of growing up will be made mostly of the everyday rituals and routines we create now even more than the big events that mark their lives. These families suggest a few ways to make every day special.

Go for walks

My son Christopher loves to go for evening walks. So we've made a tradition of loading our coat pockets with cookies and just walking around the neighborhood.

Jennifer Joyce, Sea Girt, New Jersey

Make chores fun

My son Michael loves to come with me whenever I go downstairs to do the laundry. He sits on top of the dryer (I stand in front of him to make sure he doesn't fall) and we make a game of throwing the dirty clothes into the washing machine. It's the simplest ritual, but it's becomes our thing together.

Carol Yukna, Mashpee, Massachusetts

Play hooky

I let each of my children play hooky one day a year. We plan a day of ice-skating, movies or baking cookies when there are no tests or other important events scheduled.

Pat Tierney, New York City

Play together

Whenever we can, my husband and I drive to Mount Rainier with our five children ages four, five, seven, eight and nine. We hike, walk or, in the winter, sled. Sometimes we ride our bicycles to the park. Exercising is vital for our health, and it also gives us time together without the distractions of phone calls and television.

Laura Gutierrez, Tacoma, Washington

Exercise as a family

Three times a week after dinner my wife and I and our sons, ages seven and four, run and walk together at a nearby track. We usually have a 30- to 45-minute workout.

John Joldrichsen, Rossford, Ohio

Share your day at dinner

One of our favorite family rituals is something that we have coined serendipity time. During meals at home or on summer picnics, we take turns and share the best and worst parts of our day and week. By doing this, I hope to help my children to not only understand that ups and downs are a normal part of life but also to empathize with the joys and difficulties of others as well.

Nancy S. Kaczrowski, Luverne, Minnesota

Volunteer at school

I volunteer in each of my sons' classrooms once a week. It's a great way to get to know what their day is really like. In addition, it makes the stories that they tell a lot easier to understand when they get home.

Luanne Stong, Clearfield, Utah

Be a leader

After-school activities that you can volunteer for, like Scouts and sports, have a double advantage. Your kids can develop special interests, and you can spend extra time with them.

Juanita Johnston, Youngwood, Pennsylvania

Going out—at home

Once a month, we make a fancy dinner, complete with candlelight, soft music and dress-up clothes just for ourselves. It's fun, cheaper than going out and gives our kids a chance to practice their best manners. After dinner, we watch a movie together. The grown-ups and both children really look forward to the days when we do this.

Myra Brown, Mason, Georgia

Keeping Family Time for the Family

Many family-only routines and celebrations are interrupted by friends dropping by. How can you preserve the friendships while carving out the just-us time your family needs?

Talk to the visitors

When my children's playmates show up during times that we've planned family activities, we ask the kids to leave, in a nice tone, after explaining that it is family time. Then I tell them that when we are through with the activity, we will welcome them back and that I'll send my daughter over to get them.

Selena Lewis, Bluffton, South Carolina

Make an invitation-only policy

At the beginning of summer (or any other time when uninvited guests are likely to show up), invite all the neighborhood kids over for a barbecue or party and tell them that all subsequent visits will require an invitation.

Heidi Jones, Schaumburg, Illinois

Suggest that visitors call first

Tell the kids who drop by during your family time that they're welcome to come back when family time is over, and give them an approximate time. If that doesn't work, ask the parents to have their kids call before coming over.

Susan Steinman, St. Charles, Missouri

Talk to the parents

Ask them to explain to their kids that when they see your family entertaining or eating dinner outside, the kids should not come over.

Krystal Duncan, Fort Carson, Colorado

Handling Television Viewing

Few American households don't make room in their lives (and living rooms) for television and video viewing. These tips can help your family make the most of the experience.

Watch together

Since most parents have very little time to devote to TV viewing, make a rule that the kids can only watch when you're watching together. This has three benefits: (1) It will naturally limit their TV time. (2) It will allow you to monitor the viewing and to talk over any issues that arise. (3) It will give you quiet, cuddle time with your youngsters.

Cynthia Garnet, Kansas City, Missouri

Pay for television

I solved the too-much-TV problem at my house by starting a Pay-TV policy. I raised each of my children's allowances to $5, up from $2. I then began charging each half-hour of TV-time at 50 cents during the week and 25 cents on Friday nights and Saturdays. Given the choice of cash or viewing, they chose the money. I feel it's well spent, especially since I used to spend $6 a week renting videos.

Mary Quinn, Flushing, New York

Play together

I think television and videos are a lot of fun and I can understand why my daugh-

ters enjoy them. But I've found that if after dinner I offer a choice of playing a board game or going for a walk as an alternative, they invariably choose the activity over TV. I've never made TV seem like a big reward or the loss of it seem like a punishment and therefore my kids don't treat it as any big deal either.

Rose Mayfield, Purchase, New York

Branch out

The next time you find yourself searching for a video to rent for the family, cross over to the Musicals rack and take a closer look at the old classics. I promise your kids will love movies like *Top Hat, Singing in the Rain* and *Meet Me in St. Louis.* These films have some of the qualities kids love best: music, dance, color and a fast pace. And best of all, you'll enjoy watching these movies together.

Sharon Naylor, East Hanover, New Jersey

Learn to compromise

When two kids of different ages cannot agree on a video, don't give up. Many films available on videocassette are appropriate for both 7- and 12-year-olds, for instance. Having your children choose a film that works for both of them is a good way for them to learn to compromise. If they refuse to agree, *you* should refuse to let them rent a film.

Sue Edwards, Augusta, Maine

Limit viewing time

Time spent watching videos should be limited so that it doesn't get totally out of hand. Go to the store once a week and let your child rent one movie; if you have more than one child, let them alternate weekly. While one is watching, have the other do his homework or assigned chores or play by himself.

Jeri Walsh, Elkhart, Indiana

Give special attention to a nonviewer

We take our children every week to the rental store and let them each pick out one movie. When one child is watching his tape with one parent, the other parent can involve the other child in another activity. This way each gets some special one-on-one attention, and the parents can keep an eye on what their watching.

Kathryn Bryan, Virginia Beach, Virginia

Offer alternatives

I let my son watch one video a day. Instead of watching more videos, we listen to read-along books with audiotapes.

Kim Riggs, South Bend, Indiana

Buy short tapes

I buy videos for my daughter that last only 20 minutes so that she doesn't spend as much time watching them. After the video is over, we watch public television.

Barbara Muir, Renton, Washington

Play outside

When a child is hooked at watching and re-watching a certain tape, let her watch it once a day, then encourage her to go outside with you to play.

Jennifer Stenerson, Langhorne, Pennsylvania

Away-from-Home Viewing

Having TV and video-watching standards in your own helps your children be-come discriminating viewers. How do you maintain those standards when your children are guests at their friends' homes. These parents have solutions.

Talk to parents

If your child is allowed to watch programs that you don't approve of when he's at a friend's house, talk to the other child's parents. Let the other parents know that your family maintains certain standards when it comes to television and the you hope they share your concern about TV violence.

Paula Mercer, Lonsdale, Arkansas

Tune them in

Before your child goes off to play at a friend's home, explain to the parents that while your child is visiting their home, you prefer that he not watch certain shows. If they aren't paying attention to what the children are watching, chances are they might not realize how violent some programs are and they'll appreciate your concern.

Linda Josefs, New Britain, Connecticut

The art of persuasion

Be honest and straightforward with the other parents about your television-viewing preferences for your child. Most parents will not find it a major problem to switch the channel, and it might actually persuade them to monitor their own kids' viewing more often.

Robin Clark, Rescue, California

Send a preapproved video

If you're unsure of what television programs or videos are available when your child visits a friend, ask the parents if it would be okay for your child to bring over a favorite video of his that you approve of to share with his friend. That way you can monitor what he watches without being there. Or, instead of TV viewing, maybe the parents can think of another activity for the kids.

Nancy Bueschen, Sayreville, New Jersey

Saying Thank You

Helping children show their gratitude for gifts is a special way of spreading joy in your family, as these parents know.

Say it with pictures

Whenever my three-year-old daughter receives a present, I write a thank-you note while she draws a picture for the gift giver. It is a good way to instill in children an appreciation for giving and receiving.

Krista Allen, Terryville, Connecticut

Play the name game

When my 22-month-old son was in the hospital, he received a lot of stuffed ani-mals as get-well gifts. When it came time to name each of the animals, we decided to use the last name of the friend who had given it to him. We have a Coleman, a Kennedy and an Owen, just to name a few! It's a great way to remember which person to thank, and my son has learned to associate his stuffed animals with the people who gave them.

Deborah McEuen, Fredericktown, Missouri

Help out

On holidays and special occasions, my six-year-old receives a number of gifts from relatives and friends. I want her to send each one a thank-you card, but I know she's not yet ready to write twelve or more notes. So I write fill-in-the-blank cards for her and she writes the person's name, the name of the gift and her name. I want her to be in the habit of writing thank-you notes, but I don't want to overwhelm her until she's better able to do it on her own.

Margaret Hurley, Staten Island, New York

CHAPTER TEN

Your Child's Emotional Life

*U*nlike adults, children have limited experience in the ways of the heart, mind and soul. They love fiercely and they hate with equal intensity, though, most often, they forgive quickly and completely. Children are remarkably astute, even in their innocence, and a parent's job, from the start, is to help develop all the positive characteristics children bring with them into the world. It's no small order. But seeing a child flourish and grow into the best person he or she can be is truly the greatest joy of parenthood.

Blankies and Other Security Objects

Psychologists call them transitional objects or attachment objects. Kids call them blankies.

Despite their often frayed appearance, those blankies are important. They provide important emotional benefits to children, giving them their first objects of affection and security. If you are patching together your child's worn and tattered blanket or favorite teddy bear again and again, hoping that it will somehow outlast your child's attachment to it, you're not alone. Here are some ways to help keep your child's love object in good repair and ideas on how you can ease your child away from it when the time comes.

Buy a backup

My two-year-old daughter wouldn't go anywhere without her stuffed "Bert" doll. Fearing that it would get lost or ruined from frequent washings, I purchased a backup. I'm glad I did, since she did indeed lose the original and the manufacturer stopped making that model.

Marge Kennedy, New York City

Introduce a new lovey

I was unhappy that my daughter Clair's favorite bunny was falling apart. I picked out another stuffed animal from her collection—a panda bear—and told Clair that panda needed Mr. Bunny, too. I encouraged her to let panda sleep with her and her bunny. Of course, she agreed. Soon, she was just as attached to the panda as she was to the bunny. When

the bunny fell apart, she still had her panda to hug and lug around.

Naomi Stern-Miller, St. Joseph, Missouri

Honor kids' attachments

When my older son made fun of his sister's devotion to her blanket, I reminded him of how attached he was to his model airplane collection. I was proud of him a week later when one of his friends made a wisecrack about Alice's old blanket. Brent said, "It's really no different from how we feel about our stuff." The other boy quickly changed the subject, but Alice showed her appreciation by giving her big brother a big hug.

Teresa Santelo, Arlington, Virginia

Wash it gently

I wash my son's fraying blankie inside a pillowcase, which seems to reduce the wear-and-tear of regular washing.

Janice King, Madison, Wisconsin

Turn it into a pillow

My sons used to drag around and sleep with their old, frayed security blankets. But I came up with a way to wean them from this habit: I cut a square piece from each blankie and made it into a small pillow. In time the kids went to bed without a fuss because the familiar feel of their blanket on their pillow was satisfying. Eventually, they each also stopped dragging around the remainder of the blanket.

LaDonna Barna, Sumter, South Carolina

Make it smaller

My son wouldn't go anywhere without his blankie. It was falling apart. It was

ASK THE EXPERTS

What's the Truth about Thumb Sucking?

"Thumb sucking is a healthy, self-comforting pattern," says T. Berry Brazelton, M.D.

Virtually all babies suck on their fingers at some time during the first year of life; the first time, the hands may make it to the mouth by random chance, but baby quickly learns that the fingers provide a pleasurable sensation. Eventually, many babies realize that the thumb is the most efficient and satisfying finger to suck on. Some children even stick two fingers or their whole fist in their mouths.

If your baby is a thumb sucker, don't worry. Let her indulge herself. There is no evidence that thumb sucking is in itself harmful or a sign of emotional illness.

Also, if it ends by age five, it doesn't appear to do damage to teeth alignment. Attempts to wean a child shouldn't begin before age four.

When your child is old enough and you want to help your child wean himself from his thumb, here's what pediatric dentists recommend.

- Help your child become conscious of her unconscious thumb sucking. Phrase your reminders in a neutral way. Say, "Oh, I see you're sucking your thumb," or "Did you know you are sucking your thumb?" instead of saying, "Don't suck your thumb." The point is to make the child aware, not to make him feel guilty or belittled.
- Chart your child's progress on a calendar placed in a conspicuous place. Place a sticker or star on the calendar to mark each day in which your child goes without thumb sucking.
- Cover your child's hands. This method works only after the child is made conscious of thumb sucking.

also so large that carrying it everywhere became a problem.

One day, when he was 4 years old, I decided to cut it in two. I sewed a new hem on each half and told him that half was for sleeping with and half was for keeping with him. A few days later, I cut the carrying half in half again. A week later, I cut that one in half.

Eventually, he had a four-inch square,

which he called "my big-boy blankie." When that square wore out, I gave him another small square. He carried one of the squares with him through first grade. Because he kept it in his pocket, no one picked on him for it. I'm glad I never made him completely give it up. Even today, at age 10, he still has the sleeping half with him on his bed.

Sunny Cato, Lincoln, Nebraska

Let it wear out

My daughter would not part with her blankie and I was afraid that other children would make fun of her at kindergarten. With her okay, I made the blanket into a vest, which she wore every day. By the end of the year, she'd outgrown it and gave it up.

Hillary McManus, Binghamton, New York

Tell him you need it

I didn't want to make my three-year-old feel bad about needing his blankie. Nor did I want him to continue to carry it everywhere. One day, when he was going to his Grandma's house, I told him that I was feeling a bit yucky and that I needed to borrow his blankie so I could feel better. He gave it to me. I began borrowing it regularly until he got used to going out without it.

Gigi Samson, Tucson, Arizona

Building Your Child's Self-Esteem

Contrary to popular opinion, self-esteem is not simply feeling good about oneself. It grows from being good at something and having that competence encouraged and acknowledged by the people who matter in a child's life.

Acknowledge good deeds

As the proud parents of four children under the age of seven, my husband and I like to acknowledge the good things they do, big and small. To keep track, we have a weekly chart posted in the kitchen with each of our children's names. Under their names, we write the positive things they've done each day. For our son who is often fearful, we record small acts of courage. For the one who has trouble cooperating, we note each time he listened. Other positive deeds include acts of kindness, as well as cleaning up or doing homework without being told to. At the end of the week we read the chart aloud as a family. I find this activity helps our children feel good about themselves, and helps my husband and me focus on the positive things they do.

Margie Levinson, Sherman Oaks, California

Help kids see that effort pays off

My son, age seven, really wanted to be on the neighborhood soccer team and spent most of the summer kicking a ball around the lawn. I let him know that I thought all his effort showed not only that he cared about getting on the team, but that his willingness to work so hard for something he wanted was a gift he was giving to himself. In late August, he made the team. When school started and he was faced with having to do second-grade work, which was much more demanding than first-grade, he said over homework one night, "This looks impossible, but when I first started practicing for soccer, I couldn't kick the ball at all and now I'm really good at it. So I know that if I keep practicing reading, I'll get good at it, too." Then I knew that encouraging his efforts was really paying off.

Sally Delvecchio, Buffalo

Help kids face failure

I stumbled upon a good strategy to help my nine-year-old daughter learn to accept failure and try again. When she failed a spelling test last week, instead of comforting her like I wanted to, I asked her, "What could you have done differently to get a better grade?" At first she said the words were too hard and it wasn't her fault that she failed. I told her that that attitude meant she might never pass a spelling test again. She thought about it for a minute and then said, "If I studied harder, I would have done better." When she realized she had the power to change the outcome of a situation, she felt much better about her abilities.

Cheryl Brown, Memphis

Let them know they are loved

The underlying ingredient in self-esteem is love. When a child knows that he is loved, he can risk learning, can risk failing and isn't afraid to try again. Every night, snuggle up with your kids and tell them how happy you are to be their mother and how much you love them. Even if a child acts like he's too big for your hugs, give them anyway.

Evelyn Ansel-Tardo, Morristown, New Jersey

Enlist siblings' help

I have three children, ages 2, 6 and 10. The middle one was feeling really bad about herself because she wasn't as athletic as many of her friends. She couldn't ride a bike or roller-skate or ice-skate very well, which are things most of the neighborhood kids do a lot. Her favorite activities are playing dress up and drawing.

Rather than allowing her to continue feeling bad about what she couldn't do, I signed her up for ice-skating lessons. I asked her older sister to help her learn to roller-skate, and I started spending a half-hour a day helping her practice on her bike. Within a very short time, she was good enough at all of these activities to

Building Self-Esteem: Choose Words Carefully

The most powerful tools you have to teach right from wrong are the words you use. They can either shame your child or reinforce her sense of self-worth. Here are some common scenarios and words to convey the right message when you're disciplining your children.

- *Acknowledge specific feelings.* "I know you want the doll and that you're angry that you have to give it back to Jenny. That's fine, but you can't pull the doll out of Jenny's hands while she's playing with it."
- *Be understanding.* "I know it's hard when you can't do what you want. I feel that way sometimes, too."
- *Offer reminders.* "You have a hard time remembering not to pull the dog's tail, don't you? I'll help you remember."
- *Notice improved behavior.* "You have been doing a lot better with the dog lately. I like that, and I'll bet Sandy likes it, too."

join her friends without worrying about keeping up with them. I think because her older sister learned all of these things easily, I'd overlooked how not learning these skills would hurt Darlene's self-image. I also kept encouraging her pretend play and her drawing because I wanted her to know that activities she likes should not be abandoned.

Georgia Fontaine-Meredith, Cedar Rapids, Michigan

Compliment their behavior

I frequently comment on a positive aspect of my daughter's behavior, such as what a nice person she is, how kind she is to people or how thoughtful she is. I've noticed that sometimes she even says these things to her friends now.

Jackie Burns-LaRiche, Highland Heights, Ohio

Look for inner beauty

When a child is often told how pretty she is, remind her that while it is true that she is pretty, it's more important to have an attractive inside. When she helps out or does something nice, tell her that *that* is what makes her really special.

Mary Shoupe, Arlington, Virginia

Understand the need to belong

It took me a while to figure out that sometimes being part of the crowd helps a child develop his individuality. I would not allow my son to play video games like all his friends did. He wound up being isolated from them on many days after school and was beginning to feel rejected because they chose to play at their houses instead of playing with Josh at our video-game-free home. After seeing that I was

denying him the popularity that came from knowing about the game and the effect that had on his feelings about himself, I changed my rules. Now her can play two afternoons a week and Saturdays at his friends' homes. His spirits really lifted and his sense of himself grew more positive. Because he was a part of the group, the kids started coming over to our house again. I recommend to other parents that they sometimes step back and take a look at how some rules may need loosening up.

Cybil Applebaum, Cincinnati

Watch role models—together

I have a confidence-building strategy that other parents can use: Watch sporting events together on television. Parents and children alike can learn the importance of focusing on the good try instead of the bad play by viewing professional athletes as they miss a free throw, drop a winning touchdown pass, serve a tennis ball into the net or tee off into a pond. Best of all, these mistakes will probably be replayed in slow-motion!

Janna Schoenle, Voorhees, New Jersey

Help them show talents

Every child needs to feel good about something he or she can do. Each of my three children, Eric, age 10, Nanci, age 8, and Sophie, age 5, shows special talent in at least one area. Eric is terrific at piano playing, Nanci is our family athlete and Sophie is very good at drawing. We give each of them a chance to shine. We ask Eric to play music for guests. As a family, we attend all of Nanci's gymnastics meets and soccer games. We decorate our home with Sophie's artwork. Applauding their strengths also helps each child appreciate their siblings' special talents.

Andrea Kline-Hoffman, Fullerton, California

Read all about it

Read stories that have a clear moral, such as *Aesop's Fables,* and discuss how each character's actions have an impact on the outcome of the story. My children have learned a lot from the tales and frequently refer to them to explain some of their actions. For example, when David, age nine, who has to work hard at school, got a very good report card, he said he was "like the tortoise whose slow and steady work wins the race."

Elmira Fortune, Brewer, Maine

Early Friendships

By age 15 months or so, most children are practicing the basic skills of friendship—smiling at a familiar face, offering a toy to another toddler, even comforting a crying playmate. Here are some ways to help your child handle the buddy system.

Find activities that don't involve sharing

When the playdate is at our house, I like to play records and encourage kids to dance, bang pots or stamp their feet to the music.

Kate Malchow, Fayetteville, North Carolina

Distract fussing toddlers

When the inevitable fights occur, don't fuss—distract. Show kids a toy that makes noise, or something big and colorful. Before you know it, you've taken their minds off the conflict and they're ready to play once again.

Victoria Jesiolowski, Latham, New York

Enjoy your friendships

Don't stop having playdates if you and your friends' kids seem to ignore each other. Their social skills will develop over time. Instead of constantly worrying about whether the kids are getting along, enjoy this time with their parents. Playdates are a great chance for moms to make their own friends, too.

Deborah Hemdal, Bethel, Connecticut

Let them play

Unless the kids are doing something dangerous or hurting each other, stay out of their play. Your child is more likely to discover that he has something in common with another little person if an adult isn't telling them what to do next.

Rebecca Kameny, New Haven, Connecticut

Double up on toys

There's one important rule when it comes to keeping the peace between one-year-olds: Have multiples of the same toy.

It takes a few years to develop the concept of sharing. If you try to impose it at age one, you're asking for tears.

Michelle Foreman, Dugspur, Virginia

Play in neutral places

In their own homes, kids are less likely to explore new friendships. At home, my 18-month-old daughter doesn't want another child to touch any of her toys. At the park, Caroline and other children play on the equipment instead of just with their toys.

Freida Gump, Macon, Georgia

Handling Clingy Behavior

One mother describes her son as "Velcro Boy"—a tribute to the tenacity with which he clings to her on all their outings. If your child, too, prefers your company to all others, consider these ideas.

Arrange more playdates

My son, Christopher, was very clingy as a toddler, but when he had a friend over to play with, he didn't need me to amuse him as much. He always knew, however, that I was close by if he wanted me. Today he is a very social and independent six-year-old.

Grace Cotton, Windham, New Hampshire

Get dad involved

My two-year-old daughter prefers to be with me rather than my husband. To break the pattern, I encourage her to spend more time alone with him at night or on the weekends while I'm not around. I find that she doesn't cling to me as much as she used to, and she enjoys her time with her dad more.

Linda Rowan, New Middletown, Ohio

Explain your needs

It may be a hard lesson for a child to learn, but he needs to realize that he has to share his mother, whether you want to talk with a friend or sit by yourself and read. To encourage his independence, try playing a board game or doing some other activity with him. When you are done, say, "Mommy is going to exercise now, and you have to play by yourself." Don't worry; he may cry for a few minutes, but he'll calm down soon.

Judith Mitzner, Glen Head, New York

Practice separations

I made a game of separating and returning so that I could help my son, Tyler, learn to stop clinging to me. It started out as a return to the simple peekaboo game we played when he was a baby. Then I said, "I'm going into the kitchen now and you stay here until I say 'peekaboo.'" At first, I waited only a few seconds, then a few minutes. Soon I was able to spend ten minutes or more out of his sight. Eventually, he got used to the idea of my going away and returning.

Jennifer Farber, Lilburn, Georgia

Start early

My older son screamed if I tried to go out of the house. It was very difficult for him and for me when I returned to work and left him at a day care center when he was three years old. My second son, though also somewhat clingy, has been with a sitter since he was four months old. He always understood that mommy would come back home.

Shelly Osbourne, St. Petersburg, Florida

Introduce other grown-ups

I found that each of my children learned to let me leave the house relatively easily because they were used to lots of other adults in their lives. Each of their grandmothers spend one month with us during the year. My sisters and sisters- and brothers-in-law and many friends often visit, so the kids have always been used to having other people around and paying attention to them.

Janice Cottin, Selma, Alabama

Making and Keeping Friends

As their worlds expand, so do their choices in the types of friendship that they desire. How can parents help their school-age children meet and greet new friends and help them to keep those friendships growing?

Invite a pet along

My daughter is very shy and has trouble making friends. She also has a very cute dog. We realized that when we walked to school with the dog or took him to the playground with us (always on a leash) that Samantha would soon be surrounded by other children who wanted to pet Alfie, our mutt. The dog became a great icebreaker.

Petra Demitrius, Madison, Wisconsin

Preschoolers' Social-Development Time Line

By 6 months: Babies smile at people, laugh at playful interactions with adults, may cry around strangers and may use their bodies to get adults' attention, such as reaching toward a person and touching him or her as a signal to continue interacting.

At 12 to 13 months: Toddlers imitate adult behavior, such as pretending to talk on a toy telephone.

By 15 months: A toddler becomes more responsive to others' feelings and may seek out other children to share toys with and even to comfort others.

At around 18 months: A toddler becomes more adept at regulating her own feelings; she may cuddle up with a blankie for comfort, for example.

At 2 years: He may be exuberant around those he knows but shy around strangers or in new situations.

By 3 to 4 years: More sure of herself, a preschooler becomes more outgoing and socially adventurous.

When There's Trouble Making Friends

Here are some invaluable guidelines for leading your child to friendship.

- *Avoid labeling or allowing other people to label your child.* Social skills should be portrayed as things we all struggle to learn, and any child's social characteristics shouldn't be described as a fixed state, such as shy, insensitive or aggressive. Any label tends to perpetuate the behavior that it describes.
- *Set up situations with younger kids.* Having opportunities to exercise leadership and social skills with an admiring younger child helps kids achieve the same level of social participation as their peers.
- *Take pressure off.* Children's self-consciousness is greatly intensified when attention is focused on their response to an adult greeting or query. Instead of teaching manners at the very moment that an interaction occurs, practice things such as saying hello to an adult beforehand so that a social situation isn't a setup for social failure.
- *Involve yourself.* Help your child make friends by including children in social activities. Driving other children to school, sponsoring a scout troop, baking together with your child and his

friends or joining neighborhood activities can all aid your child's social development and strengthen your relationship. These activities are likely to encourage friendships that break through the typical age and sex boundaries found in school.
- *Assess the school environment.* When you are choosing a school, try to gauge the social atmosphere. What are the school rules on behavior? Is there a kind, accepting environment for *all* children? Are children encouraged to cooperate?
- *Look at yourself as a social model for your child.* You don't have to be popular any more than your child does, but your own tendencies toward social withdrawal or interaction will have a powerful effect on your child.
- *Find professional help, if necessary.* For some children, psychological therapy can help. If your child is extremely withdrawn, consistently the scapegoat, very aggressive or easily angered, talk to a professional who can help him develop appropriate ways of relating to his peers.

Play games together

Terrence, my seven-year-old son, was a pretty bad loser at board games and things like races and this was hurting his

ability to get along with other children who considered him a sore loser. We discussed the problem and his dad and I took turns playing lots of games with him, insisting, at first, that we take turns winning and losing. We taught him to lose graciously.

Janice King, Pittsburgh

Feed 'em

Not only is it important to make your own home a place where your children's friends are always invited, but it is also important to have good snacks available for them. My son hates visiting one particular friend because his mother only serves rice cakes and other superhealthy (which he calls "yucko") foods. The kids who visit our house are treated to home-made pizza, muffins or fruit freeze pops or other kid-friendly, but still parent-approved, foods.

Cynthia Thydholm, Fairfield, Connecticut

Throw a party

When we moved into our new neighborhood, my son, Terence, was uncomfortable with making new friends. I walked around our neighborhood and met a number of families and invited them to a house-warming barbecue. That made it easy for Terence—and us—to meet new friends.

Gloria Parks, Harrisburg, Pennsylvania

Go to school

My son never asks to have friends over, but when they're here, he likes it. He's somewhat shy and is very content to play alone. To find kids that would make good after-school and weekend guests, I pick him up after school a few times a month, get to see who he's hanging out

with, meet their mothers or sitters with whom I can arrange play times, and take the kids home together. Since I've been consciously helping him expand his circle of friends, he's become much more sociable.

Darleen Mann White, Chattanooga, Tennessee

Model friendships

I think my daughter has a relatively easy time making friends because my husband and I really enjoy having our friends around. Catherine has always been exposed to us interacting with other adults and she has seen what fun friendships can bring. She has also seen us help friends in need and experienced the help of friends when I broke my leg last year and a number of our friends helped out until I recovered. Our friends picked her up after school, made us dinner a few times and pitched in with the housework.

Alison Starkey, Hornell, New York

Join clubs

I was anxious for my nine-year-old daughter to enlarge her circle of friends, which I felt was becoming too cliquey. We looked around the community for after-school programs that interested her, and we found a history club for girls at our local library. The girls there all share Melanie's interest in American history and help her feel more comfortable with her school friends because she doesn't feel the need to be invited to every party and outing that the girls in the history club get involved in.

Alice Czurnik, Menlo Park, California

When You Dislike Your Child's Friend

Sometimes parents have difficulty understanding what it is about a certain child that attracts their own child's devotion. When you dislike something about one of your children's friends, consider these options.

Talk about her other playmates' good points

Tell your child that you like "the way Jessica shares," or "how nicely Matthew says thank you." I wouldn't tell her that you don't like her friend, but simply let her know which traits you value in others.

Deborah Keith, Foothill Ranch, California

Stick close to home

Restrict playdates to your house so that you can supervise the children closely. This way if your neighbor's child starts getting obnoxious, you can tell her that if she doesn't behave, she'll have to go home.

Juliette Franklin, Lauderhill, Florida

Make your house rules clear

I had a problem with one of my child's friends. Finally, I spoke with her mother. I let her know that I expected her daughter to help pick up all the toys that she had played with before leaving my house because I expected my daughter to do the same when at her house. My neighbor's response was surprisingly positive. Apparently I helped reinforce behavior that she had a hard time enforcing at home. At first her daughter balked about cleaning up, but now she helps out automatically.

Heidi E. Morehouse, Warrensburg, New York

Check out new friends

Joining a group will give your child more opportunities to develop friendships with other children who are being raised in a way that you respect. I know how tempting it is for kids who are neighbors to get together all the time. But I am sure that if you help your child seek new friends, he or she will want to play with them more than with the closest child available.

Pamela Meoli, Northborough, Massachusetts

Keep playdates short

Limit their time together, but don't forbid your children to play with someone who's not your favorite playmate. The friendship will seem that much more desirable if you try to prohibit it. And you can't totally avoid certain kids because you live in the same neighborhood or go to the same school. For the sake of being neighborly, I'd be more tolerant.

Julia Long, Nashville

Phase out the friendship

Occasionally say no or "We're busy now" when your child wants to play with a child you find disagreeable. If necessary, explain to the child's mother that you don't think the kids play well together. (I'd blame an age difference or something else that isn't personal.) Whatever you say, don't criticize the way another parent is raising her child.

Denise Strong, Grand Prairie, Texas

Don't be overly critical

Instead, try being warm and patient, and give a pesty child positive reinforcement. When she exhibits behavior that you like, praise or hug her. With a little time and understanding you might be surprised by favorable changes in her personality. If you don't, then you'd be wise to restrict their friendship.

Michele Lipman, Commack, New York

Avoid a troublesome child

I had a problem with a neighborhood child. She hit and bit my son whenever they played together. I realize it may sound extreme, but for a little while I resorted to entertaining my son at home when I knew that child was playing outside.

Ana M. Mendoza, San Antonio, Texas

Handling a Destructive Playmate

When a visiting child's behavior includes wrecking your child's toys or damaging your property, you'll want to intervene. What are some tried-and-true methods?

Invite the child's toys along

When a particular playmate makes a habit of harming your child's possessions, speak to the child directly and ask him to bring over his own toys to play with.

Jay James, Bedford, Texas

Welcoming Imaginary Playmates

Imaginary friends give children a feeling of control in their lives. They are not an indication of any deep-seated flaw in a child's personality and, in fact, show up in the lives of many well-adjusted, creative children. Here are some ideas on accommodating your child's invisible guest.

- *Support your child's belief, but don't overdo it.* When parents get too involved, children may feel that they've lost control of their own creation. If you take the playmate too seriously, your child may become confused that you can't tell fantasy from reality.

- *Don't let the imaginary playmate take the rap for your child's mistakes.* When your child reports that it was his invisible companion who emptied the cereal box on the table, include both the culprits in the cleanup. You might say, "I know Jimmy did it, but you're Jimmy's boss, so you need to show him how to clean up."

- *Make an ally out of the playmate.* Say to your child, "Biffy brushes his teeth so nicely," or, "Perhaps you and Biffy should take a bath together."

- *Encourage your child to set a good example.* Try saying something like, "Can you show Jody how to pick up your toys?" Your child may happily do things for Jody that he would not do for you.

- *Treat unreasonable requests with common sense.* If your child asks that you set a place for his friend at an already overcrowded dinner table, you may need to say, "I think Maria will have to sit somewhere else while we eat."

Supervise playtime

Join your child and his friend in projects that don't require toys, such as coloring or playing outside, so that you can supervise their playtime while spending some fun time with them.

Sheri McCarty, Dunlap, Illinois

Plan creative projects

Plan art projects specifically for when a destructive friend comes over. Then put the toys away so that they can't be broken.

Stephanie Weidner, Racine, Wisconsin

Play "no-toy" games

When a child who has a history of breaking your child's toys is at your house, set the rule that only certain sturdy toys can be played with. Or suggest that they play imagination games, hide-and-seek, word games or charades, none of which require toys.

Lisa Orfi, Brooklyn, New York

Head outdoors

I had a problem with one of my daughter's friends, who seemed to break something of Sara's each time she visited. I solved the problem by taking both girls to the park during the times I had them together.

Joyce Yang, Houston

When Children Don't Want to Play Together

Oftentimes, children's friendships develop because the children's parents are friends. Sometimes these tagalong friendships don't work out as the parents would like. Is there any way to keep a resisted relationship going between kids?

Talk to the kids

My friend Ruth and I have been friends since second grade. Our children, both girls, are now eight. They were friendly enough until last year but have lost interest in one another. Ruth and I acknowledged that they didn't have to be best friends like she and I are but they had to be kind to each other when we were all together. They get along okay, but Ruth and I have come to accept that they won't be following our path.

Lisa Casper, Laramie, Wyoming

Try again

Invite your friend's child over to your house, where your child may feel more comfortable and can initiate activities that he enjoys. It's difficult to say for sure that the kids really have nothing in common. But if they don't enjoy playing together, maybe your friend's child isn't interested in forming a friendship with yours either.

Nancy Brooks, Bogota, New Jersey

Don't force the situation

Your child knows what he likes and does not like. Even though you and your neighbor are friends, you may have to accept that the children are not going to get along.

Johnny Sanchez, Las Vegas, New Mexico

Give it time

I would be honest with my friend and tell her something like, "My daughter is being picky this month, and she just doesn't seem to have much in common with your daughter right now. I'm sure that the situation will change in a few months, though."

Stacy Pavlick, Upper St. Clair, Pennsylvania

Take them out

If you want your friend's child to become friends with your child, engage the two in an activity outside the home that both of them might enjoy, such as going to the park or to the zoo. They could also learn a new skill together, such as bike riding or skating, to promote a friendship.

Carine Nadel, Laguna Hills, California

Draw on feelings

Drawing may be easier for him than talking, and it may lead you to uncover his reasons for not wanting to play with a particular child, even when he's the child of your best friend.

Connie Vivenzio, Raleigh, North Carolina

Plan a two-family playdate

Take the children out for the afternoon to a neutral place—just the four of you. Go out for pizza, ice cream or to the park. Going out together helped my son and my best friend's son see that they could have fun together.

Valerie Pahl, Pendleton, Oregon

Reward your child for accompanying you

Make visits brief if you must bring your child along when visiting your friend, and try to plan a fun activity for afterwards.

Marcy Hotchkiss, West Haven, Connecticut

Bring toys

When visiting a friend with a child that you want your child to get to know better, let your child take a couple of her favorite toys to your friend's house. Maybe she doesn't like the toys that your friend's daughter has.

Nel-Dina Cargill, Jacksonville, Florida

If Your Child Is Teased by Friends

Children, even ordinarily kind ones, can be cruel to one another, especially when one in the group is encouraging others to go along with teasing behavior. When your child is the recipient of others' hurtful actions or remarks, you can help.

Develop strategies together

My seven-year-old daughter was the victim of teasing by two girls in her second-grade class. Every day at recess, the two would say pointedly, "We don't want to play with you" while inviting other girls to join them. My daughter was heartbroken. I helped her to see that her reaction—crying—contributed to their abuse because it made her an easy target. I empathized about how bad she must be feeling but explained that she would do herself a favor by not showing her feelings so much. We also talked about how she could get involved in playing with the other girls before these two had a chance to hurt her. Perhaps most important, we invited the teasing girls over, one at a time, for a pleasant playdate after school. Within weeks, the teasing stopped.

Claire Boynton, Rutland, Vermont

Listen

If your child asks you to contact the parents of the children who are teasing her it means that he or she is comfortable with the idea of a confrontation. If the victim of taunting doesn't want your involvement it may be because she fears more abuse. Find out how your child wants you to handle the situation before taking action.

Julie Polak, Bucyrus, Ohio

Talk to the other kids' parents

Sometimes it's a good idea to involve the parents, since most don't want their children misbehaving. Most likely, the parents will tell their children to stop and that can put an end to the teasing.

Patricia Jesse, Princeton, West Virginia

Keep your cool

Let the parent of a child who is hurting your child know that you are not upset at her or her child, but at the child's actions.

Also, have a specific incident in mind to discuss rather than making general accusations, so she won't feel defensive.

Rebecca Lowery, Huntsville, Alabama

Appeal to the teaser's conscience

When I was young, I teased a child. Her mother told mine, and I felt terrible about it afterward.

Susan Beach, Oak Park, Illinois

Stopping Your Child's Insensitivity

If your child has participated in hurting another child's feelings, you'll want to take action before the behavior takes root. These parents offer ideas.

Act quickly

When I found out that my nine-year-old daughter had been teasing another third-grader on the school bus, making fun of the girl's appearance, I was horrified. I told her that her behavior made me ashamed, something I had never felt about her before. We talked about how the other girl must have felt and Lydia started crying. She honestly hadn't realized how mean her behavior had been. She thought she was being funny. I had her write a letter to the child apologizing for her behavior and promising not to do it again. I called the girl's mother and told her how sorry I was that these incidents had happened and what I was doing about it. She thanked me for caring and for helping to change the situation. I'm hopeful that Lydia won't do such a thing again.

Emily Swanson-Gates, Brewster, New York

Look homeward

I wasn't too surprised to find out that my son was teasing another child because my husband is always teasing him! I found out about Brad's behavior because the school principal called me to her office to explain a situation that had developed between my son and another boy. When I explained to my husband that his behavior was having serious, detrimental effects on Brad, he worked hard to change his ways. He also apologized to Brad for teaching him the wrong way to behave.

Natalie Smith, Oklahoma City, Oklahoma

Explain your feelings

Explain to your child in no uncertain terms that it is just not nice to treat a friend in an unkind way. Don't keep your feelings to yourself.

Catherine Williams, Indiana, Pennsylvania

Encourage empathy

Children often don't realize how badly they are hurting the child being picked on. It is your job to make them imagine themselves in the victim's position. Once they think about how they would feel in the other child's shoes, they will gladly stop the ganging-up behavior.

Cathy Norton, Pennsauken, New Jersey

Back off

Children have to start making social decisions, and mistakes, for themselves.

Let them work it out. Once your own child has experienced the scapegoat's role, he or she may learn to be a little nicer to friends.

Sharon Weber, Orlando, Florida

Comments That Can Hurt Your Child

From one generation to the next, labels like "crybaby," "mama's boy" and "four-eyes" have been worn by some kids like an ill-fitting jacket. Sometimes the name-calling is because a child acts in ways that some believe to be inappropriate. Sometimes people make comments that mock a person's appearance. Whatever the cause, the labels say more about the person making them than the one hearing them. Here are some ideas to help your child avoid being hurt by others' insensitivity.

Turn the situation around

When my neighbor called my four-year-old son a "mama's boy," I hugged him and said, "That's right, this is my mama's boy and I'm so, so glad that he's mine." I then told my son that being a mama's boy meant that we enjoyed each other's company. He never realized that her comment was meant to be an insult.

Wally Frankel, Evansville, Indiana

Compliment your child

When someone remarks about a physical characteristic of a child, the parent should turn her attention not to the person who says these things, but to the child. Tell the child, "As big as you are, that's how smart and pretty you are."

Bonnie Tolin, Los Angeles

Show your pride in their attributes

Try to treat all comments made about your child's appearance as compliments. For example, if someone says, "My, you're so big for your age!" respond in a way that shows the one making the comment and your daughter that you are proud of her size. Say, "Yes, she has grown to be a big girl. We are really pleased." This way, you turn the situation into a positive one.

Megan J. Pallett, Ontario

Support your child

Justin, my five-year-old son, is very sensitive and has been called a crybaby on more than one occasion. Whenever this has happened, I've comforted him—not necessarily for crying but for the situation that led up to it. For example, I'll say, "I know that seeing a sad movie can make you sad, too. It's okay to feel sad when something sad happens." That stops his crying and lets him know that his feelings are okay. I figure he'll stop crying in public soon enough.

April Wannamaker, Victorville, California

Get mad

My son is extremely small for his age and has often had to put up with people's insensitive remarks about his size. Finally, I've begun retorting, "Gee, I'm surprised that a grown-up of your age doesn't know any better than to make such a stupid comment." My wish is that I say this to enough people to make an impact!

Name withheld, Springfield, Massachusetts

Help them understand the basis for rude remarks

My daughter, age 11, has moderate cerebral palsy, which affects her gait and her ability to focus her eyes. Occasionally, her appearance or actions are the targets of rude comments. We've spoken a lot about how some people don't know any better. I've also empathized with how she must feel when she hears these comments. Nevertheless, I also say to her, "You can decide if you're going to let people's comments bother you or not. You may not be able to control other people's thoughts or how you walk, but you can control your feelings about it." I think that giving her back some control is necessary for her emotional development.

Sally Powers-Day, Alpine, California

All is well

The most important thing for you to do is to make sure that your son or daughter is comfortable with his or her appearance. Then you should let your child and other people know that yours is a happy and healthy child.

Eileen Hatzos, Berkley, Michigan

Common Childhood Fears

Beyond the monsters lurking under their beds, the daytime can offer children grist for their imaginations. Fears of lightning bolts terrify some; others are thoroughly afraid of bugs. Whatever your child's fears, don't dismiss them as groundless. Instead, work with them to put their fears to rest.

Offer a simple explanation

If your child is afraid of thunder, for instance, explain that when clouds crash together, they make lots of noise, called thunder. Then assure him that the loud noise won't hurt him.

Julie Vogl, Provo, Utah

Read about it

Buy a book or look for one in your library that explains whatever it is that's frightening your child, in words that she can understand. Then read it together. If you can't find such a book, read up on the subject yourself and then explain it in very simple terms.

Michele Warch, Baltimore

Give her tools to fight back

We live in a busy city, which is not conducive to my daughter's temperament. She is terrified of loud noises, particularly trucks and sirens. I finally bought her earplugs to put in whenever the noises frighten her.

Abby Koppeck, New York City

Distract them with a song

When thunder scares my son, we sing the itsy-bitsy spider or play ring-around-a-rosy. If that doesn't work, I put on a jazz album that he loves, and we dance.

Sharon Ghag, Edison, New Jersey

Address the fear head on

Luca, my three-year-old, was very frightened of fire-engine sirens. I went to our local firehouse and asked if Luca and I could take a tour, in the hopes that seeing a fire truck up close would help. It did! A

ASK THE EXPERTS

Is It Sadness or Depression?

Children, like adults, can suffer periods of depression. But how can parents tell the difference between depression as a temporary mood and as a true psychological disorder?

Patrick Burke, M.D., Ph.D., assistant professor of child psychiatry at the University of Pittsburgh's Children's Hospital, has studied depression and anxiety disorders in children ages 7 to 19. Following are some of the warning signs for depression.

- Chronic sadness or irritability that persists for two weeks or more.
- Boredom. While most kids experience boredom from time to time, the depressed child has lost the capacity to enjoy favorite activities.
- Persistent pessimism or self-doubt.
- Problems concentrating, including an inability to complete homework or tests.
- Sleep disorders, such as waking at four each morning and not being able to fall back to sleep. (This is more common in older children.)
- Talk of suicide. This is a major cause for concern even if only occasionally mentioned.

If warning signs do exist, parents should talk to the child's school counselor, a family doctor or a local mental-health association.

fireman let Luca wear his hat and even sit on the truck. During our second visit the next week, Luca agreed to pull the siren's cord himself. Learning where the sound came from and being able to control it made all the difference.

Linda Wilson, Northbrook, Illinois

Find out which part is scariest

My son was terribly afraid of wind for a few years. I tried everything—explaining it to him, telling him how wind was good for us, but nothing worked until I bought him ski goggles, which he could put on to keep the wind from blowing things into his eyes. The goggles helped him deal with the other aspects of his fear that weren't as strong as his fear of getting something blown in his eye.

Marissa Ansem, Nutley, New Jersey

Make the fear friendly

If your child is afraid of dogs, introduce her to one that you know is friendly. Show her that you're not afraid, but never force her to get close. With each visit, expose her to the dog a little more. See whether she'll talk to the dog, feed it a biscuit or eventually pet it. Always be reassuring by holding her hand and telling her that you won't let anything bad happen.

Cynthia Bethune, Fairbanks, Alaska

Compare and contrast

If your child is afraid of one type of animal, take him to a pet shop and ask a professional to introduce your daughter to many different kinds of animals—from a distance. Discuss the different colors, hair types, diets and sizes of each. This might pique the child's interest in animals and help him overcome his fear.

Joanne Simpson, Shelton, Connecticut

Go to the movies

If your child is afraid of dogs, watch movies with dog heroes, such as *Lassie*, *Homeward Bound* or *Benji*. Watching the movies together might be a good way to expose your child to friendly dogs in a nonthreatening way.

Martha Moore, Montgomery, Alabama

Turn fears into art

Make a collage with your children using magazine and newspaper pictures that show the thing they fear, such as pictures of dogs or lightning. This will give them a chance to express their fears creatively. The more they can open up about their fears, the more likely it is that they will work through them.

Marzee Woodward, Murfreesboro, Tennessee

Zero in on the fear

A child who's afraid of dogs may think barking means that the dog wants to hurt her. If so, tell her that dogs bark to communicate, just as cats meow, birds chirp and people talk. Although she shouldn't pet strange dogs, you can tell her that barking is also a dog's way of saying that it is happy or wants to play.

Julie Johnson, Aurora, Colorado

Teach caution

Don't go up to strange dogs just to prove a point, because you don't know if the dog is actually friendly. I know, because my son was pushed down by a big dog in our neighborhood. It took a while after that, but I helped him overcome his fear by taking him to homes that I knew had dogs with good temperaments. Now we even have our own dog, and my son loves it.

Renae Hull, Lynden, Washington

Conquer fear head-on

My six-year-old daughter developed a fear of airplane travel that had my husband and me baffled. She'd never been on a plane and so she'd never had any bad experiences on one. Since we were planning a trip to Florida by plane, we had to address her fear. She finally said that she'd seen pictures of a plane crash in one of our newsmagazines, and that she was afraid that our plane would crash. I assured her that I would never take her on a plane if I didn't completely trust its safety. That calmed her down, but she was still scared. After our arrival in Florida, she said, "That wasn't so bad." She wasn't afraid of the return trip either.

Myra Getts, Minneapolis

Making Moving Day a Positive Experience

Whether moving across town or across the country, changing residences can be hard on children. These parents have helped their kids cope.

Say good-bye in writing

This year my family relocated from New York to Kansas. To help my six-year-old daughter, Amy, cope with separation anxiety, we wrote a good-bye letter and copied it for each of her classmates. We included a stamped, addressed envelope and new pencil, and tied each writing kit together with a ribbon. So far my daughter has received six letters, and each one puts a smile on her face.

Susan Cirocco, Overland Park, Kansas

Plan a farewell party

To help my children say good-bye to their friends and feel involved in our move, we had a farewell painting party. The children decorated moving boxes with sponges, brushes, finger and footprints and even helped pack up their toys and books. On moving day, my kids were relieved to see the brightly painted boxes, filled with all of their prized possessions, being loaded into the van. When we arrived at our new house, they liked telling the moving men which boxes belonged in the playroom.

Lisa Gillon, Branchburg, New Jersey

Get pictures

To help my two daughters adjust to an upcoming move, I gave them each a camera and told them to take pictures of all the people and places they never wanted to forget. I also made business cards for each of them to pass out to their friends, putting their photos on one side and our new address on the other.

Margaret Holmes, Fairbanks, Alaska

Unpack kids' room first

Even though we had six rooms of furniture and boxes to unpack, we made a point of fixing up my sons' room as much as possible on the day we moved in. Before we did anything else, we put up their beds, hung their posters and curtains, and made it look as familiar as possible.

Jack and Miriam Coatsdale, Tampa, Florida

Save memories

I bought my daughter a huge scrapbook for all of her friends to draw in and write notes to her, and she could paste special mementos of her friends and classmates before our move.

Danielle Jacobs-Moe, Lincoln, Nebraska

Get a pen pal

Before we moved to our new town, I arranged through the local school to get my daughter a pen pal so that she would know someone when we arrived.

Noreen Casey, Farmingdale, New Jersey

CHAPTER ELEVEN

School Days: A Primer

*W*hether your child's formal schooling begins in a toddler nursery-school program or in the first grade of your local school, many of the same issues arise: How will she adjust? Will she make friends? Is he ready? What can I do to help him to have the best school experience possible? Rightly, parents take their children's schooling very seriously. Keeping in touch with your child's teachers and principal is an important step in making your child's schooling a rewarding experience.

Easing First-Day Jitters

Few kids are immune to some nervousness at the start of a school year. Here are some rituals and routines that can calm them—and you.

Plan a bus-stop breakfast

Each year, on the first day of school, a group of neighborhood parents and their children congregate 15 minutes early at the bus stop for juice and muffins. This first-day ritual helps us and the kids ease back into the school year. A week before our bus-stop breakfast, we decide who will bring the juice, paper cups, muffins and napkins.

Karen Winchell, Fort Collins, Colorado

Learn a teacher's lesson

I've been teaching fourth grade for 12 years. When I first began, I was just as nervous as my kids because I didn't really

---

ASK THE EXPERTS

What Should My Child Be Doing in Preschool?

A preschool program should grow with your child. Activities and challenges should be age-appropriate. The following guidelines come from the National Association for the Education of Young Children.

Two-year-olds

The maximum class size should be 12 children with 2 supervising adults.

- Teachers play with the children and show them how to play imaginatively, such as setting up a tea party and pretending to sip the tea.
- Teachers recognize that toddlers often play alone or alongside another child. Two-year-olds cannot be expected to play in group activities, to follow rules or to play in one place for long periods of time.
- Teachers read aloud often, either one-on-one or to small groups.
- Children are given art materials, such as large crayons, watercolor markers and large paper and are allowed to explore using the materials, rather than being guided to produce neat, finished products.
- Children have the opportunity to run around, jump, climb, swing and play with balls.

Three-year-olds

The maximum class size should be 14 to 16 children with at least 2 supervising adults.

- Teachers should help the children learn to play with one or two other classmates.
- Because they are still too young to benefit from large-group activities,

know them and they didn't know me. So I started to send "July-grams," little newspapers that tell the kids who are to be in my class next September, some things about me and about what I wanted their fourth-grade year to be like. I included jokes and riddles, too. I also enclosed a self-addressed stamped envelope and asked that each child write back to me so I would know them better when school began. Over the years, I began asking the kids to send in their self-portraits and a one-sentence description of themselves. I now compile all of these into a book that I photocopy and pass around on the first day of each year.

Michael White, New York City

Plan a big after-school event

My daughter, Cathy, was really anxious on her first day of school. I promised to meet her after class and take her downtown for a trip to the ice cream shop, where she could order anything she

children should be allowed to enter and leave a given group activity as they need to.

- Three-year-olds are ready for puzzles, beads to string, blunt scissors, paints, brushes and Play-Doh.
- There should be plenty of read-aloud nursery rhymes, finger plays and circle games such as "farmer in the dell." Teachers transcribe and read back stories that children dictate.
- Teachers will begin to impose rules, like hand washing before eating or no hitting and biting, and will gently remind children of the rules as needed.

Four-year-olds

The maximum class size should be 20 children with at least 2 supervising adults.

- Children this age are better able to understand limits, and the teachers will offer clear directives and teach problem-solving strategies when necessary.
- Children learn through active exploration and interaction with adults, other children and materials. They should use real objects (such as buttons to count), rather than workbook materials, for learning, recognize their own printed name and engage in cooking as well as other hands-on lessons.
- Teachers should spend a lot of time talking with the children, encouraging them to express their own opinions, tell stories and communicate with adults and other children.

ASK THE EXPERTS

What Can I Do to Calm My Kid's Fears?

Some kids have difficulty taking that big step toward starting school. According to Richard Oberfield, M.D., clinical associate professor of child psychiatry at NYU Medical Center in New York, these common preschool behaviors may indicate that your child may need extra reassurance.

- Unusual clinginess
- Toilet problems
- New fears
- Regressive behavior

While first-day jitters are common, parents shouldn't take them lightly. Actively helping your child cope with the fears will help her get over them more quickly. For example, try reviewing in detail exactly what will happen in school. Compare it with similar experiences your child may have had at playgroups or parties, where other children have been present. Assure your child that you or a familiar caregiver will be there for her at the end of the day.

If that doesn't work, Dr. Oberfield suggests that you attend school with your child. Talk to the teacher and plan a schedule for reducing the amount of time you spend in the class each day. Being in the classroom not only reassures your child, it familiarizes you with the setting so you can talk with her about specific fears she may have. Make such talks a part of your daily routine.

Finally, consider how your own fears may be the source of the problem. Children pick up on unspoken tensions and frustrations, and it is not uncommon for parents to have mixed feelings about sending their little ones off to school. Coming to grips with your own fears should give your child the positive reinforcement she needs to start her new school life.

---

wanted. I told her that starting school required a really big celebration.

Valerie Manuson, Kankake, Illinois

Meet with a friend

The idea of going off to his first day of first grade alone really scared my son, Nicholas, so I arranged to meet another first-grader and his mom to walk to school together. The boys helped each other out just by being together.

Margaret Harland, Highland, New York

Get enough sleep

Cynthia, my five-year-old, was very nervous about starting kindergarten and couldn't get to sleep. Even though I was usually pretty strict about her falling asleep on her own, I slept with her that night.

Xena Williams, Prospect Park, New York

Share your memories

Before Caitlin began school, I told her some stories about my own school experiences. She loved hearing the stories and it made her feel that she was ready to start.

Rachel Holchom, Des Moines, Iowa

Never use school as a threat

I learned the hard way that saying things like, "You won't get away with that at school," could backfire. My son was scared to death of school and through his tears on the night before he told me that the teachers must be very mean and that he would always be in trouble because I had told him that, in so many words. I tried to explain that I had said those things out of impatience and not because school was a terrible place. Only when he saw for himself that school was a fun place did he calm down.

Gretchen Hamlich, Naples, Florida

Handling Separation Anxiety

Many children react with tears for days or even weeks when left at the classroom door. Their anxiety is normal. You can help your child take steps toward independence by following these tips.

Make a mental map

Find out what special activities are planned for the week from your child's teacher. Then, on the way to school, talk with your child about what's on the agenda. I bet this approach will generate excitement about the upcoming day. And if a child has something to look forward to, it may lessen some of his separation anxiety.

Lanae Paaverud, McCordsville, Indiana

Be on time

Make sure that you are always on time when you drop your child off in the morning and pick her up after school. It's important that your child doesn't feel rushed before saying good-bye or anxious wondering where you are in the afternoon. Being punctual, with a few minutes to spare, will keep her calm and enhance her feelings of safety and security.

Carole Messier-Melisi, Brentwood, New York

Get the teacher's observations

Find out if your child calms down after a few minutes and begins to play. If so, don't worry. It's quite normal for a child to cry initially when a parent leaves him at school.

Nora Burgess, Alpine, Utah

Get to the root of the problem

If your child cries whenever you leave, ask him to draw a picture about his school day or play make-believe school together. These are both good ways to help him communicate his feelings about his transition to school, which may include excitement and pleasure as well as fear, anger and confusion. Perhaps you'll find that he feels left out or that another child is acting aggressively toward him. Once you get a sense of what the problem is, have a discussion with his teacher.

Karen Richardson, Swampscott, Massachusetts

Help him make new friends

Ask about the classmates he likes and what he likes about them. Then talk to those children's parents and arrange after-school playdates for the kids. If your child sees that school is about playing and making friends, he'll realize that being away from you isn't so terrible after all!

Rhonda Quidas, Preston, Maryland

Pack a reminder of home

If your child suffers separation anxiety whenever you leave her at school, let her take along a favorite small toy or stuffed an-

imal each day. It may provide her with an added feeling of security when you leave.

Lisa Petsche, Stoney Creek, Ontario

Stay awhile

For a few weeks, rather than dropping your crying child off and leaving immediately, sit down and observe the class. Help

---

Tried-and-True Separation Tips

According to former preschool teacher and director Penny Raife Durant, here are some things that will help your child adjust to the separation that school brings.

- *Don't sneak off.* If a parent disappears, the child then learns not to trust the parent and it makes the separation worse.
- *Be matter-of-fact about leaving.* Even if you are hesitant yourself, put on a brave face and tell your child you must leave—and then leave. If your child seems extremely upset, acknowledge her feelings by saying, "I know you're sad that I'm leaving. I must go to work now, but we'll see each other later."
- *Establish a ritual.* One youngster has a short routine she follows whenever she leaves her mother: She gives her mother a big bear hug and a kiss. Her mother then says, "I love you, and I'll see you after school." The child then waves good-bye.
- *Make sure your child gets enough sleep.* Most preschool children need about

11 hours of sleep a night. Kindergartners and first-graders need 8 to 12 hours, and young grade-schoolers, need 8 to 10 hours.

- *Expect lapses.* Children from three to six years of age will show distress seemingly out of the blue. Possible causes include breaks in the family routine or other difficulties at home or at school. With your child and her teacher, work to uncover and address the cause of your child's anxiety.
- *Don't berate yourself.* Distress is simply one sign of your child's attachment to you. On the other hand, don't be concerned if your child doesn't show distress; it's not a sign of a lack of attachment, just the outcome of a different personality.
- *Know the crying will stop.* Most crying episodes will stop by the end of the second week. If the crying persists, ask the teacher if the anxiety your child is experiencing is typical. If either of you has doubts, seek professional help.

him to get involved in a game with another child. Once your son sees that you are excited about and interested in his school, classmates and teachers, he will feel more positive about his school experience.

Trina Jones, Houston

Play school at home

When my son had difficulty letting go at the beginning of each day, I decided to help him by playing school with him in the evenings. We took turns as the teacher. We lined up all of his stuffed animals to be the other students. Acting gave him a feeling of control over the situation and gave me some insight into his day.

Ann Willston, Fishers, Indiana

Cures for "School-itis"

Once the initial excitement of starting a school year fades, some children slip into a kind of school-avoidance routine, commonly dubbed school-itis. Its causes vary— from simply missing home to fearing a schoolyard bully. Finding the cause is a parent's first order of business. These parents have been there and offer this advice.

Help your child understand his fears

After a good beginning to his third-grade school year, my son Brandon started to complain of stomachaches every morning and didn't want to go to school. After allowing him one day off, I made an appointment with his teacher expecting to find that the problem originated with something going on at school. We called Brandon in to ask him more about his feelings about school and he blurted out that he wanted to stay home to take care of me! I'd recently lost my job and was looking for another. Brandon picked up on my anxiety and was afraid to let me out of his sight. He believed he could help me by staying home. He then met with the school psychologist who helped him understand that his job was going to school and that I would take care of my work and him. He seemed relieved and his stomachaches went away. I urge all parents not to let their kids feel responsible for the home front.

Charlotte Zimmerman, Brooklyn, New York

Don't make sick days too pleasant

When I allow my children, ages 6 and 11, to stay home from school for minor illnesses, I make sure that their days are not too cozy. I may have them clean their rooms, do extra schoolwork or help with housework. Most of the time, they're begging to go in by lunch.

Marge Quinn, Scranton, Pennsylvania

Take school seriously

Don't let your own lenient attitude keep you from sending your child to school. Because I work from home, a missed school day doesn't really create terrible child care problems for me. When my seven-year-old daughter, Luanne, began claiming not to feel well a few days a month, I found it easy to let her stay home. What I didn't realize was that staying home was becoming a habit. She soon was unable to keep up with her classmates.

Name and address withheld

Is Your Child Ready for Kindergarten?

Readiness for kindergarten depends more on development than age, so don't assume that turning five automatically renders your child ready. It's important to be sure, because children who start school too early face a host of potential problems, including unnecessary failure.

According to the *Harvard Education Letter,* studies indicate that, at least through the eighth grade, the youngest children in a class are more likely to have academic, emotional and social difficulties than are older classmates. Perhaps as telling, an additional study found that almost half of children with learning disabilities were in the youngest third of their classes, while over 60 percent of children in a gifted program were in the older half of their classes.

How can you tell if your child is ready? Talk to her preschool teacher, whose insights can prove invaluable. A good checklist is contained in *Ready or Not? The School Readiness Checklist Handbook,* published by Research Concepts in Muskegon, Michigan. The authors suggest that parents determine if their child can:

• Zip or button her coat.
• Tell his left hand from his right hand.
• Copy a picture of a square.
• Tell in what way a sweater, shoes and hat are the same.

Keep talking

Let your children know that you are always available to talk over school issues or anything else that bothers them. In the meantime, insist that they go to school unless they are truly sick. If the issues are not too important, they'll get with the program. If the issues are serious, they'll be more inclined to tell you about them so that you can help.

Heather Ann Segal, South Richford, Vermont

Watch your own behavior

My daughter was developing a habit of getting a headache every time she had to do something she didn't want to do, including going to school. I realized that I, too, often claimed to have a headache whenever friends suggested something I didn't want to do. I had to change my own behavior before I could change Leah's!

Joanna Cooper, Address withheld

Set up a conference with your child's friends

My daughter was having a lot of trouble last year at school, often asking to stay home. Since that was not an option, I asked her to invite a few of her good school friends over one Saturday. I served pizza and took them skating in return for a 30-minute roundtable. I asked all the kids to tell me the best and worst things about school, their usual reasons for staying home and what they'd each tried to do to make a bad situation better. It was a lot of fun. My daughter also found that she wasn't the only one having to cope with school problems. Now she's more willing to look for other coping mechanisms besides staying home.

Alison Myers, Arlington, Virginia

Get past the morning

I always tell my son that if he still feels bad at lunchtime that I'll come and get him. He's never yet made that call.

Ginger Arontz, Urbana, Illinois

Get him a school-based job

My son was very lackadaisical about getting to school on time—if at all. Because he happened to be saving hard for a new computer, I had an idea that I thought could solve his problem and mine. I asked around school and found a family that needed to hire an older child to walk their first-grader to school. My son applied for and got the job. Now he leaves the house promptly every morning to walk the other child to school. He's earning $15 a week in the process, quite a haul for a 12-year-old.

Jan Speck, Madison, Wisconsin

Offer to make a doctor's appointment

If a child is really sick, he won't mind heading to the doctor's. But if his aches and pains have more to do with the fact that he's afraid to go to school because he's unprepared for a test, he's more likely to risk the test than go the doctor.

Freddi Holmes-McManus, Plains, Georgia

Give it time

My son came home from his first day of second grade and announced he was never going back because he hated his teacher. I sensed (correctly) that he was really missing his first-grade teacher so much that no one could take her place. I explained that he didn't have to love his new teacher right away and maybe never would. I also said that he might as well find something to like about second grade because he was going to school, no matter what. By around mid-October, he softened his stance on his new teacher and by June was in love with her, too.

Georgia Matts, Topeka, Kansas

Let him express himself

I told my son to draw ten pictures of how horrible, ugly, mean and terrible his teacher was and then to get over it. By the tenth picture, he was laughing at how awful he could make her look, and with his sense of humor returned, he let go of focusing on the negative.

Eileen Brannon, Ypsilanti, Michigan

When Your Child Dislikes a Teacher

Not all relationships between teachers and students are heaven-sent. These parents have helped their children deal with their negative feelings toward a teacher.

Use real-life examples

I recalled to my daughter that I'd once had a boss I really couldn't stand, but that I managed to do my work anyway. I admitted that putting up with a person I didn't like on a day-to-day basis was difficult but that sometimes it was important to do so. I reminded her that I had to work for this terrible person for more than a year; that after he was transferred my work was fun again; and that her school year was only nine months long. She agreed to stick it out without much more ado.

Hillary Barsotti, New York City

Get your own impressions

When my daughter, Kim, was in second grade, she claimed that she didn't like the teacher, so I went to the school to meet her and found her to be a lovely person. I let the matter drop. Two years later, Kim also disliked her new teacher and again I went to meet her. This time, it was clear to me that the woman was not going to help Kim have a good year. She was extremely negative—about my daughter, about the school, about life! I spoke to the administration and had Kim's class changed.

Della Brown, Grand Rapids, Michigan

Find out why

My son disliked a particular teacher because this teacher was very demanding and strict. I realized that Jonathan had only dealt with very sympathetic teachers before and that a no-nonsense teacher frightened him. I also decided it was time that he learned to get a bit more serious about school and that this teacher would probably do him some good. By the end of the year, he learned more from this teacher than he had in his four previous years. I'm glad I did nothing to change the situation.

Melissa Chin, Cambridge, Massachusetts

When Your Child Thinks the Teacher Hates Her

What do you do when your child claims that the teacher has it in for her? These parents have had the experience—and offer these ideas.

Help kids learn to deal with conflict

Ask your child if she likes her teacher. If you get the feeling that she doesn't, ask her to come up with some mature solutions. If she acts on them, she will grow as a person through dealing with the conflict.

Kim Johnson, Louisville

Have a roundtable discussion

Arrange a conference that includes your child, her teacher and you, so that any misunderstanding can be dealt with first-hand. In this setting, you can clearly see for yourself how they interact.

Cathy Clark, Phoenix

Personality conflict?

When your child complains that a teacher doesn't like her, trust your child's judgment. There must be something there, perhaps a personality conflict. Talk with your child about this type of situa-

Dealing with School-Avoiding Ills

Here are some ideas for dealing with the headaches and stomachaches that often overtake children right before the school bell rings.

- *Focus on the cause of the symptoms.* If, for example, your first-grader feels devastated by a mean teacher, it is far more important to resolve that situation through a conference with the teacher than to concentrate on your child's tension-induced malady.

- *Acknowledge your child's distress.* While his symptoms may not be due to a virus, remember that his physical discomfort may be as real as the kind you feel when overwhelmed by a tension headache. Tell your child, "Sure, you're upset—but all of us have to do things that make us feel terrible at first. Even football players sometimes feel nervous before a big game. But you'll feel better once you get started."

- *Limit the time your child stays home.* If you do let your child stay home in the morning, she should go to school later that day if her symptoms have diminished. Psychosomatic complaints should not be rewarded with a day off. When your child comes home, do something special together so she develops positive associations with school.

tion, explaining that sometimes it is difficult to get along with certain people, but she should just do her best and wait it out.

Bonnie Pluta, South Bend, Indiana

Get specific

Ask your child for specific examples of when his teacher has given him the impression that she doesn't like him. Then go to the teacher with these examples and ask her for her explanation of what happened, informing her of your child's feelings. If her responses are unsatisfactory, perhaps a meeting with the principal might prove useful.

Martha Wells, Natick, Massachusetts

Helping Kids Handle School Schedules

For very young children, school may consist of three half-days a week, which can be confusing until they adapt to the rhythm. Older children may have a particular class, such as art or dance, only once or twice a week and not be sure when to bring in special clothing. These parents have found ways to help children keep track of their schedules.

Declare dinosaur days

Going to preschool five days a week was a tough transition for my son, Daniel, who had been attending school three days a week. He constantly asked me, "When do I get a day off?" and "What do I do today?" To help him keep track of his new schedule, I initiated a bedtime ritual: He places reusable dinosaur stickers on his wall calendar to indicate what's up for the next day. A stegosaurus means a school day, a triceratops is a weekend day or a day off and a fossil sticker represents a T-ball or soccer game. Now when Daniel wakes up, he knows exactly what to expect.

Jamie Pellegrino, Poway, California

Personalize a calendar

My three-year-old daughter constantly asked me which day she went to preschool and which day she went to her babysitter. To help her keep track, I designed a picture calendar. Using a large

Does Your Child's School Make the Grade?

How can you tell if a school is good? Here is an abridged list of questions devised by R. Bruce McGill, Ed.D., of the Educational Records Bureau, that can help you decide.

- Does the school have a written statement of philosophy? For example, what does the school believe each student should achieve in terms of intellectual, social and cultural growth? Do these educational objectives mesh with your own?
- What is the student-teacher ratio for each class your child takes? (The overall ratio may include the librarian, gym teachers and aides.)
- How extensive are nonacademic offerings? What percentage of students participate?
- Are the physical facilities conducive to learning?
- Is there a built-in program for supervision of staff and in-service education of teachers?
- What objective measure is there for determining school effectiveness as applied to academic programs? How,

for example, do students rate on standardized tests, and which tests are used?
- Does the school have a system that provides a conference with parents and student? An annual conference should be a minimum.
- What evidences are there of teacher commitment? Is homework given on a regular basis? Is it promptly corrected and returned? Do teachers stay after school to work with students if necessary?
- Is there a cooperative teacher-administrative policy with procedures for ensuring appropriate student behavior? (Look for a written policy that deals with dress, tardiness, smoking, and the like.)
- Are there quick intervention strategies for helping students who fall behind?

poster board, I drew seven columns for the days of the week. Then I took photos of the places where she spends time (the babysitter's, preschool, church, Grandma's and Grandpa's home). Every night, with two-sided tape, I put the pictures in the next day's column in the order of that day's events. I think her special calendar has helped her feel more in control.

Carol Patullo, Bound Brook, New Jersey

Pack reminders

When my daughter, Emily, began kindergarten, we changed from having a babysitter every day to an after-school program three days a week. To help her keep track of where she goes after school each day, I attached different keychains (without keys) to her backpack. A Snoopy chain means the sitter will pick her up. A heart keychain means it's my day to get her and an apple keychain says that today's a day for an after-school club.

Oona O'Shea, Minneapolis

Hold a morning review session

My son got confused and frightened when he entered fourth grade and a new school where kids changed classes frequently instead of staying in their homeroom for most of the day. I asked the teacher for a copy of the schedule, which we posted to the inside of the front door. That way Jake can review his scheduled classes every morning before leaving.

Luellen Mackey, New York City

Adjust nap time

My son was used to a long late-morning nap, but at his preschool, the naps were scheduled for early afternoon. I

helped him adjust to the new schedule a few weeks before school started so that he'd be used to staying awake through lunchtime before September came.

Tracy Powell, Anaheim, California

Keeping in Touch at School

Asking children to act as messengers between you and the school is an almost surefire way to short-circuit communication. Instead, try these systems to keep abreast of what you need to know.

Check backpacks

When I ask my kids if they have anything for me from school, the usual answer is "I don't know." I've gotten into the habit of checking their backpacks every few days. I usually uncover at least one note per child that was important for me to see, such as a permission slip for a class trip.

Michelle Annaconti, Toronto

Introduce yourself

It's important for kids' teachers to know that the parents are involved in their education. I make a point of introducing myself to each of my kid's teachers early in the school year and then dropping by at least once a month and getting an informal update on their progress.

Joyce Hendricks, Annapolis, Maryland

Plan get-togethers

With so many parents working and unable to pick up and drop off their kids, our school initiated a "Second-Saturday"

Staying Informed

Here are five great ideas for keeping track of your child's school year.

1. Keep a folder in your desk for school-related information. A lot of messages will be sent home by the teacher, many of which you will want to save for future reference. Also, keep copies of your child's medical forms and other papers that your school periodically requires in this file.

2. Keep a large centrally located calendar for noting school events, such as teacher conferences, school plays and half-days. Whenever a notice comes home, immediately transfer the information onto the calendar and note those days when you or your spouse will need to take time off from work to attend school events or days when you're to pack a lunch or spending money for a field trip. Also enter reminders for making future appointments, such as scheduling a doctor's appointment early in the summer to avoid the back-to-school rush.

3. Have a family bulletin board to show off school papers and to post notices from school.

4. Join your school's parents' association or PTA; it's the best way to meet other parents and teachers and to stay on top of the latest news.

5. Enlist your child's help in periodically cleaning out her backpack, desk and bookshelves to find papers that need your attention.

get-together every month. On the second Saturday of each month, a teacher or administrative representative is available in the school library. Parents bring coffee and muffins, and we all gather to get to know each other better and see the bulletin boards and to hear about upcoming events. It's lots of fun.

Lucy Potsdam-Johnston, Miami

Put a parent in charge

In my daughter's school, each class has a class parent, and it changes for each week of school. That parent makes sure that he or she knows all the assignments for the week and about any class trips or school events that are scheduled. That parent is available for phone calls from other parents, from Monday through Thursday, between 7:00 P.M. and 9:00 P.M. This system has really worked.

Isabel Hastings, Chattanooga, Tennessee

Tracking School Supplies at Home

Looking for the backpack, lunch box, homework and library books as you rush through the morning routine can put a strained start on the day. What have some parents done to help their kids keep track of their school supplies? Here are some great ideas.

Go for neon colors

I was tired of searching high and low every morning for my children's school things. When it was time to replace their backpacks and lunch boxes, I bought

Shopping for School Supplies

What are the supplies most school kids need? Here's a list of the basics. Talk to other parents to add or subtract, according to your child's particular needs.

To create: Pencils, lined paper, erasers, pens, Scotch tape, construction paper, washable markers, assignment pads, all-purpose glue, ruler, child-safe scissors, stapler and staples

To carry and store supplies: Pencil box, sturdy backpack with easily accessible compartments, lunch box and Thermos

To store special supplies and for projects: Sturdy cardboard or plastic shoeboxes

To identify belongings: Printed cloth nametags to sew into clothing or permanent laundry markers to write on clothing, including boots and sneakers

For computer users: Computer disks, computer paper, child-friendly word-processing program

Special items to consider: Calculator, children's dictionary, special computer mouse designed for kids, age-appropriate CD-ROMs and other computer programs

neon pink for one daughter and neon green for the other. Even on a morning when we're all tired, it's easy to find things that are so visible.

Sharon Henry-Davidowitz, Wilton, Connecticut

Basket it

We keep a big wicker basket by the front door. When my kids or my husband and I get home, we drop our briefcases and backpacks into the basket. After finishing any homework, we return them to the basket where we can grab them easily on our way out the door.

Barbara Lincoln, Davis, California

Make it part of the bedtime routine

Because my second-grader, Sara, and fourth-grader, Janie, used to look franti-

cally for their school stuff in the morning, often causing them to miss the bus, I initiated a school checklist as part of the nightly bedtime routine. Before I read them a good-night story, they have to make sure that everything they need for the next day is in their backpacks and that I have signed anything that I was supposed to sign. It has made our mornings a lot easier.

Anne Cummins, St. Paul, Minnesota

Create all-in-one coats

Finding gloves and hats used to be a big problem in the morning until I trained my kids to put their hats in their sleeves and their gloves in their pockets before hanging them up. We haven't been late to school all winter!

Debbie Trabor, St. Joseph, Missouri

Bringing It All Home

As difficult as it is for parents to accept, most kids can manage to come home from school leaving things like homework assignments, boots and even winter jackets behind. "How could you lose your coat?" we ask in wonder. "I dunno," they reply. Before blowing up, try these ideas.

Double for nothing

When my son Thomas got in the habit of forgetting his homework assignment at school, I set up a new rule: The next time he forgot, he would have to do double the homework the next day. That meant that instead of reading one book, he'd have to read two. Instead of doing 10 math problems, he'd have to do 20. After just one night of this new system, he began remembering his assignment book.

Matt Preston, Shaker Heights, Illinois

Dock 'em

After losing a fourth pair of gloves at school, I began charging my nine-year-old for each pair he lost out of his allowance. Still, for two weeks in a row, he lost his entire allowance to pay for the gloves. By the third week, when he saw that I meant it, he brought them home every day. It's almost March and the glove season will soon be over, but, I'm happy to say, he's lost only one glove since he had to start paying for them himself.

Donna Campbell-Dineti, Hanover, New Hampshire

Form a phone chain

Somehow my son Jason managed to lose his homework assignment two out of three days. I collected the phone numbers of a few of his classmates so that I could call and get the assignments.

Malary Nussbaum, Santa Monica, California

Let them live with the consequences

Kimberly, my 11-year-old, had a very laissez-faire attitude about keeping track of her library books. In the past, I would scurry around the house to find the missing items or buy replacements. I talked with the school librarian who agreed on a plan with me. If Kimberly lost a book, she would have to work off its cost at the library, even if that meant missing her gymnastics class after school. As I write this, she is dusting off library books when she'd rather have been doing splits.

'Twas the Night Before a School Day . . .

Get organized at night to avoid frenzied mornings. Here's how.

- Set out the clothes your child will wear.
- Check the backpack to make sure all items needed tomorrow are packed tonight.
- Put the backpack by the front door.
- Settle on what you're planning to pack for the school lunch to avoid morning discussions and arguments over the menu.
- Get to sleep on time.

I think the lesson is having an impact, though, since this is the first time that she's really upset about losing a book!

Lorraine Kelley, Hamden, Connecticut

Logging library books

When we go to the library, we usually end up with a lot of books. I've started removing the library cards from the books as soon as we get home and pinning them up on the bulletin board or refrigerator. This way, I know how many books we checked out, when they are due back and my child doesn't lose or tear the cards.

Pam Hutchins, San Antonio, Texas

Mark the calendar

My four-year-old daughter and I love checking out books from the library. To avoid last-minute searches and overdue fines when it's time to return them, I keep track of what we borrow: When we get home from the library, I jot down the book's name, its due date and who borrowed it on a calendar in the kitchen.

Jill H. Pace, Garrett Park, Maryland

Save your money

The first time my 13-year-old son lost his winter jacket, I was upset. The second time, I was furious. Each of those jackets had been expensive football-style ones that he really wanted. I replaced the second lost jacket with a plain ski parka, which he felt was totally uncool. I explained that until he could prove to me that he wouldn't lose his things, I would only buy inexpensive, uncool clothes. Within a week, he found one of the lost jackets at a friend's house. He's held on to it for a few months now, knowing that if he loses it, he goes back to the ski parka.

Patricia Brown, Winston-Salem, North Carolina

Tips to Get Them Reading

Reading skills remain the most important ones that children will use in the classroom. Helping children become literate, of course, begins long before they're ready for school. All research indicates that the more children are read to by their parents, the more they'll love reading themselves. These parents have helped their children along on the road to literacy.

Model reading

As a teacher, I know that reading books to my children is not enough to let them know how important reading is in daily life. I've made it a point with my own two children (and I tell the parents of my students) to let children see reading in action—reading recipes together, road signs, game directions, everything that shows that reading unlocks meaning. We make it a game, reading everything we can.

Drew Valjovik, Dobbs Ferry, New York

Limit television viewing

I let my son watch as much television as he's spent time reading. In other words, if he's read a book for an hour, he can watch an hour of television. Sometimes, he's gotten so involved with reading, he's skipped TV.

Raymond Carr, Tulsa, Oklahoma

Consider outside help

I thought I did everything right by reading a lot to my preschooler. When she became a first-grader, I was upset to see that she wasn't catching on to reading as well as her classmates were. I read even more to her, but she wasn't getting it. Finally, the school had her evaluated for reading problems and, though no particular diagnosis was made, I decided to hire a tutor. Within six months, she went from being unable to read a word to reading second-grade books. I honestly don't think she would have progressed this well without individual attention from someone other than me.

Linda Peterson, Nutley, New Jersey

Relax

I've been a first-grade teacher for 12 years. I'm also the mother of three boys. Not every child learns to read in first grade. Encourage your children, but don't berate them or worry them if they take longer than their classmates. It's rare that a child can't read by third grade, and, at that point, they can catch up on whatever they may have missed earlier.

Mary Elizabeth O'Donnell, Hanover, New Hampshire

Teach phonics

My twin sons' school had a reading program that assumed all kids would somehow magically learn to read by being read to. This "whole-language" approach wasn't working for my children or for a few others in the class. I decided to buy some workbooks that taught phonics, which really opened the door for them. Putting in the time myself to do what I thought the school would do has been

---

How to Help Kids Develop a Love of Reading

- *Show your own love of books.* Let your kids see you read and hear you discuss the books you've read.
- *Give your child his own books.* Urge him to create his own library where he can store his favorites.
- *Limit television viewing.* But do look for TV-book tie-ins that can inspire reading.
- *Visit the library and bookstores regularly.* Let your child browse to see what sparks her interest. Borrow all that appeal to her and buy those you can.
- *Attend story hour.* Become part of any local events that celebrate reading.

---

worth it. Both boys are now competent readers.

Ainslee Jovan-Elsace, Shaker Heights, Illinois

Consider technology

When my daughter became turned off to books because of her trouble with learning to read, we invested in a few computer reading programs. These allowed her to play games while learning and because she had no history of failure with computers as she had had with books, she stopped resisting learning to read.

Albert Ullum, Cooperstown, New York

Take turns reading

Reading a whole book was a daunting task for my younger child. Samantha would cry whenever I suggested that she spend some time reading. So I started to take turns with her, each of us reading one page of a story. Now she looks forward to reading with me.

Mary Chevet, Poughkeepsie, New York

Follow the child's interests

My daughter wasn't really keen on reading, but she loves teddy bears. I bought her books about teddy bears, a teddy bear calendar and anything that had bears and words together on a page. Eventually, her interest in bears overrode her disinterest in reading and she began to catch on.

Emily Warner, Anchorage, Alaska

Hire a teenage helper

My nine-year-old daughter, Michelle, was uninterested in schoolwork, particularly reading assignments. She was more interested in finding out what teenagers are all about. So I hired Katie, a teenage neighbor and a really nice kid, to come over two afternoons a week to study with Michelle. Michelle really looks forward to these study sessions and Katie offers her bribes like "I'll French-braid your hair in exchange for your paying attention while you do your book report."

Barbara Hoogie, Cleveland

Play with reading

I like to show my kids that reading and writing can take place anywhere. When we're at the beach, we write each other notes in the sand. We play scavenger hunts in which the kids have to read to find the next treasure. When we go on car trips, I pass out Mad-Lib books for fun (and read-

ing). The kids are barely aware that I'm encouraging them to read a few hours a day!

Elisa Young, Winston-Salem, North Carolina

Let them be authors

I've found that a good way to get my kids reading was to encourage them to write their own books. After a visit to the zoo, for instance, each of them (ages seven and five), write a "Zoo Book." Sometimes they pick topics like "If I Could Fly" or "I Am a Monster." The books are fun to save and really help me see the progress they are making in their language skills. For instance, my seven-year-old's first book was nothing more than pictures with a few letters, like *d* to mean dog. Now his books have real plots and he uses words with mostly correct spellings.

Ann Strivor, Elvira, New York

Subscribe to magazines

Though I may wish that my three children really wanted to read classic works of literature, I'll settle for less as long as they read. I've found that letting the children each pick out a magazine that he or she wants really does the trick. One child subscribes to *Nickelodeon*, another to *American Girl* and the youngest to *Ladybug*. I found

out about the various magazines by asking our children's librarian. I was amazed that there were dozens to choose from.

Cybill Platt, Richmond, Virginia

Mastering Math

A number of ideas to help your child grasp math concepts.

Let the kids pay the bills

When my older son was little, I began letting him learn about numbers by paying restaurant bills. As he got older I gave him the responsibility of figuring out various budgets, like, "with $700 to spend for four days, how can we best spend our money on a weekend in Washington, D.C.?" Now, at age 17, he earns $40 a month keeping track of the family's bills and writing out the monthly checks

Take the Mystery Out of Math

Whether your child is mathematically talented or just average, the more comfortable she feels with numerical concepts and computers, the less likely she is to develop anxiety around these subjects. Here are some tips gleaned from the experts to help your children sharpen their abilities and gain self-confidence.

- *Be sensitive to your own attitude toward math and computers.* Even if you had bad experiences with math in school or were afraid of computers, you can encourage your child to excel. Consider taking an adult-education course to brush up on your math skills—and perhaps to find the fun in playing with numbers.
- *Buy your child puzzles, blocks and construction toys.* These are terrific tools to help your child learn spatial skills, an essential understanding about how things work.
- *Spend as much time helping your child learn math as you do helping him learn to*

read. And like pre-reading games, play pre-math games, including sorting objects, board and card games and made-up games, such as having your child figure out how many pizzas your family consumed this month? How many slices? Average number of slices per person?
- *Have the same academic standards for math for your daughter as you do for your son.* Realize that today's girls will need—and can accomplish—mathematical learning every bit as much as a boy needs these skills. Make sure that your child's school also has high expectations for *all* children.

(I sign them). His younger brother has taken over the less involved money chores.

Kelly Durant, Minneapolis

Play card games

Want to know a good way to help your child learn to add and subtract? Play cards, especially games like 21.

Christina Mayfieldl, Orlando, Florida

Buy Park Place

My son loves to play Monopoly, and it's a terrific way for him to learn about money and about basic adding, subtracting and multiplying.

Chris Farhood, New York City

Give them responsibility

Let your children be responsible for things like budgeting their own money, saving for special items and gifts and setting up long-range as well as short-term financial goals.

Michael O'Shea, Brooklyn, New York

Take them shopping

I let my children see how I plan a shopping trip by writing lists of what we need, how I clip coupons and how I choose items based on balancing things like cost and quality. These weekly trips turn into good math lessons that have helped each of my kids understand the basics of money management.

Name and address withheld

Roll the dice

I always keep a pair of dice in my pocket. You never know when you'll have the opportunity to play a few quick games with your kids! Mine love adding the dots or telling me the difference between the high and low numbers.

Kelly Atkinson, Reno, Nevada

Making the Most of Homework

Homework is a fact of life for most school kids—and their parents. When kids dawdle, do sloppy work, procrastinate or otherwise avoid the inevitable, what strategies work to get them back on track?

Start a homework club

Like most kids, my son would rather play soccer or hang out with his friends after school instead of doing his homework. The same was true for a number of his classmates. With the help of two teachers we formed a homework club as an after-school activity. The parents pay the teachers to supervise a group of kids in the lunchroom for an hour after school. The kids bring snacks from home. The club not only helps kids get their homework done, but it serves as a terrific relief for those of us whose kids are on their own after school until we parents get home from work.

Rebecca Holstein, New York City

Don't correct them

When my child began bringing home homework, I worked with her every step of the way, correcting any mistakes she made. As a result, her teacher thought she knew far more than she did. There was a big discrepancy between her schoolwork and her homework. Her teacher convinced me to let her do her homework on her own so that she would be able to judge Emma's understanding better. This has helped the teacher identify things that Emma needed extra help learning. As a result, she now makes far fewer mistakes on her homework.

Yolanda Dietz, Bronx, New York

Put time limits on dawdling

Casey, my seven-year-old, can stretch 20 minutes of homework into two hours of daydreaming and crying. After discussing the issue with her teacher, we agreed that each page of writing or math problems should take no more than 10 minutes. I now set the timer for 10 minutes and she must stop doing that page when the buzzer sounds. At first she accomplished nearly nothing, but now, after just two weeks of clock-watching, she finishes her assignments in the 20 allotted minutes.

Meagan O'Rourke, Austin, Texas

Give kids options

I have three kids in grade school and I've encouraged each one to develop a homework routine that works for him or her. I know that the parent's magazines all say that kids should have a distraction-free workplace and do their homework in a certain way, but I've found that letting each child pick the time and place to do homework works best. Every September, I tell each of them that they have until the end of the month to figure out their homework routine for the next few months. This year, one chooses to do his at school before he comes home. My

daughter likes to do hers with a friend in our house or her friend's house in the bedroom with the music blaring, and my youngest one needs to play and eat first and then does his homework in the kitchen while I clean up after dinner. Each one has the option to change their routine at the start of the second semester.

Ava Cranston, Laramie, Wyoming

Start training them early

From the first time they have homework, give your kids guidelines on getting it done and then turn over the job to them. Remind them to have everything they need—pencils, paper, books—available before they start. Be available to review directions if need be, but explain that homework is a way for the teacher to learn more about what they know and that you're not allowed to give them the answers to any questions.

Hanley Jacobs, Toronto

Stay close

My child found that homework was a very lonely experience. I began to do my homework—reading, paying bills—at the dining-room table with her. She works much better just because she doesn't feel isolated.

Cindy Hsu, Flushing, New York

Make the routine fun

My son and I had developed a routine of battling through homework. There was always something else he wanted to do once we got home. One day after school, we decided to stop off for hot chocolate on the way home and I suggested that

10 Homework Tips for All Ages

1. Support your children's efforts, but don't do their work. Check with their teachers to see what kind of help is expected.

2. Set a regular time every day for homework.

3. Establish a regular place for daily homework.

4. Attempt to understand and respect your child's individual learning style. There is no right or wrong way to learn. Some children, for instance, may work best to the sound of music in the background. If it works, let it happen.

5. Make sure that your child has all the necessary supplies for homework. This shows that you take his work seriously.

6. If possible, make homework time a time for the whole family to pursue quiet activities.

7. Focus on the positive when you review your child's work.

8. Model the behavior you want to see in your child. Make sure that your child sees you reading, writing and working at things that require effort.

9. When homework is completed, review it and then place it in a folder or other holder and have your child place it directly into her backpack.

10. Periodically check with the teacher to be sure that homework is being completed successfully.

---

maybe he try doing his homework at the booth in the diner so that we didn't have to deal with it later. He got it done in 15 minutes! From then on, we've stopped somewhere on the way home—the diner, the park, even his dad's office, to complete the homework. For some reason, he doesn't mind doing it away from home.

Valerie Vescovi, Cleveland

Talk to the teacher

Fiona, my third-grader, really struggled through her homework every night. I made an appointment to see the teacher to see why she was having such a problem. It turned out that three other parents had also asked her why their kids were having

trouble, too. She took a poll in the class and found out that most of the kids found the homework too hard. (She explained to the parents and the kids that before this year, she had taught sixth-graders and was probably expecting too much.) From the night of the poll on, the homework was much more doable and Fiona went back to handling it on her own.

Finola Dunlevy, Cambridge, Massachusetts

Make deals

To help my daughter see some value in homework, I try to extend it with something fun. We plan follow-ups to the weekly homework every Friday. For instance, if she had math homework that in-

If Your Child Is Underachieving . . .

Here are some steps to help him realize his potential.

Have a talk with your child

Adopt an attitude of support and caring. Show you understand that school is difficult; even share some of your own school failures. Ask:
• Do you think you can do the work?
• Are you trying as hard as you can?
• Do you think I'm always on your case, telling you what to do?
Don't expect clear answers the first time you start the dialogue.

Schedule a school conference

Call a meeting, if appropriate, with teachers, the school counselor, principal and your child.
Go with a cooperative attitude—we all have a problem here, no one is at fault and we all need to work together to solve it. Ask:
• What is the specific problem? Homework? Poor grades? Class behavior?

Poor influence of friends?
• Should my child be tested for physical and learning disabilities, especially if school failure is not new?
• What are my youngster's strengths and interests? Together can we design projects in these areas at home and at school that will provide positive, successful experiences?
• What are some reasonable goals for improvement? Let your child help set them and start small so that he or she can succeed. Sometimes just getting all the homework completed is a big first step.

After the conference

• Consider an agreement, written and signed, that describes what your child is to do and what will happen at school and at home when he or she meets or does not meet its terms.

volved counting money, that Friday, I gave her two quarters, two dimes, two nickels, ten pennies and took her to a toy store where she could figure out what her 90 cents could buy. (The store keeps barrels of inexpensive little toys that sell for 15 cents to 50 cents.) Then I let her spend it. When the homework involved learning about animal habitats, we planned a trip to the zoo. As a follow-up to some boring spelling

worksheets, we invited a friend over, served pizza and played Junior Scrabble.

Irene Gainer, Tupelo, Mississippi

Tips from Teachers on Volunteering

How have teachers involved parents in the schools? Here are some ideas gathered from teachers around the country.

Perhaps, for example, a periodic progress report will be required each day or week that details homework assignments, tests, grades and classroom behavior.

- Cooperate with whatever plan you work out. Consistently provide the rewards specified in your agreement if homework and studying are done and withholding them if it is not.

Consider counseling if the problem is serious

A counselor can help everyone to express his or her feelings, understand each other's point of view, and work out a cooperative plan of action. Sometimes a school counselor can play this role but private services may be necessary.

Assess some of your own behavior

Make sure that you:
- Help your child set realistic goals.

- Point out how your child's efforts result in reaching goals.
- Encourage persistence when a task is difficult.
- Allow your child to work independently, without your monitoring, guidance or suggestions.
- Do not nag or remind your child about his or her responsibilities, but do not shelter him or her from the consequences of forgetting or making the wrong decision.
- Teach your child how to accept and deal with failure by permitting your child to fail sometimes.
- Build self-confidence, not by insisting that she is capable, but by rewarding her for real accomplishments that she has made.
- Make time to do enjoyable things with your child, letting him know that you love him with or without his accomplishments.

Share your knowledge

One of the best events of the school year at our school is the "minicourse day" for the fourth through sixth grades, when parents come in and teach seminars on their respective professions. Kids choose which job courses they want to take from a class list. The classes are a perfect mix of lecture and hands-on learning—from babysitting prep classes to finding out what it feels like to be a lawyer presenting a case in court.

Nancy Torres,
nursery school through third-grade science teacher
Hunter Elementary School, New York City

Pitch in

During the school year, children order books from several student book clubs. I was delighted when one mom who works outside the home volunteered some of her

**PARENTS'
RESOURCE**

School-Bus Safety

The American Automobile Association (AAA) has a number of materials related to school-bus safety, including books, pamphlets and posters. Contact your local AAA club about availability. For an excellent brochure on bus safety, *Protecting Our Most Precious Resource,* send a self-addressed, stamped envelope to the American Federation of Teachers, 555 New Jersey Avenue NW, Washington, DC 20001.

after-work hours to process the order forms and payments and to distribute the books among the kids' classroom mailboxes when the orders arrived. She saved me many valuable evening hours that I needed to prepare for class.

Charlotte Haun, first-grade teacher,
Conant Elementary School, Bloomfield Hills, Michigan

Review schoolwork with your child

When parents reinforce lessons, children learn skills faster. I run training sessions for parent volunteers on things such as how to help kids improve their writing. Then parents come in and help children edit rough drafts of stories or reports. In a class of 28 children, this individual attention can make all the difference.

Donna Hupe, fifth-grade teacher,
Haine Elementary School, Cranberry Township,
Pennsylvania

Find time to volunteer

Parents who work outside the home are often frustrated that they don't have time during the day to volunteer, so our school found a creative way to get them involved. Parents come in at night and on weekends to help design the stage sets of plays. They build backdrops, construct props and work with students on painting scenery. The collaborative effort is a great learning experience.

Gary Allen, sixth-grade teacher,
McKinley Elementary School, Xenia City, Ohio

Packing Great Ideas into School Lunch Boxes

Just because they can subsist on a steady diet of peanut butter and jelly sandwiches doesn't mean you can't pack some fun into their lunch boxes.

No-sandwich lunch ideas

My daughter, Elizabeth, hates sandwiches, which makes packing lunches a challenge. Here are some ideas for lunches for other kids who prefer non-sandwich lunches: Microwave kids' meals in a wide-mouth Thermos, fruit salad topped with yogurt, string cheese and fruit basket, pizza (covered in wax paper and tin foil to stay warm) and cold chicken.

Teri Carpenter, Colorado Springs, Colorado

Freeze the bread

To keep kids' lunches fresh, I make their sandwiches in the morning on frozen slices of bread. The bread defrosts by lunchtime, and their sandwiches are kept cool until then.

Gail Miller, Somers Point, New Jersey

Plan a surprise visit

Last year, on my son's birthday, with the prior okay of his teacher, I showed up at lunchtime with four pizzas for him and his classmates. The surprise party was a huge hit.

Kevin Donovan, Woodside, New York

Don't bag this birthday idea

Since my son's school discourages parents from sending in sweets for class birthday parties, this year I tried something different. My son and I decorated sandwich-size resealable bags with stickers and filled them with trail mix for each of his classmates. We combined small crackers, raisins and cereal. The idea was a great success! His teacher loved it because the snack was nutritious and the children could seal up leftovers without making a mess. The kids loved it and several parents in the class have since copied the idea.

Lauren Simmons, Anaheim, California

So long, soggy sandwiches

My children love peanut butter and jelly sandwiches—they would eat them for breakfast, lunch and dinner if I let them. But they often complain that by lunchtime, their sandwiches are soggy. I found a simple solution: Spread a thin layer of peanut butter on both pieces of bread. The peanut butter keeps the jelly from soaking through.

Joan Bassler, Schwenksville, Pennsylvania

Pack a pic

If your child gets homesick at school, tape a picture of your family on the inside of his lunch box, along with a note. Your child will look forward to his surprises and he'll know that you are thinking about him, too.

Zee Ann Poerio, Pittsburgh

Great Ideas for Participating at School

These parents show that you need not give lots of time, but that even a little can be very well spent.

Make a video yearbook

I took a video camera to my daughter's kindergarten class at the end of her school term. Each of her classmates stood up and said their names and what they liked the most about their year at school. I taped storytime and interviewed her teacher, too. Then we made a duplicate of the video for my daughter to give her teacher on the last day of school.

Jana Schramm, Joplin, Missouri

Divide duties with another parent

As the mother of a toddler and a school-age child, finding time to help out at school was almost impossible for me. Then my friend and I decided to alternate days of volunteer work and taking care of the kids. Now KimAnne works at the school once a week while I watch the kids, and she watches them once a week while I go. The kids like the change of pace and KimAnne and I both get a chance to be involved in our local school.

Cynthia Nelson, Tacoma, Washington

Share your culture

My husband is American and I'm British, and we agreed that our daughter, Narissa, should learn about other coun- tries and cultures at a young age. So not long ago, I visited Narissa's school. I took along things that British kids like, such as chocolate button candies, tea, Paddington bear, models of a London taxi and a double-decker bus and the Union Jack. The international show-and-tell was a big hit; the children particularly enjoyed the candy.

Barbara Gilme, Florence, South Carolina

CHAPTER TWELVE

The Working Life

*I*f only science could clone parents, the problems of working while raising children would be solved. Since that solution isn't likely, parents must work out customized answers to the question, "How can I balance my work life and family life?" For many, working outside the home is an economic necessity. For others, work provides the emotional fuel to energize family life. But the greater the support from family, workplace and society, the better the outcome for everyone.

Making the Decision

Many moms are surprised to find they don't want to return to work as their maternity leaves draw to an end. Others find that they miss work and are eager to resume their jobs. These moms considered their options and can help you decide what's best for your family.

If the choice is about money . . .

Write down a realistic budget, showing the difference between what you earn and what your family would do without your income (and without the expenses associated with your work). I did and I was surprised to see that my $35,000 a year job translated into just $3,000 more after I'd deducted child care, taxes, transportation and other costs connected to working. And for just $3,000, it was worth it to stay home.

Lorraine Moore, Vicksburg, Virginia

Talk to others

There's no point in trying to figure out what to do all by yourself. I was greatly helped by talking to lots of other mothers, some of whom chose to go back to work and some of whom chose to stay home, before making my decision. While all of our situations were somewhat different, there were enough common threads so that I could use their experience to help me see what was best for my family.

Muriel Brown, Hartford, Connecticut

Get your spouse's support

Whether or not to return to work is a family decision. I could not have returned to work without the complete support of my husband, Mike, because I was not willing to work full time and then have full-time responsibility for the house and our son, William. He agreed to do his share and he's kept the bargain.

JoLynn Kline, Fort Lauderdale, Florida

Have a trial run

I was unsure of what was best—going back to work as planned or staying home with our son, Lincoln. I decided that I couldn't make a good decision without first testing the waters back at work. I returned to work as planned and gave myself one month of seeing how I'd feel about it, how my child care situation would work out and how the budget held up with the new expenses of child care. After this trial period, I opted to stay at work because it was working out better than I would have thought.

Sara Reilly-Moore, Binghamton, New York

Think ahead

I wrote down a list of what I want in my life five years from now, including personal and professional goals. Then I made two headings on my list: "Staying Home for Three Years" and "Going Back to Work Now." Next I put a plus or a minus next to each item, under each heading. It was easy for me to see at a glance that I'd be closer to my goals by returning to work later on.

Ronnie Harvart, St. Paul, Minnesota

Consider your feelings

I considered staying at home, but because I'd invested so much energy into my work and because I derived so much pleasure from it, I decided to go back to work. I realized that to be the best mother I could be, I had to be the best person I could be. I also realized that loving my work showed a good example to Melanie. She's six now and, like me, wants to be a teacher.

Janice Ingram, Milwaukee

Trust your gut

After the birth of my son, Jeremy, I planned to go back to work. When he was six weeks old, I began to have mixed feelings. I pretended to myself that I had made the decision not to return and listened to my feelings. I felt panicky. Then I pretended to have made the decision to go back as planned. The scared feelings went away. I took that as a sign that I really wanted to go back and I did. Sure, there are some moments when I question my decision but, overall, I believe I made the right choice.

Yolanda Grietz, New York City

Realize that it's not forever

I went back to work after my first child was born and I was glad I did. But after the birth of my second, the homeward pull became much greater, partially because the economics of sending two children to day care made less sense. Now I'm glad that I'm home full time. I plan to go back to work next year when the kids are five and seven.

Mary Dearfield, Lexington, Kentucky

Take charge of your choice

Only you know what's best for you. When other people (like in-laws, co-workers and your Aunt Tillie) offer unasked advice about whether or not you

should be home all day, tell them, "Thank you very much for your opinion, but this is a choice I have to make on my own."

Gabby Spacek, Austin, Texas

Handling Your Ambivalence

Even the right decision brings mixed feelings. Here are some ways to handle the "what ifs" and the "if only's."

Try "working" at home

I did, and I couldn't believe how worn out I felt from keeping up with my two-year-old daughter. I felt more exhausted at the end of each day of my two-week "vacation" than I ever felt after work. While I had many loving and fulfilling moments with my daughter, I'm convinced now that the at-home mother is truly a "working mom."

Joanna Evans, Baltimore

Write your feelings down

When I was adjusting to work and motherhood and feeling desperate, I would fold a piece of paper in half and head one column "Problems" and the other "Solutions." It helped me work through painful issues and brainstorm for answers. It works.

Carol R. McMahon, Chicago

Form a support group

It's important to express your feelings of sadness and anger, because they are valid. Talk with working mothers and at-home

How Can I Master Morning Mayhem?

Getting a child off to day care, another off to school and you and your spouse off to work in the morning can rival rush hour at Grand Central Station. Susan Ginsberg, Ed.D., editor and publisher of the *Work and Family Life Newsletter,* offers these tips for handling this hectic time of day.

- Do some chores the night before. Completing tasks such as making lunches, packing school bags and laying out clothes before you go to sleep will give you peace of mind when the alarm clock rings.
- Create a schedule that lets your children know when they must get up, eat breakfast and leave the house.
- Build in "cushion time" by getting up 15 minutes earlier. If your toddler is a slow mover in the wee hours, these extra minutes are an absolute necessity.
- Designate a special basket for each family member that will hold supplies, toys or class projects that need to be picked up on the way out the door.
- Establish fun morning rituals—eating breakfast together, telling a joke, saying good-bye in a certain way—to make it easier for your kids to separate from you for the day ahead.

mothers, too. It can be reassuring to know that everyone has her own frustrations.

Karen Bryan, Gardena, California

Make peace with your choice

Whenever I miss my job and the life that went with it, I remind myself that I can have another career in the future. In the meantime, I know that my daughter will only be a baby once and if I'm going to fully enjoy it, I have to be here.

Sara Lacy, Staten Island, New York

Pay attention to today

"One day at a time" is my motto. I look forward to spending the evening, or maybe the upcoming weekend, at home with my family. By staying focused on the present, I don't feel as upset about not spending more time with my children.

Dana Barnekow, Austin, Texas

Think practical thoughts

The benefits of working are easy to forget when you miss your children. Remind yourself that in addition to supporting your family with food, shelter, and clothing, you are providing them with health-insurance coverage. If you are lucky, you may also be putting money into a pension fund and savings account. And don't forget about the work ethic that you are instilling.

Lisa M. McCulloh, Mercersburg, Pennsylvania

Give it time

When my seven-week maternity leave was up, going back to work was the hardest thing I've ever had to do. I cried every day. Now I realize that I'm not the only mother who wishes she could be at home with her child and who feels guilty that she can't be. It has only been four months since I went back to work; slowly I'm adjusting.

Carol W. Bolton, Russellville, Alabama

Ease back in

Instead of going back to work full-time after three months of maternity leave, I went back part-time after six weeks and worked half-time until Sarah was four months old. Going back gradually really helped me adjust to my mixed feelings about leaving her.

Serina Martinez, Bronx, New York

Meet for lunch

My return to full-time work following my maternity leave was painful for my two children and me. So I asked my sitter to bring my then six-month-old infant and 3½-year-old daughter to meet me for lunch once a week. These midday reunions helped ease the separation anxiety we were all feeling. In fact, because we enjoyed ourselves so much, we have continued this weekly ritual for the past two years.

Jane Pianetto, Barrington, Illinois

Look on the bright side

These words of wisdom I learned from my son's pediatrician keep me going on my roughest days at work, when I really missed him: "A child should always know the joy of his parent's return."

Debbie Miller, Shelton, Connecticut

Talk to your boss

I decided to be honest with my employer about my mixed feelings. I asked to begin my time back at the office on a part-time basis. He agreed, and his support made staying with the company possible. That was five years ago and now I'm getting ready for the birth of my second child. My boss has agreed this time, too, to let me return on a part-time basis for the first month after my three-month leave.

Theresa Nelson, San Antonio, Texas

Getting Off to Work

"I feel like I put in a full day's work before I head out the door," says one working mom. Many others share her opinion— and have found creative ways to ease the morning rush hour.

Stay neat

When I first went back to work, my son, Harrison, was six weeks old. Since he frequently spits up in the morning (as babies do), I was left having to change outfits before I was even out the door. So I took an old bath towel and cut a slit in the center. Now, once I'm dressed, I slip the towel over my head and wear it until I leave for work.

Terri Dragoo, Colorado Springs, Colorado

Keep close

Try to find child care near your office. That way you can spend your lunch hour and commuting time with your kids.

Karen Turpin, Troy, Missouri

Dress to go

The best way I've found to get my son and me ready for daycare and work on time is to put him to bed partially dressed for morning. Each night, I put on his clean underwear, socks, long-johns (in winter), and sometimes even his sweat suit if I know the next morning will be particularly rushed.

Alma Usanti, Tupelo, Mississippi

Make the race fun

To help keep my kids moving in the morning, we race each other to get dressed. Who can put on socks or stocking fastest? Who's first to brush his or her teeth? Each morning, the winner gets to pick out that night's dinner dessert.

Marge Leheigh, Reno, Nevada

Get up earlier

To keep our mornings relaxed, we get up early so that my daughter can get dressed, eat breakfast, and watch cartoons without being rushed.

Carole Gerchy, Corona, California

Eat on the way

I really need peace and quiet in the morning, so I put off waking up my son and daughter as long as possible before we leave for school and work. I serve them breakfast in the car, which really helps to keep things moving in the morning.

Valerie Osbourne, Greenwich, Connecticut

Time yourself to tapes

My daughter has quite a collection of stories on tape, all of them running about 20 minutes in length. Once I wake her, I start a story tape and we try to get out the door just as the story is ending. It's a fun way to keep either of us from dawdling.

Mary Jo Trader, Mechanicsville, Pennsylvania

Maximizing Your Work Time

Time is short, but these working parents have found many ways to savor and celebrate family time.

Shut out the distractions

When I get home, I turn on the answering machine, videotape any must-see shows that are on at that time for later viewing, put aside the mail and forget about cleaning so that my husband and I can savor the time we do have with our son.

Kelly Newcomb, Summit, New Jersey

Unwind on your way home

I like to chat with friends, nap or listen to music during my commute. It helps calm me so that I look forward to the limited time I have with my children.

C. Pfeiffer, Lakewood, New Jersey

Make peace— before an argument

Working and raising two children had me stressed out. I went to hear a parenting expert who was giving a talk at my children's school and her advice changed my life. Every morning, I say to my kids, "Let's be kind to each other today." It reminds us all to cut down on arguing about silly things and to make the most of each day together.

Nancy Loomis, Ridley Park, Pennsylvania

Do chores together

Believe it or not, your kids probably find a lot of the housework and work you bring home from the office very interesting, so why not invite them to join you? My three children help me do a lot—from sorting the laundry to assisting in arranging a slide presentation for work. Not only does sharing the tasks give us more time together, but it gives my children a more realistic outlook on adult life. Mine know what I do for a living, for example, because they get to see it firsthand.

Anne Childress, Boston

Adopt a new attitude

I used to bemoan the fact that it took my seven-year-old and me about a half an hour to walk home from her after-school program, a walk I could accomplish on my own in about ten minutes. I kept thinking of all I had to do when we got home. Then one day, while she was telling me about her school day and I was telling her about my workday, she said, "Mom, today during talk time at school, I told the class that my favorite part of the day was walking home with you." I hadn't realized how this time was when we did most of our connecting. Now, I've learned to enjoy it, too.

Peggy Murphy, Minneapolis

Little moments mean a lot

Don't undervalue the time you spend with your children preparing dinner, taking a walk, singing in the bathtub or cuddling up at story time. These moments are what life is all about for parents—whether they work or stay at home.

Pam Simon, Gretna, Louisiana

Have special routines

Morning rituals with my four-year-old daughter, Meagan, help me feel more con-

nected to her. A few days a week, we go out for a leisurely breakfast together. We've even made some new friends who are also regulars at the cafe.

Leslie B. Conrad, Fairless Hills, Pennsylvania

Get housework out of the way

Waking up earlier (only half an hour before I usually do) gives me time to take care of household chores—washing the dishes, vacuuming, doing a load of laundry and even mopping the kitchen floor. The reward: When I get home from work, I am free to spend the evenings with my husband and children.

Adriana Mazutis, Chicago

Share space

I find that a good way to keep connected to my kids even though we're away from each other from 8:00 A.M to 6:00 P.M. everyday is to do what I have to do when they're around me. For instance, I clean the bathroom while they're taking their bath. I pay bills while my seven-year-old is doing her homework at the same table. I always take them with me on errands instead of doing the errands on my way home from work. I let them know that I just like being around them.

Fiona Costello, Pueblo, Colorado

Set aside a special night

With both my husband and me working and our three children in school, staying in touch as a family was getting increasingly difficult. We've begun to put aside Thursday nights to do something fun together. One week, we'll go ice-skating; another we'll go to a movie. We stay up late and talk while playing cards or a board game. We always can manage being a bit tired on Friday since we know the weekend is coming up. We all look forward to these "dates" with one another.

Paula Smiley, San Diego

Have dinner together

The old-fashioned family meal is what keeps us going. After a busy day at work or at school, our family reconnects every night at dinner.

Tamar Rosenfeld, Brooklyn, New York

Keeping in Touch While You're Working

Here are some hints for stealing time from your workday to touch base at home.

Have a question a day

My husband, kids and I have a fun game we play every day that reminds us of each other even while they're at school and we're at work. Each morning, we take turns thinking of a question and the others have all day to find the answer, which we report at dinner. For instance, today my son asked us to name the farthest planet from the sun and to find out its temperature. We all found the answers in different ways (books, asking a colleague, and on the Internet!). Sometimes, the questions are silly. Yesterday was my turn and I asked a riddle I'd heard from a child visiting my office: "Why did the turtle cross the road?" (The answer, "To get to the Shell station" was guessed by my

daughter, but everyone's answers were pretty funny.)

Lynn Delano, Glenshaw, Pennsylvania

Work together

My nine-year-old son has a hard time staying focused when he's got a job to do alone, so my husband and I take turns working alongside him. We're careful not to comment negatively on his methods, and we find that he works enthusiastically when one of us is simply doing another job in the same room or in the garage or yard.

Barbara Weigand, Kalamazoo, Michigan

Phone home

Phone calls keep me in touch. A few times a day I call my kids to talk and listen to them laugh or just babble. It reminds me that I'm working to provide a better life for them.

Denise Schulman, Bayside, New York

Leave surprise notes

My kids get home from school with the baby-sitter about two hours before I do. Every now and then, I leave them little notes to find when they get home. I put them where ever they're likely to find them—in the fruit bowl, in their toy boxes, or on their beds, for instance. They love receiving them.

Alyson Grange, Fayettesville, Louisiana

Make sure both parents keep in touch

It's automatic for me to call home and check on my kids. Sometimes, however, instead of calling home, I call my husband

Helping Kids Handle Your Business Trips

Here are some age-appropriate ways to prepare your children for your departure—and your return.

Before you go

Toddlers: Wait until the night before you leave to announce your departure, and try to do it with a minimum of fuss.

Preschoolers: Give your children a week or so to digest the idea of your absence, and use his schedule as a time frame: "When Daddy gives you breakfast, I'll be in Texas at a meeting."

School-age children: Tell your child as soon as you know when you are leaving. Then allow them to participate in planning their activities during your absence.

While you're away

Toddlers: Call at the same time every day. If your toddler doesn't want to talk, don't be upset.

Preschoolers: Call at the same time every day, and tell your child little details about your trip. He'll latch on to the fact that your hotel blanket has stripes and that you ate fruit served in a coconut shell.

School-age children: Stay in touch, and be sure to ask specific questions. "How are things?" won't elicit the same response as "What happened at the end of that book you were reading?"

When you return

Toddlers: Expect some anger, expressed indirectly. If your toddler refuses to look at you for a day, help her find words to express those feelings.

Preschoolers: Your child might be loving and clingy or slightly rebellious. Top help bolster his feelings, bring him some postcards, little soaps, a restaurant menu, or other tangible souvenirs.

School-age children: Don't expect too big a fuss about your return. If you detect an interest, tell your child what you did during the trip, but otherwise, don't force it.

and remind him to call home. It's important to the kids that they feel that we're both checking in on them and are thinking about them when we're at work.

Anne Johnson, Toronto

Tape record yourself

I tape myself reading my kids' favorite bedtime stories for them to hear when-

ever work forces me to stay late and miss their bedtimes and for when I'm away on business trips.

Carl Engleman, Van Nuys, California

Stay linked with a paper chain

When I am out of town on business, my two children, Daniel, seven, and Amy, three, always want to know when I will be returning. To give them some sense of the time involved, my wife, Nancy, created a paper chain and connected it to my photograph. Each link is equal to one day of my trip; the kids remove one link each day until I'm home. They enjoy making the chain and removing the links while anticipating my return.

J. R. Stowe, Baton Rouge, Louisiana

Have a geography lesson

When I travel for business, I usually rent a car in the city I'm in and receive a free map. When I return home, I cover the map with clear contact paper to make it into a place mat for my four-year-old daughter, Jessica. She loves locating the town I visited and pinpointing landmarks such as lakes, zoos and airports.

Marien A. Kaifesh, Mentor, Ohio

Weekend Ideas

Weekends are made for families. Here are some ideas to make the most out of your two-day time-outs from the workweek schedule.

Stay in bed

The thing I like best about weekends is hanging out in bed with my family. Every Saturday and Sunday morning, the kids climb in with my husband and me and we cuddle together, read, sometimes watch TV and even eat there. It's a wonderful break from the workweek when we're all in a rush to be someplace else.

Elaine Firestone, Hastings-on-Hudson, New York

Get physical

Nothing beats working out together to bring our family closer. Every weekend, we hike or bike for miles, stopping to eat a picnic I pack. I think when our kids are older, this will be what they remember about their childhoods. I recommend getting outdoors and moving to every family—and especially to those who spend most of the week cooped up in an office or school!

Rachel Logue-Feinstein,
North Andover, Massachusetts

Connect with a community

Each of us—my wife, my son and me—has a strong identity with our work lives.

My wife spends 50 hours a week as a dentist. I spend 40 hours as a teacher, and my son spends his time at school and in various after-school activities and clubs. We found that having a community that we all could share was essential in helping us feel like a family. We joined a church that really reaches out to families. The community gives us a feeling of solidarity with one another and with the other members, as well as providing a spiritual base and practical support.

George Davidson, Cincinnati

Declare weekends as "no-work" times

Choose one day a weekend to put aside work, errands and social obligations. My husband and I devote Saturdays to our children: We read, play, take walks and naps together and talk.

Dianne Nitzahn, Sherman Oaks, California

Fetch a sketch

Because money is tight right now, we are not able to sign our kids up for the lessons that most of their friends seem to be taking on weekends. I was looking for something neat for my husband and me to do with them that wouldn't cost a bundle, and a stroll through the park one day gave me an idea. We saw a man sketching the scenery and it looked like great fun. Now my family heads to a different location every Saturday, sketchbooks in hand, to record what we see. It gives us all a feeling of being part of the world around us and is a total stress reducer. By the way, we're all becoming pretty good artists, too.

Linda and Hollis Young, New York City

Get away from it all

On the first weekend of every month, we go out of town. Hotels have wonderful (and cheap) weekend packages that allow us to experience different areas within driving distance. They all have year-round swimming pools and other amenities. Going to a hotel makes us feel like we're taking care of ourselves.

Jackie Carter-Knewel, Peoria, Illinois

Winter at the beach

Want a great winter weekend getaway without the crowds? Do what my family does and head for the beach. It's absolutely beautiful and you don't have to fight the crowds. It's also a great stress reliever after a long week at work.

Danielle Evans, Bayside, New York

Start a grab bag

To make sure that each of my four children as well as my husband and I each get a chance to do what we like on the weekends, we have a grab bag. Every six weeks, we each write down what we want to do, and then the youngest child picks from the bag. Once that person's wish-for plans have been chosen, he or she doesn't put in an idea until everyone else has had a turn choosing. When the last person gets to do what he or she wants, we start over.

Nicole McHenry, Burlington, Vermont

Get the picture

I love taking pictures and keeping track of them would get out of hand if it were not for our regular photo weekends. Every few weeks, my kids, husband and I spend a Saturday or Sunday putting all the recent photos into albums. We also send some to friends and relatives and use the "outtakes" to make games such as jigsaw puzzles or writing silly captions. This not only helps keep the pictures in order, but it gives us a chance to review the things we've done on recent weekends. And since we are together only about two waking hours a day during the week, we get a double-dose of togetherness during these sessions, which, I think, helps my kids feel our good times even more.

Wally Day, Salt Lake City

Co-op

Like many working moms, I felt that I didn't have nearly enough time to spend with my friends or my family. Two other moms I know felt the same way and we worked out a deal: Every Saturday morning, one of us babysits for all the children (four of them), while two of us clean another's house. The next week, we switch so that every three weeks each of us gets a chance to really clean up while having the fun of company. (Knowing that a friend is coming to help also nudges each of us to keep straightening up regularly.) To top off the day, all the families do something fun together in the afternoons. This frees us all to spend Saturday evenings and Sundays with our families without having to devote too much time to boring chores.

Allison Quincy-Barnes, Des Moines, Iowa

Sharing the Caring

These parents share the pleasures—and the work—of parenthood.

Take turns

Piggyback responsibilities with your spouse when you get home. For instance, while I get our daughter's bath ready, my husband reads her a story. And while I bathe her, my husband cleans up the kitchen. This gives each of us time with our daughter. To avoid burnout, don't forget to plan an occasional night out with your spouse, with friends or by yourself. The change does me a world of good.

Rosemarie Catani-Lee, Kirkland, Quebec

Ask for suggestions

I realized that I took it for granted that I was going to wind up doing all the child care and housework even after I went back to work full-time. On one very stressed-out night, I asked my husband for ideas to help me cope. His answer surprised and delighted me. He said, "Tell me what I need to do, show me how you do it, and then let me do it however it works best for me." He told me that he really didn't know how to step in without stepping on my toes. He thought I wanted to be in charge of the whole house and family and was actually feeling left out. That was over a year ago. He's really good at doing things that I had never expected him to do. My suggestion for all working moms is not to assume that your husband is incompetent or unwilling to do his share around the house.

Kathleen Hennessy, Bridgeton, Missouri

Make a list

When I went back to work, my husband and I sat down and made a list of all the things that had to be done regularly to raise our son, David, and to keep the household running. We also made a list of those things that had to be done once in a while like taking David to doctors' appointments, making vacation plans, and rotating the tires on the car. We took turns picking out the jobs we wanted, until the items on each list had been split in two. We also remain flexible, helping each other out when needed.

Sara Ingilari, Seattle

Remember to ask and tell

My husband won't help with the housework unless I ask him to. Don't be shy, and be specific about which chores you want him to do.

Sue McGuire, Jeannette, Pennsylvania

Keep the family calendar together

Every Sunday night, Lionel, my husband, and I check our family calendar to see what has to be done that week and we make arrangements to split up who does what so that our children always get to appointments, parties and after-school activities on time and always have at least one parent present at school events.

Kathy Dietz, Prescott, Arizona

Hire a part-time sitter to pitch in

My husband used to come home from work and want to exercise and shower to unwind. But after spending the day with our four-year-old, I wanted adult conversation and time to relax, too. We agreed that both of us needed more time—to talk, to exercise, and to unwind—so we

compromised. Now a sitter comes each night to play with Laura for an hour. During this time, Pete and I take a walk and catch up on each other's day, work out problems or enjoy silent companionship. We've decided that the benefits of added intimacy, better health, and a calmer approach to our time spent together outweigh the cost of additional child care.

Claire Wise, Mentor, Ohio

Best Bets on Balancing Responsibilities

Here are parents' top tips for maintaining your job, household and sanity.

Pitch perfectionism

Juggling the responsibilities of work and family life became much easier once I accepted that my house was never going to be as clean as I would like, and my husband and I couldn't go out as often as we did before we had our daughter. She is the most important consideration in our lives now.

Maryellen R. Soell, Oakmount, Pennsylvania

Look for a good boss

I thought balancing work and family life was impossible until I changed jobs! At my last position, my boss made me feel like having a child was a major inconvenience. At my new job, my boss is happy to see my daughter drop by on occasion, is flexible about my hours and includes

Memo from the Office:
How to Save on Child Care Costs

Flexible spending accounts (FSAs) are IRS-governed programs that allow employees to set aside pre-tax earnings for child care expenses. Here's how they work.

- The employer sets up an FSA account for each employee who wishes to participate in the plan.
- The employee determines how much he or she is likely to spend on eligible child care expenses in a given year. (An expense is eligible if the money is paid to an "on-the-books" sitter or registered child care center.) The minimum annual contribution to an FSA account is $100; the maximum is $5,000.
- The employer deducts that amount from the employee's paycheck over the course of the year before income and Social Security taxes are deducted.

- The employee submits receipts for child care expenses to the plan administrator.
- The employee is reimbursed tax-free for his or her child care expenses. (The employee cannot claim the child care expense as an income tax deduction when filing, however.)
- If the employee overestimates the yearly expenses, he or she forfeits the excess payments made to the plan.

Most workers can save between 22 percent and 35 percent of their child care costs by paying with these pre-tax dollars. Separate FSAs can also be set up to cover anticipated health care expenses.

family issues in planning things like business trips. His enlightened attitude makes the world of difference to me and my co-workers.

Kerry Daniels, New York City

Streamline

If you're a working mom like I am, I suggest getting rid of anything in your life that requires your attention but that you could ultimately live without. I emptied all of the closets of debris, got rid of anything that needed dusting that I didn't

love, quit volunteering for everything and switched to cooking one-pot meals for the family. Now I can devote my limited energy where it counts—to my family and my work—in that order.

Teresa Long, Portland, Oregon

Spare yourself

Just say no to projects or committees at work, your child's school, or in the community unless their goals are very important to you.

Ruth Melheim Brubakken, Jamestown, North Dakota

Hire help

If you're working to provide the best for your family, consider using some of your income to make yourself the best mother you can be. I spend about $100 a week on a housekeeper and getting myself a massage. I don't feel guilty because I know that these luxuries allow me to give my husband and children a much nicer, happier me.

Donna Halpern, Scottsdale, Arizona

Prioritize

Make a list of the 20 most important things you must do this week and do 10 of them. The world won't fall apart if you don't do everything. You'll also find that the more you ignore, the more you find that many "important" things aren't so important after all.

Lili Armatage, Fort Lee, New Jersey

Be flexible

Being responsible for a family and a career means that you'll always have more to do than is possible and that the best-laid plans will often fall apart when a crisis intervenes. Once I came to terms with the fact that I couldn't control everything in my life, I was much happier.

Name withheld, Amityville, New York

Treat yourself

To take care of anyone else, you need to take care of yourself. That means treat yourself to some rest every week, make and keep your regular doctor's appointments, and let your family know that they, too, share responsibility for the day-to-day operation of the house. At work,

speak up if you're asked to do more than your fair share.

Lisa Morentz-Keating, Chicago

Working with Your Workplace

Sometimes the best source of help in balancing work and family life is at your place of business. After all, your company also shares your interest in making it possible for you to get to work.

Rework your work schedule

Shortly after our daughter, Chloe, was born, my husband and I negotiated with our respective bosses in order to rearrange our work schedules. Now I work part-time from 8:00 A.M. to noon, and Michael works from 1:00 P.M. to 8:00 P.M. My salary was adjusted to an hourly basis, but I'm not making much less money than I was before—and we're saving $800 a month on day care. The arrangement took some getting used to at first. Now it works beautifully.

R. J. Mortellitis, Essex, Vermont

Find other work within the company

I had been working as an executive secretary for an accounting firm for three years when my 10-month-old daughter had a severe asthma attack and was hospitalized. After Marie-Nicole's release, she was required to take medication every eight hours and visit the doctor once a week. I thought I was going to have to quit work,

How Can I Negotiate a New Schedule?

Changes in the workplace have led more and more companies to look for creative ways to hold down costs while holding on to valuable employees. If you want to cut a part-time deal, "It's important to read the climate at work to determine the best time to make your pitch," says Andrea Meltzer, of the Chicago-based placement firm Executive Options. Meltzer notes that the best time is usually while you're working full time for the company, rather than as a means to enter the workforce. To increase your chances of striking a deal, don't present your request as an ultimatum, she warns. Instead, try these negotiating tips.

- Enter the meeting with your supervisor knowing exactly what he or she must agree to in order for your goal to be reached. Anticipate the roadblocks: How will your work be done? How will important client calls be handled? Will you set up a home office to keep in touch?
- "Don't apologize for wanting to work part-time," says business consultant Kay Gurtin, also of Executive Options. "The more you treat the request as a favor, the more you lose the edge." And don't talk about your kids. Keep the conversation businesslike.
- Don't simply consider what is best for you. The new arrangement will also have to meet the needs of your employer. Present a realistic plan for getting all of your work done. Possible solutions: reorganizing staff, hiring another part-time employee and job sharing.
- Demonstrate the savings to your company of reducing your salary and benefits while retaining your skills, contacts, and knowledge of the industry.
- If your employer is concerned that your co-workers will ask for the same arrangement, explain that studies show that most people either cannot afford to work part-time or aren't interested in doing so.
- Approach your boss with a positive attitude. "Think of your request for part-time work as you would selling yourself for any job," urges Gurtin.

but my boss, sympathetic to my problem, created a new job for me as a "floating secretary." Now I work two to three days a week at my convenience, filling in for secretaries who are sick or on vacation.

Delna Parno, Brooklyn, New York

Try job sharing

A co-worker and I were in a similar position—both wanting more time with our families but both unwilling to quit work completely. We put together a plan to share one job, with each of us working two and a half days a week. Since the company was downsizing, they were thrilled to have two part-time workers instead of two full-timers. We were able to split our benefits, too, with her taking the health insurance (I'm on my husband's plan) and me taking the tuition assistance and other benefits, which I wanted. It's working well for everyone.

Dorathea Martin, Cincinnati

Ask for help

I wanted my five-year-old daughter, Katie, to take swimming lessons, but since I work full-time as a letter carrier, I wasn't able to take her to our local pool. I decided to approach my postmaster about this dilemma. She suggested I extend my half-hour lunch to one hour so I could take Katie to the pool and work the other half hour at the end of the day. Katie learned how to swim, and I learned that if you don't ask, you'll never find out how flexible your employer can be!

Nancy A. Carozzolo, Tonawanda, New York

Buy and sell your time

A number of us at work were having similar problems because our work schedules often precluded spending important time with our families. With our supervisor's okay, we planned a coverage system using coupons that we traded among ourselves for covering one another when it was important for us to be away. For example, I "cashed in" two hours worth of coverage with another worker so that I could attend a school conference. I was "paid" two hours when I worked through two lunch hours to cover for

another worker who needed to have extended lunch hours to take care of personal business.

Carolyn Harvey-Macmillan, Litchfield, Connecticut

Talk to co-workers and management

Find out if any others at work also need more help from the company and meet over lunch to brainstorm ways that might work. When some of us did this at our company, management signed us up for a consortium in the neighborhood that provides backup child care to workers in the area.

Kevin McManus, New York City

Have solutions

Telling your boss that you have problems balancing work and family life is a mistake. Instead, research possible solutions and bring those to management. Be sure that the solutions serve the company and not just yourself.

Nina Flack, Wappingers Falls, New York

No More 9 to 5!

Increasingly, parents are finding that the nine-to-five workweek doesn't match their family's needs. These parents have broken out of the mold and like it.

A split-shift arrangement

I have chosen a split-shift schedule in order to have time with our two-year-old son and save on day care expenses. I work during the day, while my husband stays home with our son and works at night. (Our main sources of communication

Organizations in the Know

The following organizations can provide information on flexible work schedules that you can campaign for at your office, including flextime, job sharing, compressed work week and working from a home office.

9 to 5, The National Association of Working Women

Call the job-problem hotline at 800-522-0925. You can also ask for the group's free information package.

New Ways to Work

Send a business-size SASE to Publications, 149 Ninth Street, San Francisco, CA 94103.

Catalyst

Send a business-size SASE to 250 Park Avenue South, New York, NY 10003, or call 212-777-8900.

with each other during the week are often notes and telephone calls.) Sometimes we feel like we're the only parents with this arrangement, but we think that it's worth it. And we truly appreciate the family time that we do have together on the weekends.

Jodi Arndt, Lakeville, Minnesota

Check out night work

I work a swing shift from 4:00 P.M. until 12:30 A.M. Night work pays more,

and I get to spend the day with my sons. I need a caregiver to fill in for only two hours a day until my husband gets home. The downside is that I don't get to tuck my kids in at night or see very much of my husband.

Judi Silva, Aloha, Oregon

Work longer hours, but fewer days

As a nurse, I know that weekends are the hardest time for hospitals to stay fully staffed. I worked out an arrangement where I work three 13-hour days, Friday, Saturday and Sunday, and have the rest of the week off. I only need child care on Fridays since my husband watches the kids on the weekend. It's wonderful to be home during the week.

Ruth Clausen, Annapolis, Maryland

Telecommute

With computers, modems, the Internet and the fax machine, staying in touch with the office from home is really easy today. I work from my home office four days a week and go in for meetings on Mondays or Tuesdays. I put in a full eight-hour day, but they're my hours. I work while the kids are at school and after they're in bed. I love being able to pick them up from school, and I'm saving a fortune on gas, work clothes and all the other expenses that go with going downtown.

Melinda Savoy-Baxter, Portland, Oregon

Take extra work home

A flexible work schedule is possible to create. Although it took me a few months to convince my boss, I now work from 8:00 A.M. until 2:00 P.M. I get in one hour earlier and eat lunch at my desk. When my work load gets extra heavy, I take home files to catch up. My boss has a happier and more productive employee, and I get to spend more time with my children

Lori J. Plotkin, Coral Springs, Florida

Bring the job home

I asked my bosses before I went on maternity leave whether I could perform my job as a computer operator from home. They said yes! I did, however, have to invest in a home computer, modem and laser printer. I learned that it never hurts to ask!

Paula Baczewski, Austin, Texas

Moms on the Home Front

Choosing to stay home to raise a family is a wise career choice for many, but getting used to the demands can take some adjustment.

Enjoy the business of being a mom

When I decided to stay at home to care for my children after working for many years, I had "business" cards printed with my name, address, phone number, and "Mother at Home" as the job title. Now when I'm out shopping or picking up my daughter at preschool and I meet another mom with whom I want to exchange telephone numbers, I just whip out my card. Being an at-home mother is the best career move I've ever made, and my business cards are one way to show how happy I am about it.

Donna Staszak, Alexandria, Virginia

Take the lead

As a spokesperson for Formerly Employed Mothers at the Leading Edge (FE-MALE), I know the frustration felt by many stay-at-home mothers that time spent with our children is undervalued by our society. But it's possible for a woman to be a feminist, a career woman at heart and a dedicated at-home mother.

Nancy Thompson, Elmhurst, Illinois

Dress for success

I was happy to give up my business suits and panty hose, but, at first, I went overboard for the sake of comfort and wore only sweatsuits when I became a full-time mom. I happen to catch my reflection one day in a store window and was pretty horrified to see that I looked like a soft, comfortable sofa. I started to wear trimmer corduroy slacks or denim jeans and nice shirts. Now I feel more comfortable in other ways—like I'm not afraid of running into a former co-worker because I no longer look sloppy.

Lindsy Gauk, Bethlehem, Pennsylvania

Prepare for your new role

I decided to approach being a full-time mom in the same way I'd approached any new job: I prepared myself by talking to others in the position, made a schedule that included meetings with other at-home moms and decided ahead of time that I was going to love it.

Betsy Connors, Kissimmee, Florida

Make new friends

When I first became a full-time mom, I tried to keep in touch with my former co-workers but eventually, we had little in common. I found it was more important to get to know other moms at home. Otherwise, you'll just feel isolated. Let go of your former life and get on with this one!

Carol Burke, Staten Island, New York

Enjoy your choice privately

I was so thrilled when I began staying home that I made the mistake of telling everyone who would listen how happy I was to be at home all day. It wasn't long before I was "volunteered" to sign for deliveries, to watch others' children when their child care fell through, and to fill in for a million other tasks. I quickly learned to say "enough!" After all, I made this choice so I could make my life and my son's life easier.

Pamela Short-Cuminski, St. Louis

Don't compare lifestyles

When I was working full time, I wondered what full-time moms did all day. Now I know! And now when I hear full-time moms putting down working moms or working moms saying nasty things

---

Preparing to Stay at Home

Here are some guidelines to get you ready for making the switch from salaried worker to home.

- Make a budget that realistically reflects your new circumstances.
- Hook up with a parent resource group or start your own.
- Don't overschedule all of your "free" time.
- Find an occasional babysitter so that you can have some time for yourself.
- Make a promise to keep up with at least one outside interest.
- Check out local exercise possibilities.
- Remember that it's not forever.

---

about at-home moms, I simply say, "Every mother is a working mother," and refuse to get caught up in the debate. I've done both and each has its rewards and hassles.

Opal Ruben, Boulder, Colorado

Educate yourself

I was a bit at a loss as to how to entertain my two kids and myself when I first began staying at home. I began to subscribe to magazines that offered good ideas for family activities and bought a few books on projects to do with kids. I also joined the local library (something I'd never had time for before) and got involved in the reading program there. Now I'm never without a plan for keeping us busy in productive ways.

Lorraine Kelsey, Concord, New Hampshire

Form a club

I loved becoming a full-time mother, but I missed my old life so much. I especially missed working and having lunch with adults. At first, I tried to set up lunch dates with my former co-workers but as time went on, we had less and less to talk about. So I set up a neighborhood mothers' group. We meet every Wednesday, talk about the kids, have lunch and plan something special. One week, we all decided to read the same book to discuss at our next meeting. Another time, we held a backyard toy-cleaning party. Having a set agenda and a regular meeting time keeps us all feeling much better about ourselves and helps us enjoy our lives more.

Lauren Cole, St. Joseph, Missouri

Dads at Home

Though it may seem so at times, you are not alone. More and more dads are stepping out of their traditional roles to discover that nothing quite beats getting to know your kids better.

Consider how lucky you are

Whenever I am feeling as if I am the only stay-at-home father in the world, I listen a little more closely to my 16-month-old daughter Larisa's laughter, cra-

PARENTS' RESOURCE

Just for Dads

Full-time fathers can find support here.

Full-Time Dads

A magazine that includes interviews, advice and a forum for the exchange of ideas. For information write to the magazine at P.O. Box 577, Cumberland, ME 04021, or call 207-829-5260.

At-Home Dad Newsletter

The newsletter includes stories, resources and tips for home businesses. For subscription information, write to the newsletter at 61 Brightwood Avenue, North Andover, MA 01845.

The Fatherhood Project

This organization offers information about seminars and a list of the best books on fatherhood. Send a SASE to 330 Seventh Avenue, 14th Floor, New York, NY 10001.

dle her in my arms and think how few fathers have the opportunity to experience such a close bond with their child. Doing this usually gives my spirits a quick lift.

Israel Lopez, Boca Raton, Florida

Find fellow dads

I ran an ad in the local paper to find men who were at-home fathers or just interested in forming a talk group. You may be surprised at how many at-home dads you're able to round up in your own area. Make the effort, it can't hurt.

Theodore D. Manley, Colorado Springs, Colorado

Don't worry about what others think

Who cares what anyone thinks? I have been a stay-at-home father since my son was three months old. If my family and I are happy with our lifestyle, that's all that counts.

H. L. Martin, Longwood, Florida

Get involved

I have done volunteer work to feel less isolated since I started to work at home and care for my now 18-month-old daughter. Once a month, I work on low-income housing with Habitat for Humanity. I helped organize a reunion for my high school class, and I do some admissions and career counseling at my college alma mater. And once a week I invite a buddy over for pizza and backgammon.

David Tausig-Edwards, New York City

Find a welcoming playgroup

Try different types of playgroups with your child until you find one that you like. I love staying at home with my eight-month-old son and teaching a parent-tot swim class at the local YMCA. I've noticed that it draws a lot of fathers.

Robert W. Linens, Sr., Burlington, North Carolina

Read all about it

Go to the library and look up back articles (especially those dated around Father's Day) in your local newspaper. Often newspapers run articles about at-home dads in the lifestyle section. Four months ago, I read about a stay-at-home dad who ran a support group, and I called him. He said, "Come on over." This group has been a lifesaver. It's great to connect with other like-minded dads.

Peter Baylies, North Andover, Massachusetts

Roll with the punches

I sometimes have sensed that people are looking down at me for not being the main "provider" in my family, but I take solace in the fact that I feel like a pioneer for other fathers. My wife and I made our decision in the best interest of our child. What could be more important than that?

Matthew Franklin, Bergenfield, New Jersey

Enjoy your equality

I'm happy that my wife can pursue her master's degree while I stay at home with our three-year-old. I worked for many years and think it would be selfish if I didn't allow her time to develop her career skills.

Robert C. Stewart, Tucson, Arizona

Home-Based Business Ideas

For many parents, working at home is the best of all worlds. Most who have done it caution that kids and business each require a separate space and some time apart from one another. Here are some inspiring ideas from mothers of invention.

Child safety is big business

I do room-by-room home inspections for parents, educate them on accident prevention and sell safety products. I com-

PARENTS' RESOURCE
Connecting with Others

These organizations can put you in touch with others who have chosen to stay home with their children.

Family Resource Coalition

This national clearinghouse lists more than 1,000 parent-support organizations and supplies information for parents who wish to join an existing organization in their community or who want to start their own. For more information, write to the coalition at 200 S. Michigan Avenue, Chicago, IL 60604.

National Association of Mothers' Centers

This grassroots network has more than 100 centers, each owned and operated by its members, that run workshops and other group activities. To join, write to 336 Fulton Avenue, Hempstead, NY 11550, or call 800-645-3828.

Mothers at Home

This organization publishes books and a monthly magazine called *Welcome Home,* through which stay-at-home moms can communicate. Write to the organization at 8310-A Old Courthouse Road, Vienna, VA 22182 for more information.

FEMALE (Formerly Employed Mothers at the Leading Edge)

This national nonprofit organization has a network of 70 local support groups for at-home mothers. The annual membership fee includes a subscription to the monthly newsletter. If you're interested in joining a chapter or starting one, send a business-size SASE to FEMALE, P.O. Box 31, Elmhurst, IL 60126.

---

piled most of the guidelines I use based on free research material from the Consumer Product Safety Commission.

Chris Cullem Pouch, Aurora, Colorado

Transcribe medical records

Medical transcriptionists are in big demand. I have been in this lucrative business for five years. I interpret and transcribe dictation by doctors concerning the condition of their patients. Check for courses in medical terminology and transcribing at a community college near you, or those given through a home-correspondence program.

Lynne M. Gill, Woodland, Washington

Start a typing service

I type term papers and resumes. I advertise in the local university newspaper and by posting fliers around my neighborhood. With very little effort, I make great extra money. If you own a word processor, you're in business.

Leslie Sholly, Knoxville, Tennessee

Plant a garden

Grow herbs in your backyard and then sell them to neighbors or to local farmers' markets. A woman in our area was so successful at this, she eventually rented out a

A Business Plan Pointer

Every working mother would love to have a Deborah Wax in her town. The Springfield, Virginia, mother of three has created her own business by solving a problem that many families face: getting kids where they need to go. Whether that be to soccer practice or the babysitter's house, Wax makes sure they get there, five days a week, in her shiny red van. "There are so many activities for children these days, but no way for parents to get them there," explains Wax. "Most baby-sitters won't transport children."

Called Kids Express Transportation Services, the business was born in April 1993, out of Wax's own frustration. An accountant who worked full-time, she could not figure out how to transport her daughter, then 6½, to and from her various activities. So Wax decided to take matters into her own hands: She quit her job and bought a van for $17,000. After starting with just one desperate client, she now makes more than 100 trips each week carting kids—even preschoolers—all over town, never leaving them until she is sure "they are where they are supposed to be." She charges $1 a mile; a typical ride costs about $6. Business is so good now that Wax is already expanding, recently adding another van to the fleet. She has hired two other mothers to do the driving (with herself as backup). "It is the ideal flexible part-time job," she explains.

warehouse and marketed her herbs to major spice companies.

Joy Lawrence, Squamish, Washington

Capitalize on calligraphy

I learned calligraphy at a community college. Now I write addresses on envelopes for wedding invitations and fill in names on certificates and diplomas from local schools.

Hinda C. Bodinger, Bayside, New York

Bake

I bake on consignment for a local health food store. Every day since I took a chance and gave the owner a taste test, I have brought in four baskets filled with muffins, mini loaves of bread and assorted cookies. In addition, through word-of-mouth, I've picked up business for holiday-gift packages and party platters.

Name withheld, New York City

Extra! Extra!

Are you a very early riser? If so, try a newspaper route. I have one, and it takes me only about two hours a day. I get an early-morning workout and make extra money. Best of all, day care is never necessary for my children because I make deliveries before my husband leaves for work.

Kendia Styron, Lynnwood, Washington

Tackle taxes

I'm taking tax classes and plan to launch a tax-preparation business. For home-correspondence programs write to the National Tax Training School, 4 Melnick Drive, P.O. Box 382, Monsey, NY 10953.

Dawna Mavel, Edgerton, Kansas

Do makeovers

I took makeup courses, and now I do makeovers for women before weddings and other special events. I advertise in church rectories and bridal shops. Then I show potential customers a portfolio of before and after photos of my clients.

Name withheld, Massachusetts

Do your homework

Some firms recruit people to work from their homes. For information write to the National Information Corporation, P.O. Box 5385, Spring Hill, FL 34606-5385. I earn extra money making hair bows.

Vicki Singer, Detroit Lakes, Minnesota

Make bouquets

I design bouquets with balloons and candy for weddings, bridal showers and parties. In three months I made back the money that I invested. Business is so good that I now have a credit-card machine!

Name withheld, Penbroke Pines, Florida

Start a local paper

I publish the weekly *Public Record Bulletin* for our county. One afternoon a week, I go to the county courthouse and

---

PARENTS' BOOKSHELF

The Working Life

The Work at Home Sourcebook (Live Oak Publications) shows how to pursue a career that you can manage at home.

The Working Parents Handbook, by the editors of the UCLA Childcare Services Newsletter (Fireside/Simon & Schuster), offers practical solutions to common dilemmas.

The Home-Based Entrepreneur: The Complete Guide to Working at Home, by Linda Pinson and Jerry Jinnet (Upstart Publishing), provides the nitty-gritty information on starting a home-based business.

The Second Shift: Working Parents and the Revolution at Home, by Arlie Hochschild with Anne Machung (Viking Press), explains the shifts in roles and social attitudes and what women can do to find balance in their lives.

What's a Smart Woman Like You Doing at Home? by Linda Burton, Janet Dittmer, and Cheri Loveless, founders of Mothers at Home, contains supportive stories by stay-at-home moms. To order, call 800-783-4666.

---

tape-record information that's available to the public: small claims, divorces filed and granted, marriage licenses, deaths, real-estate listings and bankruptcies. The next day, I transcribe the information, make copies and deliver or mail the bulletin to local businesses that subscribe.

Peggy Siegrist, Miami, Oklahoma

Tutor

As a former teacher, I started a tutoring service. I contacted the local school boards and put out the word that I was interested in tutoring students in English. In time, the boards started to send me referrals.

Patrice E. Gilbert, Enfield, Connecticut

Start a diaper service

It's not glamorous, but I began a diaper-cleaning service. I do pick-ups and delivery at night, and laundry during the day. Currently I have 15 customers, but my goal is to have 50.

Carol Kalmes, Onalaska, Wisconsin

Sew long

Since I was seven years old I have loved to sew. Two years ago, I decided to turn my hobby into a business. With $1,000, I launched Quinn's Quilts & Crafts from my den. I cleared out a corner of the room so that I could keep an eye on my kids while I sewed. I started out by making quilted wall hangings and crib quilts. My inventory now includes table runners, place mats, pillows, vests and friendship quilts. In my first year of business, I made a $2,000 profit, and this year my revenue doubled. I market my work at crafts shows, consignment shops, and through word of mouth. By the time my kids are in school full-time, I'd like to generate enough income that I can keep on being my own boss.

Diane Quinn, Springfield, Virginia

Design with your computer

With a computer and a laser printer, I design fliers, invitations, programs, and brochures for local businesses. You may find *Home Office Computing* magazine a good resource. For subscription information call 800-288-7812.

Beverly J. Colar-Credelle, Sauk Village, Illinois

Pump iron

I love ironing, and as we know, most people hate it, so I established an ironing service. Between the ads that I've posted on local community bulletin boards and word-of-mouth, my business has turned into a gold mine.

Jan Delsesto, Fort Lauderdale, Florida

Brush up on nail care

By doing manicures in my home, I earn good side money. It's also a great way to get to know my neighbors.

Suzanne Bennett, South Plainfield, New Jersey

Be entertaining

Entertaining at parties is a great sideline. I love to dress up as a clown, perform simple magic, do face painting and sing and dance at kids' birthday parties. Trust me: With a little imagination, there's lots of money to be made in this business!

Alisa Allen, Centerville, Indiana

CHAPTER THIRTEEN

Household Hints

*U*sing *time and money well are the built-in challenges* of running a household. They may not be the most fun, but the rewards are many. Time saved from housework helps ensure that you have precious minutes each day to spend together enjoying family life. And money saved on the necessities allows you and your family to relish some extras.

No-Mess Habits

Often, the best way to clean up starts with not making a mess to begin with. There are ways to limit the upheaval and keep children from undoing all your hard work.

Paint in the bathtub

My son loves to fingerpaint, but more than once he has gotten paint on the furniture, rugs and all over himself. Now I put him in his bathing suit and set up a plastic tray for fingerpainting in the bathtub. I tape the finished art to the bathroom tiles until it dries and can be moved. After he's finished, I just hose him and the tub down with the shower head.

Jennifer Pigeon, Santa Monica, California

Limit games to one at a time

My two kids have about a dozen games (each with a few hundred pieces, it seems) between them. Often, they would pull out a game, get tired of it and pull out another. They'd make a big mess and mix up all the pieces. Now I place the games on the top shelf of the closet and let them have only one at a time.

Kerry Kennedy, Lancaster, Pennsylvania

Child-lock drawers

Do your children drive you crazy when they fling things out of dresser drawers? To deter my 18-month-old, I attached a colorful toy with interlocking links through the handles.

Paula Repp, Okemos, Michigan

Make use of baskets

I have a big basket right inside the front door for dropping anything that is brought into the house. When my kids come in, they drop their jackets, bookbags, toys and anything else that would otherwise wind up on the floor or kitchen table into the baskets. This basket has kept my house from always looking like the Marines just landed!

Michelle Levy, Bayside, New York

Leave no paper trail

The biggest mess in our house is made by papers, so I bought a three-tiered box and put it on the desk in the foyer. I put bills in one tier, school papers in another and things to file in the third.

Janet Larson, Minneapolis

Use drop cloths

To prevent messes and to make the inevitable ones easier to clean up, I use plastic tablecloths in a variety of ways—under my toddler's high chair, under my four-year-old's play table and under our dining-room table. It's a lot easier to pick up and shake out a tablecloth than it is to constantly sweep up crumbs and mop up spills.

Vivian Sampson, Laramie, Wyoming

Discourage stacking

The best way I've found to eliminate clutter is to do away with almost all furniture (end tables, dressers and so forth) that has a top on which my family can stack things. I've replaced the end tables with floor lamps. Instead of dressers, my kids have hanging rods and hooks for all their clothes. Between meals, I keep a huge flower arrangement on the dinner table so that there's no room to plop down books and other things that the kids cart in.

Emma Longfeather, Kingston, New York

Space-Saving Storage

The maxim "A place for everything, and everything in its place" is especially noteworthy for parents of young children. Here are some tips for keeping your kids' possessions in place.

Tackle the mess

Are you looking for a convenient way to organize your child's small toys, such as rubber balls, action figures and race cars? Buy an oversize plastic fishing-tackle box that has two or three levels of compartments. It makes storage and cleanup much easier.

Joyce Shannon, Muncie, Indiana

Create parking spaces

My children's bicycles and ride-on toys were always in the way whenever I wanted to back out of the garage. So I painted colorful parking-space lines and my children's names on the garage floor. Now, like Mom and Dad, they can pull into their respective parking spots.

Marie Sabo Recine, Hamilton Square, New Jersey

Recycle boxes

I recycle oatmeal canisters to store my children's crayons, action figures and toy cars. I decorate each container with contact paper or self-adhesive fabric that co-ordinates with the decor in the kitchen or my children's bedroom. They also make good wastebaskets in the car.

Tessa W. Aquino, Buffalo Grove, Illinois

Use a shoe organizer for Barbies

My three daughters, Noelle, 10, Lauren, 8, and Jacqueline, 5, have accumulated quite a number of Barbie dolls.

When their collection outgrew their Barbie cases, I bought a long, clear, plastic shoe organizer and put each Barbie in her own pocket. Now, when my daughters want to play, they simply open the closet and pick their favorite dolls at a glance.

Mary-Jo Scott, Cary, North Carolina

Bag those mittens and gloves

To organize our mittens, hats and scarves, I hung a shoe bag on the inside of the closet door. The smaller children use the lowest pockets, and the older children use the upper ones.

Barbara Westbrook, Spartanberg, South Carolina

Hang your kitchen utensils

I use a clear shoe bag that fits over the pantry door to store my kitchen utensils and spices.

Kristina Blakely, Pueblo, Colorado

Find toys instantly

Keeping track of my children's little toys and game pieces has become a lot easier since I installed over-the-door shoe bags. Each pocket contains something that used to wind up in a big box, where the children could never find it. For instance, one pocket holds a jump rope, one a deck of cards, one has a few small balls. Since the pockets are see-through, the kids can find things when they need them.

Michael Daley, Sioux City, Iowa

Ditch big toy boxes

Toy boxes are great looking on the outside, but it's impossible to keep toys organized inside them. When we redid my sons' room, we threw out the toy box and replaced it with shelves. We then put all their little toys in see-through boxes on the shelves. Now the boys can find what they want easily and they don't dump out the entire contents of a large box to get to a toy figure at the bottom!

Shelby Dianopolis, Astoria, New York

Play picnic style

My five-year-old son, Ryan, loves playing with his blocks, but he hates to pick them up when he's done. To solve our daily dilemma, I store them in a large plastic container. At playtime, I pour the pieces onto a picnic tablecloth on the floor. When he's finished, I carefully lift the cloth and pour the blocks back into the container while he picks up any stray pieces. Because I set limits on where my son can play, cleanup has become hassle-free.

Laura Basila, Concord, California

Storing Your Child's Art

Kids produce artwork faster than most museum curators—or parents—can store it. Instead of trying to display it all or tossing it, try these creative uses to show off and preserve your child's masterpieces.

After-Art Cleanups

The materials kids use to create their artwork can create a special kind of mess. Here's how to remove the marks that were never intended.

Crayon

On wallpaper: Gently roll a kneaded eraser (the kind sold at art-supply stores) over the marks. If the stains remain, crush some white chalk and mix it with dry-cleaning fluid (available at most supermarkets). Lightly sponge the paste against the crayon marks, but do not rub. When dry, brush off the excess with a tissue. If you have washable wallpaper, continue to wipe off the area with mild soap and water. If you have nonwashable paper, follow by gently rubbing the spot with baking soda on a damp cloth.

On walls and woodwork: Dab at the marks with a cloth dipped in household cleaner. If this is unsuccessful, sprinkle baking soda on a clean, damp cloth and rub gently.

On blackboards: Place a cloth over the mark and apply a warm iron. Repeat until clean.

Marker

Washable markers usually wash out of cloth and off most surfaces with soap and water. For permanent markers, try going over the stains with a clean cloth dipped in liquid detergent and lukewarm water.

Water-based paint

Before allowing your child to paint with a brush or fingerpaints, add ¼ teaspoon of

Transport it in tubes

Save the cardboard tubes from paper towels, wrapping paper and posters to store or transport your child's prized artwork home from school.

C. M. Wegner, Minneapolis

Hang it from clotheslines

Artwork seems to grow in my house like moss on trees. Every day, it seems, one of my two children comes home from school with a bunch of drawings. To keep the artwork from taking over our home, I hung a clothesline in each child's room and use clothespins to display the most recent drawings or their favorite work. The rest gets packed into large paper portfolio cases that I bought at our stationery store.

Sue Chin, Fairfield, Connecticut

Use as wrapping paper

At the end of each school year, the kids and I decide which 10 drawings to save. We use the rest for wrapping paper.

Anna Weintraub, Colorado Springs, Colorado

Photograph structures

My son loves to build terrific structures that take over half the house. To let him know I appreciate his efforts even though

liquid dishwashing detergent to the paint to make mishaps easier to clean up.

Paint

On walls and woodwork: Dab the area with a damp cloth to remove as much as possible, then rub gently with baking soda on the damp cloth.

On rugs and carpets: Immediately blot the paint with a dry towel. Let the paint dry, then carefully comb out all excess with a stiff brush. Dab at any remaining stain with a clean cloth soaked in a mixture of one teaspoon of liquid dishwashing detergent and one cup of warm water. Blot with a dry towel and repeat until clean.

On washable fabrics: Let the paint dry; then brush off surface accumulation with a stiff brush. Wash the item as usual but don't put it in the dryer, since the heat may set any remaining stain.

On nonwashable fabrics: Blot the paint with a dry cloth. Once dry, brush off any remaining paint with an old toothbrush. If any stain remains, have the item professionally dry cleaned.

Ballpoint pen

On walls and woodwork: Dab at the marks with distilled white vinegar. Blot frequently.

On wallpaper: Dab with a damp cloth. Then spray lightly with hair spray and blot with a dry cloth.

On fabrics: Place a paper towel under the stain and spray with hair spray. Launder as usual.

I have to ask him to disassemble the work, I take pictures of it and display the photos on his bulletin board.

Carol Pizzaro, Leonia, New Jersey

Frame the triumphs

Because I can't possibly save all the great artwork that my daughter creates, we pick out our favorite every year and have it professionally framed. We've dedicated one dining-room wall as the Caitlin Gallery. It's wonderful to see how her artistic style has evolved from her first scrawls to her current masterpieces.

Marge Kennedy, New York City

Present some as gifts

Both of my son's grandmothers love to know what Jonathan is up to lately. Since he's too little to write letters, I include samples of his latest artwork in each card I send them. They love it and I reduce our collection somewhat.

Rosalyn Treuber, Stockdale, Arizona

Create place mats

I cover some of my children's artwork in plastic contact paper and use it for place mats and playmats.

Terry Garvey, Milwaukee

Clever Cleanup Tricks

If only we could wave a magic wand to make the messes disappear! Unfortunately, most cleanups require elbow grease, not secret spells. These parents have discovered ways to mix in a little magic to make housecleaning a bit easier.

Erase crayon marks on wallpaper

After my toddler drew on my favorite wallpaper with crayons, I found a good way to remove it. I held a hair dryer, on the hottest setting, over the crayon marks until the wax warmed. The crayon was then easily wiped off with a damp cloth and a small amount of oil-based soap.

Jayne Zito, Sterling Heights, Michigan

Baking soda cleans wallpaper

My mother-in-law taught me this one for taking greasy kids' fingerprints off our washable wallpaper, since regular soap and water did not work: She made me a baking-soda-and-water paste, which I put onto the wall and let it dry. Then I brushed off the remaining powder. It really worked!

Nancy Higgens-Armondo, Massapequa, New York

Soap down the walls

An accidental spill of dishwashing detergent showed me that it's the best

Getting the Drop on Gum

The key to removing gum from clothing, furniture, walls and other surfaces is to freeze it. Simply run an ice cube over the gum several times, then scrape if off using a dull knife. Dab at any remaining stain with dry-cleaning fluid.

cleanser for painted walls. I'd mixed a bowl of detergent and water to let my children make soap bubbles in our family room, when my daughter tripped with the bowl and the soapy water landed on the walls. Drying the mess revealed a very clean wall! So I made more and washed down the entire room. Now, it looks like it's been repainted.

Malory Browne, Redwood, California

Housecleaning Shortcuts

Housecleaning may never become a thing of the past, but it doesn't have to take all of the present either. These parents have discovered some nifty time-savers that can work for you.

Create a cleaning carryall

So that I don't have to gather the cleaning products I need for each room when I clean, I put all the supplies and a roll of paper towels in a single bucket and carry it with me. This saves me many steps and I always have what I need when I need it.

Una Conway, Forest Hills, New York

Use the dishwasher . . .

I used to spend a lot of time cleaning toothbrushes, hairbrushes, small toys and a million other things by hand until I realized that these things could be better washed in the dishwasher. Now, almost once a week , I do a totally nondish dishwashing. I use twist ties to secure small items that might slip through the dish racks.

Metta Rish, Detroit, Michigan

. . . or the bathtub

Cleaning bikes, dollhouses and other big toys created a real mess in our rather small apartment until I copied a friend who did this big-job cleaning in the bathtub. Now all the mess goes right down the drain and rinsing, using the shower, is a snap.

Jan Engle, Fort Worth, Texas

Baby wipes to the rescue

When my son outgrew his baby wipes, I was left with a few boxes that I had bought on sale. I found that they were great for cleaning appliances, telephones, countertops and bathroom sinks and pipes.

Emily Durant, Kingston, New York

Dust off those old socks

After my wrist was cut while dusting metal miniblinds with a rag, I started putting an old pair of tube socks over my hands for this kind of cleaning. Then I realized that all dusting was easier with the socks than with traditional rags. I can even dust two-handed and finish in half the time.

Gisela Birnbaum, Honolulu

Old diapers do the trick

I've found that nothing makes a better cleaning rag than an old cloth diaper. They leave no lint, are easy to clean and are extremely absorbent.

Marty Everston, Akron, Ohio

Are Crayon Stains on Clothing Permanent?

Crayons in kids' pockets have a way of working themselves into the clothes dryer, where they can create a lovely mess. The folks at Binney & Smith, the creators of Crayola crayons, have some tips for removing these stains: Place the stained fabric surface face down on a pad of paper towels and spray with a petroleum distillate such as WD-40. Wait two minutes, turn the fabric over, and repeat the process. Next, apply liquid dishwashing detergent to the stain and work it into the fabric. Replace the toweling as the stain is absorbed. Depending on the fabric, wash in hot or warm water with laundry detergent and powdered bleach for about 12 minutes and rinse in warm water. To rid the dryer of any remaining wax residue, spray the drum with WD-40, wipe with a soft cloth and run a load of dry rags through the drying cycle.

Everyday Time-Savers

These parents share their strategies for making chores less time-consuming.

Buy services—and time

I save about two hours a week by having my laundry done by the local Laundromat. I save another two hours by shopping for groceries by phone from my desk at work and having the food delivered to my home. Another hour savings comes from ordering anything I can by phone, such as postage stamps and prescription drugs. The costs are minimal—about $20 a week. And the extra five hours or so a week I have to spend with my family makes it worth it.

JoAnna Hook, Maplewood, New Jersey

Do a room a day

Every night, after the kids are asleep, my husband and I tackle one room and completely clean it. Working together, it only takes about 15 to 20 minutes to do it. This way, our weekends are free of housework (mostly), and we never really feel that we're devoting that much time to cleaning.

Joy Jamison, Salinas, Kansas

Start a cleaning co-op

With 16 children between us, my friends Susan, Amy, Kathy and I were always moaning and groaning about how impossible it is to keep up with household chores. Finally, during one of our playgroup discussions, we came up with a solution—a cleaning co-op. Here is how our co-op works: Each week, on a rotating basis, one of our homes becomes the cleaning target. The hostess provides refreshments, lunch and—most important—a to-do list. We fold laundry, change linens, clean out garages, defrost refrigerators, organize videos, toy car and doll collections, and, of course, vacuum, scrub floors and clean toilets. On occasion we take on special projects such as canning peaches, polishing silverware, landscaping and doing light carpentry. The hostess keeps our kids entertained with arts-and-crafts projects. Our rule is that we work a total of three hours and then stop to eat and chat. Best of all: Once a month, one of us doesn't have to clean her own house.

Wendy Von Zirpolo,
Danville, New Hampshire

Freshen beds

I used to change the sheets every week, but on top of all my other work with my job, house and kids, I was looking for ways to cut back without anyone feeling deprived. I've found that just changing the pillowcases each week makes the beds fresher and I reserve complete changes for every other week. (With six beds to make, this is a real time-saver.)

Karen Street, Address withheld

Especially for Working Moms . . .

Lunch hour can be put to more uses than just eating lunch, as these moms know.

Do errands at lunchtime

Instead of taking an hour to eat and socialize, I do some of my home chores at lunchtime. Things like going to the post office, dropping off a prescription, getting my clothes to the cleaners all can be done much more easily near my work than near home.

Sarah Lipsig, Roosevelt Island, New York

Get mail at the office

I have most of my mail sent to my office address. That way I can easily pay bills, renew magazine subscriptions and read the mail during my lunch hour, which is much easier than doing it at home.

Kate Horvath, San Francisco

Kitchen Time-Savers

The kitchen is usually the hub of the family—and the place that most housework is needed. Cut down on the time spent preparing and cleaning up after meals by taking some of this advice.

Erasing Scratches from Wood Furniture

First apply a coat of wax- or oil-based furniture polish. If scratches remain, clean the area with a cloth dampened in mineral spirits (available in hardware stores). Then apply one of the following coloring agents to the scratched surface. (Test first in an inconspicuous spot.) Coloring agents include: (1) Crayons. Find a shade that matches the finish and fill in the scratch, blending with your finger. (2) Wax sticks. Melt wax in a saucepan and carefully drip it into the scratch, then blend with your finger. (3) Shoe polish. Apply with an artist's brush or cotton twisted around the end of a toothpick. If you get a darker color than desired, dab on a drop or two of mineral spirits. After applying any of these camouflage techniques, finish the wood with a wax- or oil-based furniture polish.

ASK THE EXPERTS

How Can I Keep Silver Sparkling?

Tarnish can't be eliminated entirely, since it's the result of a natural chemical reaction occurring when silver comes in contact with sulfur dioxide in the air. It can be minimized, though, and here's what the Soap and Detergent Association recommends.

- Don't let salt or high-sulfur foods such as eggs or mayonnaise remain on silver for long. Salt can corrode silver while eggs and mayonnaise hasten tarnishing.

- Wash silver as soon as possible after use with dishwashing liquid and hot water. Rinse in hot water and towel dry to avoid spots. And don't drain on a rubber mat—contact with rubber promotes tarnishing.

- If your flatware is dishwasher safe, follow this procedure: Don't overload the silverware basket or sprinkle detergent on the silverware; use water at least 130°F.

- Store in specially treated bags available where silver is sold, and don't use rubber bands to close them since the sulfur in the bands will cause tarnishing even through the bags. (When storing for an extended time, wrap pieces in wax paper and keep in a clean, dry place.)

- Don't place or store silver near heating ducts.

Make TV dinners from leftovers

I've found a way to skip cooking one night a week. After dinner I store a complete meal of leftovers in a microwave dish in the freezer. After five or six nights, I've stored up enough TV dinners to serve everyone. And for a bonus, each member of the family gets to have his or her favorite meal twice in one week.

Darlene Moorehead, Elmira, New York

Make one-pot meals

No more complex recipes for me! Now I use my Crock-pot and my microwave to help me save time for what I love most: spending time with my son.

DeAnne C. French, Austin, Texas

Form a cooking collaborative

Four of my neighborhood friends and I agreed that cooking dinner consumed too much of our time, so we came up with a solution. Here's how our cooking co-op works: Once a month we meet to plan 30 menus for the month and to assign which weekday we'll cook. On our cooking day, we prepare and deliver five identical meals, one to each family. Some co-op rules: Our budget is $40 for five dinners; we never eat the same meal more than once a month; dinners must arrive hot and ready between 5:30 P.M. and 6:00 P.M., and include a main and side dish, bread, salad and fruit. It's a luxury having to cook on only one weekday and sitting back and waiting for my dinner to arrive on the other days.

Judy Hilton, Rochester, New York

Go the paper route

Once a week, I serve dinner on paper plates and use disposable cups. That gives me an extra 20 minutes with my family. It may not be much, but I enjoy it.

Francie Delano, Nutley, New Jersey

Cook once a week

The after-work crunch of cooking dinner while supervising homework and simply finding time to relax with my children was making me crazy. One Sunday, I decided to cook six dinners ahead and freeze the food in reheatable containers. It worked so well that I now do it every week. What a difference this has made! By investing about two hours a week (the same time I was spending on Sunday dinners alone) I have an extra 40 minutes every evening.

Rita Marshak, Indianapolis, Indiana

Serve water at dinner

One of the biggest jobs I used to have after dinner was cleaning up milk, juice or soda that my kids spilled. It seemed they couldn't get through a meal without knocking over a glass while reaching for something on the table. Now I serve only water with meals and the cleanup is much easier. They can have other drinks any other time.

Marita Jimenez, Fort Worth, Texas

Enlist a mealtime cleanup crew

To get our two kids, ages 9 and 12, to clean up after meals, we came up with the plus-three solution: Each family member is responsible for cleaning his own dishes and place setting, plus putting away three other items from the table.

Robert S. Onufer, Laguna Hills, California

Housework: A Family Affair

Sharing the workload of housekeeping benefits more than the one who is usually stuck with the job. When each family member has appropriate chores to do, everyone learns to take responsibility for his or her share of the housework. These parents have found terrific ways to assign chores and to help kids get their jobs done.

Make it a game

My children often complain about doing the same household chores over and over again. To add a little fun and suspense to cleanup time, I made a wheel-of-fortune type job distributor. I cut out an arrow and a circle from cardboard and attached them with a push pin. Then I wrote down a variety of jobs along the circle. At least the kids get a little excited now when it's time to clean up.

Christine Gibson, Evansville, Indiana

Let kids form clean teams

My daughter, Samantha, like most 10-year-olds, would rather spend her time with her friends than cleaning her room. One day she came home from her friend Lisa's house and told me that they had come up with a plan: On Saturday mornings they would both clean Lisa's room and on Saturday afternoons they'd tackle Sam's. They have fun and the work actu-

15 Ways to Cut Minutes a Day from Your Cleanup Schedule

1. Set up a shelf in the laundry room, and put each member's folded laundry above his or her name on the shelf. Let it stay until the person who owns it puts it away.

2. Teach your children to sort dark clothes from light before the clothes reach the laundry room. Consider placing two hampers—one for each—in the bathroom.

3. Allow your older children to start supper before you get home from work. They can start washing greens for a salad and can set the table for dinner.

4. Take 5 minutes in the evening (and save yourself 20 minutes the next morning) to locate your keys, glasses and anything else you tend to search for as you rush to get ready for the day.

5. Organize your clothing accessories to speed up morning dressing time. Throw away stockings with runs; find all the backs to your earrings, keep scarves ironed and the night before you plan to wear a particular outfit, put the accessories that go with it on the hanger.

6. Keep your library books and your children's on one shelf in the house. Put them back there between readings so you won't have to search through other books when it's time to return them.

7. When packing grocery bags at the supermarket, put similar items together (frozen foods, paper products, canned and boxed goods, for instance) to save time unpacking at home.

---

ally gets done! Their system's been in place for nearly a year.

Amelia McIntyre, Ames, Iowa

Use a child's impatience

My son, age seven, loves when we have company over for dinner, but he is very impatient until everyone arrives. To pass the time, I ask him to make centerpieces or place mats for our table. He designs unique arrangements out of Legos, Bristle Blocks and Tinkertoys and sometimes he draws personal place mats for everyone.

He enjoys his role in preparing for guests and he loves to show off his creations—and I'm happy that he has something to keep his busy while I prepare.

Julie C. Martin, Omaha, Nebraska

Work to music

My daughter, husband and I take turns choosing the background music to our Saturday morning housework. An added bonus is that we grown-ups get to keep up-to-date on our child's musical tastes.

Dottie Moe, Cleveland

8. Separate forks, knives and spoons as you load the silverware compartment of your dishwasher and as you put away the utensils.

9. Buy a clear, plastic storage container with multiple compartments and fill it with picture hooks, nails, screws, thumbtacks and other items used for home repairs.

10. Draw an outline of your tools on the wall to mark where they hang. Make sure you put them back as soon as you are finished with them.

11. If you commute by car or have to park at meters, keep a roll or two of quarters or tokens in your car so that you won't be caught short on your way to work.

12. Color-code your keys (with nail polish or plastic jackets) for easy identification and store extras on a key rack. Give a set to a neighbor in case of an emergency.

13. Keep an extra car key in your wallet. That way, if you lose your key chain, the only spare won't be sitting at home in a drawer.

14. If you have a circuit breaker, figure out which switch controls which room(s), and label each accordingly so you won't have to guess which switch corresponds to which outlets during an emergency.

15. Put your coffeemaker on a timer and set it so that the coffee is ready to drink when you get up in the morning.

Hide treats and surprises

To make cleaning up a bit more fun for my two children, ages 6 and 10, I hide little treats and coins and stickers around the house for them to find as they clean.

Lorraine Chapman, Iowa City, Iowa

Offer a payoff

Whenever my children, ages six and seven, have to do extra chores such as helping with spring cleaning, I make sure that I pay them back with extra time to do something fun. For instance, after helping to choose and pack items to give away, the whole family played Monopoly, their favorite game.

Margee Hanson, Baltimore

Let kids choose their chores

I often fought with my two teenage sons about helping around the house. Finally the older one suggested that they choose their own jobs instead of doing what I wanted when I wanted it. I agreed to the experiment, telling them to keep me posted. I was surprised when Charlie,

Vinegar and Baking Soda—Not Just for Cooking

White vinegar is good for a lot more than making salad dressings. It's one of the best household cleaners around. And don't worry about the vinegar making your house smell like a pickle factory. It evaporates quickly, taking the smell with it. Here are some ways to use vinegar as a cleanser.

- Full strength on a cloth, it's great for polishing chrome and stainless steel. Or use it to remove soapy buildup from basin fixtures, however, you'll need to use a mixture of one teaspoon of salt dissolved in two tablespoons of vinegar.
- Toilets and bathtubs require slightly different treatment. For toilets, pour vinegar in, let stand for about five minutes, then flush. For stubborn stains, spray with vinegar and then brush vigorously. Bathtubs should be wiped first with vinegar, then baking soda. Rinse with clean water.
- For bathroom tiles, mix a solution of one part white vinegar to four parts water. Rinse well. (Clean the grout with a mixture of ¾ cup of bleach and one gallon of water; use a brush and rinse thoroughly.)
- Add a cup of vinegar to the rinse cycle when you're washing a plastic shower curtain (which should always be washed with a large bath towel). For quick cleanups of plastic shower cur-

---

13, decided he wanted to cook dinner instead of washing dishes every other night. It turns out he's a pretty good cook. And Peter, 15, decided on his own to clean the garage from top to bottom. It's never looked so good. My advice to other moms of teens is to give the kids more options. You might just discover that they're good at more than you would have guessed.

Teresa McNeil, Seattle

Thank your children

I refrain from redoing any work that my children do with sincere effort. So what if the bed is made a little crooked or the knives and spoons are on the "wrong" side of the plate? As long as they do a job willingly and as well as they are able, all I say is "Thank you."

Marianne Kerr, Lexington, Kentucky

Brag

My daughter loves overhearing me brag about what she's helped me do around the house. For instance, last week when I wasn't feeling well, she cleaned her room and the living room. It was a big job for a seven-year-old and I was really grateful. She was so proud of herself and I was proud of her. I told everyone about it and made sure that she heard me bragging.

Natalie Umberto, Santa Fe, New Mexico

tains, wipe off soapy film with a cloth dampened with vinegar and then rinse.

Baking soda does more than eat up odors in the refrigerator.

- A handful of baking soda in the bottom of the dishwasher will help absorb odors.
- To remove traces of food odors, soak plastic food containers overnight in a baking soda solution or rub dry baking soda into your wooden cutting boards with a damp sponge and rinse clean.
- As a paste made of three parts baking soda and one part water, use it to pol-

ish silver. Just apply the paste with a damp sponge, rub until clean, rinse and buff to a shine.

- Clean away corrosion buildup on your car's battery terminals using the same paste.
- In your bath, use baking-soda paste to smooth away rough skin on elbows, feet and knees.
- Out of deodorant? Apply a small amount of baking soda to your armpits.
- In a solution of four tablespoons of baking soda and one quart of water, use baking soda to clean chrome car bumpers and trip as well as vinyl upholstery.

Go fish

I keep the names of tasks on folded index cards inside an old fishbowl. Every week, my three kids take turns fishing for what housework they'll do. Each child takes a turn, choosing three tasks. The one who does them first (and to my satisfaction) gets a dollar.

Yolanda Melker,
Princeton, New Jersey

Helping Toddlers Get in on the Act

It's never too early to involve children in housework, as these parents have found.

Appoint your child Deputy Housekeeper

Give your young child a choice of two tasks that he can help with. My son loves to put away silverware, stack bowls or find the socks from the clean-laundry pile.

Lesli Drucker, Charlotte, North Carolina

Provide creative tools

My three-year-old son loves to help me clean up, so I give him a thick, soft-bristle

Easy-Does-It Cleanup Tips to Involve Children in Housework

- Be sure that you have your child's full, undivided attention before you ask him to clean up.
- Be specific. Instead of giving your child vague directives such as "Clean up this mess," try "Put all the blocks in the blue basket." When that's done, go on to the next item on your list, such as "Now let's put the books on the shelves."
- Break big jobs into smaller, more manageable ones. For instance, instead of asking your child to get the table ready for dinner, ask her to put out the plates, then the silverware and napkins. Then ask to set the drinking glasses and certain items from the refrigerator.
- Turn cleaning into a game. Say, "Can you put all the books on the shelf before this timer goes off?" or, "I bet I can get the bed made before you put all the cars in the bin."
- Label shelves (with pictures for non-readers) so kids can remember what goes where.
- Keep your child's room arrangement consistent. It's hard to remember where to store things if the storage space keeps changing.
- Create an easy-care room by providing open shelves at your child's level. Cover the floor with an easy-to-clean mat or opt for bare floors that can be damp mopped faster than it would take to vacuum a carpeted room. Paint walls with washable paint.
- Accept a certain amount of clutter.
- Close the door on teens' rooms if you can't stand looking at the mess and they don't choose to clean it themselves.

paintbrush to "paint" the dust away. It keeps him busy while I do the housecleaning and it's a help, too.

Elaine Potter, Jacksonville, Florida

Turn the high chair into a child-size desk

I set my son up at his high chair with crayons and supplies so that he can do his paperwork when I need to pay bills or write letters. When I'm preparing dinner, I give him a bowl of water and a few spoons to play with, which seem to keep him busy and happy.

Donna Lipton, Fort Campbell, Kentucky

Keep them busy with playthings

Separate your child's toys into different boxes in each room of the house; this way he or she can look forward to having something new to play with while you're working in that room.

Christine Dickinson, Towaco, New Jersey

Find age-appropriate tasks

My three-year-old son is my biggest helper around the house. He loves to push the clothes into the dryer. He hands me the clothespins, gets the diapers and baby wipes when it's time to change his sister, helps set the table and picks out vegetables.

Tammy Jones, Brockway, Pennsylvania

Find child-size tools

I bought child-size housecleaning tools for my three-year-old son so that we can work together. He likes to use his miniature broom and feather duster while I do my housework. Sometimes I even let him help me push the vacuum or use a small handheld one. It is a good way for us to spend time together and to get work done, too.

Kim Erickson, Lincoln, Nebraska

Beat the clock

When my son, Jared, is underfoot, I set the kitchen timer and turn folding napkins or cleaning up toys into a series of timed games. He enjoys himself and the housework gets done faster.

Teresa Jarrell, Corpus Christi, Texas

Reward your child for his patience

Sometimes I make a verbal agreement with my three-year-old son, David. I explain that if he lets me complete my chores in the morning, he can choose a special activity for us to do together later. As a result, he understands that sometimes he must compromise in order to get what he wants.

Elizabeth Rios, El Centro, California

Be a role model

I'm a tugboat sailor, and I try to involve my two-year-old son in everything I do when I come home after being away at sea. If I'm sweeping the garage, I give him a small broom to mess with. If I'm working with my tools, I give him a safe one to carry around. Sometimes he loves to play with a set of keys or open things. When I do dishes, I put a chair up to the sink and let him help. When my son was an infant, I'd sit him on my lap when I worked on bills. If I made a call, I gave him a play phone to play with. Be creative and encourage your kids to love life and people.

Sean S. Waterbury, Littleton, Colorado

Schedule baby breaks

Have a big box of distractions ready—filled with items such as toys, colored paper and crayons to amuse your child while you're working. Then take an occasional break to play together.

Shayna Russum, Pearl, Mississippi

Share dad's work, too

My daughter loves to watch her dad working and to hand him each of his tools as he asks her for them. A child's set of tools lets her pretend to be working alongside her father.

Debra Ullmann, Adkin, Texas

Tackling Preteens' and Teens' Rooms

The most important thing for parents to know about their preteen's or teenager's room is that all those lessons you've taught

Sharing the Housework with Your Spouse

Sometimes it's the other grown-up, not the children, who needs reminders to pitch in. Here are some typical resistance scenarios and how they can be overcome with some imagination.

- *Your spouse complains that your standards are unrealistic.* Maybe he's right. What's the use of having a kitchen floor that's so clean you could eat off it—unless you plan to dine on the floor? Most likely there is room for compromise here. Standards are something you can negotiate.

- *The old, "You're so much better at all of this than I am."* (Which means, of course, "Maybe I should just watch you and take notes for the next 10 years.") Experts say that if women are better at housework and child care, it isn't because they were born that way. It's just that they have had more practice. Offer to allow your spouse more practice so that he, too, can become an expert.

- *The chores get done—badly.* The worst thing you can do is to try to control your mate's work around the house. Given time and practice, most people's standards will rise as long as they feel responsible for a job. In the meantime, bite your tongue.

- *Your spouse "forgets" to do something.* This is one reason couples should be specific about the chores that they agree to do. If forgotten tasks continue to be a problem, you need to talk about it.

- *You sense increasing resentment to requests.* You may find that conflicts between the two of you are growing. If you are unable to resolve these matters, counseling can be helpful.

them about cleaning up are not completely forgotten. Your kids will remember them again when they have their own children. For now, however, your best bet may be to close the door.

Lend a hand

My daughter's room is tiny so there isn't much to do; but the mess can be overwhelming and she will get upset sometimes that there is so much picking up to do. So I suggest that we do it together. I hope my willingness to help will instill better habits for the future.

Wendy Rosenblum, Medford, Massachusetts

Stick to your guns

I told my daughter that I wouldn't buy her any new clothing until she started taking care of what she had by picking up clothes from the floor and putting them in their proper places. I stuck to my promise for about a month and she began to cooperate with my request. As she grew older I threatened to clean her room for her and then she would clean it right away, since she didn't want her privacy invaded.

Diane Watson, Nassau County, New York

Forget it

I didn't bother to ask my daughter to clean her room. It was always a mess and I just shut her bedroom door. We were both too busy to have endless fights about keeping it clean.

Holly Repp, Baltimore

Be firm

My 13-year-old son doesn't like to clean at all; he would rather read or do artwork. I told him that before he does something he really enjoys a lot, he has to clean his room. I tell the same thing to my step-daughter and it works for both of them. It's an effective way to get them to pick up after themselves and once they set out to clean up, they do a very good job.

Susan Farmer, Jacksonville, Illinois

Strike a deal

If you give your children an allowance, set up a deal with them. If they don't have their rooms clean by bedtime or by 10:00 A.M., for instance, then you will clean it for them, but they will have to pay you to do it. It may be only 25 cents, depending on their allowance. Then they will think, "Gee, I don't want to have to pay Mom all my allowance," and they will do it them-selves.

Renee Hoffman, Lansing, Michigan

Bracing for the Big Jobs

Spring cleaning, preparing the house for holidays, getting the house winterized—these are the big jobs that require special attention. Make the most of these annual rituals in ways that save time and include some fun.

Storing Winter Woolies

To pack away winter clothing, follow these easy-care tips.

- Clean all clothing, as well as your storage space, before you begin packing. Clothing that is dirty attracts moths and other insects.
- Store clothing in a cool, well-ventilated area, such as a large, dark closet. (Light may cause colors to fade.) Avoid spaces with extreme temperatures and humidity levels.)
- Use cedar chests, airtight containers, cloth or canvas bags or cardboard boxes. Never use plastic containers which hold in moisture and may cause mildew to form.
- Mothballs do not kill moth larvae that are already in your clothes, but they do work as a repellent. Don't let mothballs touch the clothing.
- Potpourri, wrapped in netting and stored between sheets of tissue, will keep clothes smelling fresh.
- If you store clothing by hanging it in a closet, drape a sheet over it to keep out dust and light.

ASK THE EXPERTS

What Are the Best Methods to Prevent Mildew?

Mildew, a fungus growth caused by molds, is easier to prevent than to cure. Molds like damp, dark, warm and poorly ventilated spaces. Your best bet, according to the Soap and Detergent Association, is to create an environment in which mildew can't exist.

- Keep areas susceptible to mildew cool and airy.
- Don't store clothes or linens if they're dirty. Molds are attracted to stains on fabrics.
- Don't store damp fabrics, including those clothes that are rolled up for future ironing, or leave damp items in the hamper.
- Prevent mildew in closets by allowing air to circulate. A 60- to 100-watt bulb should be left on in the closet periodically to discourage mold growth. Be sure the bulb is not touching anything.
- If mildew does develop, brush spores off outdoors, dry-clean items that can't be washed, wash others immediately with detergent and bleach or soak items that can't be bleached in nonchlorine bleach and then wash.

Have a yard sale

Once a year, I go through each room of the house and pack up all the things that have been outgrown, underused or otherwise ignored. Then I pick a day for a yard sale. Before the sale, my kids price their own items and I price mine, we post notices around town and go to the bank to get rolls of quarters and single dollar bills for change. Early that day, we set up in the driveway. Each year, we earn about $600 for our work, which we always use for our summer vacation.

Marlee Raine, St. Charles, Missouri

Give yourself a break

When it's time to do the spring cleaning, I start to feel overwhelmed. But I've found that if I tackle just one room a week for six weeks the job gets done. Each time I finish a room—laundered curtains, waxed floors and everything else—I give myself a treat. I might go out to dinner with friends, take in a movie by myself or anything that feels like a reward. I keep the reward in mind as I clean to motivate myself.

April Urkin, Albany, New York

Hire your teens and their friends

When it's time to do a big job like the garage or attic, I hire my son and his friends for the day. I provide pizza and soda and they do the rest. It's great fun and a good way for the kids to earn money. I even hired them to paint the master bedroom, which they did very well. Their labor cost $150 ($50 each for the day). A professional wanted $800.

Nancy Holmes-Delacy, Grand Rapids, Michigan

Have an old-fashioned bee

I recently decided to make new slipcovers and drapes for the living room and two friends offered to come over and help. Together we got the job done in just one day. We decided to do each other's rooms over in turn. We've completed rearranging furniture and painting in one of their living rooms and next week, we're redoing the third friend's bedroom.

Jackie Montgomery, Tulsa, Oklahoma

Get inspired by magazines

Before getting into spring cleaning, I go to the library and look through all the decorating magazines for ideas to freshen the look of our home. While I can't redecorate every year, I always find some things I can do to make the house look different and new. Little things—like replacing a curtain tie with a big ribbon—can really spruce up a room. The ideas I get from magazines always inspire me to get busy cleaning.

Susan Jacobson, Fort Lee, New Jersey

Kid-Friendly Decorating Ideas

As important as it is to keep a child's room organized, it's equally important that the room be welcoming and as special as the child who lives there.

Make handprints

While decorating our son's nursery, we were low on money but wanted the room to look special. We decided to "handprint" the wall. We took red and blue paint and put our handprints around the wall near the ceiling. As our relatives come to visit, each puts up a yellow handprint. We have the prints of our son's uncles, aunts, grandmothers, grandfathers—even his great grandma. Each print is labeled with its owners name. This is an inexpensive, very personal and special way to decorate a child's room.

Christine Shebroe, Sarasota, Florida

Build fences

My two daughters, Amy, nine, and Emily, seven, share a room. To divide the room, we installed a white picket fence down the center of the room, complete with a swinging gate. On both sides of the fence, we hung window boxes decorated with wooden cutouts of flowers. Behind the cutouts and inside the boxes, the kids store their little toys, dolls and art supplies. We completed the garden look by painting the floor green and painting a border of flowers around the baseboards. The ceiling is painted sky blue with clouds. A wooden wheelbarrow holds Amy's stuffed animals and dolls and a small homemade wishing well holds Emily's. The girls love showing off their secret garden and the fights over space are a thing of the past now that each girl has her own clearly marked half.

Rose Marie Nussbaum, Lansing, Michigan

Support sports

Gregory and Adam, my seven-year-old twins, are basketball fanatics, so I turned their room into a minicourt, complete with a real hoop (which I installed over a laundry basket to encourage tossing their clothes in the right place). Each boy's bedspread shows his favorite team. Other features include bleecher seats along one wall, under which are large plastic crates for holding their stuff; a row of hooks on the wall for hanging their clothes, and a locker each with shelves instead of dressers.

Faith Finbar, Whitestone, New York

Build a bookcase/dollhouse combo

To accommodate my daughter's growing collection of little dolls and dollhouse furniture, as well as her library of books, my husband built a combination dollhouse/bookshelf along one wall. Now everything is neat and her collection is shown off and easily accessible for play.

Ruth Keeler, Clinton, Maine

Get an aquarium

My husband works at an aquarium and his love for aquatic things has rubbed off on my son. We decorated his room with a real 60-gallon aquarium, hung shower curtains that show an undersea scene in his window and painted the whole room deep blue. We also hung stuffed animals of whales, dolphins and sea turtles on fishing line from the ceiling. He stores his sports equipment and other big toys in a fishing net hung in one corner.

Diane Lipsig, Orlando, Florida

Bringing Old Toys Back to Life

Because they're so well used, toys can show signs of wear and tear long before kids are ready to give them up. Here are some ways to lengthen the life of favorite playthings.

Revive a chalkboard

Has a young artist in your home ruined a chalkboard by drawing on it with crayon? Try erasing the board with extra-fine flint or sandpaper. Chalk will be able to leave its mark once more.

Jane Young, Mansfield, Massachusetts

Beautify dolls

I found that the best way to comb my daughter's doll's hair is to use a wig brush. It works much better than one of our regular hair brushes, since it keeps the dolls' hair from being pulled out.

AnaLee Kennedy, Middleton, Wisconsin

Pump up

The local bicycle shop is a great place to put compressed air back into deflated basketballs and footballs, which, in our house with four boys, always seem to need repair.

Janet Florio, Hartford, Connecticut

Protect stuffed animals

Whenever I put my children's stuffed animals in the washer and dryer, they came out worn and ragged-looking—until I discovered the pillowcase. Now I load a pillowcase with stuffed toys, tie it closed, and put it through the wash and dry cycles. The toys come out looking fluffy and new. If the animals are clean but dusty, I run them through the dryer on the fluff cycle with a sheet of fabric softener inside the pillowcase.

Ellen Bilofsky, Brooklyn, New York

Recycling for Every Day

The three Rs—reduce, reuse and recycle—are today's lessons for both parents and kids. Here are some terrific ways to save the earth—and money.

Gift cards from old greeting cards

Make gift tags out of used birthday and Christmas cards that you have saved. Cut out hearts, squares and triangles from the fronts of the cards. Next, punch holes in the corner of each cutout and thread a ribbon through it. Then write To: and From: on the back of the tag and sign it. Stash a batch away so that you have them on hand for all occasions.

Nancy Lang, Wichita, Kansas

Compost to go

To give my children a recycling and gardening lesson, I have them replenish the soil naturally. The kids fill a half-gallon milk carton with carrot and potato peelings, apple cores, orange rinds and eggshells. When the carton is full, we dump it into a bucket in the garage.

When the bucket is full, we bury the contents between the rows of our garden. *Voilà!* Enriched soil at no cost. (Be sure to omit meat scraps and grease; they attract undesirable animals.)

Anita S. Kellerby, Cody, Wyoming

Share the wealth

I make a point of finding out who can use all (or much) of our junk. For example, my son's preschool teacher collects all of our paper-towel and toilet-paper tubing and used stationery (with one clean side) for art projects. Used clothing and furniture go to the Salvation Army. Every year, we bring our old Christmas tree to a company that recycles the wood chips. I donated a used computer to a local grade school (and got a tax deduction for it), and I give used and cleaned stockings to an older woman who lives in our complex, which she uses to make braided rugs.

Lenore Gaston, Indianapolis, Indiana

Teach Earth Day lessons at home

Last year I thought Earth Day (in April) would be an opportune time to teach my two-year-old daughter, Samantha, about the three Rs: recycle, reuse and reduce. First we read *The Lorax,* by Dr. Seuss, and *The Paper Bag Prince,* by Colin Thompson—two books with a nature theme. Then we sorted through her toys and clothes and decided which things to give away to the needy. I cut up stained or ripped clothing to use as cleaning rags.

Sandy Yujevic, Sylvania, Ohio

10 Ways to Save Energy and Water at Home

1. Seal window and door frames with caulking to prevent drafts and heat loss.

2. Close the shades during the day in summertime to reduce the need for air conditioning.

3. Install water-flow restrictors on faucets and shower heads.

4. Put a timer on your water heater.

5. Reset the heater temperature to 120°F and drain it every few months.

6. Wrap the heater in an insulating blanket especially designed for home heaters.

7. Insulate your attic.

8. As you replace appliances, buy only energy-efficient models.

9. To prevent heat loss, close fireplace dampers when not in use. Use kitchen and bathroom vents only when absolutely necessary.

10. Insulate all hot-water pipes that run through unheated spaces.

Give green gifts

I buy miniature pine trees at the local nursery as inexpensive and ecological gifts for my children to give to their friends and teachers. Sometimes they draw pictures of birds or squirrels to put in the pine needles. If the tree is a winter gift, it can be nurtured indoors until the weather is warm enough for it to be planted outside.

Shawn Messner, Battle Creek, Michigan

Make recycling a family affair

Recycling isn't just a mom-and-dad responsibility: Let your children get into the act. My two-year-old daughter loves helping me stomp on cardboard boxes and bags to flatten them and tie string around stacks of newspapers. These simple hands-on lessons stimulate my daughter's interest in recycling and at the same time help me get the job done!

Jacqueline A. Vigotty, Woodstock, New York

New Treasures from Old

There's more to recycling than saving the earth. Sometimes, old treasures can be made into new ones, as these parents have discovered.

Pillows from an old quilt

My grandmother's quilt meant a lot to me but it was in such bad shape that it could no longer be repaired. I hated to just store it away, so I cut out the still-good parts and made throw pillows for each of my children's beds. I think Grandma would like that.

Anne Marie Cunningham, Prescott, Arizona

A special jacket from old clothes

When my daughter left for college, I was compelled to go into the attic and look through all of her baby clothes. Most were in pretty awful shape, but each piece had something worth salvaging. I cut shapes from all the old clothes—hearts, stars, squares—and bought a denim jacket that I then appliquéed all the cutouts on. I used many old buttons for additional designs around the collar. She loves her "baby jacket," and I love seeing her in it.

Evelyn Nunetz, Chapel Hill, North Carolina

A christening dress from a wedding-gown train

When I was pregnant with my son, Michael, I made a christening dress for him using the detachable train of my wedding gown. Then for the finishing touches, I sewed two blue satin ribbon bows onto the front of the dress. I hope this heirloom will be cherished by future generations of my family.

Mary Lou Cuomo, North Babylon, New York

A big-bed comforter from a crib quilt

After my son grew out of his crib, his comforter was still like new. Instead of packing it away, I made it larger by adding a fabric border lined with cotton batting. My son enjoyed his familiar blanket and

my husband and I enjoyed the money we saved.

Michelle Shepherd, Rochester Hills, Michigan

A patio table from broken dishes

During our move last year, we dropped the box that contained our wedding china. I was heartbroken because every piece was shattered. My husband collected all the little pieces and created the most beautiful mosaic table for our porch. Everyone comments on it and can't believe it when I tell them that it's our old china.

Linda Wares-Thomson, Richmond, Virginia

Homemade Toys

You'll not only save a small fortune by recycling household items into toys, but you'll give your children unique and creative toys that they couldn't find elsewhere. Just be sure that none of your homemade creations have sharp edges or contain small parts that children could swallow.

Back to the drawing board

I've found three handy uses for a cardboard storage box. Try one as a table for kids to lean on when they paint or draw, a work space to draw directly on or a place to store art supplies.

Rhonda Doherty, Brentwood, California

Blocks from empty boxes

I created a homemade set of blocks for my one-year-old daughter because regular blocks were to heavy for her to play with. I covered empty cookie boxes, milk con-

10 Ways to Reuse Empty Disposable-Wipe Containers

1. Store babies' socks; they fit perfectly.
2. Store toy cars, baseball cards and doll shoes.
3. Store crayons, markers and colored pencils.
4. Keep loose buttons all in one place.
5. Store audiotapes in the car.
6. Make a slit in the top for a piggy bank.
7. Punch a hole in the bottom, string cord through and hang as a birdfeeder.
8. Store small bottles of perfume, nail polish and makeup.
9. File recipe cards, bills, receipts, photo negatives.
10. Make your own first-aid kit for home, car or work.

Cheri Webb, New Lenox, Illinois

tainers, formula cans and paper-towel rolls with colorful contact paper. My daughter can now safely throw her blocks across the room!

Susan Kolnitys, Higley, Arizona

An alphabet game from a coffee can

Here's a fun way to help your toddler learn her ABCs: Cover an empty coffee can with decorative contact paper. Cut a slit in the plastic lid wide enough for magnetic letters to fit through. As your child familiarizes herself with the alphabet, she can drop in the letters or use them to decorate the sides of the can.

Marie McEnery, San Jose, California

Art supplies from trash

I've discovered that some things I typically thought of as trash can be used for art supplies. For artsy paintbrushes, experiment with toilet-paper rolls, berry baskets, ice cream sticks and newspapers or bubble wrap rolled up and taped at one end and shredded at the other. As alternative painting surfaces, try egg cartons, cardboard, used sandpaper and wood scraps.

Shelly Cook, San Diego

New crayons from old

Recycle old broken crayons using candy molds. First, melt an equal amount of candle wax and crayons in a saucepan until the mixture is soft enough to pour into a candy mold. Chill for 30 minutes, then pop them out of the mold. For crayons that really stand out, add glitter to the mixture. My children love coloring with crayons shaped like rabbits, bugs, eggs, hearts and stars. Sometimes they just display their special crayons on a shelf as knickknacks.

Cathy Deaton, Allardt, Tennessee

Doll dresses from old socks

My three-year-old daughter, Jessica, wanted new dresses for her dolls because she decided that they were all getting married! Since wedding clothes weren't in our budget, I was inspired to make her dolls gowns. First I rummaged through her drawers for white socks with lace, bows or beaded trimmings that were missing their mates. I then cut off the toe, sewed a hem and made spaghetti straps from the leftover scraps within 20 minutes. All my daughter's dolls had one-size-fits-all wedding dresses!

Charlene Cattley, Auburn, Massachusetts

Throwaways become new playthings

As part of my family's effort to help the environment, we recycle many throw-aways into toys. Using glue and construction paper, we cover milk cartons and transform them into trains or tiny villages. Oatmeal canisters are perfect for drums and rocket ships. Milk jugs can be cut into space helmets and paper-towel rolls make great telescopes.

Lisa Ray Turner, Rio Rancho, New Mexico

Money Savers

Saving money is on top of every family's priority list. Here are some ways to get you started.

Swap toys among friends

A group of friends and I who have children around the same age started a toy-swapping program. Every month we fill a bag with the playthings that our children have lost interest in and we swap. After a month we swap the items again. Often, by the time our children get their toys back, they have a renewed interest in them. It's

Reuse Your Baby-Food Jars

Here are four great ways to reuse all those glass baby-food jars.

1. Snowballs. Use non–water-soluble glue to attach plastic animals and other tiny toy figures to the underside of the lid. Add a drop of dish-washing detergent to the jar and fill with water. Add tiny slivers of aluminum foil. Seal the lid with waterproof sealer, such as adhesive cement—and shake away!

2. Workshop organizers. Use wood screws to fasten the lids face up to the underside of workshop shelves.

3. Party favors. Decorate the jars by gluing on felt or by attaching stickers; fill the jars with treats.

4. Dessert containers. Fill jars with flavored gelatin or pudding for individual portions.

Anita Schoniger, Keystone, South Dakota

been a great way for all of our families to save money.

Andrea Sekel, Mesa, Arizona

Collect coupons

In our church nursery, we set up a box for congregants to drop in coupons for baby products that they don't need, such as diapers and baby food. Each week interested mothers come by and pick and choose the coupons they need. I found

Money Savers Just for Parents

- Before purchasing a car seat, check to see if you can obtain one free or for a low rental charge from a government or private agency. Check with your local hospital or state health department to see if such a service is available to you.
- Buy gently used clothing, toys and sports equipment at rummage sales.
- Split babysitting costs with another family.

- Buy baby furniture used. Make sure, however, that all items meet current safety standards.
- Buy store brands of often-purchased items such as diapers, baby soaps and canned foods.
- Use the library instead of buying all new books.
- Buy next year's clothing at the end of this year's season.

that it saved me money when my children were little.

Sheila Barlow, Amelia, Ohio

Swap coupons

My son and my neighbors' children were all born within six months of one another. To help our families save money on baby products, we created a coupon co-op. Once a week we meet to exchange coupons on items that we need most. Our co-op helps us to be thrifty and gives us a chance to exchange war stories with other new parents.

Deanna L. Barrett, Wilton, Iowa

Start a library of toys

To save money on games and toys for your children, find out if your community has a toy library. Toy libraries let people borrow and return items just like in a regular library. For the location of one near you, send a SASE to the USA Toy Library Association, 2530 Crawford Avenue, Suite 111, Evanston, IL 60201.

Kathryn Stein, Kensington, California

Barter

Organize a barter system at work, your place of worship or your mothers' support group. Here's how: Take down the names, telephone numbers and a list of goods, such as film, food or clothing and services, such as home repairs, house cleaning, baby-sitting, tailoring, catering, computer training, photography and accounting, that interested participants can provide. Distribute the list among the members. When you need something, call and arrange for a fair trade. Be sure to draft and sign an IOU. Bartering arrangements are a great way to save money and meet people.

Dee Dalasio, Bridgeport, Pennsylvania

Keeping Track of Easily Misplaced Items

One of the most annoying everyday occurrences can be misplacing important items. Here are some ideas for keeping track.

Photograph your address for film processors

Anyone who has had film lost by the developing company has experienced the disappointment of losing important pictures such as baby's first Christmas. To prevent this occurrence, take a snapshot of a large card with your name and address on it with each roll of film. That way, if the pictures are sent to the wrong party, they can be returned to the rightful owner.

Linda Harris, Munnsville, New York

Tie keys to shoelaces

Often in the summer I don't have any pockets to hold my house key. One day I found a solution. I put my shoelace through the hole in the key, slid the key down to the top of my shoe and then tied the lace. Then I tucked the key between the shoe tongue and the side of my shoe. The key is in a safe, tight place.

Zeta Ann Strickland, LaPorte, Colorado

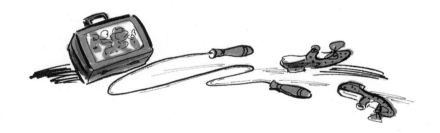

CHAPTER FOURTEEN

Fun and Games

A *child's day often includes stretches of time looking for* something to do. Scattered among these usual days are special occasions—the days and seasons that bring the family together to create and celebrate traditions. Through the opportunities parents create and the choices children make, kids learn about the world around them and, of course, about themselves.

Here's how to engage your children on even the worst "Mommy, I'm bored" days—and how to make sure that their activities are positive and rewarding.

Better Birthday Parties

Kids consider their birthday the best day of the year. They don't have to share gifts or attention with anyone else—just fun and laughter. Creating birthday celebrations that meet your child's expectations is a tall order, but there are almost as many ways of making a birthday special as there are kids looking forward to it.

Make an autograph tablecloth

At your child's next party, buy an inexpensive tablecloth for all the guests to sign. Then outline the names in permanent dye, or, if your handiwork is up to it, embroider over each signature. You can either save the cloth as a remembrance of that party or use it again year after year, adding names of the new party guests.

Suzan L. Wiener, Spring Hill, Florida

Create a stand-out invitation

Because kids get so many birthday-party invitations, I wanted to make sure no one misplaced my daughter's. As insurance that it would be noticed and not forgotten, I adhered a small square piece of magnetic tape to the back of each invitation. Now her guests' parents can immediately attach the invitation to their refrigerator for quick and easy reference.

Cindy Lippencott, Bel Air, Maryland

Celebrate a different date

My son's birthday, unlike his friends', is in the summer, which means he usually misses out on the fun of being the big cheese at school. To give him the same chance, we came up with an alternative day. We calculated that on December 8, he would be 2,000 days old. His kindergarten teacher loved the idea and celebrated it as his special day. She now encourages other children with summer birthdays to find another date to celebrate. Other possible dates to try are half-birthdays or the number of weeks, months or minutes your child is.

Suzy Awe, Pawnee City, Nebraska

Put presents aside

I have found that until they are about six, it is too stressful for kids to watch the birthday child open presents. I put the presents away as the children come in and have my son or daughter open them later. I also send a postcard to each child with my kids' thank-you note—I do the writing and my children scrawl their name.

Toni Barlow, Ames, Iowa

Match the guests

My sons prefer parties that involve taking their guests out, to the ice-skating rink, the bowling alley, a baseball game or the movies. To keep track of my group, I give party favors of brightly colored T-shirts. The kids put them on before we set out and I have no trouble tracking everyone in the group.

Devra Gherardi, New York City

Self-frame the art

A surefire hit for your child's next birthday party is art at the table. Use a four-foot roll of white craft paper as a tablecloth and then, at each place setting, hand paint several "frames" to accommodate an 8½-by

An Age-by-Age Party Guide

Your child's age determines a great deal about whom you should invite and what activities kids will enjoy at their birthday party. Here are suggestions for celebrants from age 1 to 10.

1-year-olds

Invite two guests for one hour. To eat, serve small pieces of banana, ice cream and miniature waffles. Children can play pat-a-cake, itsy-bitsy spider and catch with rolling balls. Party favors for this group might be bibs with their names, bright-colored sipping cups or oversize balls, also with their names painted on in nontoxic markers.

2-year-olds

Invite three guests for a party of 1 to 1½ hours. Feed them ice cream, small pieces of fruit and perhaps some finger sandwiches. Games for this group include ring-around-a-rosy, "London Bridge" or a parade in which everybody marches. Be sure to enclose the party area with gates and leave lots of open space within the safe area for running. For party treats include pails and shovels marked with the children's names, crayons and coloring books.

3- and 4-year-olds

Ask four or five kids to a party for 1½ hours. Feed them bite-size vegetable

11-inch picture. Bring the kids to the table and let them draw within the lines. This way they can see how their masterpieces look framed. For a party memento, laminate each child's best picture with clear contact paper, cut out the framed picture and it's ready to go home.

Cynthia Hall Searight, Fairfield, Connecticut

Invite Mom and Dad, too

So many parents of young kids are reluctant to leave their child for a party that I've decided to turn that into a blessing. I invite the parents to come along, saying how much I'll enjoy having the extra help. I provide refreshments for the parents, too—and I also take advantage of the help they offer.

Carol Britter, San Jose, California

Games That Enhance Your Child's Learning

Children learn all day. From a walk with you to "helping" to make lunch, they are observing, absorbing and making sense of the world. One of the best ways for them to learn is through play.

strips with yogurt dip, miniature rice cakes and ice cream in wafer cones. Favorite games include "Duck, Duck, Goose," "Pin the Tail on the Donkey" and freeze dance. Avoid competitive games; instead, make sure that every child "wins." For party favors, this group enjoys stickers, Play-Doh, crayons and coloring books and slinking spiral-spring toys.

5- and 6-year-olds

Let children invite six or seven kids to the party and keep it going for 1½ to 2½ hours. For treats, serve such things as apples on a stick, pizza and individual cupcakes or cake. Play games like "Simon Says," tag, treasure hunt, limbo, hot potato and 20 questions. Favors that will win favor include jump ropes, sidewalk chalk, marbles, costume jewelry and miniature flashlights.

7- to 10-year-olds

Eight to 11 children is a good number of guests. Have them stay two or three hours. Feed them pizza, make-your-own sundaes, chocolate-dipped strawberries and bananas. Older kids enjoy scavenger hunts, bingo, peanut hunts, bubble-gum blowing contests and limbo. Party favors could be key chains, trading cards, colorful erasers, anything slimy and hats.

Have a letter for lunch

My son and I have a letter of the day for him to learn his alphabet. We talk about it first and when he sits down to lunch, there it is on his plate in his favorite condiment—ketchup. From eating his letters, he has become interested enough to start designing letters in such nonedible forms as his Lego pieces and toy cars.

Sandra Slade, Burnaby, British Columbia

Customize a dictionary

Create a personal dictionary for your prereader. You can start by cutting pictures of his favorite things from magazines and take pictures of family and friends, from A to Z. Put all of these together in an alphabetized scrapbook with the letter on top of the page, the word under the picture.

Catherine Jasinski, Amherst, New York

Turn play into practice

I've combined some of my son's favorite pastimes with alphabet learning. I wrote big, uppercase block letters on a piece of cardboard with a marker. My son takes a box with beads, string or Play-Doh—from which he rolls balls—and places a variety

Making Your Own Play Dough

It's easy to make play dough in your own kitchen.

- 1½ cups flour
- 1 cup salt
- 1 tablespoon cooking oil
- 1 tablespoon alum (located in the spice aisle of the grocery store)
- 1 cup boiling water

Mix all ingredients together except the water. Gradually add boiling water, stirring until mixture cools. Knead in food coloring until completely blended. Store in plastic margarine tubs keeping colors separate.

of these over the letters. He's having a good time while learning a great deal about the alphabet.

Sarah Baker, Yelm, Washington

Put time in kids' terms

Since young kids have so little sense of what time means, I wanted to find for my four-year-old son a concept of time he could readily understand. To do this, I began to place time frames with activities and routines he knows well. For instance, I tell him, "Grandma is coming to visit in two sleeps," instead of, "Grandma is coming on Saturday." He seems to be getting it easily.

Lidia Toledo, Tampa, Florida

Mention left and right

To help my daughter learn left from right, I casually incorporate them as often as I can during activities. I'll say, "Put your left arm in the sleeve," or, "Use your right hand to pick up the cards." My parents did this when I was little, and as a result I never had to learn left from right—I just knew.

April Clark, Archer, Florida

Mark a carton

An empty egg carton is the means for a game my three-year-old daughter enjoys. I write a number on the inside bottom of each cup of the carton which I then give to her. She then picks from beans, rice or sometimes jelly beans to fill the cups of the carton—matching the number of items to the number printed on the bottom. I check her answer at a glance, and she can—and does—play this game over and over again.

Rebecca Clarke, Ramer, Alabama

Put a dot on the shoe

My four-year-old daughter had a terrible time remembering which shoe went on which foot. To get her past this quandary, I colored a small black dot on the outside of each shoe next to the arch. I explained to her that if the dots touch after she has put her shoes on, that means she has them on correctly. Each morning we have a game in which she goes looking for the dots—it seems to have done the trick.

Peggy Benz, Vista, California

Use a timer

I find a cooking timer is useful to teach my five-year-old son about time. When he asks how much longer he can play a particular game or stay in the tub, I tell him and then set the timer so that he can see for himself. That gives him a visual sense of what 5 minutes means in the space of an hour. He is gradually getting a stronger sense of what it means when he has 10 more minutes to play before bedtime.

Christine Gibson, Evansville, Indiana

Show a flower drinking

Kids can easily learn how plants absorb water in this simple experiment. Fill a small jar with water to which you have added several drops of food coloring. Explain how plants take in water through their stems and place a white carnation in the colored water. Periodically check the flower with your child and watch how gradually the blossom takes on the shade of the colored water.

Susie Harrold , Thomasville, North Carolina

Turn words into puzzles

To aid new spellers, try a new kind of puzzle word game. Cut out large geometric shapes from construction paper and break the shapes by cutting them in half with a zigzag or wavy line. Next write the first letter or letters of a word on the left side of each shape and the remaining letters on the right—for example, "ba-by" or "c-an." Your child will know he has spelled the word correctly because the pieces fit together.

Tonya Duriez, Indiana, Pennsylvania

Teach from menus

Playing restaurant with your children is a good way to teach them more about reading. We cut out pictures of food from magazines, mount them on construction paper and write the name of the food under each one. The kids play waiter and waitress, taking our orders by copying the food names on their menu. By including prices you can help your children practice math skills as well.

Mary-Ann Watson-Bonsall, Port Elgin, Ontario

Give clues in books

When a group of kids are over playing with my two daughters, I organize everyone for what we call the Book Game. I start by removing some of the children's books off my girls' shelves and placing them on the floor. I then ask the children to find a picture of a dog, or the number five or something red and purple on the same page. The object of the game is for the children to be the first to find the picture. It's fun watching their eyes light up as they hunt for and recognize the requested items.

Janice Goodrum, Bloomington, Minnesota

Set a number for the day

Our three kids, six and under, love the number-for-the-day game. We post a number in a creative fashion—macaroni glued to construction paper is one favorite—on the refrigerator. The kids look for the number when they get up and then the fun starts. We search for that particular number all day. Say it's a seven: We cut sandwiches at lunch into seven pieces, build towers of seven blocks, count cars in groups of seven. By the end of the day, seven has become a good friend—and a number the kids know well.

Elizabeth Pantley, Kirkland, Washington

Match color cards to nature

Children can learn much more about the wide variety of colors while they gain an appreciation for the amazing range of hues nature has to offer. Collect some paint-chip cards at your local paint or hardware store, then cut out the squares and mount them on bigger index cards with the name of the color. When the kids are ready to go for their color hunt, give a few cards to each child in a paper bag. Have the children collect leaves, twigs and rocks that closely match the colors on the paint squares—you'll be amazed at how many colors they will find. Once home, have the kids mount the color squares and collectibles on poster board along with the names of the colors.

Dawn Gillen, Hamilton Square, New Jersey

Publish your child's book

Children take great pride in developing their own work and creating a showcase for it. To help your child become published, take some quiet time to discuss possible story topics—an autobiography or original fairy tale are good to start. The child can then write—or dictate—the story for you. When that is finished, get out some art supplies and two pieces of poster paper or other sturdy stock for the covers. The child should decorate the cover any way that seems to fit the story. The books that follow are sure to be among favorite childhood treasures.

Lori Beth Murray, Columbus, Ohio

Read first to ease the way

To make reading a challenging book less frustrating for my eight-year-old son, I read it aloud to him first, often at bedtime. The next day I let him read it aloud to me. Words that were unfamiliar to him are now friendlier and easier for him to remember and to sound out. I find that he doesn't balk as often as he used to about reading a big boy book.

Elaine Konyha, Medina, Ohio

Be a weather watcher

You can teach your child a great deal about the weather through a refrigerator calendar. Either make or find a calendar with big spaces for each day which your child can use to draw pictures that describe the weather. As your child becomes more interested in the details of weather, he can plot daily temperatures on a colorful bar graph.

Kathryn C. McGowan, Yorktown Heights, New York

Blast off in the kitchen

Make a volcano in your kitchen and introduce kids to basic science principles. Start by cutting the neck off an empty 20-ounce plastic bottle. Place three tablespoons of baking soda inside the bottle and add red food coloring to heighten the drama of the lava. Pour vinegar slowly into the bottle and watch your volcano erupt.

Karen Michaelson, Northome, Minnesota

Have book-based picnics

To beat the summer blahs and keep my children's love of books alive, I started weekly story readings—on picnics. I take books from the library that have unusual characters. Based on these, we all make simple costumes and decorations and cook treats that go with a particular book's story. Out in the fresh air and sunshine, my kids play out fantasies of being airplane pilots, Mexican dancers and gypsies. Best of all, these picnic readings have encouraged them to make additional trips to the library, reread their favorite books and practice basic research skills.

Terri Quillen, Indianapolis

Write an account

When my 10-year-old son is recounting some especially interesting events in his day, I'll suggest he might try writing them down by saying, "That would make a great story." He may write only a few sentences or sometimes he'll be inspired enough to give a complete account. Whatever the result, I keep them all in a file which I think he'll find both interesting and entertaining as he gets older.

Rini Ranbom, Columbus, Ohio

Make a scrapbook journal

I gave my eight-year-old daughter a large photo album in which she puts any scraps that are important to her—birthday cards, tickets, pictures and other items dear to a child's heart. To go with her memento, she writes something about it or the occasion on a small piece of paper which we attach to the page. She finds it more fun and less intimidating than keeping a standard journal, because she doesn't feel that she has to fill up a whole page with writing.

Leslie Ford, North Augusta, South Carolina

Turn everyday events into math

I started a math journal of story problems for my six-year-old daughter who is just starting this concept. While she is at school, I write down a few problems in a notebook based on our day. The problems waiting for her to solve later might include, for example, adding the number of books and videos that her younger brother and I checked out of the local library (three books for him plus three books for her, plus one book for Mom and two tapes). She may try her hand at subtraction by figuring out the number of cookies we ate during the day.

Sarah Shatzer, Dubuque, Iowa

Keep the microscope handy

We have a microscope in our kitchen along with the pots and pans so that our kids can take a closer look at anything that interests them. They've inspected everything from dead bugs to leaves, seeds, grass, onion skins, paper, animal fur, fingernail clippings and hair. My kids have gone a step further—taking notes of their findings and keeping them in a science journal for comparisons and reference.

Deborah Staub Bartell, Shaker Heights, Ohio

Use baseball cards

Baseball cards have vital stats on the player that kids like to know to impress each other. The stats can work for you, too, to teach math. My seven-year-old son collects baseball cards and I use his passion. I select from his favorites, note the players' birthdates and my son then has to figure out how old the player is now.

Bob Steiner, Brooklyn, New York

Demonstrate density

Using water and common household objects, children can experiment with the property of density by discovering what floats and what sinks. Place a variety of items on a tray, for instance, a plastic bottle with a cork, a piece of wood, a straw, a bar of soap, polystyrene, a sponge, shells, nails and coins. Fill a shallow basin with no more than three inches of water and have your child take one item at a time from the tray to guess if it will float or sink. By dropping the item into the water, your child will immediately see what was the correct answer.

Annette Wallace, Spencerport, New York

Guess how many

All of my second-grade students love guessing games, and the games are good for their observation, logic and spatial skills. I ask them general questions such as, "How many books are on the bookshelf?" but the activity that they particularly enjoy is guessing how many marbles are in a jar or how many cups of water a container holds. After the kids estimate the answer, they like to empty and fill the container to see how close they are.

Stephanie Vallin, St. Peters, Missouri

Start a kids' book club

I started a book club for my children and their friends which is working well to keep them reading and interested in books. Each week we rotate houses and let the junior host choose a book of the week, often with a holiday or seasonal theme. The older children lead a discussion about the story and take turns reading to the younger ones. The kids in the book club also have time to practice reading silently or just to look at the pictures.

Lori B. Murray, Columbus, Ohio

Name that leaf

My son loves to pick up leaves that have fallen from trees. We glue them to five- by nine-inch cards, write the name of the tree each leaf fell from, and cover the cards with clear contact paper. These provide us with many pleasant afternoons, reviewing the cards and trying to identify the name of the tree without looking. Other times, we take the cards with us when we're walking outside and try to match the leaves with the trees they came from.

Sarah Langfeldt Baker, Yelm, Washington

Turn spelling into stories

Make studying for weekly spelling tests fun for your child by turning it into a game. Write each spelling word on a strip of paper which you put into a bowl. Have your child draw out three or four of the words at random. Then challenge her to write a short story using all the words she has selected. This study game worked beautifully in our house—my refrigerator door is filled with spelling tests marked "100 percent!"

Kimberly Evanovich, Santa Cruz, California

Beyond the Books:
Activities to Stretch Young Minds

For kids who need help with verbal skills, try the following:
• Make up songs putting new words to old tunes.
• Dance or dramatize a story or poem that you have read aloud.
• Record a story your child makes up. Write it down so that you can read it together or tape record it for later listening.
• Talk over dinner plans for the week, then write menus that cater to family tastes and schedules.
• Keep a written record of the scores and progress of the family's favorite baseball, hockey or basketball team.

• Spell words with blocks.
For children who need help with number skills, try the following:
• Measure and compare various items in the home, such as toy fire trucks, race cars and the family members' shoes.
• Measure ingredients for a recipe that you read together.
• Plan and help shop for a birthday party. How many guests will there be? How many plates, napkins, hats, party favors?
• Think about how to spend an allowance—or make plans about saving for a special purchase.

Sharpen skills through the mail

Since there isn't a child who doesn't enjoy getting mail, here's a way to turn the mail into practice for kids' penmanship and correspondence skills: Write fan letters to celebrities, ballplayers or toy-company executives. (You can usually find these people's addresses in books such as *The Address Book,* Berkley Publishing.) Often kids will get back autographed pictures or even personal replies which they find thrilling. Kids can find free samples of such things as games and stickers through the magazine *Freebies*. For ordering information, write to P.O. Box 5025, Carpinteria, CA 93014. This is an excellent demonstration for kids about how a clear, succinct letter (with a properly addressed envelope) can get results.

Suzanna Caperton, Columbus, Ohio

Give a word a day

When my sister and I were little, our mother increased our vocabularies by telling us a funny-sounding word every night at bedtime. After she tucked us in and started to close the door, we'd beg her for a "funny word." We would shriek with delight when we heard words such as "surreptitious" or "preposterous"—words that make sense to adults but sound silly to kids. Soon, though, we had powerful vocabularies and could use the words in the right context.

Barbara Coyne, Carmel, Indiana

Rainy-Day Fun

"There's nothing to do!" It's a complaint mothers have heard for generations and at no time do moms hear this more than on rainy days. In fact, there's plenty to do even when it rains all day—creative pastimes indoors and, when the rain is warm, some delightful activities out of doors with slickers on.

Indoor camp-outs

To make rainy days fun for my children, I have an indoor camp-out for them. The kids put on their favorite camping clothes and hats and I pitch a tent—blankets draped over chairs do just fine—and line with sleeping bags, all in our family room.

I equip their campsite with a radio, flashlights, pots and pans, snacks and board games. Naptime at camp is a breeze. I turn out the lights, the children snuggle into their sleeping bags and take a snooze under the "stars."

Deborah A. Davis, Troy, New York

Bathtub water play

With all that water outside, my children like to play with water indoors. I put them in their bathing suits and into the bathtub with fingerpaints. When they've finished their fun, I clean kids and tub by turning on the shower.

S. Seifert, Englewood, Colorado

Enjoy the wet world

A summer shower provides refreshing activities—out of doors. The children love splashing in puddles, getting as dirty as they want making mud pies and squishing wet grass between their toes. They have fun and they also learn a little more about the world, this time when it's wet.

April Clark, Archer, Florida

Pick by picture

Having to stay inside with a toddler who doesn't yet know a lot of words can be challenging. To help direct my boy to which activities he would enjoy, I took pictures of him at play—riding his fire truck, coloring, reading, playing with blocks and finger-painting. I then taped them to the refrigerator. Now when the weather keeps us in, I ask him, "What would you like to play today?" He can choose the activity that suits his mood by pointing to the appropriate photo.

Melissa Hudson, Berea, Kentucky

Beautify the indoors

For families with fish tanks, add to the fun of looking at your fish by letting your child draw pictures for his underwater pals. Cut a piece of white poster board the same size as one side of the tank or bowl. Then have your child draw fish, plants, waves, rocks and sunshine with brightly colored markers. Attach the picture to the back of the tank facing the fish.

Charlene Pulliam, Stevensville, Montana

Keep a box of reminders

We have made a fun box full of activities that the kids and I like to do together.

Using index cards, we write down ideas and color-code them. For example, red is for art activities, green for places to go and yellow for crafts. We've made the box fun to look at, too, with all sorts of colorful decorations. Whenever I hear that old refrain—there's nothing to do—I pull out the fun box.

Sandra Clarke, Mississauga, Ontario

Sick-Day Activities

There's a time in children's illnesses when restlessness reigns supreme. When they are too sick to go out, but well enough to have some energy, kids need help, which is to say, activities. These should entertain, amuse and, most of all, engross.

Fill a toy basket

At night when my boy is sick and after he has gone to sleep, I fill a basket with quiet toys—books, puzzles, crayons and anything else that involves peaceful play. When he wakes up he can look forward to an assortment of pleasing toys that will bring a smile to his face and cheer him throughout the day.

Shelley O'Hern, East Syracuse, New York

Sew a pretty picture

Sewing takes little energy and provides immediate satisfaction of a job well done.

Schoolwork in the Sickbed

Kids who are out of school because of minor illnesses can still keep up with their schoolwork. This not only helps them stay current with their studies, it also helps them understand that illness is not an excuse for ducking responsibilities.

• Get in touch with the teacher or teachers and ask for specific homework assignments.

• Arrange for a classmate to bring home books and papers that your child needs to complete assignments.

• Look for ways to keep your patient involved in the course of studies. Young children can practice reading skills by having picture books at hand; videos, documentaries or television shows about subjects that older kids will be covering in school are also good sick-day pastimes. The goal is to keep kids thinking even when they're sick.

• If your child will be absent for a week or more, consider hiring a tutor to help him or her keep up. If you can't be the at-home teacher, ask a high-school student to come over after school to help guide your child through the work, explaining any areas of confusion.

I save the front of our prettiest greeting cards and punch holes all around at about one-inch intervals. I give the cards to my patient, along with either colorful shoestrings or yarn and a large plastic needle. After she makes her color selections, I thread the needle and knot the string and then demonstrate a hem or basting stitch to loop the thread through the holes. The child can keep the cards "sewn" with the colorful frames or, when things get boring later, pull out the string and sew some more.

Maija Johnson, New York City

Make move-around stickers

Sticker play can provide long periods of quiet play, but it can be frustrating for a child not to be able to move the stickers around as the story develops. To lower frustration in our house, I put the stickers on wax paper. This allows my daughter to remove the stickers again and again.

Maria Gaddis, Flemington, New Jersey

Create letter-writing fun

What better time to write letters than when you're stuck sick in bed? To make letter-writing more fun, for both our daughter and the letter recipient, we got her a pad of paper to design her own letterhead. She draws pictures across the top and then writes her name alongside. Between the designing and the corresponding, she is busy for hours.

Gene Candeloro, New Hartford, New York

Pick a puzzle

My five-year-old loves puzzles and they're great for in-bed entertainment. But tackling new, challenging puzzles can be really frustrating for young kids. To keep the puzzle from being overwhelming, I divide it into several sections. I then put the pieces for each section in a small plastic bag and label it for my child by where it goes in the puzzle. As mastery of the puzzle begins to develop, I break it up into fewer bags, until finally my child is able to work with all the pieces at the same time.

Eleanor Kowalchik, Randolph, Massachusetts

Have a magic bag

I made what we call a magic bag for my four-year-old daughter. It's black velvet, lined with cream satin and it opens with a satin cord. I decorated the outside with costume jewelry, shiny buttons, glitter and puffy paint. Inside are small books, wind-up toys, colored chalk, necklaces and other trinkets. When she is sick, reaching into her magic bag is guaranteed to give her something that will brighten her day.

Jody Petersen, Quakertown, Pennsylvania

Indoor Play All Year Long

There are only so many days of the year—and hours of the day—when children can play out of doors. That means parents need a wide assortment of indoor pursuits to keep kids engaged. A balance is helpful here: activities that involve an adult presence and those that can leave you with some free time to take care of your day. "I love being an active part of my children's games and such, but I'm thrilled that there are some the kids can enjoy doing on their own," says one mother.

Free Art Supplies

You may be able to get some useful art supplies for your children without spending a dime. Try these.

Home-decorating stores: They often have free outdated wallpaper books and the large pages are ideal for wrapping gifts, decorating dollhouses and designing stationery.

Cabinet and furniture makers: There are always many small wood scraps around. Perfect for creative wood sculptures.

Printing shops: Here you'll find a steady supply of paper scraps in various shapes, colors and textures. Children can create bookmarks and paper sculptures or just cut and color.

Upholstery shops or custom fabric stores: These have out-of-date fabric samples to give away. Use them for doll clothes, collages and more.

Newspaper printers: Ask for leftover ends of plain newsprint rolls, available for free or at a nominal cost. Most rolls are 20- to 25-feet long and wide enough for large murals, body tracings or any giant-size art project.

Design nature's jewelry

For hours of indoor fun—and some wonderful jewelry, too—have your child collect pretty things when out of doors. Such items as colorful pebbles, blades of grass, leaves or feathers make an ideal collection. Keep the items in a box for jewelry-making day. A simple band of masking tape, with the sticky side out, is all you need around your child's wrist. Then she can decide among nature's bounty what will look just right for the day.

Lori Maunsell, Brandon, Manitoba

Make a play rug

I created a play rug for my kids that offers a multitude of indoor activities. Using stencils on an inexpensive carpet remnant, I randomly spray-painted numbers and letters in bright colors. I personalized the rug by adding the kids' names as a border around it. They use their rug to dance, exercise and generally clown around, but the game they love best is musical hop. When I stop the music, I call out a number and whoever is standing on it wins the round.

Helene Lesel, Los Angeles

Whip up some finger paint

I save money by making my children's finger paints at home. To do this, mix one-fourth cup cornstarch with two cups cold water, bring it to a boil and continue until the mixture thickens. Cool and pour into containers—baby-food jars with screw-on lids are perfect. Add food coloring and you're ready to paint.

Chris Givson, Fontant, Wisconsin

Etch away

For an easy etching, have your child color the surface of a small piece of tagboard with crayons, as many different colors as he wants. Then have him paint over it with a solid-color poster paint. Once that dries, your child can create an etching by scratching through the surface poster paint with toothpicks. He can make a simple sketch or something more elaborate—it's up to the artist to choose from all the colors under the surface.

Aimee LeMountain, Westport, New York

Hand-paint special gifts

Both of my children's grandmothers love to cook. To make a special present for them, my children hand-painted aprons. I bought two inexpensive white aprons and put them alongside pans of nontoxic fabric paint on the kitchen table. My kids dipped their hands in the paint and put their handprints all over the aprons—my daughter chose red prints for hers, my son chose blue. Later, I added their names, the date, and gold glitter fabric paint. My kids had a ball creating their special gifts and their grandmothers loved them.

Sandra Dennis, Victoria, British Columbia

Preserve paper dolls for more play

The problem with paper dolls and their clothes has always been that they fall apart so quickly. To preserve these for many days of your child's play, cover all of them with clear contact paper. All you then have to do is cut the paper following the shape.

Jeanine Smith, Oregon City, Oregon

Put on a puppet show

My four-year-old daughter loves putting on puppet shows and they can keep her occupied for entire afternoons. To create new stars for her productions we cut out her favorite coloring-book characters and glue them on popsicle sticks. I reinforce the backs of the characters with cardboard—this way they stand up easily and last longer. To make it more fun, she and I make up stories based on pictures from the coloring books as we go along.

De Brandt, Excelsior, Minnesota

Outdoor Play: Summertime Favorites

Warm days when the sun doesn't set until after dinner. No homework, no tests, nothing to worry about. It's no wonder that summer is a favorite time of year for kids. Even with all its bonuses, though, summer sometimes needs ideas from mom and dad to get the fun rolling.

Rub textured surfaces

My four-year-old loves taking walks with me in our neighborhood. To make them especially interesting, we take along crayons and paper. He stops at anything with a surface that intrigues him and makes a crayon rubbing. To make one, place the paper over the object—be it the sidewalk, a fallen leaf, a rock or brick—anything with texture. Then rub the side of a peeled crayon across the paper a few times. If you want an especially good rubbing, anchor the paper first with masking tape.

Linda Foust, Oakland, California

Make a backyard waterfall

To keep my children happy during Louisiana's hot summer days, I make them a waterfall. I hang our garden hose, with a spray nozzle attached, over a tree branch in our backyard. To add to the good times, I put a splash pool below it. The kids love running and squealing under their waterfall and splashing around in their pool.

Sharon Parker, Shreveport, Louisiana

Create music from nature

Go for a summer nature walk and show the kids how to compose their own music on instruments they can create. Blow on a blade of grass, while holding it between your thumbs, and listen to the buzzing sound it makes. Fill an empty can with seeds and shake it like a maraca. Cut a hole in a hollow stick or reed and you've turned it into a flute. Tie fishing line around a piece of wood and then strum it—with the end of a bird's feather. Sing along and your children will have an instant nature band parade.

Diane Stanton-Rich, Address withheld

Put in sandbox extras

When my husband designed a backyard sandbox for our sons, he added several unusual items that have been huge hits. He found a steering wheel and a bicycle horn at a local junkyard and brought them home. Our kids play in the sandbox for hours, transforming the box into a school bus, space ship, dump truck and race car.

Dorothy Murray, Troy, New York

Take the scooper

The next time you head for the beach, tuck an ice-cream scooper into your beach bag. You'll be amazed what a great tool it is for building sand castles.

Louella Antley, Sylva, North Carolina

Signal the kids

What do kids like more than playing outside with their friends? We devised a system to call in the neighborhood kids for play without having to have my daughter go around looking for them. We bought a small, colorful windsock, and our daughter hangs it on the fence or door whenever she goes out to play. The neighborhood kids know the signal and their moms know this means it is okay to send them out to come into our yard.

Susan Knott, Grand Haven, Michigan

Tell stories in the sand

Pop some cookie cutters of animal shapes in your beach bag and have the kids make up stories in the sand. First they smooth out a few patches of sand for pages and create pictures with cookie cutters. The author writes a few lines under each picture or, more typically, tells his story aloud. With all the different kinds of cookie cutters we bring along, including a reindeer, the stories take some unusual twists.

Donna Daniele, West Chester, Pennsylvania

Go for a secret excursion

One of my kids' favorite summer activities are the mystery daytrips we take. I pick out different destinations within an easy drive from our home and prepare the clues. We have gone to a local fort, an art museum, a car show and an aquarium. To give the kids ideas about where we may end up, I give the older kids secret code words or mark a trail along the map. The younger ones get pictures cut from newspapers and magazines. I pack the kids, the clues and a picnic lunch in the car and off we go.

Diane Stanton-Rich, Mayodan, North Carolina

Splash the duck

On a hot day at the beach or in your backyard, your kids will particularly appreciate this variation of "Duck, Duck, Goose." Have the child who is "it" walk around the circle with a bucket of water and splash the "goose" before the chase begins. The kids have a million giggles, and it's a quick way to cool off.

Susie Neevel, Alexandria Bay, New York

Wintertime Fun

Winter brings its own magic. It is a season of surprises, when you can wake up in the morning to discover not the world you knew the night before, but one that is white and wondrous. Childhood memories are filled with recollections of play in the snow. These are the memories your children are making for themselves now.

Be a trailblazer

When my family takes a walk in the new-fallen snow, one parent heads out first to create a trail for the rest of us to follow. Lots of zigzags, circles and patterns make the going especially fun.

Estelle Gersh, Minneapolis

Study snowflakes

To give children a way to study snowflakes up close, I made a snowflake catcher. Here's how: Stitch two pieces of black felt together on three sides (about five inches square). Slide in a plastic square that can be cut from a plastic milk bottle to give the item support. Then stitch the fourth side closed. Next, attach a piece of yarn to the square. Finally, tie an inexpensive plastic magnifying glass to the end of the yarn. The kids can now go out any snowy day and discover the beauty of snowflakes with their intricate and ever-different patterns.

Lynn Conover, Rochester, Michigan

Color a snow canvas

Snow makes an amazing backdrop for kids' art. I fill squirt bottles with water and then I add a few drops of food coloring. My kids love spraying colorful designs, making interesting drawings and writing messages to each other in the snow in our backyard.

Vicky Nissen, Puyallup, Washington

Bring the outdoors in

Sometimes when it's just too cold to play in the drifts outside our door, we bring the snow inside. To beat cabin fever, I collect big bowls of snow and put them in the kitchen sink. I pull chairs up to the counter, give the kids spoons and cups and they play with the snow. They build anything they like to do outside—snowmen, forts, cities—but in the tiny variety.

Barb Knisley, Rockwell City, Iowa

Lift a finger

Children are always hearing on weather reports what direction the wind is from, but it has no meaning for them. You can demonstrate much more vividly yourself and teach them something about the weather at the same time. On a cold and windy winter day, wet your child's finger and have her hold it up. The side that gets cold first is the direction the wind is coming from. This also teaches what the

Answers to Common Winter Questions

Kids have many questions about winter's weather. Here are the answers to the usual "What makes . . . ?"

Snow

Very small amounts of water, even smaller than raindrops, that freeze and stick together.

Freezing rain

Rain that falls onto the ground that is cold enough to turn the raindrops immediately into ice. The ground is then very slippery.

Sleet

Raindrops that go through atmosphere that is cold enough to turn them into ice on the way down. Sleet stings when it hits you because each bit of sleet is as heavy as a raindrop, but it's made up of solid ice.

Hail

Bits of sleet that are carried back up by strong, rising air currents. Before they fall again, they are covered with a new layer of water, freeze again and then fall once more. The process is repeated sometimes many times, making bigger and bigger pieces of hail.

---

weather people mean by wind chill. The reason behind wind chill—and why it is usually lower than the actual temperature—is that the wind makes skin moisture evaporate faster and the result is feeling colder than you would otherwise.

Lara Tunisia, Memphis

Sports: Should My Child Join a Team?

It's well-established that children need exercise and most of them need more than they are getting. A popular way parents can encourage children to accomplish some running around is through team sports. But that isn't without questions of its own. What team sports are good, and for what kids?

Look to the game

It's popular in my neighborhood to start even five- and six-year-olds on soccer and baseball teams. Before I signed my five-year-old daughter up I researched what was available. Many of the leagues have greatly simplified versions of the particular game for little ones. I waited until I found one that focused on kids having fun together and not the competition of the team. My daughter is pleased with the whole thing, from the uniform to running up and down the field with her new friends.

Kathy Kross, Shirley, New York

Should I Be My Child's Team Coach?

Being the coach of your child's team sounds like a terrific opportunity to share time and experiences, but for many families, the situation can create more problems than benefits. "If you can truly be objective coaching your child's team, it can be wonderful," says Linda Bunker, Ph.D., professor of sports psychology at the University of Virginia, in Charlottesville, and co-author of *Parenting Your Superstar* (Human Kinetics). The problem is, she continues, that "it's often difficult for parents who are coaches to be objec-

tive." Consequently, you might criticize your own child too much or overpraise him or her, allow your player too much time on the field or bend the rules.

Keep in mind as well, notes Bunker, that "children benefit from the opportunity to experience other adult role models." Kids also appreciate it when their parents are supportive spectators. What this all adds up to is that you should give the matter careful thought before you say yes; you may find that coaching another team in the league is a better way to go.

Check out the coaches

Little League can be a wonderful activity, but sometimes it's not. When the coach is one of those intense people who takes everything personally, it's hard on everyone, including the kids on the team. Before I let my two kids join any team, baseball or otherwise, I check out the coaches. Better to have the kids sit out a season than be under one of the overambitious team leaders.

Darlene Cruse, New York City

Wear the right safety gear

Many kids today, including my 10-year-old son, are heavily into roller hockey. Some of us were worried about kids getting injured in such a fast sport, but we didn't get far in getting the kids to go along with such safety measures as wearing their helmets and pads. We de-

cided we were going to have to come up with a way to make safety more attractive. One of the dads agreed to coach them two evenings a week in exchange for the players' obeying all safety regulations in their practice sessions with and without him. The kids are thrilled to have real coaching and the teams and are now very cooperative about playing it safe.

Janene Hiltzer, Ithaca, New York

Holiday Magic

Children bring a unique and unrivaled joy to any holiday, from watching them take on the face of Halloween ghosts and goblins to becoming careful artisans, creators of lacy valentines. There are a multitude of unusual and creative pastimes that make welcome additions to your year-round holiday calendar with kids.

Valentine's Day

There's no better time to remind kids how much you love them than on this special day for love.

Go on Cupid's treasure hunt

My mother always held a Valentine's Day treasure hunt, a tradition I've continued. I prepare a special Valentine's Day dinner, and once we finish, the kids lift their plates for the first of five rhyming clues. It might say something like, "You'll find a box in the drawer with your socks," and off they go in search of the next clue. All are hidden in the house, as is the treasure—a special Valentine's Day present.

Sandra Lee Skordalos, Baltimore

Put out a valentine heart

Every year I make my children a Valentine's Day pouch. I cut two heart-shaped pieces of red felt and sew them together with gold thread, leaving four inches open at the top. In the hearts I place little gifts—candies, action figures or coupons redeemable for time together. My kids love this tradition because it feels like they're getting another Christmas stocking, but this time in February.

Beth S. Kotz, Newman, Georgia

Give valentines at home

My two children love to give valentines to everyone in the class. Of course, they almost never get back anywhere near the number they give out—sometimes by a lot. To ease any hurt feelings about this, we started a special at-home valentine box. About a week before the big day, each child decorates a shoe box with a slit in the top. Then we attach a note pad and a pencil tied to a string. We encourage family friends and neighbors to leave a note or drawing to place in the kids' boxes. On Valentine's Day, just before dinner, the children sit down and go through their broad collection of cards. There are never hurt feelings after this.

Marjean Verhuse, Napa, California

Start a breakfast tradition

When my youngest was just old enough to hold a cup, I started a valentine tradition that I've kept up with three more children. Each year at breakfast, I put out special decorated cups full of valentine candy and treasures. No one is allowed to eat the candy until later in the day, but they play with the stickers, pins and other small gifts right away. The mugs have become more and more colorful through the years and each child has a special shelf filled with them.

Verna Strong, Orem, Utah

Easter

At winter's end, Easter celebrations should be full of colorful enjoyment for everyone in the family.

Watch those bunny prints

While the Easter bunny doesn't have quite the same magic as Santa Claus, your kids can still get a big kick from his visit. I dab bunny prints on the wood floors with washable white ink leading toward the carpeted living room. Then it's up to the kids to go looking for their basket somewhere in that room.

Megan Kingston, St. Louis

Hide one basket

With five kids in my family, I needed to come up with a way to give Easter some special fun. My solution: Each year I hide one basket someplace truly difficult to find. Naturally, I started with the older kids so I wouldn't have frustrated pre-schoolers on my hands! The children don't know whose turn it is each year to be the recipient of the "hidden basket," so finding out is part of the mystery. It can take hours to turn up the missing basket, and all the kids follow along.

Alexa Elkington, Las Vegas

Let young kids design

My younger child wanted to help his brother and sister decorate Easter eggs so I came up with an approach that allows him to take part in the fun. I give him a hard-boiled egg and have him dab non-toxic glue on it with a cotton swab. Then he takes bits of colorful tissue paper and attaches them to the glued spots. To better show off his Easter creation, I give him a toilet-paper roll which I have first covered with construction paper to place his egg on top.

Dawn Kunz, Norman, Oklahoma

Hold a hunt

What would Easter be without an egg hunt? In our neighborhood full of kids, a few of the parents get together to hide eggs at a nearby park early that morning. After church services, we all gather at the park with parents stationed around the periphery of the area in which we hide the eggs to be sure no child strays too far. We also hide one special egg. The child who finds the "king" egg—decorated with an aluminum-foil crown—gets to claim a small prize. After the hunt, we head off to someone's house for a potluck brunch. It's a really special day for everyone.

Leigh Ann Porter, Rochester, Minnesota

Mother's Day, Father's Day

It's important for children to learn the importance of giving back. Mother's Day and Father's Day are great places to start.

Look to the generations

We use Mother's Day and Father's Day in our home to celebrate several generations. On Mother's Day we go to my parents' home and on Father's Day, to my in-laws'. We exchange gifts among the generations and spend the day going through family albums and talking about our own growing-up years. Our children have a really good concept of what it was like in our families in the "old days" because of these annual celebrations.

Marion Crawford, Stockton, Massachusetts

Ask someone to step in

Since I am a single mother, I haven't been sure how to handle Mother's Day without the other parent there to help plan the celebration. I asked my sister to help me out with this and she has turned it into a wonderful shared time for her and my son. They plan an afternoon together on the Saturday before to go shopping and have lunch. She takes him to places he loves and they talk about what gifts would be good choices for me. I think this has helped him appreciate me more and I know it has brought them closer.

Jane Shapiro, Los Angeles

Handprint a tie

Ties are predictable gifts on Father's Day, but this one brought big smiles in our house last year. I purchased a plain, cream-colored tie and had our two-year-old decorate it. She placed her hands in non-toxic paints and carefully stamped her hand prints all over the tie. Dad wore it with great pride to the office!

Linda Newman, Dallas

Make a "mom card"

My family made this card for me last year and it is so special I recommend it to everyone. From construction paper, they made a two-foot strip of paper folded lengthwise so that is was in six equal sections. They then decorated each panel with something they think is great about me—pancake maker, jogger and family cheerleader were the first three. They decorated each panel with drawings and photos illustrating the particular characteristic. This is one card I'll save forever.

Ariel Robbin, Spencertown, New York

Halloween

This may be everyone's favorite small holiday. It's a day for nothing but fun and parents can enjoy it as much as the kids.

Have a party treat

Little kids are quickly worn out by trick or treating from door to door. I have found that it is both easier and more fun

to treat them to miniparties as we go. I contact three or four neighborhood mothers and we each plan a small-scale party in our home. The host child runs

ASK THE EXPERTS

What Do I Do When Halloween Is on a Work Night?

Halloween often falls on a work night, which means parents might prefer to put off the activities. But kids can't wait and so you need strategies around it. Here is advice from Susan Ginsberg, Ed.D., former director of the Work and Family Life programs of New York's Bank Street College of Education.

- Make Halloween plans early. "If you let it go to the last minute, the kids will get anxious about it. Halloween is a hot topic of discussion among kids at school," says Ginsberg.
- If your commute keeps you from getting home in time to paint faces and put on costumes, consider taking a personal day or ask ahead if you can leave work early that day. If that's not possible, says Ginsberg, ask a neighbor to help get your kids ready; in exchange, you can take all the children trick-or-treating when you get home or for a special outing on the weekend.

Halloween Entertainment

Add some thrills and chills, not to mention many laughs, to your child's Halloween party by having guests play these games.

The slime game

Set out small amounts of cottage cheese, cold cooked pasta, applesauce, peeled grapes and other foods with interesting textures. In turn, each guest is blindfolded and asked to dip a hand into the bowls and guess what it is.

Jack-o-lantern painting

Guests supply the pumpkins and you supply the paints and markers to make the faces. Prizes can be for the funniest, scariest, most original or even silliest—but be sure every child wins something.

Pass the pumpkin

Using a small pumpkin with the stem cut off, have children in teams of three or more pass the pumpkin to each other. The pumpkin must be held between each child's chin and chest and no one is allowed to use hands. The first team to pass the pumpkin down the line and back again wins.

---

the show demonstrating any special decorations and giving out the goodie bags to guests. It's important to keep each party brief so that the kids will make it through to the final stop.

Bethany Kandel, New York City

Freeze some of the loot

As kids get a little older the amount of Halloween candy they accumulate can be astounding. I put about three-quarters of their loot into the freezer. This way they enjoy their Halloween goodies for months to come and I don't worry about excessive sweet-eating.

Joyce Smith, Boise, Idaho

Dress a chess king

My son loves to play chess, so of course he wanted to be his favorite piece for Hal-
loween: the king. To make his costume I sewed a full-body cape of black satin. I designed a chessboard grid for the front of the cape with black and white contact paper which I also put around the neck and bottom of the cape. I outlined simple drawings of chess pieces on the back of the contact paper, cut them out and affixed them around the board. The crown, my son's head piece, was from cardboard and contact paper. It's easy to do and the costume looks great.

Hemda Aharoni, Petah Tikvah, Israel

Collect treats without sweets

Since kids get so much candy at Halloween, I'm doing something different. I keep a large coffee can in which I store little trinkets that turn up during the year—

barrettes, plastic figures, key chains, new pencils—any small item that might strike a child's fancy. On Halloween, I put them out on a tray and give the children a choice of a small prize or candy. The trinkets are always gone long before the candy.

Deborah L. Whitehair, West Chester, Ohio

Thanksgiving

Children quickly learn that Thanksgiving is more about family togetherness than it is turkeys and pies.

Hold a round-robin of thanks

Each year between dinner and dessert, we sit around the table and discuss something that we are particularly thankful for in the previous year. The kids usually focus on something they got while the older family members talk about an event or something special someone did. Whatever "it" is, we all applaud its place in our family's life. Seeing how the round-robin changes every year helps us realize how we are changing and growing.

Hayden Clark, Rochester, New York

Entertain in the kitchen

Holidays almost always mean many hours in the kitchen. To keep my son busy and near Mom—which he always seems to want when I am especially busy—I give him a variety of kitchen implements to use. This could include spatulas, cookie cutters, potato mashers, wooden spoons and the like. He traces the shapes of these interesting objects onto a piece of paper, intertwining and overlapping the shapes

to make intricate designs. Then we take out the crayons and he stays busy even longer.

Kathy Vogt, Las Vegas

Put turkeys on the table

An ideal placecard for your family's Thanksgiving table can also be a wonderful art project for one of your family's youngest members. You or your child can draw a picture of a turkey head on a piece of construction paper and cut it out. Glue the head to a toothpick and insert it into a plump and round raw potato. Poke four toothpick legs into the potato so that it can stand up on its own. Skewer cranberries, colored marshmallows and cereal with toothpicks for colorful feathers. Then write the name of those coming to dinner on the side of the potato turkey with a marker.

Kimberly Blum, Lansing, Michigan

Cut-out place mats

A pre-Thanksgiving activity that my kids and I enjoy doing together is making place mats for the feast. We gather magazine pictures of food, leaves and turkey shapes that the older kids and I trace onto different colors of construction paper and then cut out. We lay the shapes on paper place mats and laminate them front and back with clear contact paper. They are a warm and welcoming addition to our table.

Sara Lebens, Stacy, Minnesota

Hold a Thanksgiving bowl

On Thanksgiving Day, outdoor activity not only passes the time, it creates healthy appetites and is an opportunity for adults and kids to have some fun together. You might try a backyard football game (touch football, of course), relay races or let the kids pick out some of their favorites. Everyone comes back in rosy-cheeked and fired up to eat.

Annie Rosen, Harrisburg, Pennsylvania

Go to the movies

We have found a grand way to entertain ourselves and family guests when we are sitting around feeling far too stuffed after Thanksgiving dinner. If you have a camcorder, you can show a movie that will make everyone smile. This started when my kids were two, four, five and six—they liked the story "Three Little Kittens," so we decided to film it with them as the main characters. To avoid having to edit, we shot each page in order and did no retakes. Before each take, I gave directions and reminded them of their lines. Since the successful premiere of "Three Little Kittens," making movies has become one of my family's favorite activities. If you need more actors, invite the children's friends—especially if they are kids who will also be at dinner. You can film a classic story or make up your own—but remember this important caveat: The shorter it is, the easier it is to make.

Deeanne Gist, Spring, Texas

Christmas

The highlight of the year, Christmas is like nothing else for children. All the time and hard work are worth it when you see their joyous response.

Give from the heart

In our family, we give each other "gifts of love" every year. They include reading to a younger sibling, doing a chore without being asked and taking a child on a special outing. We write our gifts on slips of paper and tuck them into each other's stockings. Amid the toys and candy of Christmas morning, our gifts of love remind us of the true meaning of the holidays.

Amey Vance, Salt Lake City

Wrap up empties

The youngest children always like the colorfully wrapped boxes better than anything that might be inside. I make sure to wrap some extra (empty) boxes. This way the toddlers are busy playing with their treasures while the rest of us finish unwrapping ours.

Kathy Keller, Leslie, Michigan

Put together a holiday wish book

As the holiday season nears, my children begin to discuss what gifts they want. Instead of making a list for me, I ask them to create a book. They decorate two pieces of construction paper for the covers, and I put in a few pieces of white paper for the pages. For the next month or so, the kids spend many hours leafing through catalogs and magazines, looking for pictures of things they would like. They cut them out and glue the pictures into their books. When Santa needs to know which gifts they have in mind, "he" has an easy reference.

Diane Arnold, Temple Terrace, Florida

Leave an early gift

As our family is busy eating Christmas Eve dinner, Santa's elves sneak in and leave a present for each family member to open right away. They are always Christmas pajamas—and they make Christmas morning pictures festive and colorful.

Sally Haskell, Houston

Hold a diversity dinner

My family traditionally has a buffet-style dinner for the holidays. Last year we made it a diversity dinner. We invited some Chinese friends who brought a Chinese dessert. My sister, who had just returned from Thailand, made several Thai courses. We rounded out the fare with Swedish and Italian entrees and Greek baklava. It's easy, educational and fun to have a diversity dinner—invite friends from different cultures and ask them to bring a traditional dish. Conversation is never a problem since talking about holiday traditions in different countries is a natural.

Linda Demaris, Shoreview, Minnesota

Prepare a Christmas countdown

To add to the holiday fever, our family makes a "gingerbread-man Advent chain." Here's how: Get 12 pieces of brown construction paper big enough for two gingerbread men and fold them in half; place a gingerbread-man cookie cutter on the paper with its head at the folded edge and trace. Be sure to leave the heads connected when you cut out each tracing. On the front of each one, place numbers from 1 to 24. Inside, write down a surprise activity to do with the kids before Christmas: Sing a holiday song, bake cookies, go see the town's Christmas tree, go caroling. The kids can decorate the gingerbread men with crayons, markers, sparkles and anything else that adds to the spirit. Hang your gingerbread men along a string and drape on

Teaching Kids True Holiday Spirit

Family Matters, a program of The Points of Light Foundation, based in Washington, D.C., offers the following ideas to help you help the less fortunate during the holiday season.

• Help disabled or elderly neighbors shop, wrap gifts and write holiday cards.

• Offer to drive a homebound person to his family for the holidays.

• Read holiday stories to people with vision or literacy problems.

• Repair or paint the home of a needy family.

• Serve a holiday meal at the local homeless shelter.

• Coordinate a clothing or canned-food drive.

• Sing holiday carols at a nursing home.

Holiday Ideas and Crafts

Special Easter eggs

Make a Humpty-Dumpty egg. From construction paper, draw arms, legs, collar and tie all of sizes suitable to attach to an egg; cut out. For the body, a tube the egg sits on, cut a five-inch by two-inch strip, and tape or glue the ends together. Cut colored yarn into three-inch lengths and tie one piece around the middle of a cool, hard-boiled egg. Gently glue on yarn hair and paper body parts. Use a marker to draw a mouth and small, round stickers for eyes and cheeks and to decorate the tie. Adults can make Humpty's wall by cutting off the top of a milk container. Wash it carefully and let it dry. Have your child help cover the sides and tops of the container with construction paper and draw bricks on the wall using a marker. Place Humpty on the top.

Prepping a happy pumpkin face

You don't need to be an expert with a knife to provide the kids with a satisfying pumpkin face. Start by choosing a pumpkin that's firm and unbruised. (Store it in a cool place to preserve freshness longer.) When you're ready to work, wash the pumpkin and let it dry. Cut below the stem for the lid and, using a sharp knife, cut around the inside rim, but not too deep. Scoop out the flesh and seeds with a serrated spoon.

Have the kids use acrylic paint to make a face; it's fast-drying and washes off small hands easily. If you're starting with a base coat, allow it to dry completely before you paint details. Kids can attach paper, fabric, yarn and other decorations with craft glue. Pipe cleaners make zany additions—parents can poke holes with nails for attaching.

A children's holdiay table they'll love

The big holidays that involve having a sumptuous dinner usually mean an overly crowded table. You can help your young children feel good about having a table of their own—thereby freeing up the adult table—by encouraging them to take over the table decorations. Add seasonal touches for the centerpiece, such as small pumpkins, fall leaves, gourds and apples in autumn. For winter feasts, start with pinecones and evergreen branches. Spring tables might have a bouquet of daisies and in summer, try shells and driftwood. Whatever the season, encourage kids to make individualized placemats. When it comes

the fireplace or a bookshelf and open one a day until Christmas.

Susan Ossim, Cincinnati

Put on Christmas story plays

On each of the four Saturdays before Christmas, our family puts on a Christmas

time to light the table, select a battery-operated lamp to give a totally safe glow.

Pumpkin serving bowls

Kids over the age of six can entertain themselves at fall and winter feasts and create some useful serving bowls for you. Here's how.

Carefully cut off the tops of several small pumpkins, scoop out seeds and wash out the inside. Place pumpkins on separate plates and have the kids create their own sculptures by using toothpicks to attach raw vegetables, nuts, miniature marshmallows and dried fruits to the outside of each pumpkin. After decorating, fill pumpkins with salad, cranberry sauce or, better yet, pumpkin soup. Use pumpkin sculptures the same day so that they will retain freshness. Younger kids can fill pumpkins with flower or leaf arrangements, great for creating a colorful holiday home.

Your personalized holiday wreath

Children will take special pride in a holiday wreath that they help make themselves.

- Start with a simple evergreen wreath, 18 to 22 inches wide.
- Use cookie cutters as stencils and trace hearts, stars, houses, reindeer, and other interesting shapes on heavy colored paperboard. Cut out shapes and make holes with a punch at the top and bottom of each shape for hanging.
- Make a wreath centerpiece, the village tree, of a Christmas tree shaped–wooden ornament or draw your own with paperboard with holes top and bottom.
- Tie ornaments and shapes to the wreath with ribbon or colored yarn
- Nestle wrapped candy canes and dried flowers around the shapes on the wreath. Baby's breath will create the illusion of snow falling on the "town."

Paper snowflakes

Children six and older will enjoy this.
- Parents should start by cutting out a seven-inch circle on construction paper. Fold in half; fold half in thirds.
- Have children cut small shapes out of folded paper and then unfold to reveal a unique snowflake.
- Parents can attach flakes to windows by spraying a quick coating of adhesive to back of each flake, allowing it to dry and pressing on window.

play. We light the Advent wreath and the children narrate a small part of the story, using props to illustrate it: a halo for Gabriel, a blue cloth for Mary's head, a baby doll for Jesus and chocolate coins for the wise man's gift of gold. Last year by

Christmas Day, our three-year-old son could recite almost the entire nativity story for the family by himself.

Linda Carroll, Forest, Virginia

Have a cookie bake-in

Nothing beats the smell of cookies baking at Christmas time. Every year, about a week before the big day, we bring our extended family together for a day that fills Grandma's home with that wonderful smell. Aunts, uncles, cousins and friends—as many as 25—gather for cookie day and we bake from dawn to dusk. The kids have a communal good time decorating the cookies, and we all have dozens of holiday cookies to take home.

Madeline Herzog, Lynwood, Washington

Talk about giving

Since kids can't possibly get everything they would like, we talk to them ahead of time about their gift wishes. We discuss the giving aspect of the Christmas season and about the good memories Christmas creates. This seems to help them see that Christmas is about more than what you get. Love comes in many forms.

Arlene West, St. Paul, Minnesota

Let the kids make gifts

A great gift your young children can make is a special Christmas T-shirt. Have the kids dip their hands in green fabric paint; place their hands and fingers on a prewashed T-shirt in a pyramid effect to make the shape of a tree. Once the prints are dry, the kids can go wild decorating the tree with crystal fabric paint and other kinds of sparkles. Brown fabric paint will give the tree a trunk.

Terri Brown, Stuart, Florida

Paint your window

Instead of buying holiday decorations for our windows, we paint them with poster paints mixed with a drop of liquid dishwashing detergent. That way, when the holidays have come to an end, we can use ordinary window cleaner to wipe away our holiday reminders.

Sara Bonner, Mohawk, New York

Personalize ornaments

Our favorite kinds of ornaments are those which have some family history. To make your own: Tie a ribbon to the top of a wooden curtain ring. Cut an index card to fit the inside circle of the ring, and have your children stamp their thumbprints—one per ornament—in the middle of the card. With fine-point markers, the kids can transform the print into a person, animal or creature. Write a holiday greeting, design or child's name and the date on the card and glue it to the back of the ring.

Kay Miller, Minneapolis

Start thank-you habits

Even children too young to write can form the habit of saying thank you with a note for their Christmas gifts. Save some of the nicest wrapping paper, and cut out pictures from it. The kids can paste their favorite pictures onto plain notepaper—and parents can do their part by writing the child's message.

Debra Kodger, Montville, Ohio

Hanukkah

Lighting a candle on each of the eight nights is one way Jewish children begin to understand their ancient history.

Bring a menorah

On one of the eight nights of Hanukkah, I have a party for my children and their friends. Everyone brings a menorah from home. We eat potato pancakes, exchange gifts, light a candle and say the Hanukkah prayers. We get a chance to admire all the menorahs and tell a little about them.

Jan Schwartz, Wellesley, Massachusetts

Adapt the dreidel game

Young children have a tough time spinning a dreidel in the traditional fashion so we adapted the game for Hanukkah into what we call the Dreidel Slide. We make a ramp with toys, but we put a bump at the bottom that will make the dreidel flip. This allows even the youngest in the family—13 months old—to play dreidel with the rest of us.

Marcy Levy, Newtown, Pennsylvania

Read together

An excellent bibliography that I found when searching for quality children's books on Jewish holidays and other aspects of Jewish life is "Light a candle! The Jewish Experience in Children's Books." This booklet is available for $4, plus $1 for postage and handling. Write to the Office of Branch Libraries, The New York Public Library, 455 Fifth Avenue, New York, NY 10016.

Susan Pine, New York City

Teach their history

It's tough for Jewish children to understand why their homes don't have colorful trees and Santa filling stockings. We stress all the wonderful stories that lie behind Hanukkah and its traditions—from the dreidel to lighting the candles—to help our kids develop more interest in "their" holiday. Each night after lighting a candle and exchanging a gift, one of the children tells a part of the Hanukkah story.

Denise Raimi, Bel Air Beach, Florida

Computers and Your Young Student at Home

Children today have a wide world of education literally at their fingertips with a computer. They're now a fixture in schools and a valuable addition to every home.

Arrange group play

I have quite a bit of educational software for my kids, ages seven and five. I've found that they do more with it and seem to enjoy the programs more when they are in group play. Twice a week now I have computer hour. Several neighborhood moms send their kids over and we have a class. I'm there to help or suggest, but for the most part the kids work on their own. They respond really well to the friendly competition, other kids' suggestions and the team play that being in a group gives them. Afterwards we all have a snack.

Francine Johnson, Eugene, Oregon

Compose on computers

My son has had a lot of trouble with book reports and other school material that require him to write more than a page. He really struggles to form letters and make his writing legible. Now I put him on the computer to do any kind of report and the work is starting to flow. For his last book report I printed out six pages and he has started writing a book of his own.

Jana McClean, Austin, Texas

Let kids explore

I was nervous when we first got our computer that my children—all under age eight—would break it. I've learned that this is pretty much impossible. It really pays to let your kids explore the computer to discover the many wonderful things it can do. The computer is also invaluable to help them get stronger in their weak areas. My eight-year-old would be lost without Spellcheck.

Margaret Sweeney, New York City

Monitor computer time

My nine-year-old son would happily spend entire days in front of the computer. I'm delighted that he enjoys it so much, but I had to come up with some ways to keep it from taking over his life. I started by putting the computer where I could easily see him instead of in his room which helps me keep track of his time. We also determine each day how much computer time he needs for homework and how much he gets for the games he likes. I let him trade off outdoor time against additional computer time—45 minutes on his bike or rollerblading buys him an extra 45 computer minutes over the weekend.

Chrystal Pennar, Hoboken, New Jersey

Photos and Other Memory Savers

At no time has it been easier to save your family memories through photography. Cameras are simple to use and camcorders make it possible to capture motion and sound along with your child's amazing growth. Now it's up to you.

Bring bubbles to the picture.

Whenever I take my three-year-old daughter to have her picture taken, I carry along a bottle of soap bubbles for added insurance. We are guaranteed a perfect smile for each shot as the bubbles are popped, as well as a much more relaxed photo session.

Sandra Britto, Plymouth, Massachusetts

Hold gallery viewings

Every few months I videotape my daughters giving me a showing of the artwork in their gallery. This gives me not only a chance to have each girl's drawings on tape, but I also capture their adorable comments and observations at each of these ages.

Fran Miller, Wheaton, Illinois

Give grandparent picture gifts

For something every grandparent will love, cover some special photos of the grandkids with clear contact paper or have them laminated. Send them to grandma and grandpa who can then keep them in their wallet or, as one grandmother did, use as bookmarks. That keeps the kids constantly in mind.

Tiffany Orensky, Wilmington, Delaware

Save each year

Every year until our daughter turns 18, my husband and I plan to record her for a few minutes on a special birthday video-tape. Someday, all of three of us will be able to watch her grow up before our very eyes.

Georgine A. Takatch, Cleveland

Send a photo bouquet

When my husband's father was in the hospital, fresh flowers weren't allowed in the intensive care unit. Inspired to send him something, I came up with a better bouquet idea. I purchased artificial daisies and ad-hered pictures of each of his grandkids to the center of the flowers. You can also make a photo daisy bouquet by making daisies and leaves from oaktag and attaching them to wooden sticks, colored green.

Debi Bunting, Rochester, New York

Make your own refrigerator frames

To put small photos of the children on your refrigerator in fittingly attractive frames takes only some slide holders, available at a camera-supply store. Deco-rate the borders with paint, glitter or stars and after the frames dry, slip in the photo. Glue a magnet to the back and your child's smiling face is ready for kitchen display. These also make great gifts for relatives.

Michelle Godbout, Cocoa, Florida

CHAPTER FIFTEEN

On the Road

*B*efore you were a parent, getting around was easy. You had no need for the multitude of bags and equipment that make parents look more like packhorses than people. There was no careful organization and planning to work around children's schedules—or, for that matter, no kids in a variety of moods to tote along with you. There's little question that getting out and about is harder now, whether it's for a shopping expedition or a family vacation.

But, of course, having children can't stop you from taking care of business outside your home. And it shouldn't stop you from taking family vacations. Even with organizing, packing and other hassles, family travel gives you valuable time to relax, to share exciting activities and to know each other in new ways.

First Outings

Those first few ventures out the door with your new baby in tow are at once exhilarating and terrifying. You'll encounter obstacles you never did before—doorways too narrow for a carriage, steps too steep for a stroller. And you'll have to make adjustments determining how much is absolutely necessary to carry. It won't take long, though, for you to know just how to get around, what you both need, and how to relax in the company of your own baby.

Spray away messes

One item I've come to value among my baby's going-out things is a spray bottle filled with water. I use it to rinse off pacifiers, teething rings, bottle nipples and sticky hands when we're away from home.

Lorraine Nazareth, Lake Forest, California

Send up a stroller signal

Walking my daughter in her stroller from the car through parking lots always made me nervous. I was afraid cars could not see her since the stroller is low to the ground. I've attached a neon flag on a long stick to the stroller; anyone can spot it in a second.

Betty Ann Grundfast, Missouri City, Texas

Always be ready to go

I'd heard it was a good idea to have your baby bag filled and ready to go, and it works. I keep diapers, baby wipes, a changing pad, blanket, burp cloth, plastic bags for dirty diapers, a change of baby clothes and a back-up bottle of ready-to-feed formula in my bag. I tuck a small camera in there, too—you never know when the next photo opportunity will come along!

Allison Easton, Cambridge, Massachusetts

Get a better grip

When I carried my daughter around in her car seat, the plastic handle often dug into my hands and made my palms sore. I found the solution in a sporting-goods

---

Teach Your Child What to Do When Lost

Kids must know the rules of what to do if they become separated from you. Before you go anyplace, tell them in a calm manner so that they don't become overly fearful about the thought of being lost. Explain that they should stay put and let you come to them—otherwise you'll end up chasing each other in a circle! Point out that if you are someplace with uniformed attendants, such as an amusement park, they should alert one of the employees of their predicament and that person will help them out. Finally, if you are in the great outdoors, on a hike or nature walk, give all the kids a whistle to wear around their necks. They should blow this loud and often if they stray away; this will give you the signal you need to find them.

store: tennis-racket grip tape. I used it to cushion the handle and it provided great relief.

Christine Mok, Columbia, Maryland

Double-duty fanny packs

I've discovered my fanny pack works perfectly as a shopping-cart seat belt for my daughter. I belt her in and both she and my wallet and keys are safe and secure.

Diane McBride, Corinth, Mississippi

Bring your own clean eating utensils

When you're leaving for a restaurant with your baby, put his spoon in a toothbrush holder before it's packed in your diaper bag. It stays clean this way and it's also easier to find in your bag.

Pennye Pucheu, Lafayette, Louisiana

Play car tunes

It's frustrating to have my son fussing in the car and not be able to soothe him because I'm driving. I made a "mommy tape" for those moments. I recorded myself singing his favorite songs and then filled out the tape with tunes from his music boxes and various toys. The tape has proved itself invaluable for calming him when I most need to.

Rosemarie Dooner, Macedonia, Ohio

Use a net for backpacker protection

The elasticized netting sold to use over strollers and playpens works wonders in other ways, too. We like to hike but the bugs were a problem for my seven-month-old son. I slipped the netting

ASK THE EXPERTS

Should I Feel Nervous Taking My Baby Outside?

Some parents are reluctant to take their new baby away from the snug security of home. "I've known new parents who refused to take their babies out in public or who would go to shopping centers only late at night after almost everyone else had left," says Edward R. Christophersen, Ph.D., chief of behavioral pediatrics at Children's Mercy Hospital, in Kansas City, Missouri. "But unless your child's physician recommends otherwise, you don't need to worry about taking your baby to shopping centers or family functions." To help parents get past new-baby travel jitters, Dr. Christophersen advises them to take the baby with them on a few training trips— short hops to the corner store and back—before setting out on a three-hour excursion to the mall.

around him in the pack and now he is protected from bug bites without having to use bug repellent.

Diane Rushton, Scarborough, Ontario

Calm the car-seat critics

My father-in-law made continuous remarks about how silly I was to insist that our infant daughter travel only in her car seat. I was able to stop his criticism by pointing out that I knew it was his love for her and his concern for her comfort that was behind his complaints. But we love her too, and the best way we feel to show our love is to give her the best protection she can possibly have when traveling—her car seat.

JoAnn Eastman, Ames, Iowa

scowling or sleeping? A fellow hiker friend came up with a small mirror on a string I wear around my neck. I can check on my son whenever I want and he squeals with delight when he sees me making funny faces at him in my "rearview mirror."

Judy Rosen, Estes Park, Colorado

Traveling with Babies and Toddlers

Really young kids are wonderful to take traveling in many respects—they're easily portable and they are happy just to be with you, wherever you are. At the same time, all parents know that babies and toddlers require a seemingly neverending supply of toys, bottles, food and equipment. There is also the problem of keeping young kids happy as the road stretches before them, for which parents soon find solutions.

Fasten toys in place

Our two-year-old was constantly dropping his toys on the car floor—retrieving them from the front seat is a physical feat! We now avoid the problem by getting him toys that attach to the car seat. They're always there for him and we don't have to worry about play and retrieve or worse—flying toys.

Peggy Rutherford, Sacramento, California

Hang a mirror

I like the convenience of taking my son in his backpack when we are sight-seeing or hiking. But not knowing how he was doing made me anxious. Was he smiling,

Build in break time

Toddlers get so restless in the car that we now regularly program breaks every two hours or so. Whenever we can, we stop someplace where our twins can run around and burn off some of that nonstop energy. But even walking around the fast-food places on the interstate is generally enough to calm them for the next two-hour haul.

Edward Simpson, St. Louis

Protect your car from messes

With two small children traveling in the back of our car, the upholstery can get awfully dirty. To avoid having to clean it constantly, I put a crib sheet over the back seat. It's just the right fit and I can whip it off in an instant when we get home to go right into the washing machine.

Laura A. Layden, Beaver Dam, Kentucky

Have tapes tell a story

Story cassettes are lifesavers when it comes to long hours in the car. I'm so grateful for the peace my daughter's favorites bring the family I don't even mind hearing them again and again.

Roger Shipman, Idaho Falls, Idaho

Search for trucks and such

Toddlers are enchanted with trucks and buses, which is decidedly in your favor on car trips. Point out the trucks and buses as you go along—especially bright yellow school buses, which are particularly noticeable and fun. Older toddlers will learn to look for them on their own.

Deborah Youngman, Seattle

Best Vacation Ideas

Family travel is a dramatic shift from the days when you traveled as a couple. Now, in addition to finding kid-pleasing destinations, you must devise strategies to keep peace and happiness en route, to help children feel safe and secure while there—and, on top of it all, to get in a little relaxation yourself. Without question it's a challenge, but one you can meet successfully.

Research the trip before you travel

If our trip includes sights that are educational, I discuss them with my son well ahead of time. I point out what I think he will find most interesting about them and I offer him a special treat during our trip for an oral or written report on any aspect that he finds particularly interesting. He starts researching before we leave home

Vacation Child Care

Most resorts and many hotels now offer child care as a regular service. Don't make any assumptions, however, about either its availability or its quality. Ask when you call for reservations if you can obtain child care services.

If it's there, follow up with questions concerning quality. "Parents should ask for the details of any type of kids' program or baby-sitting services, just as they would for any child care used at home," says Barbara Reisman, executive director of the Child Care Action Campaign, in New York City. She suggests you ask the kids' program director or hotel manager the following questions.

- What are the caregivers' qualifications? Have they received child care or first-aid training?
- What is the adult-to-child ratio?
- What activities are provided for the children?
- Are the kids' groups separate or mixed-age?
- How do caregivers help a child adjust to the new environment?

and by the time we get going, he is really excited by the idea of actually seeing what he has been reading about.

Suzy Gershman, Westport, Connecticut

Schedule for success

On our vacations, I keep enough of a schedule that the kids are comfortable knowing what to expect, but it's one that's loaded with fun. I plan the first half of the day around sight-seeing. I then pick out a place I know the kids will enjoy for lunch—fast food or someplace with an eye-catching theme that makes it special for children. After lunch we do something that is active, usually swimming. Late in the afternoon, when the kids are hungry but not yet ready for dinner, we have tea and I let them include a sweet treat for themselves.

Arlene Taylor, Biloxi, Mississippi

Pin down the memories

A wonderful way for kids to remember every trip is with a scrapbook. Pack a glue stick, a spiral notebook and a plastic bag for collections—postcards, leaves and the like—so your kids can make their own scrapbook of the trip. This even lets kids who are too young to write create a journal of their vacation.

Dorothy Jordon, New York City

Stay close to your vacation home

Once we get to our destination, we keep the amount of time we're in the car to a minimum. Our rule is that day trips can't be more than one hour away from our hotel or guest house; otherwise the kids start picking on one another because they prefer to be doing active things.

David Spiegel, Washington, D.C.

How to Deal with Motion Sickness in the Car

Motion sickness is one of the biggest problems for families traveling by car. Fortunately very young children aren't usually bothered by it, but when kids hit the preschool years, it can become a real nuisance for you and discomfort for them. Have kids who are prone to motion sickness keep their heads still and their gaze forward, preferably fixed on something far up the road. They should snack frequently, since empty stomachs make the problem worse, and stop often enough for them to walk around and get air regularly. Of course you won't let them read or do other close work in the car, which in itself can bring on motion sickness.

If the familiar nausea strikes in spite of your precautions, a good remedy for that queasy stomach is ginger powder. You can buy this in capsule form from a health food store.

Give everyone a fanny pack

I take individual fanny packs for each member of the family. I pack them with essentials such as snacks, sunscreen and sunglasses. The kids have all they need easily at hand and I don't have to carry everything.

Rhonda Berkshire, Lancaster, Ohio

Make the Most of Disney World

Walt Disney World (WDW) in Orlando, Florida, is the top vacation destination of American families. With three major theme parks (Magic Kingdom, Epcot and Disney/ MGM Studios) plus some of the country's best water parks (Typhoon Lagoon, River Country and Blizzard Beach) it has something for everyone. Here are some tips to make your Disney getaway a happy experience for all.

For everyone

- If at all possible, choose to go during off-peak seasons (September through early November, January through April—except for spring-break weeks that coincide with school closings—and May). The park hours are longer during peak seasons, but the lines are longer, too.

- Check with your travel agent, membership organizations (such as AAA), your union and credit card issuers to find out about any special deals they might have.
- If anyone in your party is celebrating a special event, such as a birthday, check with your resort and/or travel agent for possible perks.
- Bring a stroller or rent one at each theme park. It will be a well-spent $5. Even kids who gave up traveling in a stroller years ago can't keep up with the demands of foot travel.

Most visitors leave WDW with strong feelings. Some can't wait to go back; others are so exhausted that they dare not think of trying it again. For most, however, the experience is wonderful. The most essential things to bring with

Create an at-home vacation

My wife and I were reluctant to take another summer road trip with two kids under eight cooped up in the car, so we decided on an at-home vacation, our "holiday in." We drew a circle with a 100-mile radius around our town and gathered brochures for points of interest. Then we made up a two-week vacation itinerary: a children's concert, a boat trip, a crafts show, bullhead fishing, a ball game and hot-dog dinner, an inner-tube trip, planetarium show, rock-and-mineral hunt, a day at an amusement park, a na-

ture walk, a dinner in an exotic restaurant and a couple of movies. Was our at-home vacation a success? You bet. My wife and I were more relaxed, and our kids gathered a wealth of material for their back-to-school projects.

Donald A. Haines, St. Paul, Minnesota

Write on

Each afternoon my son and his dad sit down together to write about what they did that day in a special trip diary. This not only makes a permanent record of the family trip, it also keeps life calm during

you are a sense of humor, flexibility and a reasonable agenda.

Best rides and attractions for the youngest visitors

At the Magic Kingdom: Dumbo's ride, the Carousel, The Mad Hatter's Tea Party and Mickey's Starland

At Epcot: The Image Works playground

At MGM: The Little Mermaid show

Best rides and attractions for school-age visitors

At the Magic Kingdom: Splash Mountain, Big Rock Thunder Railroad, Space Mountain, Pirates of the Caribbean, the Raceway, The New Tomorrowland and the Hall of Presidents

At Epcot: Explora—Innovations East and West, AT&T's World of Communication, Spaceship Earth and "Honey I Shrunk the Audience" 3-D show in Futureworld, and Norway and Mexico in the International Showcase

At MGM: The Twilight Zone Tower of Terror (really scary, but a thrill for most), the Monster Sound Show, Muppet 3-D Show, Indiana Jones Spectacular, the Great Movie Ride, SuperStar Television, The Animation Studio and the Backstage Tour

For older teens and adults

Individual tastes and abilities will lead different visitors to different attractions. But it's good to know that:
• The water parks are particularly appealing and appropriate for teens.
• You can plan on at least one fine-dining experience either at your resort or within the parks, such as one of the international restaurants at Epcot.

the downtime at the end of the day when kids usually get cranky. Having his dad's full attention is definitely an attraction for my son.

Amy Reif, McLean, Virginia

Packing Basics

Packing for the family requires serious planning—everyone needs a sufficient amount of clothes but you don't want to be stuck with mountains of luggage. First-aid items must be in there right along with sandals and T-shirts. Plus, you'll have to make room for certain "friends" who, as kids know, simply must be part of the trip.

Carry comfort on the road

Of course you won't forget security objects, be they a blanket or a bear. But remember to put them in an accessible place wherever you are—the airport, the car or anyplace in between. Children really appreciate having something from home to keep near them. Even the smell reminds them of home when they feel disconnected.

Gail D. Hoffman, Cincinnati

Bag those outfits

To avoid a jumble of clothes every time you open the kids' suitcases, place complete outfits together (shorts, pants, sweater, shirt, underwear and socks) and put them in their own plastic bag, preferably a sealable one. You can leave more room in your suitcase if you squeeze the air out of each plastic bag before you place it in. In the long run you'll save lots of time looking for socks and such and when clothes are dirty, they can just go back into what is now the laundry bag.

Betty Waldron, Hollywood, Florida

Have provisions on hand

You never know when a flight is going to be delayed and you're stuck with a hungry and wet baby. Tuck enough baby food in the diaper bag to make it through a long flight with lots of delays and put in several more diapers than you think you'll need.

Bill Echelberger, Richmond, Virginia

Are We There Yet? Dealing with Impatience on the Road

For children used to having rough-and-tumble days, sitting for hours in the car can be grueling. As excited as they are about their destination, getting there isn't half the fun. Smart parents can turn the time on the road into fun for all—diversionary tactics are the answer.

Introduce storytelling in the round

We create round-robin stories in the car. The first person starts off with key charac-

PEDIATRICKS

First-Aid on the Road

Families should always bring along a first-aid kit for traveling. Here are some items you should include.

- Adhesive bandages, in a variety of sizes
- Antibiotic ointment or Mercurochrome
- Calamine lotion for bites, stings, sunburn and skin rashes
- Sunscreen that's at least SPF 15
- Insect repellent
- Gauze and cotton balls
- Scissors
- Tweezers
- Acetaminophen, in both adult and children's varieties
- Decongestant or antihistamine
- Cough drops or throat lozenges
- Lip balm
- Petroleum jelly
- Antidiarrhetic
- Thermometer
- Facial tissues

ters and the setting. At a "cliffhanger" moment, the story is turned over to the next person. We get from one to three minutes each and naturally we all make it as dramatic as possible. We laugh a lot, it's imaginative and it really passes the time.

Sherry Weidenbaum, Massapequa, New York

Soothe the savage beast

Music! It has been a wonderful travel tool for our family. We buy a new tape we

Dress for Success

Along with the shorts, T-shirts and bathing suits, pack one really nice outfit for each child in case you need them to look their best—for Grandma or a restaurant. For the journey, though, dress them in their most comfortable clothes. The fancy duds can wait until you arrive at your destination.

Select clothes to promote peace

When you're packing for children, choose their favorite clothes and colors, not the ones you like and they don't. Why spend time arguing about clothes on vacation? Select items in three mix-and-match colors to give you the greatest number of outfits.

Cynthia Bell, Beacon, New York

Pack tightly to reduce shifting

Fit as many clothes as you can into each suitcase to keep the contents from shifting around en route. This will help avoid clothes getting wrinkled.

Nancy Butler, Oakhurst, New Jersey

Keep shoes to a minimum

Since shoes take up so much room, take as few pairs as possible. Always have at least one spare pair for everyone, though, just in case. Small items such as hair bows and toiletries fit nicely into shoes; then wrap the shoes in tissue or bags so that they won't soil other articles in the suitcase.

Linda Meltzer, Breckinridge, Colorado

all listen to, plus we have the kids bring along a portable cassette player with their own favorite music.

Rinah Judith Karson, Little Rock, Arkansas

Elaborate on "I spy"

For our long car trip, I made up a more elaborate form of "I spy" for my children, ages six and eight. Before we left, I went through magazines and newspapers and cut out pictures of things that I expected to see along the road: buildings, statues, farmhouses, cars of different styles and colors, animals and tractors. I wrote down route numbers and road names that I knew we would pass and then I glued each picture to a three- by five-inch index card. In the car I dealt out five cards at a time to each child. The first child to spot all the items in his hand won the round. I was glad I had thought to laminate the cards with clear contact paper, which meant they held up for the ride home.

Linda Ellinwood, Marcellus, New York

Sing childhood favorites

I teach my kids old favorites such as "She'll Be Coming Round the Mountain," songs from the days when I was traveling

PARENTS' ALERT

Car-Seat Safety

Automobile accidents remain the leading cause of death and injury to children, according to the National Safety Council. Those who suffer the highest passenger death rates are infants under six months.

To make sure your child is as safe as possible:

- Use a car seat manufactured after January 1981, when strict federal safety regulations went into effect.
- For infants weighing under 20 pounds, use a car seat that is designed so that the child faces backward. This is the only safe way for a baby to ride. In case of an accident, the pressure of impact will be evenly distributed along the baby's back, not on his fragile chest and abdomen.

- Try to install your car seat in the middle of the rear seat. It is the safest place in the car in the event of an accident. In any case, always keep the car seat in the backseat, away from air bags which can, when inflated, crush and even kill a small child.
- Use the car seat until the manufacturer recommends discontinuation—usually when the child is four or 40 pounds, whichever comes first. Then consider a booster seat for the child, which generally affords better protection than seat belts alone.
- If you inherit a used car seat, you can check to see if it meets safety standards by calling the National Highway Traffic Safety Administration at 800-424-9393.

with my parents. They get a big kick out of hearing about my days as a child and we all sing at the top of our lungs—with the windows rolled up, of course.

Anna West, Golden, Colorado

Keep toys for the car

I bought a special toy for my daughter that lives in the car at all times. When she gets into the car, it's the first thing she sees and it entertains her for many hours. Naturally, she'd like to take it with her when we leave, but I remind her that this is where the toy lives and that it will be wait-

ing for her on our next trip. I change toys periodically so she doesn't get bored.

Lisa Dezenzo, West Orange, New Jersey

Don't fool around

Many times when kids fight, it's to get attention. I stop the car and tell them flat out that this is a safety issue and I can't be distracted by their antics. I also let them know I'm not going to get in the middle to resolve their dispute so they'd better take care of it themselves. After a few minutes they generally do just that.

Deborah Rowell Legan, Shoreview, Minnesota

No-Fuss Auto Safety

Car seats and seat belts have made a dramatic safety difference in the United States. In fact, all states now have laws requiring car-seat usage for kids, and many mandate seat belts for all others as well. But the problem of how to keep kids happy once in them remains.

Give your child company

I strap in my daughter's favorite doll in the seat belt next to hers. This shows my daughter I'm serious about seat-belt use, and it gives her company when she gets lonely in the back of the car by herself.

Rachel R. Raczka, Pottsville, Pennsylvania

Don't give in to unbucklers

When my boy was a toddler, I thought it would be okay for me to let him occasionally sit outside his car seat. Once was enough to get me in trouble—from then on it was a fight every time we went someplace. I learned my lesson and with my daughter, I have never wavered for a second. She doesn't even ask to sit elsewhere, because this is just what we do: We get in the car and she sits in her car seat.

Tiauna Ward, Sandy, Utah

ASK THE EXPERTS

How Can I Make Sure My Car Will Start?

One scenario that unnerves just about every parent is the thought of getting the kids finally and safely buckled in, putting in and turning the car key—and having nothing happen. Fortunately, there are a number of ways you can prevent this from happening to you, says Arthur Nellen of the Car Care Council. His advice to help you be sure your car will always start is this:

- Push the gas pedal to the floor and then turn on the ignition when your foot is halfway up. Pumping can result in a flooded engine—though this is not true for all cars. Check your owner's manual for specific advice on your car.
- Check your battery if it's more than three years old—especially if the cold weather is about to set in. Batteries need replacing as often as every three to four years.
- Ask your mechanic if you should switch to a lighter-weight oil for winter. By offering less resistance, a lighter oil can make it easier for the engine to turn over.

Demonstrate safety

My son started complaining about the way I always insist he buckle up. Because he was old enough to have some sense of cause and effect, I showed him what could happen if he was not in the seat belt. I demonstrated on myself, falling forward and bumping my head on the back of the driver's side. He still occasionally complains, but I remind him of what can happen and he quickly gives up the fight.

Ann Marie Longbardi, North Haven, Connecticut

Buy for comfort, too

It only makes sense to get a child the most comfortable car seat you can find. Because kids must sometimes spend many hours in these seats, they are going to be aware of a seat's comfort. If they associate the seat with feeling good, they are much less apt to fuss.

Dolores Swanson, Fargo, North Dakota

Plane Travel

More and more families are taking advantage of air travel. As comfortable, quick and efficient as airline travel is today, there are still many restrictions for children. The greatest of these, of course, is their having to sit still for hours at a stretch. Fortunately, airplane seats are well designed for entertaining activities, with trays that pull down and windows that can be used as stages.

Ask for more legroom

If extra legroom is important to you—and you don't mind giving up storing bags under the seat in front of you and being able to lift arm rests between seats—ask for bulkhead seats. These are the first rows in each cabin, which are always the ones with the most leg room. And do take ad-

PARENTS' ALERT

Prevent Ear Pain during Flight

Infants and young children often suffer discomfort during landings due to otalgia, or ear pain. Increased air pressure during descent causes the eustachian tubes, which link the nose and throat to the middle ear and normally equalize ear and atmospheric pressure, to collapse. This blocks the flow of air into the middle ear and creates a vacuum that sucks the eardrum inward, creating a stretched eardrum, muffled hearing and ear pain.

The best way to get the eustachian tubes to open up and relieve the pressure is by swallowing. Older children should chew gum, but you'll need to give a younger child a bottle. The most effective time to give a baby a bottle is at the onset of descent, when you first feel air-pressure changes in your own ears.

Babies who have colds should not fly at all. If there is no way to avoid it, ask the doctor about an antihistamine, a decongestant or both.

vantage of early boarding calls offered to families. The last thing you need when you're trying to get little kids on board and into their seats are hoards of adult passengers bumping into you with their carry-on baggage.

Irene Haber, Glenns Falls, New York

Bring plenty of finger foods

I make sure to bring lots of juice for my son to drink throughout the flight as well as his favorite finger foods. Chewing and swallowing help keep his ears clear and they stave off any grouchiness he might have from hunger while he waits for the service. I try to get crackers or cookies that have shapes—animal crackers are a good choice—because they entertain him, too.

Amy B. Brown, Winter Park, Florida

Save some steps

Instead of parking and then dragging your luggage to the terminal, drop everything off at curbside check-in. Then you're free to go the distance to long-term parking without the exhausting chore of getting your luggage checked before you.

Judy Grey, Montclair, New Jersey

Tote a bag of tricks

Bring along a bag filled with items that will entertain and occupy your child. Pack a few of her favorite toys and books and be sure to add some new surprises as well. You can keep the action going for hours—the hours it takes to get you to your destination.

Kelly Bougalis, Hibbing, Minnesota

Encourage window play

Reusable vinyl stickers have plenty of play appeal. Give your child these and the window seat so that he can use the window as his stage, turning his stickers into characters for whatever story he wants.

Randy Kramer, Monroe, Connecticut

Beware the exit rows

Kids under the age of 16 are not allowed to sit in the exit row—an emergency precaution. If those are your assigned seats, you'll need to move and should the flight be full, the family may have to split up. When you call for your boarding passes, be sure to tell the clerk how old your kids are and remind him not to give you that row.

David Kempler, Washington, D.C.

Reserve a choice flight time

I know that a lot of families prefer to fly when the kids usually sleep, but we have found this doesn't work so well for us. We need to be fresh and wide awake to enjoy the flight and avoid being cranky. Whenever possible, we book morning flights.

Gilliam Littlehale, Cincinnati

Call for a meal pleaser

At least 24 hours in advance, call the airline to order a children's meal. These are usually terrific, consisting of foods that kids really like.

Roger Stanger, Provo, Utah

Tell the kids about flying

Discuss with kids before you get on board about what flights can feel like. If they know that airplanes sometimes shake or bump and that the engines shift and make different kinds of noises, when that actually happens they won't be frightened. Even kids who have flown before may need to be reminded.

Theresa Ramsey, Lawrenceville, Georgia

Visit the airport's play areas for happy waiting

Some airports have play areas for kids—the Kidport at Logan International Airport in Boston, for instance. These are terrific places for kids to run around in a contained area. We get a breather and the kids can play off some of their excess energy.

Patricia Mahon, Dublin, Ireland

Let kids be kids

Don't be embarrassed—or punitive—when your kids behave in ways that are strictly kidlike such as hanging over the seats to see the passengers behind them, crying or running up the aisles to visit new friends. That's not to say you should let them run wild or be obnoxious, but kids have to have some leeway even if some fellow passengers give them a look or two.

Bill Bercow, Boulder, Colorado

Feeling at Home in Hotels

For a few days or weeks, your hotel or motel room is your home away from home. There is something delightful about having this contained and cozy space as your own for a period of time, especially with small bottles and other gifts that are common in hotels today. It's important, though, to take some precautions in terms of maximizing both family comfort and safety.

Child-proof all the time

When my husband and I take our toddler son out of town for an overnight stay, I tuck a few childproofing items into my bag. Socket protectors and a toilet lock go into my diaper bag along with our boy's other provisions. It's well worth the small effort to put these items in place—as we all know, it only takes seconds for little ones to start exploring and having them more protected goes far in assuring peace of mind. I also check to be sure the windows are secure.

Connie Reese, Greenville, South Carolina

Snap the memories

Our kids think staying in a hotel or motel is one of the high points of life. To preserve the memory we have them decide what is their favorite spot or part of the room. Then we take a picture of them in it. Last year it was the oversize bathtub that won my five-year-old son's heart and that's where we got him on film.

Nancy Snyder, Austin, Texas

Recreate a bit of home

The minute we get to our hotel room, I show my son where he's going to sleep. I always bring his quilt with us and put that—along with a stuffed toy he has selected to carry on the trip—on his bed. By the time he's ready for sleep, he feels comfortably at home.

Louise Goldstein, Ithaca, New York

Call ahead for cribs

Be sure to reserve a crib in your room at the same time you make your hotel reservations. We have had to do without when a hotel had given its last crib to a family before us.

Jamie Kincaid, Fargo, North Dakota

Arrange the exit plan

All hotel rooms have diagrams on their doors that show the floor plan and exit routes for the hotel. We go over these with the kids and explain our emergency plan.

When Kids Travel Alone

In this age of easy jet travel, it's not unusual for kids to cross the country—themselves—to visit grandparents or spend time with the other parent. The airlines have strict regulations about children traveling on their own. These typically involve several forms you'll need to fill out, which include giving relatively detailed information about the person picking the child up at the other airport. That person usually needs photo ID before airline personnel will release the young passenger. Allow plenty of time before the flight to take care of these matters.

You may be allowed to go on board with your child. It's up to the attendant at the gate. Your child will be assigned a flight attendant who will be responsible for delivering him or her into the waiting arms at the end of the flight—provided, of course, there is photo ID waiting as well. Don't leave the airport until the airplane has taken off; unforeseen delays could mean your child will have to spend more hours at the airport and you should be there to take over.

Since regulations change from time to time, check with the airlines when you make the reservations to be sure you'll have everything you need to get your child off smoothly.

We then go out into the hall to be sure we understand the directions and the plan correctly. My husband and I also ask at the desk to be sure the smoke detectors' batteries are checked regularly. We keep it very matter-of-fact so that the kids don't get alarmed, but they are aware of safety measures.

Chris Berresford, Ventura, California

Traveling Solo with Your Kids

Almost every parent is faced with traveling alone with the kids. The demands can be difficult—kids may need generous amounts of time and attention when there isn't enough of you to go around. Solo travel is definitely manageable, but it requires a greater degree of planning and ofttimes more patience, especially when everyone seems to need you at once.

Lighten your load

When you need to bring a lot of packages or gifts, spare yourself the trouble of dragging them and your luggage with you and let a parcel service do it for you. Call a few days before you are leaving and the extra baggage will be waiting for you when you get there. This is also a good way to handle the problem of toting strollers and other bulky equipment, which are too much when there is just one of you.

Steven Murphy, Brooklyn, New York

Become day-trippers

I like to take my two children on short getaways. I scout out things like petting zoos, restored villages and the like, places that are entertaining and really different from being at home. It helps us all feel we have gotten away, but our day trips don't require the kind of work that a real trip does.

Catherine Carr, Pittsfield, Massachusetts

Adults do matter

Single parents often feel they have to go someplace just for their kids. They should remember that vacations are for them, too. Places that offer weekly packages usually have the same people for the week. This means families get to meet each other right away and have a chance to become really friendly as the week moves on. Whatever you do, always try for a place that has communal dining—it forces you to meet other adults.

Dorothy Jordon, New York City

Enjoy the kindness of others

Before we leave on any trip, I get a stash of dollar bills so that I have ample tip money. Help is everywhere around you—sky caps, bellboys, parking-lot attendants—and taking advantage of them makes my life much easier. Traveling alone with kids is demanding enough without adding any extra strain.

Ruth Bonner, Madison, Connecticut

Provide easy access

I keep a mesh bag in easy reach of my daughter in the back seat and I fill it with her car toys, a juice bottle and nonsticky finger foods. I also put in a colorful book or two that she can easily handle. This way I never have to turn around to help her out when we are on the road.

Barbara Lunde, Buckley, Washington

Traveling with Teens

Teenagers are a particular challenge for traveling families. Too old to need you, too young to be strictly on their own, teens often go from being terribly grown-up to acting

Giving Teens Some Independence

Teens need independence and separate time from their family. Look for travel destinations that give them the opportunity to be on their own a good part of the time, perhaps even the whole day. This might be places with ample sports facilities, especially if they include ways for teens to interact, such as group tennis or scuba lessons. Keep evening activities in mind, too—discos, arcades or rec rooms for darts and table tennis. Naturally, you'll want to be sure that there is some supervision and that independent activities don't stretch safety rules before you give the okay. Most of all, don't take it personally when your teens consider family togetherness something to avoid at all costs. They'll enjoy it again someday.

Romance and the Family Vacation

Finding romance with your spouse may seem like a near impossibility when you're vacationing with children—picking up half-eaten sandwiches doesn't do much for feeling flirtatious. But couples can find quiet time for themselves if they use some imagination. First of all, give yourself some space.

Book a suite

All-suite hotels, such as Embassy Suites and Guest Quarters, are ideal because parents can enjoy a quiet conversation in one room while the children play or sleep in the other.

Ask for adjoining rooms

You may be able to negotiate a lower rate for a second room (assuming your kids are old enough to be on their own). Many Hyatt Hotels, for example, offer 50 percent off the second room for children, if one is available.

Use a nursery monitor

You can relax on the terrace, a nearby patio or pool and still keep tabs on your sleeping tot.

Quarter, please

If your children are old enough to play without supervision, send them to the game room with a large stack of quarters.

Vacation with another family and share the child care

Do you have friends whose children are the same age as yours? Consider having the families take a trip together. They can take your kids for an afternoon outing or sleepover; then you can take theirs the following day.

---

more like their younger siblings. Teens also bring zest and energy to a family—to say nothing of the help they can offer with brothers and sisters—that adds a valuable dimension to the vacation. You just have to know the tricks to helping your teenage travelers have a good time their way.

Bring a buddy

Whenever possible, we allow our teenage daughter to bring a friend with her on a trip. They sometimes shut themselves up in the room for hours, but they are having a good time. They entertain each other and having company keeps our girl in a good mood.

Harriet Goldberg, Los Angeles

Remember a reality check

I've learned from raising two teenagers not to expect them to get excited about anything that might really interest adults or younger kids on a given trip. Teens shrug off just about everything with a who-cares? attitude. Now that I expect it, I don't allow my kids' attitudes to interfere with the satisfaction I get from seeing the sights. I don't get mad at them either—this is the way of teens.

Tom Elkins, Reno, Nevada

Give the budget lowdown

My teens have trouble containing themselves when it comes to expensive souvenirs, so I make souvenir budgeting part of our pre-vacation discussions. We decide together exactly how much money they can have for the extras like fancy T-shirts. We've been able to avoid all arguments about vacation spending money since I started this.

Anne O'Brien, Hempstead, New York

Go for the action

Teens need other teens and they need action. We look for destinations that have a lot of organized activities, the kind that keep the kids busy and give them access to other teens. Dude ranches are a great idea.

Belinda Carter, Chicago

Parent Time on a Family Vacation

With so much attention paid to the pleasures and comforts of traveling children, it's easy to forget that vacations are for parents, too. Don't let that happen. On vacation you and your spouse have the rare pleasure of leisure time together—it's an opportunity to be around each other in the slower paced way you were before there were kids. It's a chance to have some time just to yourself as
well, to explore interests that are perhaps only yours. Take advantage and enjoy!

Give yourselves a touch of class

Treat yourselves at least one night of your vacation to dinner at a first-class restaurant—just the two of you. We get a sitter lined up when we make our hotel reservations to be sure we'll be able to have our night out. Then we look for the restaurant in our price category that sounds the poshest. We get all dressed up and behave with our best manners—it's like dating again.

Deanne Nelson, Norman, Oklahoma

Enjoy family favors

Summer trips with our four-year-old son to see my husband's parents can be hectic because his mom and dad often have many visitors. At the suggestion of my in-laws, my husband and I frequently escape for an overnight stay at a local hotel. We feel rested and recharged after having this opportunity to go for a swim, eat a nice dinner and sleep late. It doesn't cost us much and we love it, but I think Grandma and Grandpa enjoy it even more—they get to have their only grandson to themselves.

Bethany Kandel, New York City

Take turns taking care

My husband and I trade off several hours of each day we are on vacation being the primary caretaker of our three kids. This gives us both a scheduled time to relax, knowing that there is a parent meeting the kids' needs and supervising their safety.

Stephanie Wells, Ojai, California

Bring the sitter along

We have found that it doesn't cost us much more to bring a sitter with us on vacation. The main thing is to find someone our kids really like being with and a young person we enjoy, too. We've had some real success with this—if you find someone who is enthusiastic about your trip and responsible about your kids, it can add more to the vacation than just babysitting.

Tricia Brakeman, Atlanta

Use kids' camps

Pick a vacation spot that has a children's camp during the day. There is so much for the kids to do during the day that it leaves us free to play tennis, go sailing or simply loll on the beach by ourselves. The children are also happy with their activities and we spend the late afternoon and evenings with them. Everybody wins—we all have our own pursuits and time together.

Cindy Stewart, Philadelphia

CHAPTER SIXTEEN

Time for You

*B*eing *a mother is a 24-hour-a-day responsibility. The job* description, were there such a thing, would read "Must meet others' needs continuously; requires thinking about others' well-being even when else-where."

Even so, it is possible for you to find time and energy for your life sepa-rate from your kids and in spite of hectic schedules. It's also healthy for you and for your family. Enjoying your marriage, your friendships and pursuing your private interests makes a happier you and when mom's happy, so is the whole family.

Great Ways to Get Back to You

It's all too easy to become so involved in being Mom that the rest of you gets lost. "I'm not sure I even remember what I liked to do before the children were born," sighs one mother of two. She's not the first mom to forget her pre-kids life. In fact, one of the first things you should do in thinking about getting back to you is to create a list of what you would enjoy with more time off—and you can't say sleep.

Run with the baby

Since I returned to my job when my son was six months old, I thought I wouldn't have the same complaint that other stay-at-home mothers have about losing their sense of self. I was busy and productive in the office, had many friends and a job I liked. I found, though, that once I had a child to take care of, my entire life centered around him. I didn't want to see my work friends after hours because I wanted to get home to my son. I was also reluctant to go away on weekends without him.

Yes, it was happening to me. I had work and being a mommy and that was it. Recognizing that my life was getting awfully limited didn't change the fact that I wanted to have as much time as I could with my son, but I knew I needed to get out more. The answer for me was a jogging program. We got a special jogging stroller for the baby, one that you can push in front of you as you run. He loves it and is totally content as I put in my three miles four or five days a week. Getting out in the fresh air with the world quiet around me has made me so much more content and I've lost every bit of baby weight, at last.

Sharon Parke, Beaverton, Oregon

Develop an at-home learning plan

As the mother of two toddlers, I found my life consumed by neverending tasks—laundry, diapers, dishes and housecleaning. I realized that if I didn't make a conscious effort and a plan to do something, that I'd be consumed, too—by boredom. I promised myself right then to learn one new skill each year. The first year, I tried knitting and made scarves for my kids. The second year I tackled something a bit harder—quilting—and I succeeded in making a simple quilt. This year it's Chinese cooking, and thus far I've learned to make terrific egg rolls. Without question, it takes creativity and a great deal of determination to use my rare free moments to work on my current project. It gives *me* back, though, with a real sense of accomplishment that makes every bit of effort well worthwhile.

Julie M. Ellis, Anderson, South Carolina

Go to school—again

After five years staying at home with my two children, I felt hungry for more intellectual stimulation. I turned to a local college, enrolled in a continuing-education biology class and realized how important school was to me. Much to my delight, the college gave me credit for the three semesters of classes that I had at-

Little Luxuries That Boost Morale

When you spend most of your energy caring for others, it's especially delicious—and important—to splurge occasionally and have others do for you. Yes, it takes some of your hard-earned money, but who better deserves a wonderful treat? Here are some indulgences that cost little but bring big satisfaction.

• A half day of beauty at a salon or spa. For about $100 you can choose two or three services, such as a facial, manicure and pedicure or an aromatherapy massage. Or you can have a massuese come to you. Just be sure you select one that is licensed by the state. (To find a masseuse, call the American Massage Therapy Association at 847-864-0123.)

• Hire a professional organizer to declutter your space. Sessions range from $35 to $75. But even one meeting can help you put order in your surroundings. "I do more than organize people's spaces," says professional organizer Stephanie Schur, of White Plains, New York. "I help organize their lives." For a list of organizers in your area, send an SASE to the National Association of Professional Organizers, 655 N. Alvernon Way, Suite 108, Tucson, AZ 85711.

• Enjoy the arts. Buy a series of concert or ballet tickets or enjoy a night at the theater. Sign up for tap-dancing lessons, modern jazz or ballet lessons. Beginner courses are offered at dance studios and your local YMCA.

• Send yourself fresh flowers. Put in an order to cover a month of regular deliveries at your home or office.

---

tended prior to having children. It then went even further and awarded me life-experience credits for my work history—which included my responsibilities and skills as a mother. And an added bonus, I was granted a scholarship reserved for mothers returning to school. As for child care, I am fortunate that my husband can work at home two days a week and take care of our children, but child care shouldn't hold any mother back. You may be able to find on-campus care (sometimes at no cost) or, by posting a sign in the student union, child care exchanges with other back-to-school mothers. Check too if there are any scholarships available for returning moms. By next year I will be certified to teach high school English. Mothers who are thinking about returning to school: Go for it.

Leenie Hobbie, Points, West Virginia

Form a best-seller club

Having three children was a dream come true for me, but three kids under

More Roles, More Happiness

It stands to reason that being a parent, wife and worker triples a woman's burden. Not so, says new research. In fact, it triples her joy. The study, by Toni Antonucci, Ph.D., professor of psychology at the University of Michigan in Ann Arbor, found that despite the everyday strains and stresses of raising a family, mothers are physically healthier and have higher self-esteem than single or married women without children.

"The more roles a woman takes on, the more opportunity she has to obtain satisfaction, success and rewards," says researcher Dr. Antonucci, who measured the quality of life, frequency of depression and self-esteem of 2,500 women.

Although the study focused on mothers with jobs, Dr. Antonucci believes that any outside activity—whether it be volunteer work, a hobby or even regular exercise—can lead to a healthier emotional life. In fact, Dr. Antonucci reports that multiple roles may also help alleviate stress. "For instance, if your job is unrewarding but your kids are blossoming, the situation at work doesn't seem so devastating," she says.

Mothers are also physically healthier because they tend to take good care of themselves. "They are the people who buckle their seat belts, don't smoke, don't drink, eat regularly and don't snack as much," Dr. Antonucci observes, "probably because they know that there are others—namely their husband and kids—who depend on them."

five was turning my mind to mush. Even though I have always loved to read, I usually spent any free time, especially after the kids were finally in bed, sitting like a lump in front of the TV. A book review in the newspaper for a new novel got me thinking—I knew it would be hard for me to devise a reading program on my own that I would stick to, but becoming part of a group reading the same book, well, that would be a great incentive.

I checked with some of my friends and neighbors who I felt would make good reading buddies. Most were enthusiastic about being part of a reading club. We meet every two weeks, pick books from the best-seller lists and then hold discussions about our current book. Now and then we throw in a classic author, such as Jane Austen, as well as guest speakers (professors and an occasional local author).

It's been very exciting to develop what I call my "grown-up" part and to get back to something I love. Our reading club has also provided me with a mini social life separate from my family which has given them a certain new respect for me. When I get dressed for club night, my five-year-old watches with obvious pride that Mom's going out to read.

Priscilla Wallace, Lansing, Michigan

Balance your life

I left behind a career as an engineer which I very much enjoyed to stay home with my son. I love him dearly and have no regrets, but by the time he was a year old, I was becoming increasingly unhappy. I had no life apart from him and I had to give my life more balance. My solution was somewhat unusual, but it has been wonderful for me. I enrolled in a weekly tai chi class. Tai chi is a form of movement, somewhat like a very slow dance, that is actually a way of meditation, which has been practiced in China for centuries. It is amazing what tai chi has done for my peace of mind. My smile is back and I have a renewed feeling of inner peace and happiness. By making time for myself, I have more love and energy to give to my family.

Laura A. Hunter, Bossier City, Louisiana

Join the Y

Until my family and I had to relocate a few years ago, I had no idea what an amazing resource the YMCA and YWCA are. I started investigating our local Y's programs as a way of becoming involved with our new community. Much to my surprise, I discovered that the Y offered financial aid and a work program that I could use to cover our membership fee. I started out by volunteering in the youth department, and in return I received

Create a Marriage Memory Board

You no doubt have many souvenirs stashed away from particularly wonderful moments in your marriage—matchbooks from your favorite restaurants, a postcard from your honeymoon, theater stubs from a weekend away. Instead of keeping them out of view, why not display them on a marriage memory board? Inexpensive and easy to make, a memory board ensures that reminders of the joyful moments of your married life are always there, even during the low times.

Your memory board could be a bulletin board or a piece of plywood that you can prime and paint. Decorate with items that have meaning to you and your spouse. Include photos of the two of you, perhaps a pressed flower from a bouquet he sent you, a cartoon or two on the state of marriage.

Keep some space open for future additions. You may prefer to keep the board in the privacy of your bedroom, but it also makes a wonderful conversation piece in the kitchen or another area where friends can admire it.

great discounts on family membership and programs. To my surprise, our Y also provides low-cost, on-site child care. This gave me a way to take some courses and last year, I became a certified aerobics instructor and learned CPR.

Melissa Husband, Lansdale, Pennsylvania

Sign up for free classes

The county home-extension office, listed in the White Pages, frequently offers free classes on a variety of subjects that can make your home-life more interesting. Look for such topics as cooking, crafts and landscaping.

Diane Davis, North Vernon, Indiana

Recharging Wedded Bliss

While parenthood is a wonderful part of enhancing the bonds you share with your mate, raising a child together also can place considerable stress on a marriage. There's much to do, not much time to do it in and both partners end up rushing from one chore to another. Romance and the quality of your relationship can easily slip between the cracks, but it doesn't have to be that way. There are many ways, big and small, to keep the romance alive.

Consider professional help

After our marriage hit an all-time low, my husband gave me an ultimatum: marriage counseling or separation. At first I was afraid to talk to a therapist, but I agreed to go with him and, to my suprise

PARENTS' RESOURCE

If You're Looking for a Therapist

Professional help has saved many a marriage, but finding a therapist you both like and can afford is sometimes difficult. Average per-session fees charged by psychiatrists, psychologists and social workers range from $60 to $100.

Your medical insurance may cover part of the cost of therapy or a specified number of sessions. Check your policy for particulars. If you must bear most or all of the cost and this represents a financial burden, discuss the fee with your therapist; he or she may be willing to work on a sliding scale.

To find a professional therapist in your area, contact the following:
- American Psychological Association, Public Affairs, 750 First Street NE, Washington, DC 20002-4242. Call 800-374-2721.
- National Association of Social Workers, 750 First Street NE, Suite 700, Washington, DC 20002. Call 202-408-8600.
- American Association for Marriage and Family Therapy, 1100 17th Street NW, 10th Floor, Washington, DC 20036. Call 800-374-2638.

(and my husband's), I was very comfortable. It was a great relief to confront problems that we had never discussed in the

ASK THE EXPERTS

Is There a Good Way to Fight?

Fighting is part of any close relationship, including marriage. Ron Taffel, Ph.D., psychotherapist and author of *Why Parents Disagree: How Women and Men Parent Differently and How We Can Work Together* (Morrow), points out that there are rules to turn fighting into a productive activity. He adds that these can also help children see that when handled well, fighting can be good.

Here are the rules he suggests.

- Keep away from any name-calling. (And, of course, no physical attacks!)
- Avoid placing blame on each other.
- Don't drag your kids into the argument or ask them to take sides in any way.
- Stick to "I" statements. Say, "I feel upset when you do . . . ," rather than "You're so lazy." This helps move the fight away from blaming each other.
- Try to be as specific as possible about your particular gripe. Say, for example, "I hate it when you forget to do the laundry," instead of "You're so forgetful."
- Make sure that neither of you is always the winner.
- Forget trying to find a perfect compromise. Many times there is no such thing. Bring the fight to a resolution of some sort. If possible, let the children see you come to this resolution, one that you can take action on.
- If you're fighting anywhere in the house and the kids are there—even in their rooms or on another floor—keep in mind that they'll hear every word you don't want them to hear. If you really don't want them to know about your fight, take it outside.
- Make up. Preferably, make up in front of the kids if they witnessed the fight, so that they see that love can coexist with anger.

10 years we had been married. Thanks to therapy and family support, our relationship was saved. If we hadn't sought professional help, I suspect we would be divorced today, not the happy couple we now are.

Name and address withheld

Know what to attack

We have found our key for effective communication. It's simply this: Even though it's sometimes difficult, attack your problems, not each other.

Monica Cosinga, Bronx, New York

Talk about the little things, too

Each night before we go to sleep, my husband and I ask each other one last question: "What did you love about me today?" Our answers can be quiet gestures, the way we looked at one another at a particular moment, the way he dressed our two-year-old that morning, or perhaps that I put toothpaste on his toothbrush. Sometimes it's bigger things, time spent with a hurting friend or going out of our way to do a favor.

Our bedtime ritual is a daily reminder of how much we appreciate each other in so many ways. It keeps our marriage fresh and vital.

Michele Sbrana, Alameda, California

Have a date night

Shortly after our first child was born, my husband and I recognized that we had almost no time that was just for the two of us. We made Thursday night our date night and booked a sitter for that night on a regular basis. There have been times when we've had only enough money to go for coffee instead of out to dinner, but that hasn't mattered. The real purpose is to have quiet time to talk and to concentrate on us. We do have one rule for our nights out—we aren't allowed to discuss the kids, the house or any of our routine tasks. After all, this is our night!

Kelly Crawford, Des Moines, Iowa

The Value of Friendships, New and Old

Having a child presents a seismic change in your life. Your priorities, your interests, your goals and dreams now all center around the presence of this small newcomer. This shift oftentimes results in less focus and time spent with friends. But friends, new and old, offer a special bond and understanding that is invaluable.

Start a dinner club

My husband and I organized a potluck dinner club with three other couples we met at our church. The eight of us get together once a month for anything from a sit-down elegant dinner to Chinese takeout or a picnic. We take turns hosting, but we all hire babysitters. This is a night for adults only and it's a great way to stay close and a chance to get away from life's daily pressures.

Tammy Smith, Springville, Utah

Organize a girls' night out

As an at-home mom of two young children, I felt that I deserved an occasional night out with the girls. I called another mom I didn't know that well but whom I liked to ask if she would be interested. Was she ever! We agreed that we needed more adult conversation and I told her to spread the word. We were starting a Mom's Night Out. New moms seemed to spring up from everywhere, and now, two years later, there are more than 20 women in our group. One Tuesday a month we see a movie, play bingo,

Cast a Wide Net for New Friends

For mothers staying home with young children, isolation can be a real problem. Mothers who continue to work outside the home struggle with a different angle of the same problem—meeting women who, like them, are also balancing work and the needs of small kids. Women in either situation find the going much easier once they have a circle of like-minded women with whom they can share problems and experiences, laughter and insights.

Potential new-mother friends are everywhere. If you are religiously inclined, look for a house of worship that attracts young families. Sunday school and its variations are great places for the kids to mingle and for parents to meet each other. Parent-child classes in your town are another place to look; try your city parks and recreation departments or

the Y. Go grocery shopping! Everyone in town gets to the store sooner or later and striking up a conversation on the merits of brand names is an easy icebreaker. And don't overlook storytime at the library, a great way to meet other moms.

One activity which you may dismiss at first because of the time commitment is volunteering. Even though you are time-crunched, give it serious thought. Check around at your church, local libraries, schools, political groups, museums or hospitals. This can be a wonderful way to make new friends while making a difference.

Whatever you do or wherever you are, don't be shy about meeting others. Speak up, introduce yourself to someone who looks compatible and make a plan. You have nothing to lose but your loneliness.

dine out or work out at a hotel health club and then relax in the whirlpool. Whatever we do, we get a chance to talk, laugh and dream. It's easy to start a Mom's Night Out, just grab a friend and spread the word.

Heidi M. Funk, Brainerd, Minnesota

Get to know the neighbors

In the last few years many more families with young children have moved into the development we live in. Although people said, "hello," none of us really

knew one another. After a number of months of nodding at each other, I rallied together a few of the neighbors I did know and we decided to host a block party. First we printed and distributed fliers to determine community interest. Then we held a meeting to iron out the logistics: the day, the location, a rain date, refreshments, entertainment and the legalities of blocking off the street. I'm proud to say our block party was a huge success and we plan to make it a yearly event. Best of all, now when we see one another, we stop and talk. We truly are neighbors now.

Debra A. Warner, Blackwood, New Jersey

Keep the old

After my son was born, I lost interest in many of my single friends. It wasn't that I didn't care about them, I just didn't care much anymore about a lot of things they were involved in. Parenthood was everything to me and I began to neglect those friendships. One night a woman who had been a close friend for many years asked me over for dinner—alone. She told me straight out how much she missed me and how sad she was that I didn't seem interested in being friends any longer. That night turned my thinking around. Yes, I was in a new phase of my life, but the people and things I had enjoyed before would be important to me again. I decided to keep up with my old list—even though I can't see any of them that often right now, I call regularly. I also see to it that I don't go on and on about my adorable child. It's actually nice to hear what they are up to, none of which is baby talk.

Katia Kornuber, Boise, Idaho

Enjoy friends of all ages

My four-year-old daughter and I like to go for long walks in our neighborhood. Through these we have met many elderly neighbors and some have become good friends. They tell me about raising their own children and their marriages—it's fascinating and has really broadened my understanding of life.

Patti Fignar, Easton, Connecticut

PARENTS' BOOKSHELF

The Blue Jay's Dance: A Birth Year, by Louise Erdrich (HarperCollins). A poignant, lyrical odyssey of the joys and frustrations of pregnancy and motherhood. Erdrich, a keenly spiritual observer, records the rhythms that bind families and nature together.

Let's Always . . . Promises to Make Love Last, by Susan Newman (Perigee Books). A collection of thoughts and ideas to keep relationships romantic, loving and intimate.

Meditations for New Mothers, by Beth Wilson Saavedra (Workman Publishing). Meditations that address the emotions, doubts, conflicts, anxieties and wonders of living with a newborn.

The *Woman's Comfort Book,* by Jennifer Louden (Harper San Francisco). A self-nurturing guide to a woman's emotional well-being.

Start shared motherhood projects

My friends and I found that we hadn't made nearly as many entries in our second-born children's baby books as we'd made in our firstborns'. We had piles of their baby cards, photos and artwork in closets. As an incentive to have fun together and accomplish a task we were all ignoring, we planned a baby-book party. We all showed up with our stacks of memories and we spent hours sorting through pictures and memorabilia and filling in the missing baby-book entries. Not only did we have fun sharing birthing experiences with one another, but our second- (and a few third-) borns now have a complete record of their babyhoods.

Victoria Wilkinson, Charlotte, North Carolina

Help yourself by helping others

When I was a new mother living far from family and friends, my mother advised me to join a group called Beta Sigma Phi. This is an international philanthropic women's organization that raises money for breast-cancer research, disaster relief and scholarships. As it turns out, many of the women in my local chapter were young mothers also, which helped me develop a very satisfying social life. I made many dear friends I still have. To get information about a chapter near you, call 816-444-6800, or write to P.O. Box 8500, 1800 West 91st Place, Kansas City, MO 64114.

Cindy Herman, Kennewick, Washington

Make specific plans

When you summon up the courage to invite another mom to get together, make your invitation specific. When I say something like, "Can you come for coffee Thursday at 10:00 A.M.?" it almost always works out. When I open with a vague "Come over for coffee sometime," sometime never comes.

Gina Rozon, Saskatoon, Saskatchewan

Make new friends

In the first lonely months of staying at home with a new baby, I was determined to meet other new moms who could relate

to what I was going through. The solution: a notice I put up on a community bulletin board in my neighborhood supermarket. It read: "I wish to meet moms with preschool children to have coffee, share stories and start a babysitting co-op. Call Barb at . . ." It worked.

Barbara Duguay, Seattle

Bubble Baths to Beauty Rest: Breaks That Rejuvenate

Days crammed with work, errands, appointments and chores, evenings filled with more—finding strategies to give you much-needed breaks can seem impossible. Yet these regular breaks built into your day or week can make an astonishing difference. "I don't get resentful of my many responsibilities as long as I have something for me at least every few days or so," admits one mom. "This is what keeps me sane and, yes, satisfied."

Take a spin on the ice

When I was a child, I dreamed of being an ice skater at the Olympics. I never got

Easy, Inexpensive Rechargers

It doesn't take a big investment, in time or money, to give yourself a recharging break. The key is to find activities that are strictly for you, not the kids, and that are truly different from the usual rhythm of your day. Some of these may be just the thing to recharge your energy.

- Exercise outdoors. Take a bicycle ride, jog along a lake, practice yoga in your backyard. Combining exercise with being outdoors will refresh your spirit as it puts a glow in your cheeks.
- Get a haircut. Can't afford the fancy salon downtown? Ask about the services of their trainees; many salons make their trainees available to the public once a week at a reduced rate. This may not be the way for you to achieve the new you for a special occasion, but it might be just what you need for a good trim and an hour of pampering.
- Play tourist. Sign up for a hike at your local nature preserve or other point of interest in your community. Call the Chamber of Commerce for brochures on the sightseeing opportunities in your local area and select the ones that interest you.
- Watch for lectures and speeches given by authors, public figures or experts at bookstores, local colleges or libraries.
- Get a free makeover at a department-store makeup counter. It's a good opportunity to sample new products and maybe even find a new look.
- Visit a museum on the free night.

lessons then, but when a new ice-skating rink opened near our home, I made up my mind to go for it. I took lessons for the first few months, but now I can do the spins and twirls without instruction. I won't ever make it to the Olympics, but I get out several hours a week and enter a world that belongs only to me. I go home refreshed and eager to help my children find their dreams.

Diane O'Rourke, Huntington, New York

Tell the kids

At those moments during the day when I feel I can't go further, I'm reminded that children can be sensitive to adult feelings. All I have to say to my three-year-old son is, "Mommy needs some time and when I get done we'll play trucks." He gets it and he is wonderfully cooperative about letting me spend some time reading, sipping a cup of tea with my feet up or chatting with a friend on the phone. Even ten minutes of this mommy time can make a world of difference.

Catherine Cummins, Monroe, Wisconsin

Learn mini-meditation

I always thought meditation was a wonderful way to relax and get your

How Can I Get Sounder Sleep?

Daytime breaks won't help anyone who is overwhelmed by fatigue. The key: a good night's sleep. Some advice from the Better Sleep Council in Washington, D.C., for ways to help you sleep well: keep the temperature of the room in the mid-sixties; avoid alcohol or anything with caffiene—coffee, tea, colas and chocolate—for several hours before bedtime; make sure your mattress is still comfy (not more than 8 to 10 years old) and big enough.

Even under the best conditions, sleep may still elude you. When that happens, the Council suggests:

- Close your eyes and recall your favorite relaxing fantasies. Concentrate on the details.
- Starting at your toes, first tense, then relax each muscle group in your body.
- Select a truly dull book or magazine to read.
- Have a soothing beverage. Milk, for example, contains L-tryptophan, an amino acid that seems to trigger sleep. (You can also find it in eggs, tuna, cottage cheese, cashews, chicken and turkey.) Some herbal teas are also helpful.
- Take three deep breaths, exhaling fully after each. After the third exhalation, hold your breath for as long as is comfortable. Repeat series five or six times.
- A warm bath (not hot) relaxes muscles and reduces tension, which helps create drowsiness.
- Counting sheep works as it involves both sides of the brain in a repetitive, boring task. Hate sheep? Build a wall, brick by brick.
- If you're still wide awake after 15 minutes, get up, leave the room and do something else. Don't return until you feel sleepy.

Two free booklets on the subject are available. For the Better Sleep Council's "A Guide to Better Sleep," write to P.O. Box 13, Washington, DC 20044. For DuPont's "Get a Good Night's Rest," write to DuPont Sleep Guide, Dept. 5119, Ronks, PA 17573.

mind off the stresses of the day, but who has 20 minutes twice a day? Even though that's what the experts advise, I decided to adapt what I read to a 5-minute break once or twice in my day. When I can build in 5 uninterrupted minutes—or when I'm at the end of my rope—I sit in a big easy chair. Keeping my feet flat on the floor, my eyes closed and my body relaxed, I concentrate on calming my mind. Then I picture myself walking on a beautiful beach. I can hear the waves and feel the warm sun and the soft sand. I take myself on that walk for the next 5 minutes and when I come back, I am so relaxed I can handle anything. Some days, for variation, I picture myself in the mountains or sitting on a lush, green hill. It's wonderfully empowering to know I can give myself such rejuvenating visits every day.

Martha Carter, Rockville, Maryland

Savor quiet beauty

After a hard day, it's amazing how replenishing a walk alone with the moon, frogs and crickets can be. A wonderful read that reminds me of the joy of solitude and the world around me is Anne Morrow Lindbergh's *Gift from the Sea* (Random House). I read it again and again.

Elena Jarvis Jube, Haines, Oregon

Soak away the tension

It sounds cliché, but I really do take a long bubble bath to get my break. I wait until weekends or holidays when my hus-band is home to supervise the kids. Then I fill the tub, pull out my current novel and slip into the bathroom for a long afternoon rest. I was always a shower person before I became a mother, but I've discovered time in bubbly, hot water is truly refreshing. Besides, when I lock the door, everyone knows Mom isn't to be disturbed.

Devra Gherardi, Roosevelt Island, New York

Find morning moments

With three preschoolers, I often have long, stressful days. I function so much better when I have some quiet time that I decided not to leave the opportunity to chance. I get up an hour before my children wake, and, even though it's sometimes hard to greet the world at the crack of dawn, having that time to myself transforms my attitude. I drink my coffee, eat a leisurely breakfast, read, catch up on housework or look through the mail. This energizes me for the rest of the day.

Leann Husband, Minneapolis

Index

Leg warmers under nightgown, 102
Lessons in lieu of after-school care,
    205–6
Lethargy in infants, <u>33</u>
Letters, writing. *See also* Correspondence
    to child on birthdays, 33
    to ease transition of moving, 288
    fan, 381
    as sick-day activity, 384
Libraries
    as alternative to buying books, <u>370</u>
    keeping track of materials from, 304,
        305, <u>354</u>
    love of reading and, 306
    as place to meet people, <u>432</u>
Lice, head, 82
"Light a Candle! The Jewish Experience
    in Children's Books"
    (bibliography), 401
Light bulbs, red, as night light, 101
Lighters, safe storage of, <u>135</u>
Lightning, fear of, 286
Linens. *See* Bedding
Lip, fat, <u>144</u>
Liquids. *See* Fluid intake
Little Engine That Could, The,
    <u>35</u>, <u>100</u>
Little League, 390
Lost child, 180–81
Lotion, warming, 78
Love, self-esteem and, 271
Luggage tag on diaper bag, 200
Lunch
    creative ideas for, <u>58</u>, 314
    doing errands during, 351
    meeting children for, 321
    packing the night before, <u>320</u>
    school, 314–15
Lying, 229–32
Lyme disease, 170, 173

M

Magazines, children's, 307–8
Magic Kingdom, 410–11
Mail, receiving at work, 351
Maintenance, household, <u>135</u>
Makeovers, 341, <u>435</u>

Makeup, entertaining baby during appli-
    cation, 29
Make Way forDucklings, <u>100</u>
"Mama's boy," 283
Manicures, as home-based business, 342
Manners, 66–67, 181, 255, 263, 266
Markers, removing marks from, <u>346</u>
Marriage
    counseling, 429–30, <u>429</u>
    "memory board," <u>428</u>
    recharging, 429–30
Massage
    for fussy baby, 25
    treating oneself to, 331, <u>426</u>
Matches, safe storage of, <u>135</u>
Math skills, encouraging, 308–9, <u>308</u>,
    379–80
Mattresses
    allergies and, <u>159</u>
    on bunk beds, <u>103</u>
    on floor, 102
    as play place, 36
    protecting, from bed-wetting, <u>127</u>
Maturity, signs of, in adolescents, 233
Meal planning and preparation, <u>49</u>,
        61–62, 64–65, 246. *See also*
        specific meals
Measles-mumps-rubella (MMR) vaccine,
    <u>34</u>
Measuring spoon for baby spoon, 63–64
Meat, as choking hazard, <u>60</u>
Medical emergencies, <u>195</u>
Medical transcribing, as home-based
    business, 339
Medications. *See also specific*
        medications
    for bed-wetting, <u>129</u>
    discarding old, <u>138</u>, <u>158</u>
    easier administration, <u>30</u>, 155–59, <u>156</u>
    measuring accurately, 158
    safe storage of, <u>134</u>, <u>138</u>
Meditation, 428, 435–36
Meeting place, pre-arranged, in case of
    separation, 181
Menorah, 401
Menu
    ideas, <u>62–63</u>
    kid-planned, 64
    in teaching reading, 377

pets and, 261
privileges and, 209–10
Restaurants, 67–69
babies and, 406
feeding kids first at, 68
games for, 68
introducing in stages, 68–69
naps before visiting, 68
stroller in, 68
Rewards
for getting to bed on time, 99, 112
for good behavior, 214–16
sticker system of, 215–16
for toilet-learning, 120, 130
Ribbons, replacing buttons with, 89
Rice cakes as snack, 57
Rice for cleaning bottles, 43
RID (head lice treatment), 82
Rollerblading
bicycle helmets for, 175
clothing for, 169
learning with child, 168
safety, 176
Roller hockey, 390
Routines
adjusting babies to, 29–30
bedtime, 98, 99, 104
homework, 311
mealtime, 66
Rudeness, 255, 256
Rugs
allergies and, 159
personalized play, 385
removing spots from, 347
Rummage sales, 37
Runaway Bunny, The, 100

S

Sadness, as sign of depression, 285
Safety. *See also* First-aid
accessories, 5, 137
appliance, 134
away from home, 136–38
backyard, 136
bathroom, 72–73, 75, 134

bicycling, 174–76, 174–75, 183
car-seat, 414
checklist, 134–36
child care and, 188, 189, 195
crossing streets, 176–78
day care centers and, 188, 189
driveway, 177
furniture, 141-44
garage, 136
high-chair, 53
in-line skating, 174, 176
inspections, 338–39
kitchen, 134, 141
laundry-room, 136
playground, 178–80, 178–79
school-bus, 314
skateboard, 175, 176
skating, 174, 176
strangers and, 182
swimming, 136, 169, 171, 172-73
traffic, 176–78
vests, water, 172–73
walking alone and, 182
winter, 165
Salt
baby food and, 52
poisoning potential of, 139
Sand
in eyes, 173
removing from wet hands, 81
Sandals, hazards of, 169
Sandboxes, 387
Sandwiches
alternatives to, 314
keeping fresh, 314–15
made from heels of bread loaf, 59
peanut butter, 50
unusual, 58, 62, 63
Sauces, 62–63
Scalding, preventing, 72, 73, 75
Schedules
calendars for keeping track of,
299–301, 302
first-year vaccinations, 34
infant feeding, 44–46
sticking to, 246
work, 331–34

460 *Index*

Timer, kitchen
for housecleaning games, 359
for learning sense of time, 376–77
for time-outs, 211, 212
Tobacco, poisoning potential of, 139
Toddler beds, 103–4
Toddlers
books for, 100
fights of, 273
friendships of, 273–74
multiple, 245–47
sharing and, 273
social development of, 275
traveling with, 407
Tofranil (imipramine) for bed-wetting,
129
Toiletries for newborns, 4
Toilets, 134, 356
Toilet-teaching, 113–31
bathing suits and, 169
fears associated with, 125
nighttime, 124–31
medications for, 130
moisture-sensing alarm for, 129,
131
signs of readiness, 127
readiness, 113–17, 114, 115
Tools, 171, 355, 359
Tooth Fairy, 86
Toothpaste for stain removal, 65
Towels
in baby bathtub, 72
child's own, 74, 78
to protect clothes from spit-up, 321
warming, 78
Toy(s). *See also specific toys*
bathtime, 73, 74
in car, 407, 414
cereal-box, 241
for children with disabilities, 162
cleaning, 349
in different rooms, 358
duplicates, 273
glow-in-the-dark, 105
homemade, 367–69
illness and, 383, 384
lending libraries, 370
play kitchen, 64
saying goodnight to, 99

separation anxiety and, 294
storing, 345
swapping, 369
used, 370
Toy boxes, 345–46
Transitional objects, 268–70
Travel, 407–22
business, 325, 326
safety accessories and, 137
toilet-learning and, 121–23
weekend, 327
Treasure hunt, 391
Trees, as gifts, 366
Tripping, as sign of vision problem, 157
Trust, establishing, 231
T-shirts, 238, 240, 400
Turmeric, in meals, 63
Turn-taking, 216–17, 239
Tutors, 306, 342, 383
26 Letters and 99 Cents, 35
Typing service, as home-based business,
339

U

Umbilical-cord stump, 20, 21
Umbrella, as alternative to hat, 171
Underwear, baby's, 87
Urination, as indication of dehydration,
32, 148
USA Toy Library Association, 370

V

Vacations. *See* Travel
Vaccinations, 34, 148–49
Vaccines for Children program, 34
Vacuum cleaner noise to soothe fussy
baby, 25
Valentine's Day, 391
Vaporizing cream, for colds, 152
Varicella (chickenpox) (VVV) vaccine, 34
VATER syndrome, 164
VCRs, safety considerations, 135
Vegetable(s) , 62-63
cupcakes, 51
encouraging eating of, 49, 54